ENEMIES OF THE BAY COLONY

Puritan Massachusetts and Its Foes

SECOND EDITION

Philip Ranlet

University Press of America,® Inc.
Lanham · Boulder · New York · Toronto · Oxford

Copyright © 2006 by
University Press of America,® Inc.
4501 Forbes Boulevard
Suite 200
Lanham, Maryland 20706
UPA Acquisitions Department (301) 459-3366

PO Box 317
Oxford
OX2 9RU, UK

Library of Congress Control Number: 2006923336
ISBN-13: 978-0-7618-3486-1 (paperback : alk. paper)
ISBN-10: 0-7618-3486-9 (paperback : alk. paper)

This book is dedicated to my brother,
David Ranlet.

Anno 1688. . . . One J. Brodbent an Exciseman and a Hectoring De-
bauchee, Residt in Boston (where too many of the same stamp, have
lately multiplyed) meeting an Honest, Ingenious [Puritan] Countryman
upon the Road, enquired of him, what Newes Countryman? who Replyed,
I know none: the other then Replyed, I'll tell you som . . . The Devil is
Dead: How? said the Countryman, I believe not that; Yes, said the other,
he is dead for certaine: Well then, said the Countryman, if he be dead,
he hath left many fatherless Children in Boston.

—Lawrence Hammond,
Diary of Lawrence Hammond,
Massachusetts Historical Society,
Proceedings, 2nd ser., VII (1891-1892), 147.

Contents

Tables

Preface

This second edition of *Enemies of the Bay Colony* has gained more than a new subtitle. Two additional biographies—that of the Narragansett sachem Miantonomo and Satan—have been included. Miantonomo's life revolves around the infamous Pequot War, while Satan's story is actually an account of the Salem witchcraft outbreak.

All of the original chapters have been revised. King Philip has been modified the most; Joseph Dudley's biography has been revamped to aid its readability. Sources published after the appearance of *Enemies* have been incorporated where relevant, but older works I have since examined are also now part of the foundation supporting this book.

Each chapter can stand by itself. However, the inclusion of the Pequot War and the Salem witchcraft trials now makes *Enemies of the Bay Colony* into a narrative history of Puritan New England from its very beginnings to the mid-eighteenth century.

Philip Ranlet
June 29, 2005

Acknowledgments

Ever since this book was first dreamed of, Alden T. Vaughan encouraged me. Not only did he read the original manuscript, he bore my criticism of one of his class reading lists with his usual grace. Alden Vaughan is the epitome of a superb teacher and scholar, which is why my biography of Richard B. Morris is dedicated to him. My good friend James Baughman has helped me in so many ways I can not list them. My colleagues at Hunter College, Florene Memegalos and Angelo Angelis, have given helpful advice. My thanks also go to Sunil Mehra, M. D., for taking time out from his busy schedule to read my Salem chapter. And my brother David has always provided his support.

I am grateful that the New England Historic Genealogical Society allowed me to reprint my essay on Thomas Morton, which was the foundation for chapter 2. A chunk of chapter 5 first appeared as "Another Look at the Causes of King Philip's War," in the *New England Quarterly*, v. 61, March 1988. Copyright held by the *New England Quarterly*. Reproduced by permission of the publisher. I also thank the Huntington Library for permission to quote from its collections.

PR

Chapter 1

The Resurgence of the Puritans

When Perry Miller was a graduate student, he announced his plan to study the Puritans of New England. His choice of a subject dismayed some of his teachers. As Miller later wrote, they cautioned him that he was just "throwing my career away: that field, they said, was exhausted, all that wheat had long since been winnowed, there was nothing but chaff remaining."[1]

By all appearances at the time, Miller's professors seemed to be right. In the 1920s the study of Puritanism seemed to be a dead end for a beginning scholar. Debunkers such as H. L. Mencken, who saw little good in anything, had unleashed their venom upon the Puritans and depicted them as dreary zealots. Scholars Charles Beard, Vernon L. Parrington, and James Truslow Adams had also attacked them as intolerant moralists.[2]

Despite all that, Miller, ignoring his atheism, forged ahead and produced a mountain of scholarship on the Puritans, which made him, Edmund S. Morgan believed, "the greatest historian of ideas that America has ever seen." During Miller's long career at Harvard, though, he inspired few students to work on Puritanism. After serving in the Second World War, the bored Miller seemed to exhibit signs of depression. By the 1950s he may have privately felt he had failed. In 1956 he wrote: "after three decades of endeavor, though we have shaken a few complacencies, we have not arrived at the comprehensive understanding we presumptuously proposed." As for himself, he was "sadly deficient" for the task. Some years later, in 1963, Perry Miller committed suicide.[3]

If Miller did, indeed, think that he had failed, he was wrong. According to Michael McGiffert, "it is possible in the 1960's to speak of

American Puritan studies as a field of scholarship, and to appraise its estate and activity, because Perry Miller, above all others, made the American Puritans studiable."[4] Miller had shown other scholars the exciting aspects of Puritanism. He was especially pleased to note the work of Bernard Bailyn and Edmund S. Morgan. These two historians—Bailyn at Harvard and Morgan at Yale—had numerous students, all of whom absorbed Miller's view of the importance of the Puritans.[5]

This Harvard-Yale alliance (along with many other scholars) produced a flood of work on early New England. Counting from 1939, well over a thousand publications about the Puritans have appeared, and over two hundred of these writings were books. In 1966 Morgan suggested that scholars examine some less-explored areas. Yet the outpouring continued, with an especially big deluge in 1970. Twenty-one years after Morgan's suggestion, David D. Hall had to lament the sheer "impossibility" of keeping up with the increasing flood of Puritan studies. Although interest in Puritanism abated a bit in the 1990s because of the fascination with multiculturalism, Puritanism is clearly on the rebound in the twenty-first century. In 2004 Morgan observed that "The Puritans have now become the most closely examined group of people in American history."[6]

Within this mass of scholarly literature is much criticism of Perry Miller. Yet, as McGiffert pointed out, this scholarship "takes many of its cues from Miller's writings." Similarly, Francis T. Butts insisted that "few real differences" existed between Perry Miller and those who have followed in his wake. Puritan studies are still largely amplifications of his work.[7]

Miller, however, was not the only historian who helped make Puritanism the most popular subject in early American history. Credit has to be shared with another Harvard professor, Samuel Eliot Morison. In his first important work on Puritanism, *Builders of the Bay Colony* (1930), Morison used the tools of biography to reveal representative Puritans as "human beings." Morgan called *Builders of the Bay Colony* "a tour de force." Throughout Morison's long life, he produced many other important studies of early New England.[8]

Miller, Morison, Morgan, and the other scholars of Puritan New England have done American history a great service. Nevertheless, being human, their work has gaps and flaws. Morison, for example, tended to forgive too easily the faults of his ancestors. Other historians of the Puritans were equally "fascinated by these people," to use Morgan's phrase. In 1987 Morgan was asked how he could be "so utterly fair-minded about the Puritans." He responded: "Maybe I bend over backwards in being 'fair' to them—maybe I'm too favorable to them." That statement could probably be said about much of the scholarly literature on New England Puritans.[9]

It is a truism that "Every new generation of historians of Puritanism will discover hiatuses, blind spots, limited perspectives, and errors in the work of its predecessors."[10] In my case, my first real contact with the subject came in 1977 at Columbia University when I took a graduate colloquium on the Puritans. All the readings were able works, but, in my opinion, the authors shared one basic flaw. They liked the Puritans and I did not. I was rather amazed at the sometimes rough treatment the foes of the Puritans received. For example, I could not accept Bailyn's picture of Samuel Maverick.[11]

My research paper that semester, a biographical account of Thomas Morton of Merry Mount, gave me the idea for this book. I resolved to do similar biographical reassessments of other "enemies" of the Bay colony, much as Morison had done for its builders. Accordingly, this book contains nine biographical accounts of opponents of the Puritan system of New England. Along with Morton and Maverick, the other subjects are: Anne Hutchinson, Miantonomo, King Philip, Sir Edmund Andros, Joseph Dudley, Benjamin Colman, and Satan, who made quite an impact on Massachusetts during the Salem witchcraft trials. These subjects are a sampling of the foes of Massachusetts. Morton and Maverick were among the "old planters" who arrived before the Puritans and clashed with them. Hutchinson sparked the Antinomian crisis. Miantonomo and King Philip represent the local Indians who struggled with the Puritans. Andros and Dudley typify the imperial resistance to Puritanism—Andros was the imperial outsider, Dudley was opposed to the Puritan government from within. Colman embodies the later resistance to the Puritan religious orthodoxy. As for Satan, all Puritans (except for an occasional turncoat) saw the ruler of hell as a dangerous enemy.

The characters' public careers are the main focus of each account. For the most part, their private lives are not examined. I trust that these foes of the Bay colony will be judged on their own merits and mistakes, not on the Puritans' (or the Puritans' later champions') opinion of them. Nonetheless, readers are encouraged to condemn Satan and all his works.

Both Joseph Dudley and Benjamin Colman might be seen as curious "enemies" of the Bay colony. Dudley, however, became a leading light of the Dominion of New England, an evil deed in the eyes of many Puritans. And the memory of his offense was still alive when he became governor of Massachusetts. According to Richard Bushman, the "hatred" of Dudley "still burned brightly in the minds of the old charter party in 1702" and they remained suspicious of him.[12] Dudley's later career was affected by his earlier opposition to the Puritan political regime. He is a fitting subject for this book.

As for Colman, a reader might object to him being among the assorted worthies. Colman himself surely would have objected, but his opposition to the Puritan church as it stood in 1699 justifies his inclusion. His inclusion also permits the time frame of this book to extend from the earliest days of settlement to beyond the end of Puritanism's ascendancy in the Bay colony. Besides, Morison, in *Builders*, included an account of Robert Child, whose great importance is as an enemy of the Puritan state, not as an architect of it.[13]

The Mathers would have agreed that Colman was an enemy to the old ways of Massachusetts. Anyone who upset the Mathers as much as he did deserves a place of honor in this book. Certainly, if Cotton Mather had prepared an enemies list, Colman—and Joseph Dudley—would have been on it. Perhaps Satan would have ranked higher on Cotton Mather's list, but not by much.

This work's emphasis is on the Massachusetts Bay colony and its neighbor, Plymouth. After Plymouth's early days of glory, it sank into a secondary position (Joseph Dudley once, in jest, called it a "Dukedom")[14] and was eventually incorporated into its northern neighbor. The other areas of New England—Connecticut, Rhode Island, New Hampshire, and Maine—are discussed as circumstances dictate.

Two peculiarities of the colonial period require a mention for the benefit of those readers not well-versed in the subject. I prefer to give quotations as they were actually written. In some cases, though, where the spelling or punctuation is too bizarre for modern readers, the obscure sections have been modified. Colonial Americans also had a different calendar, the Julian, than that of the present day. The Julian calendar year began in March and was ten to eleven days behind the calendar being used in Catholic countries. In the text of this book, the Julian day will be retained, but the year will be written as if the calendar year started in January. The notes will give the Julian year when it is known for certain, with the modern rendering of the year. Therefore, in the notes a reference to February 1, 1687/8 means that, when the letter in question was written, its English author in Boston was still in the Julian year of 1687, while a resident of Mexico City, who was using the modern calendar, was already in 1688.

Chapter 2

Thomas Morton of Merry Mount

Of all the characters in this book, Thomas Morton is by far the most colorful. His erection of a maypole in Puritan New England has aroused the interest of many historians and has begotten much literature.[1] As fascinating as Morton's maypole is, however, it should not obscure the rest of his colorful career as an enemy of the Bay colony. Thomas Morton of Merry Mount, the Lord of Misrule, was an early and vigorous foe of the Puritans.

Little is known about Morton before the early 1620s. The year of his birth is uncertain although 1579-1580 has been suggested as an approximate date. According to his book, *New English Canaan*, his father was a soldier. The future host of Merry Mount may have attended Oxford.[2] His career, though, is well documented. Trained as a lawyer at Clifford's Inn,[3] he practiced in the West Country of England, where in November 1621[4] he married Alice Miller, a wealthy widow.

After the death of Alice Miller's first husband, her eldest son, George, deprived her of her property rights. George Miller had a hostile personality as the following incident demonstrates. The Phipps family had allowed the Millers to use the Phipps church pew, but only while the Phippses did not need the extra space. Eventually, the Millers could no longer sit in that pew, but young Miller could not accept its loss. One Sunday he

> came into church during service and the pew door being locked he proceeded violently, with many oaths, to break it open, whereupon Mrs. Phipps in ordering him to desist called him "Boy." In his rage Miller replied: "Dost thou call me boy? Gods wounds! If I were in bed

with thee thou shouldst knowe that I were no boye." He then leaped
over the door and tumbled on the heads and necks of the gentlewomen
seated with the Phipps family, finally landing in the lap of Mrs. Phipps
where he sat despite her protests. Then he picked her up bodily and
threw her over the railing into the aisle. . . .[5]

Alice Miller, confronted by this "younge man of an untemperate
condition and most incorrigible," hired lawyer Thomas Morton, whom
she had known for several years, to represent her.[6] Not surprisingly,
Morton found much that was desirable in this widow with claims to a
comfortable estate, and he courted her successfully. But her son suspected Morton of coveting the estate for himself, a very likely possibility. Before her remarriage, Miller convinced his mother to lease the
property to him as a test of Morton's affections. After signing the lease,
she changed her mind, but her son refused to return the land deed. Sub-
sequently, Morton and Alice Miller, by then man and wife, became em-
broiled in litigation with her son.[7]

Young Miller won the court fight and retained control of the property, although his mother was granted a yearly income of £ 50 from the
estate. Obviously disappointed by the outcome, in February 1623 Morton
deserted his wife, which has been called "sufficient confirmation of all
that has been said against him."[8] Certainly, desertion is not commendable, but the marriage had a considerable problem facing it—George
Miller. Not only had Miller opposed the marriage, he sought to prevent
it by hiring women to talk against Morton.[9] Furthermore, Miller obviously hated his stepfather. Even after Morton had left his wife and had
gone to New England, his stepson spread a false rumor that Morton had
fled to escape a murder charge.[10]

During 1624 Morton, "being then minded to travel," obtained a patent
from the Council for New England—dominated by Sir Ferdinando
Gorges—which granted permission to settle in its domains. At this time,
such patents were easily available, because the Council for New England
knew of the reluctance of even its paid employees to live in the wilderness.[11] Those men willing to go could hardly be turned away. But Morton,
who usually seems to have been short of cash, probably could not afford
the expenses of the voyage across the Atlantic or the various necessities
needed for survival in the New World.

Somehow or other, Morton met Humphrey Rastall, a disreputable
English merchant. Rastall, one of those entrepreneurs who met the Vir-

ginian need for workers by selling the labor of indentured servants, had a long history of flirting with the law. He had been charged in the past with a string of offenses, including piracy. Such a man required the services of a lawyer, and Morton likely drew up the various contracts concerning Rastall's commercial venture of 1624—a voyage to Virginia to sell servants. Part of the enterprise involved a trip to New England to obtain a cargo of fish.[12] This business trip perfectly suited Morton's plans. As payment for his legal work, Morton apparently got free transportation to New England and the supplies he wanted.

Also connected with this expedition was a Captain Richard Wollaston. On this venture, Wollaston was only in charge of the servants themselves. Another captain commanded the *Unity*, the ship that would bring the party to America. Although Wollaston had no authority concerning the *Unity*, he did control the servants' provisions, which were reserved for them and could not be used by the ship's crew.[13]

The *Unity*, with Rastall, Wollaston, and Morton aboard, departed from England in March 1624. During its difficult voyage across the ocean, the ship leaked badly and many provisions spoiled. In addition, Rastall decided to change their destination. Instead of going to Virginia first, they were now to go to New England to meet the *Zouch Phoenix*, another ship engaged in the venture, which would be in that area.[14]

Towards the end of June 1624, the *Unity* arrived in the wilderness of New England. The ship's shortage of provisions had gotten worse. During the first weeks after its arrival, the ship's passengers received only one biscuit per day plus some "bad" meat twice a week. Wollaston thought he just barely had enough supplies to get his men through the winter months. Meanwhile, Rastall went to Virginia in another ship, and the *Unity* took on a cargo of fish, most of which rotted long before it could be sold.[15]

From Virginia, Rastall ordered that the servants be brought to Virginia for disposal to the planters. Wollaston seems to have decided that, because of the shortage of provisions, some of the servants should be left in New England temporarily, to lessen the strain on the ship's supplies during its voyage to Virginia. Wollaston may have assumed that the servants staying behind in New England could hunt or fish and so needed very few of the provisions. Reportedly, Wollaston had obtained a patent from the Council for New England; leaving some people in New England might have been a contingency anticipated before the party left England. Perhaps Morton suggested getting a patent to avoid any legal problems. It is known that Rastall's men left salt and fishing gear on shore near Cape Ann. With a patent in hand, the expedition had every right to leave people or property there. Later, when settlers of the Dorchester Company removed some of the salt, Morton protested vigorously.[16]

Whatever the plan was, it miscarried. The *Unity*, with Wollaston aboard, sailed for Virginia in early December. Because of unfavorable winds, after about a month at sea the ship, low on provisions, was not near Virginia. To avoid possible starvation, the *Unity*'s captain headed to England and reached it in February 1625.[17]

Wollaston had put a Lieutenant Fitcher in charge of the remaining servants. Morton stayed with them. Colonizing the present site of Quincy, Massachusetts, they called their settlement Mount Wollaston. But Wollaston overestimated Fitcher's ability to maintain order as the scarcity of supplies had shortened the tempers of the servants. By the terms of their indentures, they were entitled to sufficient food. As a lawyer, Morton knew this—he may have drawn up the indentures himself—and told the servants about it. Morton also knew that, according to law, indentured servants who had been mistreated could even be set free. For example, in 1626 a court in Virginia released one of Rastall's apprentices whose contract he had violated. Morton's additional information that they were entitled to their freedom sparked a revolt among the servants, and Fitcher was thrown out of Mount Wollaston. Now that the former servants considered themselves free men, they accepted Morton's leadership.[18]

Morton and his friends soon annoyed their English neighbors, especially the Plymouth colonists. The most famous incident involved the erection of a maypole, accompanied by "revels and merriment after the old English custome," to celebrate spring's arrival. Enlivened by the consumption of "a barell of excellent beare," the servants danced around the maypole with Indian women. Morton saw no wickedness in "this harmeles mirth made by younge men (that lived in hope to have wives brought over to them. . .)."[19] But his celebration of "the feasts of the Roman goddess Flora, or the beastly practices of the mad Bacchanalians" dismayed William Bradford and the Pilgrims. Especially disturbing were several poems composed by Morton, the "Lord of Misrule," which tended to "lasciviousness . . . and scandal." Merry Mount (as Mount Wollaston had been renamed by the merrymakers) had become "a school of Atheism."[20]

Not surprisingly, servants of surrounding settlements flocked to Merry Mount, the scene of "drunkenness, riot and other evils." Morton entertained all comers and so was charged with "inveigling of men's servants away from them." As a further jolt to the sensibilities of the Plymouth residents, several of Morton's followers had relationships with Indian women, or as Bradford put it, some were "abusing the Indian women most filthily, as it is notorious."[21]

Exactly when Morton's maypole was erected is unknown. The usual date given, 1627, is unlikely. The revolt of the servants probably happened in early 1625. Bradford suggested that the maypole was built shortly after the takeover when the merrymakers had started trading with the natives. Young Englishmen of the 1620s just freed from servitude were surely overjoyed by spring. Would it have taken these lusty lads two years to think of putting up a maypole? Most likely, they erected the 80 foot high maypole for the festivities of May 1, 1625.[22]

Morton's merrymakers were lustful in their frolics, but historians have blown the affair out of all proportion just as the English Puritans generally over reacted to May day. In England, there was no surprising increase in births nine months after May 1. In New England, some scholars insist, the Pilgrims wanted to expel Morton because of the revels at Merry Mount. According to Michael Zuckerman, "Morton's offense" involved engaging the Indians "in a . . . more erotic mode" than the Pilgrims thus demonstrating to them that their "most haunting anxieties" about their "own impulses" would come true. John Seelye extended this theory to Morton's book, *New English Canaan*, supposed "geopolitical pornography."[23]

These scholars overrate the moral dimension of Morton's maypole and the festivities at Merry Mount, which were hardly "terrifying portents of the collapse of European civility."[24] However, maypoles had already become a royalist symbol in England. Whenever Englishmen wanted to annoy Puritans, they often built a maypole, which symbolized the very different societies that Anglicans and Puritans preferred. During the English Civil War, for example, maypoles commemorated Puritan military defeats. And when Charles II was restored and crowned, maypoles were erected in celebration.[25]

When someone such as Bradford or John Endicott looked at Morton's maypole, they did not just see an old pagan relic. It also represented to them other things the Book of Common Prayer, bishops, vestments— which were far more upsetting to them than Morton's "erotic mode."

Eventually, maypoles became closely connected with followers of the Archbishop of Canterbury, William Laud, a great enemy of Puritanism in both England and America. Not surprisingly, Morton dedicated *New English Canaan*, in which he wrote about his maypole, to Laud's colonial commission.[26]

But Morton did other things which went far beyond providing upsetting symbols. His successful fur trade with the Indians only worsened his relations with his neighbors. His prosperity came partly from outwitting the Pilgrims; he once journeyed to the Kennebec before them, and his "boate . . . gleaned away all [furs] before they came," much to their surprise. Primarily, though, Morton prospered because he sold guns and powder to the Indians. Neither the first nor the only trader then arming the natives, the Lord of Misrule was the most conspicuous. Not only did he sell guns—he carefully taught the Indians how to use them.[27]

Bradford believed, probably correctly, that Morton had ordered more guns from England for the Indians, but Morton depended chiefly upon selling gunpowder and shot to bolster his Indian trade. In 1629 the Puritans inventoried his possessions and found only two guns, which were likely his personal weapons. In contrast to the few guns, the Puritans found nine pounds of gunpowder, a substantial supply of bullets and lead, and tools used to form molten lead into bullets. Morton had only three pounds of a more traditional Indian trading item, beads. Although Morton had plenty of competition in the sale of firearms from Dutch, English, and French traders, he provided a nearby source of ammunition and powder which undoubtedly brought him much Indian business.[28]

Faced with the "terror" of armed and well-supplied Indians, Morton's neighbors tried to "admonish him to forbear those courses," but he rejected all their supplications with "scurrilous terms full of disdain." When a second attempt also failed, the Plymouth inhabitants and other nearby colonists decided to expel him from the area. The planters contributed funds to pay for his removal, and Plymouth dispatched Miles Standish with eight men to arrest Morton. Whether he surrendered to avoid bloodshed, as he later wrote, or whether he was captured while too drunk to load his gun properly, as Bradford claimed, the result was the same— Morton's sojourn at Merry Mount had ended, at least temporarily. In 1628 a messenger, armed with letters to the Council for New England describing Morton's conduct, conveyed him to England.[29]

Although the planters banished the Lord of Misrule himself, they allowed "some of the more modest" of his followers to remain at Merry

Mount. They apparently continued their revels until Puritan John Endicott, while "visiting those parts, caused that maypole to be cut down and rebuked them for their profaneness. . . ."[30] That rebuke quieted the "modest" remnant.

Despite the letters of complaint, Morton escaped punishment. Bradford believed that Morton had "fooled of the messenger" and so lessened the force of the charges. Whatever the English authorities thought about him, they did not prevent his return to New England in 1629. Plymouth's own agent in England, Isaac Allerton, brought the host of Merry Mount back to America "for base gain." To make Allerton's offense still worse, he boarded Morton and even employed him as a scribe. But upon discovering Plymouth's hostility, Morton returned to Merry Mount, his "old nest."[31]

In 1629 Merry Mount fell within the patent of the Massachusetts Bay colony, and Morton quickly irritated the Puritans. Continuing "to advance the dignity of the Church of England,"[32] his activities caused Edward Johnson to write in 1654:

> The third Church of Christ gathered . . . at Dorchester [in 1631] . . . ; neere about this Towne inhabited some few ancient Traders, who were not of this select band, but came for other ends, as Morton of Merry Mount, who would faine have resisted this worke, but the provident hand of Christ prevented.[33]

Morton created other problems for Massachusetts. Governor John Endicott summoned the inhabitants to Salem and asked them to sign an agreement which declared that in both political and religious matters "wee should follow the rule of Gods word." The Lord of Misrule rejected the agreement because it should have specified that "nothing be done contrary or repugnant to the Lawes of the Kingdome of England." Despite being good law, his objection did not endear him to Endicott, who liked Morton as little as his felled maypole. In general, lawyers were unpopular in the early days of the colony. The Puritan leaders preferred to interpret the law as they saw it; lawyers could only get in the way. Some years later, even Thomas Lechford, a lawyer who had defended English Puritans against arbitrary justice, had a difficult stay in Massachusetts. With no such favorable record, Morton was an annoyance that Endicott could do without.[34]

Word soon reached John Winthrop and the chief officials of the Massachusetts Bay Company about the annoying lawyer in their territory. By that time, Winthrop had heard George Miller's old rumor. As early as November 1627, Winthrop had been told that Thomas Morton had murdered a business associate and fled to New England.[35] If Morton truly was a murderer, then an arrest warrant would be an excellent way to rid the colony of a troublemaker. The Puritan leader, a former justice of the peace, certainly knew how to procure the issuance of a warrant. Winthrop brought the document to New England in 1630 and planned to use it at the earliest opportunity.[36]

Morton himself provided the opportunity. During the summer of 1630, he accidentally shot a gun at some Indians who had not brought him a canoe. Although the wounded Indian was not severely hurt,[37] Morton was in serious trouble. On August 23, 1630, the magistrates, during the first meeting of the Court of Assistants, ordered him to appear before them. According to Samuel Maverick, they believed Morton to have had "a design to sett the Indians at varience with" the colony, and on September 7 the magistrates accordingly tried him "for his many injuries offered to the Indians." The court, complying with the warrant, ordered that he be returned to England to answer the murder charge. In addition, since Morton allegedly had mistreated the Indians, his house was to be "burnt down to the ground in the sight of the Indians for their satisfaction. . . ."[38]

In December 1630 the Puritans sent Morton back to England once more. Before the ship left the sight of land, they set his house on fire so that he could see the smoke. Infuriated by the scene, he later wrote that the burned traces of Merry Mount cried "for recompence, (or else revenge,) against the Sect of cruell Schismaticks."[39]

Once cleared of the groundless murder charge, Morton complained to Sir Ferdinando Gorges of the Council for New England. Gorges did nothing. However, Gorges took notice when Sir Christopher Gardiner— a man of considerable social status—and Philip Ratcliffe voiced their protests. Gardiner, whose title came from military service for the Holy Roman Empire, had become a Catholic but had since returned to Protestantism. In order to escape from his two supposed wives in Europe, he journeyed to Massachusetts with his mistress. After the discovery of his alleged bigamy, Gardiner was jailed. Then the Puritans learned that Gardiner was in communication with Gorges if not actually one of his agents. Meanwhile, Gardiner's mistress had married someone else. After Gardiner's release, he visited his former mistress and her new husband; Gardiner eventually left for England. No doubt disappointed at having lost his latest love, Gardiner resented his treatment by the Puritans. The other complainer, Philip Ratcliffe—treated far worse than the love-sick knight—had been critical of both the Massachusetts Bay government and the Puritan churches. Accused of sedition, his ears were cropped. Expelled from the colony, he added his resentment to Gardiner's. Moved by these charges, Gorges and his associate, Captain John Mason, pressured the Privy Council for action against the Bay colony.[40]

Morton, Gardiner, and Ratcliffe presented an extensive complaint to the Privy Council, which charged the Puritans with being hostile to the Church of England and to the very laws of the nation itself. Some Puritan supporters in the mother country defended Massachusetts. Thomas Wiggin, who worked for Gorges but would soon be employed by a Puritan nobleman, did his best to impugn the character of the colony's foes. A charge of bigamy and consorting with a "harlot" discredited Gardiner. Ratcliffe had committed a "horible blasphemy" and deserved his punishment. As for Morton, Wiggin talked to that unreliable source, George Miller, and got specifics about the murder Morton had supposedly committed. In addition to Wiggin, Sir Thomas Jermin, an old foe of Gorges, used his influence to aid the cause of Massachusetts.[41]

On December 19, 1632, the Privy Council appointed a special committee to examine the charges of Morton and the others. Announcing its opinion a month later, the committee declared that regardless of

> the faults or fancies (if any be) of some particular men upon the general Government, or principall adventurers (which in due time is further to be enquired into) [we] have thought fitt in the meane time to declare, that the appearances, were so faire, and the hopes so great that the Countrie would prove, both beneficial to this Kingdome, and profitable to the perticular Adventurers, as that the Adventurers had good cause to go on cherefully with their undertakings. . . .[42]

The Privy Council's decision surely stunned Morton and the others. If this defeat was not bad enough, the committee criticized Gorges for having joined in with Morton and his comrades.[43]

Nevertheless, by 1634 the situation had completely changed. In April 1634 Archbishop Laud became head of a new Privy Council Commission for Foreign Plantations, and Gorges, Morton, and the others had found a powerful friend to aid their cause, for Laud's committee had authority over colonial charters. The Archbishop sought a strengthening of royal influence in the colonies and the charter of the Massachusetts

Bay Company was a hinderance to his plans. The enemies of Massachusetts had done their best to turn Laud against the colony and they succeeded.[44]

Because of the determined foes of Massachusetts Bay, Laud's committee reexamined the charges against the colony. In testimony before the committee, Edward Winslow tried to defend the Puritans, but found it necessary to defend himself. Unfortunately for Winslow, Morton had informed the committee about some of his religious activities in New England. The Puritan layman had to admit that, because of Plymouth's lack of ministers, he had preached and had performed marriages. Unable to explain his actions away before the Archbishop of Canterbury, Winslow, in a petition, later resorted to attacking his critics, "enemies to all goodness," such as the "Jesuited gentleman," Gardiner, and the supposed murderer, Thomas Morton. This time, such tactics failed. Laud, angry at a layman doing the work of a cleric, had Winslow jailed for over four months. And the committee declared the charter of Massachusetts void.[45]

Morton, gleeful over the verdict, described his own work against the charter in a letter to William Jeffreys, an "old planter" who lived near Merry Mount. The Lord of Misrule added that Ratcliffe "was comforted by their lordships with the cropping of Mr. Winthrop's ears which shows what opinion is held amongst them of King Winthrop. . . ." That prospect delighted Morton almost as much as it did Ratcliffe. When Jeffreys received the letter he brought it to Winthrop, who alerted the magistrates about Morton's "railing speeches and threats against this plantation, and Mr. Winthrop in particular."[46]

There is a deeper meaning to Morton's letter. The Lord of Misrule probably sent it to Jeffreys in the hope that the Puritans would learn about his actions against them. Indeed, he claimed that he had sent several such letters into New England. To Morton, revenge seemed sweeter when those who had wronged him knew how he had triumphed against them. Rather than just sending a nasty note to Winthrop, Morton could not resist a pun, a literary device he delighted in. His salutation to Jeffreys was "My very good gossip." Winthrop assumed Morton was using "gossip" in the sense of "a familiar acquaintance." But Jeffreys could not have been very friendly with Morton—Jeffreys had contributed to the fund to pay for Morton's expulsion in 1628. Morton was likely making a joke about Jeffreys's character—"gossip" had already taken on the modern meaning of "tattler." Perhaps Morton had sized up Jeffreys correctly; he did not keep the letter secret and acted like a tattler.[47]

Thomas Morton did more than pun the Puritans. In May 1635 the Council for New England hired him to bring in the courts a *quo warranto* proceeding against the Massachusetts charter, and so end the existence of the company that had created the Bay colony. Although the suit was brought under the name of the crown's attorney-general, Morton actually did the legal work, which, according to Charles M. Andrews, was "conducted . . . with considerable skill." Morton concluded the action successfully.[48]

About the same time Morton began writing *New English Canaan*, an obvious attempt to create additional difficulties for New England. Andrews declared that "No man who wrote" that book "could be as vile as Bradford and Adams make him out to be." *New English Canaan* is memorable for its depiction of Morton's foes under humorous names. Miles Standish, for example, is "Captain Shrimpe," and John Endicott is "Captain Littleworth." In a more serious vein, the book detailed its author's complaints about Massachusetts Bay and Plymouth colonies. He conveniently listed twelve of their "many unwarrantable Tenents," all certain to inflame Laud. These beliefs included their failure to use the Book of Common Prayer, their refusal to wear a wedding ring, the performance of marriages by magistrates, the baptism of only the children of church members, and the limitation of the Eucharist to church members. Anyone, wrote Morton, who did not accept those tenets "they say is a very reprobate." He also mentioned some of their political variations, such as the issuing of warrants without the king's name. Moreover, "mine Host of Ma-re-Mount" showed how the New Englanders took "the Law in their owne hands, (there being no generall Governour in the Land . . .)."[49]

New English Canaan is also a vivid account of the New England landscape and environment. Morton had explored the countryside of Massachusetts, that "very beautifull Land." As he observed, "The more I looked, the more I liked it." Comparing this wilderness to the biblical Canaan, Morton decided that it was far superior to England. Greatly intrigued by the natives and their civilization, he commented that the Indians were "more friendly" than the Puritans, a reflection upon his experiences with both groups.[50] Despite his ill feelings toward the Puritans, he admired what they had done with this new Canaan. Far from the Puritans despoiling the land, he declared that "they have deserved (in mine opinion) some commendationes, in that they have furnished the Country so commodiously in so short a time; although it hath bin but for their own profit, yet posterity will taste the sweetness of it, and that very sodainly."[51]

Published in 1637, the book received censure from the Puritans and their supporters. In England Matthew Cradock "utterly disliked" it and sent a copy to Winthrop.[52] Bradford believed it to be "an infamous and scurrilous book against many godly and chief men of the country, full of lies and slanders. . . ." On the other hand, Samuel Maverick, no friend to the Puritans, saw it as "a good description of the Cuntry . . . , only in the end of it he [Morton] pinched too closely on some in authoritie there. . . ."[53]

While the offensive against Massachusetts Bay was underway, the English government and Sir Ferdinando Gorges were making plans for the next logical step—a new political structure for New England. In 1634 Gorges, as an experienced soldier, believed that the various New England colonies should be combined to make them easier to defend. This new administration needed a royal governor and, of course, other officials such as a bishop. Immigration of those "Scismatically inclined"— that is, Puritans—had to be restricted. Most important, the new governor had to have "such authority with competent power"—military might— "to prevent the scornes and insolencies, that in default thereof might be offered" by the Puritans.[54]

The next year, Gorges learned that he had been selected as the first governor of New England. But when he planned to leave for America, his ship suddenly fell apart. Why this mishap occurred is unknown. Gorges liked to try experimental ship designs and perhaps this ship had been one of his least successful experiments. The ship may also have been poorly built because Gorges was close to bankruptcy. He had put much of his not very substantial wealth into colonizing the New World and this risky gamble had not paid off for him.[55]

By 1636 a new complication had arisen. Sir Ferdinando Gorges, then in his seventies, had "growne a little doubtfull of the state of my owne bodie, not able to indure the Sea any long time." A trip to America could have caused his death. Nevertheless, he insisted upon going through with his mission and received his royal commission as governor in 1637. However, he continued to find excuses for not leaving England. He wished to see the king before embarking, Gorges claimed. Then he wished to delay because of an important meeting of Parliament. Gorges never left for New England—he may have been too proud to admit to himself that he was just too old for the job. And royal officials may not have wanted to humiliate the old Elizabethan knight by telling him that.[56]

Gorges's hesitancy may have been increased by another fear, that his original plan emphasizing military force would not work. In 1638 he suggested that the Puritans of New England be won over by offering to them "all favour and freedome." Instead of first sending a governor aided by troops, he urged that a special commission be created to determine "by what meanes" New England "may best be ordered for the quiett peace and content of the planters." A colonial proprietor—of a non-Puritan area—would head the commission, which would include some New Englanders "of the most discreete and temperate sorte." Only then should a royal governor be sent.[57] This suggestion, similar to what was tried in the 1660s, came to nothing.

Morton's role in these maneuverings is uncertain. He apparently became involved in the colonial land dispute between Gorges and George Cleeve. Cleeve, who favored Puritanism, came to England and employed Morton to assist him with the legal aspects of his claim in Maine. In 1637, because of Morton's connection with Cleeve, Gorges cashiered the Lord of Misrule from any connection with him. This split had been healed by 1640 as Morton then signed one of Gorges's land patents. The following year, Morton signed the charter of Agamenticus, Maine, one of Gorges's settlements. Seemingly, Gorges had accepted Morton being on both sides of the dispute as he had continued to do legal work for Cleeve.[58]

Morton, in these days immediately before the English Civil War, was very busy changing sides. From being an advocate of the king and Laud, he switched to the cause of Parliament. Cleeve had convinced Alexander Rigby, a leading member of Parliament, to purchase an old land patent in Maine for the "Province of Lygonia." With Rigby's aid, Cleeve interested Parliament in his land claims. When in April 1643, Parliament sought information on the matter, Morton and Winthrop were two of those who were selected to investigate. As the English Civil War had broken out the preceeding year, Morton's allegiance was clear. No royalist would have been given such an assignment.[59]

Meanwhile, in Massachusetts, events had not boded well for Gorges or his supporters. Frightened by reports of the proceedings underway against New England, the Puritan leaders planned to resist. Boston was fortified, troops were armed, supplies were stockpiled. The colony also stalled the actions against its charter by refusing to send the document back to England. This strategy of delay was crucial. With the passage of time, Laud and other royalists were distracted from colonial affairs by the far more important internal problems in England. The royal government, according to Richard Arthur Preston, did not have "a clear, vigorous colonial policy and the passive resistance of the Puritans created a situation for which the government was unable to find a ready solution." The Bay colony escaped from the crisis with its charter intact.[60]

As early as 1641, Morton planned to return to New England. Sir Ferdinando Gorges had given the charter of Agamenticus to Morton's care. Morton then wrote to Maine asking for a substantial sum of money to compensate him for his "payns and travell" in return for the charter. The Lord of Misrule, once again short of money, needed a way to pay his way across the ocean and the delivery of the Agamenticus charter was a convenient excuse. Thomas Gorges, Sir Ferdinando's nephew then in charge of Maine, was very annoyed by Morton's request although he complied with it. Thomas Gorges, who had Puritan sympathies, complained to his uncle: "I conceave Mr. Moorton to be an able man, yet I know not whither it be a policy for a Lord of a province in N. Ing. to countenance him that hath declared himself an enemy to the land."[61]

Morton had several reasons for coming back, once again, to Puritan New England. He wanted to "looke after" his land in America and Rigby had hired him as one of his agents there. Perhaps the most important reason was that Morton did truly love the area. Before leaving England, he made out his will—suggesting that he planned to stay in America for the rest of his days.[62]

Arriving in December 1643, Morton wintered at Plymouth and continued to irritate its residents. For example, he hunted illegally on the property of his old foe, Miles Standish. But Edward Winslow, who had been jailed in England because of Morton, was the most upset at his reappearance. Winslow doubted that Morton had really changed his colors and abandoned the royalists. If Rigby had actually hired this "serpent," Winslow fumed, then he was not worthy of trust. Winslow also sounded a familiar Puritan warning:

> Morton is the odium of our peop[le] at present, and if he be suffered
> (for we are diversly minded) it will be just with God who hath putt him
> in our hands [that he be punished] and [if] we will foster such an one
> that afterward we shall suffer for it.[63]

Despite Winslow's doubts, Morton at that time had no devious plans up his sleeve. All he wanted was to settle around either New Haven or the Narragansett country, which were still sparsely populated. Hoping to attract some others to join him, Morton offered land but found few takers. As of yet, Morton had no land in those places. The lands he claimed in his will are either in Maine or offshore islands including a dubious claim to Martha's Vineyard. Presumably, Morton planned to buy land in southern New England. But where could he have found the money to do so? While at Plymouth, Winslow had observed, Morton had so little money that he was unable to buy liquor, quite a comedown for the Lord of Misrule.[64]

The answer to the puzzle lies in Morton's will. Among all the places claimed, there is no reference to Merry Mount. He seems to have left it out of the will because he planned to sell it to finance his new ventures. Because of the continuing growth of Massachusetts, Morton probably assumed that, unlike his property in Maine, there was a great demand for land in the Bay colony, and especially for land so near the coastline. He seems to have expected a sum of £ 200 for his old haunt, but he was in for a great shock when he arrived at Merry Mount. In 1634 Boston had taken over the area and settlers had moved in. The town of Braintree, created in 1640, had absorbed Morton's territory. He could hardly sell what was already in the possession of others. His claim to Merry Mount had been ignored.[65]

Bitterly angry, Morton once again sought revenge against the Puritans. This time he decided to rouse royalists in New England. Rhode Island—filled with those who disliked Massachusetts Bay—seemed like a rich recruiting site to Morton. Upon his arrival in Rhode Island, he commented that "he was glad to meet with so many Caveleres." To increase support for Charles I, Morton offered land all over New England—which he did not have—to potential recruits and did find some men willing to take up the king's banner. Such activity, Morton believed, would be rewarded when Gorges arrived as governor of New England. Morton confided in William Coddington, a former supporter of Anne Hutchinson, whom he thought was a fellow sufferer at the hands of Massachusetts. The Lord of Misrule had misjudged Coddington, who informed Winthrop of what he had learned. Morton left Rhode Island and headed for Gloucester, whose fishermen seemed like another pool of royalist recruits. From there, he planned to go to Maine, where royalists could work in more safety.[66]

Yet Morton had not reckoned with the alertness of Governor Endicott of Massachusetts, which in May 1644 had prohibited helping the royalist cause. Endicott had become aware of "a great partie for the Kinge" in Maine. Some of these royalists tried to steal a ship in Salem, Endicott's own community. Now that he realized that royalist plots were possible even in New England, the governor immediately guessed that Morton was formenting trouble. Having learned that he was going to Gloucester, Endicott ordered his arrest. Soon afterward, another Puritan, John Browne, demanded that Morton be punished for *New English Canaan*.[67] Thomas Morton was arrested, exactly where and how is not known.

During Morton's trial in September 1644 before the Court of Assistants, the magistrates confronted him with his letter to Jeffreys, his book, and his prosecution of the *quo warranto* against the colony. Hoping to receive additional evidence from England, the Court decided to jail him until it arrived. In November Morton petitioned to be released, but the magistrates refused "unlesse hee find sufficient bayle" which he could not. When in May 1645 Morton petitioned again for his freedom, he complained that he had been jailed for "manie Moneths and laid in Irons to the decaying of his Limbs." The deputies became interested in his case and the lack of the English evidence was becoming embarrassing to the magistrates. But they again rejected Morton's petition. Finally, after a year as a prisoner "without fire or beddinge . . . [during] a very cold winter. . . ," the magistrates fined him and allowed him to leave the colony. Morton traveled to Agamenticus, where he supported himself with his legal trade. Whether or not he aided the royalist stirrings in Maine during 1646 is unknown.[68]

Morton died in Agamenticus in 1647. The Lord of Misrule died "haveing as he said and most believed received his bane by hard lodging and fare in prison. This was done by the Massachusetts Magistrats. . . ."[69] After over twenty years, the Puritans had silenced Thomas Morton.

Chapter 3

Anne Hutchinson

When John Winthrop called Anne Hutchinson an "American Jesabel," he thought he had damned her forever by linking her to an immoral prophetess mentioned in the book of Revelation. But the phrase is used almost as a badge of honor by scholars when they write about her. Indeed, even nineteenth century historians often took Hutchinson's side. How could they seem to oppose an icon of religious freedom? Twentieth century historians depicted her as a heroic symbol for the need of and the legal right to a fair trial. During the 1970s and 1980s she evolved into "Ms. Hutchinson," the feminist victim of male oppressors. Whatever viewpoint of Anne Hutchinson one may choose, she was an enemy to the Massachusetts Bay colony.[1]

Anne Marbury was born in 1591. Her father, Francis Marbury, a minister, educated her in religious matters. Among her first books were, surely, the Bible and the *Book of Martyrs*, a compilation about devoted Protestants who had suffered because of their faith. Her father suffered too when he voiced his displeasure over the quality of some clerics of the Church of England. Eventually he regained favor with the church because he was not a Puritan.[2]

William Hutchinson, a tradesman, married Anne in 1611. This successful marriage produced fifteen children. Winthrop believed that William was a weak man dominated by his strong mate. However, the Puritan governor's opinion of her husband reflected his great hostility towards Anne Hutchinson. Her husband did believe that she was "a dear saint and servant of God." He must have taken great pride in her religious learning and theological bent. At the same time, he believed that a wife was "the weaker vessel" and she, no doubt, obeyed him. Somehow or other, the Hutchinsons managed to reconcile such potentially clashing beliefs.[3]

Perhaps there was little dispute between the Hutchinsons over a woman's role. English businessmen tended to treat women better than other groups did. And Puritans saw a married couple as partners, each with duties to the other. Some wives helped their husbands conduct their business. By the time of the Hutchinsons' marriage, ideas about women were changing. Not only were women learning to read, intelligence was something a woman no longer had to hide (although Roger Williams believed that females should be veiled). There was even at least one female preacher in Ely, England, Elizabeth Bancroft, whom Anne Hutchinson greatly admired although she never listened to her oratory.[4]

But Mrs. Hutchinson admired a more conventional preacher as well. During her occasional visits to the English town of Boston, listening to John Cotton inspired her. Rapidly, he became her spiritual guide. When Cotton deserted old Boston for colonial Boston, she decided she had to follow him. In July 1634 she and her family arrived in Massachusetts.[5]

It took some doing, however, before Boston's church admitted Mrs. Hutchinson as a member; her husband had no problems. She had stated some unusual opinions during the voyage to America and she was informed on. Nonetheless, she managed in Boston to convince everyone that she was an orthodox Puritan and in November 1634 she was declared to be a visible saint of Boston's church.[6]

With that problem out of the way, Hutchinson devoted herself to absorbing the spiritual lessons provided by Cotton. She started a meeting (properly referred to as a conventicle) at her home for other women. At this conventicle, a long-standing Puritan tradition in England, she expounded upon Cotton's sermons and tried to clarify the more mysterious sections. Her meetings started out with only a few people, but as her reputation grew, more and more attended. Gradually, she began to express her own religious tenets and criticized those ministers she disapproved of. Motivated by a belief that the end of the world was near, she could afford to waste no time. Erring preachers had to be exposed.[7]

Before Anne Hutchinson's preachings can be understood, the basic beliefs of the Puritans must be summarized. An orthodox Puritan believed that God's elect had been predestined by the Creator to be saved from the torments of hell. How these lucky individuals lived their lives did not matter. It was assumed that saved individuals would perform good works and lead good lives. Mrs. Hutchinson believed in a heresy called Antinomianism, which had several important differences from the norm. First, Antinomians believed that the Holy Spirit actually resided within them. Second, as they had been irrevocably saved, how they lived was of no matter—moral laws were meaningless and good works were unnecessary. Third, as God was within them, they could "infallibly" decide if another person was a true saint; only a brief chat was required. Fourth, anyone who disagreed with them were practitioners of the hated "Covenant of Works" and were not true visible saints. Only those who accepted the Antinomian "Covenant of Grace" were really saved.[8]

According to Mrs. Hutchinson, every Massachusetts minister—save Cotton—propounded the erroneous Covenant of Works. Startling as that claim might be for a Puritan colony, Antinomianism spread with amazing rapidity. Soon women impressed by Hutchinson brought their husbands to her meetings, which swelled to about 80 participants. John Winthrop, who lived "across the lane" from the Hutchinsons, could see her increasing popularity. A large faction of Boston's church accepted her viewpoints, but Winthrop was not one of her admirers.[9]

During October 1635 John Wilson, the other minister of the Boston church, returned from England, and Hutchinson quickly grew disgruntled with him. He preached a Covenant of Works, she believed. Her comments at her meetings blistered every one of Wilson's sermons. Nor was she respectful of the minister during the church services. Mrs. Hutchinson sometimes led walkouts when Wilson spoke; other times the Antinomians physically turned away from him. John Cotton obviously did not like such behavior, but he later claimed those involved—largely female— always gave credible excuses for their actions. On the other hand, Wilson discerned that something was seriously amiss among the church members. He learned Hutchinson's opinion about him.[10]

But the Antinomian assault on Wilson was just the most obvious attack upon the religious establishment of the colony. As Philip Gura commented, the Antinomians' attack upon the ministers "displayed a strong anti-institutional, if not anti-intellectual, bias." One of Mrs. Hutchinson's admirers insisted that she was more fulfilling than the Massachusetts "black-coates that have been at the Ninneversity." This curious remark suggested that the college-trained clergy had studied at a university that was no better than Nineveh, the capital of ancient Assyria, where pagan gods had been worshipped.[11]

All of the settled ministers came under assault in one way or another. When the Antinomians' beliefs became known to the ministers, they preached against them only to have their statements opposed by some of those present. Sometimes the clerics were publicly insulted by being called "Pharisees" or "Baals Priests." Her followers preferred Anne Hutchinson to any of those unsaved ministers. And the ministers grew to detest her. She had constructed an anticlerical system—God was within each Antinomian so the ministers were really just useless middlemen. [12]

The Antinomians gained two important supporters. The first, Sir Henry Vane, a recently-arrived young man with very impressive connections in the mother country, leaned towards Mrs. Hutchinson's religious doctrines and participated in her meetings. Because of his social status, in May 1636 Vane was "too suddenly chosen governor" according to a critical minister. His victory gave the Antinomians a measure of political influence. [13]

John Wheelwright, the second important new figure, was related by marriage to the Hutchinsons. When he settled in Massachusetts during 1636, Mrs. Hutchinson joyously welcomed him for he was the only minister besides Cotton who seemed to back her religious views. Wheelwright would help to stir the colony in the months ahead. [14]

By the middle of 1636 the beliefs of the Antinomians were no longer secret. Wilson knew what was happening and eventually even John Cotton understood what had been going on, supposedly, without his knowledge. Or, at least, he may have realized the extent of Anne Hutchinson's differences from orthodox Puritanism. Cotton's behavior will remain quixotic. He later insisted he had been caught by surprise because of his "sleepines." Whatever Cotton actually thought, by October 1636 other clerics were telling him the truth. Cotton met with Mrs. Hutchinson; she denied what he had been told. For Cotton, that ended the matter. [15]

The mounting crisis, which Cotton tried to stay out of, had already ensnared Governor Vane, who could not handle it. At first he wanted to leave for England to escape. But the Antinomians in the Boston church begged him to stay. With the likelihood that Vane's deputy governor—their foe Winthrop—would be elected in his place, the Antinomians wanted to keep their hero in the colony. After exerting much pressure, they persuaded Vane to stay and fight as well as he could—which would not be very well. [16]

In an attempt to calm the religious dispute, the colony's leaders proclaimed a fast day "designed for peace" on January 19, 1637. Cotton preached a non-controversial sermon. Wheelwright followed; his previous sermons had been mild-mannered and the foes of the Antinomians expected something "gentle." To their great surprise, they heard just the opposite. [17]

Wheelwright denied the validity of a Covenant of Works, but, he declared, those who believed in that error were powerful. Still, they would be defeated in this "battle" because God was on the side of the Antinomians. The preacher admitted that this fight would cause commotion, not only in the Boston church, but in the colony itself. There was a need for a "Spirituall burning" to destroy the "whore" entirely. Although he urged Hutchinson's followers to live good lives and obey moral laws, he charged that when their foes lived good lives they made themselves worse in God's eyes. Wheelwright's harsh sermon started Winthrop and his allies on a campaign to rid the colony of the Antinomian heresy. [18]

In March 1637 the General Court—already dominated by Winthrop supporters—moved against Wheelwright and tried him for sedition. He attempted to defend himself, but his cause was hopeless as Vane and his comrades could do nothing to help him. Although Wheelwright was found guilty, the General Court did not sentence him. Winthrop hoped to quiet the Antinomians by this demonstration of "moderation." As Winthrop's forces had the numbers in the General Court to destroy the Antinomians, he assumed they would realize that fact and remain silent. Furthermore, the site for the election due in May was shifted to quiet Newtown (later Cambridge) instead of Antinomian Boston. Vane, who opposed the move, was, again, totally helpless and outmaneuvered. Despite such obvious signs of weakness, the Antinomians did not give up. A remonstrance that protested the Wheelwright verdict was submitted and ignored (for the moment) by the majority. Wheelwright and others continued to voice their opinions. [19]

The winner of the May 1637 election should have been obvious. Various Antinomians gave fiery campaign speeches and fist fights broke out. Such tactics did not sway the electorate, who elected John Winthrop governor, with Thomas Dudley as deputy governor. Vane and other Antinomians were not even picked as magistrates. Winthrop's forces had made a clean sweep of the election. Defeated, the Antinomians were not gracious. Six Boston militia sergeants—all Antinomians—refused to carry ceremonial halberds for Governor Winthrop; two of his servants were drafted for that duty. Ex-governor Vane turned into a model of a bad loser. In July 1637 Winthrop gave a dinner to honor a visiting nobleman.

Vane diverted him away from the governor, and the visitor dined with the genial Samuel Maverick instead. The following month Vane left Massachusetts.[20]

When the Antinomians refused to abandon their beliefs, a synod of the ministers was called to begin to heal the religious rift. The synod, which convened in August 1637, was especially notable because Cotton agreed completely with his colleagues. He understood that he had to take a public stand in support of the united clergy or become a target himself. Cotton condemned the Antinomian heresy. With that "new light" now also opposed by Cotton, there remained just one minister who supported it, Wheelwright, dismissed by another cleric as "a man of a . . . stiff conceit of his own worth and light."[21]

In early November the isolated Wheelwright finally received his punishment from the General Court for his sedition—banishment. He promptly appealed to the king, a useless gesture; the Puritan leadership did not acknowledge that principle. When informed that such an appeal was invalid, Wheelwright did not pursue it further and accepted the sentence. Given a choice of an almost immediate departure or staying confined until the weather improved, Wheelwright impulsively wanted to leave Massachusetts for the uncertainties of New Hampshire. Probably not realizing the danger of such a trip in November, he trekked through "deep snow in which he might have perished." Wheelwright later thought his survival on that difficult trip was something to marvel at.[22]

Dealing with Wheelwright was only a start. Winthrop and his associates had already decided that they and the Antinomians were so radically different as to be unable to coexist in one colony without dire consequences. Wanting to root out the followers of Anne Hutchinson, they grasped at the old remonstrance protesting Wheelwright's treatment as a convenient tool. This curious document had suggested that Wheelwright was a prophet and that the devil himself, "that old serpent," had been behind the General Court's actions. Winthrop had complained that many of the signers had gotten involved in governmental matters that were beyond their state in life. Most of the culprits were men who did not know the meaning of words such as "sedition," "remonstrance," or "contempt." The Court deemed that losing their right to vote was sufficient punishment for most of them.[23]

At last, the time had now come to grapple "with the head of all this faction"—Anne Hutchinson. The General Court, in November 1637, tried her for sedition. The trial began with Winthrop being completely frustrated by her nimble defense of her actions. She could cite the Bible as well as her accusers could. The ministers, led by Thomas Shepard of Cambridge, joined in the trial as well with as little success as Winthrop. The determined ministers related details of an earlier, private talk they had had with Mrs. Hutchinson about her beliefs. She denied the ministers' account of the meeting.[24]

During an overnight recess, Mrs. Hutchinson perused notes, compiled by John Wilson, on her meeting with the clerics. When the trial resumed, she declared that the notes backed her version of the meeting and insisted that the ministers should be required to make their statements under oath. A donnybrook ensued. Finally, Winthrop asked a nervous John Cotton to give his opinion about the controversial meeting. Cotton was, as Richard B. Morris commented, "in a way . . . as much on trial as the prisoner." Cotton, after all, was her spiritual mentor. Cotton declared that his recall of the ministers' talk with Hutchinson was different from his colleagues. She had not impugned their religious ideas in the way they remembered it. Except among her most bitter foes such as Winthrop and Dudley, the case against her was dead.[25]

But in the midst of Cotton's testimony, he happened to mention Thomas Bilney, one of the early English Protestant martyrs who had been eulogized in the Protestant classic, the *Book of Martyrs*. Mrs. Hutchinson must have read it as a child. Perhaps a memory of an illustration from it flashed before her—of "Bilney being dragged from his pulpit by the friars" in England. Such a scene sharply contrasted with what she was doing. Instead of boldly declaring her beliefs as Bilney had done, she was withholding the truth from a gathering of antichrists. Suddenly, she decided to act more like a Bilney and state her true beliefs. She realized the consequences of being truthful because her destiny had already been foretold to her.[26]

Mrs. Hutchinson jumped in just as Cotton was demolishing the case of his fellow ministers. She stated "what in my conscience I know to be truth," announcing that God had told her "by an immediate revelation" that her fate would be like that of the Old Testament figure, Daniel, who was placed in a lion's den and was unharmed because God protected him. When Daniel's accusers were put there, the lions killed them. She would similarly triumph over the leaders of Massachusetts, who would themselves be destroyed. Hutchinson said all this in a very determined manner, which made Winthrop quip that she seemed more like a lion than another Daniel.[27]

The trial was all but over. Her gleeful foes had all the evidence they needed right from Anne Hutchinson herself. They saw it as a gift from God. Cotton repudiated her, calling her supposed revelation merely a "delusion." Some of the judges diverted their attention to Cotton, but Winthrop stopped that line of questioning. After all, Cotton was no longer willing to be tied to her in any way. The court convicted her of sedition and she was to suffer banishment. She would be confined until the weather improved.[28]

Did Mrs. Hutchinson receive a fair trial? A modern American court would never be the scene of such a spectacle, but, of course, the seventeenth century was different. In the 1630s a political trial such as Hutchinson's was common enough. The trial did conform to English standards of that age.[29]

Hutchinson's talk of revelation presented Winthrop and his comrades with a great deal of worry. During the trial, Thomas Dudley brought up a well-known case where supposed divine revelations brought turmoil in their wake. In 1534 radical Anabaptists seized control of the German city of Munster—a religious revolt had turned into a political one. The Anabaptists expelled all those of other religious persuasions from the city, destroyed physical traces of other faiths, and burned books. Monogamy was frowned upon in radical Munster. For example, the chief leader of the Anabaptists had sixteen wives. Protestants and Catholics united long enough to rescue the city in 1535. Dudley was uncertain whether the Antinomians in Massachusetts were inspired by Satan as the Munster Anabaptists had been, but he was convinced that Hutchinson's revelation came straight from the devil.[30]

The government of Massachusetts had no intention of allowing Boston to degenerate into another Munster. On November 20, 1637, the Court declared:

> Whereas the opinions and revelations of Mr. Wheelwright and Mrs. Hutchinson have seduced and led into dangerous errors many of the people here in New England, insomuch as there is just cause of suspicion that they, as others in Germany, in former times, may, upon some revelation, make some sudden irruption upon those that differ from them in judgment, for prevention whereof it is ordered, that [the Antinomians] shall . . . deliver in . . . all such guns, pistols, swords, powder, shot, and match as they shall be owners of, or have in their custody. . . . Also, it is ordered . . . that no man who is to render his

arms by this order shall buy or borrow any guns, swords, pistols, powder, shot, or match. . . . [31]

Concerned about the strength of the Antinomians in the militia, the General Court rendered them harmless. As a further precaution, military stockpiles were taken out of Boston. For good measure, Antinomians in Salem, Newbury, Roxbury, Ipswich, and Charlestown were also disarmed.[32]

With the colony now safe from any possible coup attempt, only one more act had to be played. Because Anne Hutchinson had espoused heresies, she had to be tried by the Boston church. Two ministers, Cotton and John Davenport, had been talking with her and had succeeded in their mission to redeem her to a surprising degree. She was tired and ill. By the time of her church trial in March 1638, Mrs. Hutchinson was pregnant yet again. All the physical travails of pregnancy no doubt caused her to want to lessen the burden she was about to face. In a religious age, the prospect of excommunication from a church was a weighty sentence and one most individuals would try to avoid.[33]

At the trial itself, Hutchinson presented a written statement that seemed to be repentant. During the proceedings, she even declared she was against criticizing ministers. Nor did she favor the libertine views of some extreme sects and declared she abhorred sexual misconduct. None of her comments did her any good.[34]

The ministers wanted Hutchinson excommunicated and they would stop at nothing to gain that objective. They seized upon what was seemingly a minor point—exactly when she held some of her beliefs. Accused of lying, it was merely a matter of time before the actual words of excommunication were pronounced.[35]

Cotton's comments at the trial had to be the hardest for Mrs. Hutchinson to hear. He called her ideas evil and compared them to gangrene. She was full of pride and "puft up." Probably most upsetting to her was his declaration: "though I have not heard, neither do I think, you have been unfaithfull to your Husband . . . , yet that will follow" from her beliefs.[36]

John Wilson's statements were in the same spirit. He called Anne Hutchinson Satan's tool whose apparent repentance was not real. The minister formally excommunicated his former tormentor. Wilson surely relished telling her she was now no better than a pagan and so should be shunned by the members of the Boston church.[37]

After the dreaded words had been spoken, the ordeal was over. A great weight was lifted from her shoulders. Hutchinson gloried in her martyrdom. Unlike Bilney, she still lived. As she left the meetinghouse, one of her followers, Mary Dyer, walked with her. (Mrs. Dyer eventually became a Quaker and was hanged by Massachusetts, but that martyrdom was well in the future.) When Hutchinson reached the door of the church she had been expelled from, she observed that it was "better to be cast out of the Church then to deny Christ." Clearly, Cotton believed, "she had changed only her Expressions, but not her Judgment."[38]

Meanwhile, William Hutchinson and others were trying to find a new home for the Antinomians. Not permitted to settle within the Plymouth colony because of their Antinomianism, they went to Rhode Island instead. That colony had enough "Elbow roome" for the unorthodox. Roger Williams helped to pave the way for them and they purchased Aquidneck island from the Indians. Near the end of March 1638, Mrs. Hutchinson left Massachusetts to join her comrades there.[39]

Soon afterward, the Massachusetts authorities learned that Anne Hutchinson, acting with Cotton's advice, had concealed that Mary Dyer had delivered a stillborn, ill-developed fetus. The production of a "monster" suggested to Winthrop and others that God had punished Dyer for her religious views. When Hutchinson had a miscarriage, her enemies declared, God had spoken a second time in confirmation of the actions undertaken by the government of Massachusetts Bay. Winthrop eagerly spread the news about the monsters, even to England. John Wheelwright looked rather askance at this delight in writing about the deformities. Such failed pregnancies, he insisted, had a "naturall cause." As for the hostile writing about "defects of Nature," Wheelwright asked, "must it needs be in print?"[40]

As time passed, not many hostile passions inflamed by Anne Hutchinson had cooled. Thomas Dudley believed that the government's chief mistake was allowing the Antinomians to go untouched as long as they did. As for Winthrop, he delighted whenever he could record that one of her former disciples had strayed into immorality, and he soon suspected that she had dabbled in witchcraft. His evidence for this involved her association with Jane Hawkins, who supposedly was on good terms with Beelzebub. Wheelwright ridiculed the thought of Hawkins in league with the devil. According to Wheelwright, she was "a poore silly woman" who only attended Hutchinson's meetings for the free food she received there.[41]

Anne Hutchinson returned the angry sentiments of her foes. When she left Massachusetts, she reportedly repudiated her statement admitting religious error. Along with her closest supporters, she believed the Boston church to be a "strumpet" and participated in religious activities as if she had never been excommunicated. Hutchinson and others yearned for the return of Sir Henry Vane in a position of power as a general governor over New England. Their dream of having control over the government of Massachusetts went unfulfilled.[42]

The Antinomians had to be content with Rhode Island as their home. During March 1638 the leading male Antinomians signed a compact creating a religious government that would be run according to Christ's "perfect and most absolute lawes." The Antinomian settlement in Rhode Island would be the future Portsmouth. But Mrs. Hutchinson soon disapproved of the conduct of William Coddington, their ruling judge. Allying themselves with another religious radical, Samuel Gorton, in 1639 the followers of Anne Hutchinson removed Coddington from his position and put William Hutchinson in the office instead. Coddington left Portsmouth and established his own community at Newport. However, Coddington was soon back in charge.[43]

Religious affairs on Aquidneck island were as changeable as the government. Many curious ideas floated about, including the notion that females lacked souls, which must have distressed Anne Hutchinson. Her disappointment with Rhode Island grew as her following gradually depleted. She lost some people to the Quakers, others to the Baptists. Her world seemed vastly different when William Hutchinson died in 1642. Tired of the years of strife, she decided it was time for a change; she would settle somewhere else.[44]

Hutchinson opted to live in the Dutch colony of New Netherland. She picked a wilderness area later named Eastchester (now part of the Bronx). The colonists there were easily outnumbered by the Indians, who twice warned a carpenter not to build Hutchinson's house, an omen of the future. Yet she was not at all concerned about living in almost complete isolation. During August-September 1643 hostile Indians killed some of the Dutch. Anne Hutchinson knew nothing about it. When some apparently friendly Indians arrived at her door, she welcomed them and tied up the household dogs at the Indians' request. With that possible means of defense eliminated, the Indians killed Hutchinson and most of those with her. Mrs. Hutchinson's enemies saw her violent death as another sign of God's verdict against her.[45]

About the time of Anne Hutchinson's demise, John Wheelwright started to repair his relations with the Massachusetts Bay colony. He regretted getting involved with the Antinomians. After he admitted his error, in May 1644 his banishment was revoked. The following year he summed up Hutchinson as "a woman of a good wit" who "had many strange fancies, and erroneous tenents."[46]

If Hutchinson had still lived, she probably would not have been surprised by Wheelwright's repudiation. After all, John Cotton's defection had occurred in the midst of the Antinomian crisis. His role is murky: He likely held similar beliefs as Mrs. Hutchinson on many matters, but he held them "obscurely." Cotton could not accept his friend Anne Hutchinson tearing the colony apart because of doctrinal differences. Whatever Cotton's true feelings, he could not have been proud of his role. Just before his death he made arrangements to destroy his documents relating to the Antinomians.[47]

Hutchinson's activities also stirred up the mother country. In 1638, for example, one Antinomian foe wrote to an Englishman that "Mrs. Hutchinson was and is a woman who led aside silly men and women into strange conclusions." But her admirers sent their own letters to England that were favorable to her. Her death did not abate the controversy because in 1644, John Winthrop's *Short Story*, an attack upon the Antinomians, was published there. But Winthrop's book backfired—it hurt the reputation of the Congregational system in England and made Presbyterianism seem more attractive.[48]

Finally, was Mrs. Hutchinson persecuted because of her sex? There are certainly plenty of references to the fact that she was female and acting very differently from the customary female role. She behaved like a minister or even a government official—male roles—instead of being submissive. One must remember, however, that the Puritans moved against many male Antinomians including Wheelwright. If the chief leader had been male, the Puritans would have given other biblical citations instead of Saint Paul and proceeded as they did with Anne Hutchinson.[49]

Nobody can be certain as to the actual source of Hutchinson's revelation. But, in a sense, it came true. She did triumph in the end. Her name, if not her cause, lives on.

Chapter 4

Miantonomo

Samuel Eliot Morison thought that the Puritans' involvement in the death of the Narragansett sachem (or leader) Miantonomo was disgraceful.[1] A supposed "victim of Puritan land hunger," the Indian has even been transformed into an ecological prophet by historians who have followed in Morison's wake. Both Miantonomo's execution and the Pequot War are used as weapons to attack the colonists by scholars thinking mostly of "the present day."[2]

Almost forgotten amidst the host of criticism hurled at Puritan New England over Miantonomo's fate is that American Indians had their own rivalries and wars. Miantonomo and Uncas, the chief sachem of the Mohegans, became bitter foes, eventually dooming the Narragansett leader. By comparison, the colonists were but secondary players in this epic of an enemy of the Bay colony. Truly, Miantonomo's "Head was cut off by Uncas."[3]

All of the early colonists agreed on one thing: the Narragansett Indians were "a great people." They dominated the western shore of Narragansett Bay and had many tributaries among surrounding tribes including some in Massachusetts and Long Island. Their manpower made them especially powerful; they had far more warriors than their neighbors. Because the Narragansetts had somehow not been hit by a deadly epidemic that decimated two of their ancient foes, the Wampanoags and the Massachusett, Miantonomo's people became still more powerful. Massasoit of the Wampanoags had to submit to them as his overlords.[4]

The Narragansetts were also wealthy. One Puritan was amazed that, despite poor soil "yet they have good corne without fish" as a fertilizer because they regularly rested their land. But most of their wealth came from their control of wampum, a product made from shells that Indians highly prized. The Narragansetts profited in the fur trade as well.[5]

A famous custom of the Narragansetts is what has been called their dual sachem system. Two preeminent, closely-related leaders divided power. One sachem, an older man, took care of more sedentary matters while a younger, more vigorous, sachem served as the warrior. If necessary, the younger sachem travelled away from the Narragansett territory for warfare or negotiations with friend or foe. Roger Williams referred to the young leader as the "marshal" and "executioner." Apparently, as the young warrior aged he eventually took over his senior's role and a younger warrior took over military affairs. This unusual system had been in place before European contact.[6]

Roger Williams, who observed the dual sachem system close up, noticed how the two leaders had to take each other into account: "The old Sachim will not be offended at what the young Sachim doth; and the young Sachim will not do what hee conceives will displease his Uncle."[7] Without such careful consideration of the other sachem, the system could not have worked.

By the 1630s Canonicus was the elder sachem. His much younger counterpart abandoned the name Mecumeh for Miantonomo, which in the Narragansett tongue meant "the people's choice." Edward Johnson described him as "a very sterne man, and of a great stature, . . . causing all of his Nobility and such as were his attendan[ts] to tremble at his speech." Miantonomo knew how to intimidate other Indians.[8]

As neither sachem could read or write, they made marks, displayed in Table 1, on various documents produced by the colonists. Some of these marks demonstrate the relationship between Canonicus and Miantonomo. The elder's sign usually consisted of a bow and an arrow. The arrow, however, never had feathers and thus was not really functional. An arrow without feathers would not have a stable flight. Unfeathered arrows could, in real life, only be used in religious ceremonies. Sometimes Canonicus used a bow for his mark. This sign meant that Canonicus was incomplete without his partner, for Miantonomo's usual mark was a fully functional arrow, with a sharp point and equipped with feathers. Such a weapon could be employed in war and hunting; the arrow would travel a great distance. This mark symbolizes his own duties. By 1639 Canonicus's arrow even lacked a point, making his arrow as useless as a toy. Two years later, Miantonomo was being called chief

Table 1
The Sachems' Marks

1A. Canonicus

1637   1637   1637/8

1638   1639

1639

Table 1
The Sachems' Marks

1B. Miantonomo

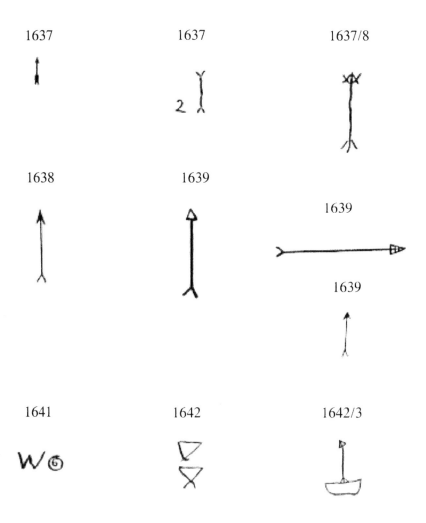

1637   1637   1637/8

1638   1639

1639

1639

1641   1642   1642/3

Sources for the Sachems' Marks: John Russell Bartlett, ed., *Records of the Colony of Rhode Island and Providence Plantations in New England* (Providence, 1856), I, 18, 46, 49; Howard M. Chapin, ed., *Documentary History of Rhode Island* (Providence, 1919), I, 48, 62, 77, 143, 167, 170; *ibid.*, II, 73.

sachem and, soon after, he utilized a mark like Canonicus's except that its arrow had a sharp point and feathers. Miantonomo had become the first of the sachems as Canonicus had been during Miantonomo's youth.[9]

Indeed, Canonicus first appears in the earliest days of New England. In 1622 the planters of Plymouth had a curious encounter with a messenger from him. Earlier, he had wanted peace with the new arrivals, but that year a Narragansett appeared at Plymouth with a known Indian friend of the Pilgrims, Tokamahamon. The messenger, looking for the absent Squanto (the Wampanoag who had joined forces with the colonists), left an odd item at Squanto's abode, "a bundle of new arrows lapped in a rattlesnake's skin." Puzzled by this unusual gift, the planters asked Tokamahamon for its meaning. He answered "That he could not certainly tell, but thought they were enemies to us." This vague response suggests that he really did not want to get involved. Intrigued, the English questioned the Narragansett messenger who promptly smeared an earlier courier for misrepresenting what he saw at Plymouth.[10]

When Squanto returned, he quickly expressed his concern over the wrapped arrows which, he declared, represented "enmity and it was no better than a challenge." The settlers responded with their own challenge—they filled "the skin with powder and shot" and returned it to the Narragansett sachem. Canonicus reacted with shock, Edward Winslow related. The bundle "was no small terror to this savage King" who "would not once touch the powder and shot, or suffer it to stay in his house or country." Eventually, it turned up back at Plymouth.[11]

The shock Canonicus experienced can be imagined, but not for the reason the Pilgrims thought. The rattlesnake-skin bundle of arrows was, indeed, meant as a challenge, but not to the Pilgrims. The threat was delivered to Squanto, after all. As a Wampanoag, Squanto was a traditional enemy of the Narragansett and Canonicus wished to intimidate him. Not surprisingly, Squanto expanded the threat to the English colonists for his own protection. Canonicus was quite willing to frighten a single Wampanoag Indian, not the strangers with the equally strange weapons.[12]

Far from being a warlike individual, Canonicus was an advocate of peace, highly unusual for his day. When the Pequots tried to convince him to ally with them against the English, Canonicus "instead of taking part with them, labours all he can to hush the War in hand, laying before them the sad effects of War; sometimes proving sad and mournfull to the very Victors themselves, but always to the vanquished." To the English,

Canonicus proclaimed that they "had rather make choice of Peace than Warre, provided it may stand with Truth and Righteousness. . . ." Miantonomo's father, Mascus, had held similar views about war.[13]

Although Williams called Canonicus "a wise and peaceable Prince," his commendable attitude about war had some unforeseen consequences. Because the epidemic that hit the Indians around 1617 had spared the Narragansetts, they could intimidate most of their neighbors by their vastly superior numbers. The Narragansett could get their way without war. Younger men such as Miantonomo had no practical military experience beyond quick raids. The warriors had plenty of bluster and bravado but nothing to back it up. Such inexperience counted for nothing when the Narragansetts intimidated one of the depopulated easterly tribes. When Miantonomo confronted Uncas and the Mohegans, who were related in some way to the Pequots, Miantonomo would be overmatched. Uncas had far more considerable military experience—even though he kept losing to the Pequots—than the Narragansetts and the Mohegan warriors, "though not so numerous," were willing to fight. The factors that doomed Miantonomo were in place from the start.[14]

Miantonomo first appears in history during 1632 when he journeyed to the Massachusetts Bay colony to sign a friendship pact. He stayed a few days and attended a Puritan church service. What he thought of the sermon, given in a language he could not speak, has not been recorded. Nor would a plain Puritan meetinghouse have been very appealing. Meanwhile, three of his hungry men, wanting food, forced their way into a closed home. Causing consternation among the Puritans, they insisted that the culprits be punished. A reluctant Miantonomo had them beaten and they returned to their homeland. The sachem had been hesitant to punish his men for something that was considered normal behavior among his people; strangers could enter an Indian home at will. Miantonomo departed Boston promptly afterward, no doubt to the relief of his hosts.[15]

Things went much better in the colony of Rhode Island, which "was obtained by Love," as Williams testified. Canonicus and Miantonomo sold much land to Williams and his followers, both in 1637 and in the future. When Williams settled in what became Rhode Island, Canonicus was at least 70, and Miantonomo, no longer youthful, was about 40.[16]

The two Narragansett sachems and Uncas soon occupied center stage in the infamous Pequot War. The Pequots, who dominated the central region of what became Connecticut, were enemies of the Narragansetts. The origins of the Pequot War have been discussed elsewhere.[17]

Intensely unpopular with other Indians, the Pequots had been war-ring with the Dutch. The death of some English traders ignited the war. John Oldham had been killed by Indians within the Narragansett sphere, so Miantonomo vowed to lead a substantial force to punish his erring subjects. Eventually, one hand was sent to Boston. As with other reports of Miantonomo's military prowess, the result was not awe-inspiring, to say the least. He also paid an assassin to deal with one of the murderers and then expected the colonists to refund the wampum expended. "His warrs keepe him bare," Williams explained. The request seems to have been ignored.[18]

Miantonomo feared that the New England colonists might blame the Narragansetts for Oldham's death and tried to shift their attention to his own enemies, the Pequots, who, he claimed, had sheltered some of the murderers. (Uncas also pointed to the Pequots.) In spite of Miantonomo's fears, the Puritans absolved both of the dual sachems from any blame. On October 21, 1636 Miantonomo, who had been treated royally in Bos-ton, signed an alliance there directed against the Pequots, who had killed a different trader. The perpetual league provided for war against the Pequots, the death of murderers, and even "Free trade between us."[19]

At this time Miantonomo and the Narragansetts seemed to be brim-ming with martial spirit. By early 1638 his arrow mark, depicted in Table 1, seemed fiercer than usual with barbs (probably supposed to be eagle talons) projecting from the arrow head. At the end of April 1637 Williams travelled to the Narragansett encampment to talk with the dual sachems. Canonicus, however, was sullen as he suspected the English had tried to kill him with disease. Miantonomo, though, was more recep-tive. He and other Narragansetts gave some military advice, which has been praised, and Williams passed it along to Boston.[20]

Miantonomo and his associates advised the Puritans that a serious attack on the Pequots should take at least a month and be at night "by which advantage the English, being armed [i.e., wearing armour], may enter the houses and do what execution they please," an apparent fore-telling of part of the strategy of the assault on the Mystic fort. Miantonomo preferred the English handle the most dangerous part of the hoped-for battle. Included among the advice was the suggestion "That it would be pleasing to all natives, that women and children be spared, etc." Women and children constituted a major part of the booty the Narragansetts ex-pected from a successful war against the Pequots. When Incorporated into the Narragansett tribe, the human booty would swell Narragansett numbers even more.[21]

Along with that counsel, Williams urged that a substantial supply of sugar be sent to sweeten the sour Canonicus. Regarding the progress of the Narragansett war effort so far, Williams reported: "They pass not a week without some skirmishes, though hitherto little loss on either side. They were glad of your preparations. . . ."[22]

Although the Narragansetts were thrilled with English military preparations in April, by mid-May the atmosphere had changed. They had been eager "to take a full Revenge of all their former Injuries upon their inveterate Enemies," but where were the promised English soldiers? "The Narragansetts are at present doubtfull of Realitie in all our promises," Williams wrote, and he tried to explain the lack of "speedie performance."[23]

When soldiers commanded by Captain John Mason finally came to the Narragansetts, they were still "discontented" that the English had come "no sooner." Miantonomo seems to have been more concerned about their numbers. He warned the English that they did not have the numbers needed to make an impact upon the Pequots. To Miantonomo and his people, war was merely a question of numbers of warriors. Although he gave his own suggestions on how to deal with the enemy—no doubt along the lines of what Williams had already been told—Miantonomo did not volunteer to accompany Mason's force. Since the sachem thought that the expedition would be either doomed or ineffectual, there was no logical reason for him to go. No possible reward or glory could be obtained. Miantonomo did send some Narragansetts and Eastern Niantics, who were his subjects.[24]

Among the allied Indians, there was plenty of militant talk. Miantonomo even urged that the English merely ferry his warriors to the Pequots and do nothing else. Mason knew that boast to be meaningless and ignored it. Such talk contradicted Miantonomo's earlier advice. His warriors did their own boasting. An exasperated Mason wrote that the Narragansetts "had frequently despised us, saying That we durst not look upon a Pequot, but themselves would perform great Things." Yet, as the expedition moved closer to Pequot territory, more and more Narragansetts and Niantics left. Clearly, the Narragansetts feared the Pequots. One Puritan noted, "It was credibly reported that these Indians had gotten such a power from Satan, by God's permission, that an arrow should not pierce their skin." Faced with such a powerful foe, many Narragansetts preferred to leave.[25]

As Mason's army melted away, he came to depend upon his other allies, Uncas and the Mohegans. While the others were boasting, Mason asked Uncas a simple question: "what he thought the Indians would do?" Uncas's response was truly prophetic: "The Narragansetts would all leave us, but as for Himself He would never leave us." Uncas soon found he had dependable friends in Mason and the colony of Connecticut.[26]

Mason targeted the Pequot wooden fort at Mystic. No typical Pequot settlement, it was built on high ground, and had more wigwams within than usual. Archaeological work reveals that such forts were new adaptations to European colonization. Earlier villages were not built or sited primarily for defense. Located inside a fort created specifically for defense against Europeans, the Pequots were very confident. They had already warred against the Dutch and, clearly, had not been impressed. As for the English, the Pequots dismissed them as women.[27]

The attack on the fort at Mystic remains controversial. Some scholars refer to Indian "outrage," and that many Indians "left the field rather than participate in such a slaughter." A reexamination of the evidence suggests a somewhat different scenario.[28]

On May 26, 1637, Mason and some English soldiers entered the Mystic fort as Miantonomo had originally advised. Confronted by fierce Pequot resistance, Mason, a professional soldier, decided to set afire the highly combustible wigwams and thus the fort itself. Encircling the inferno, the English killed those who tried to flee; another circle of the Mohegans and Narragansetts dispatched those who had slipped past their allies. Hundreds of Pequot men, women, and children died either in the burning fort or in a futile attempt to escape. Although new to the Indians, fire was an old European weapon. The destruction of Mystic was comparatively mild compared to the horrors of the Thirty Years War then still raging in Europe.[29]

One drawback of fire as a weapon is that there is no booty. When the fort was destroyed, about fifty Narragansetts left the battlefield because nothing could be seized until, suddenly, another Pequot force attacked them. John Underhill, another professional soldier, related:

> Then came the Narragansetts to Captain Mason and myself, crying, Oh help us now, or our men will be all slain. We answered, How dare you crave aid of us, when you are leaving of us in this distressed condition, not knowing which way to march out of the country?[30]

Together, the reunited allies killed about one hundred more Pequots.[31]

The English reaction to the destruction of Mystic was not as dog-matic as some imply. Not all the English there were professional soldiers who knew what had been happening in Europe. England, after all, never became enmeshed in the Thirty Years War. Underhill noted that "Great and doleful was the bloody sight to the view of young soldiers that never had been in war."[32]

Indian reaction was more complicated. "Our Indians," Underhill wrote, "came to us, and much rejoiced at our victories, and greatly, admired the manner of Englishmen's fight, but cried Mach it, mach it; that is, It is naught, it is naught, because it is too furious, and slays too many men." This often quoted sentence was deconstructed by Francis Jennings who insisted that the seventeenth century meaning of "admire" suggested merely that the Indians were astonished by European tactics, and that "naught" implied that the Indians believed the destruction of the fort to be evil.[33]

Such meanings are, indeed, in the *Oxford English Dictionary*, but Jennings chose not to look very closely at the entire entries. Already by the time of the Pequot War, admire had taken on its modern meaning: "To regard with pleased surprise, or with wonder mingled with esteem, approbation, or affection; and in modern usage, To gaze on with plea-sure." Shakespeare had used that definition of the word in the 1590s. In addition, while naught could suggest evil, it probably meant the word nothing. That definition, although archaic now, was acceptable usage in the seventeenth century. In fact, a fuller account of Underhill's passage indicates that Jennings picked the wrong meanings:

> Our Indians came to us, and much rejoiced at our victories, and greatly, admired the manner of Englishmen's fight, but cried Mach it, mach it; that is, It is naught, it is naught, because it is too furious, and slays too many men. Having received their desires, they freely promised, and gave up themselves to march along with us, wherever we would go.[34]

What did the allied Indians at the scene actually believe? They were astonished at what they saw and would have preferred to have taken many Pequot women and children alive thus strengthening their tribe. On the other hand, their Pequot enemies had been thoroughly vanquished. Therefore, although the Narragansetts and Mohegans would not have fought the way the English did, they appreciated the finality of the result.

That explains why they continued to march along with the colonists. Finally, was Miantonomo outraged? There is no evidence of it. In fact, in July—some weeks after the destruction of the Pequot fort—Roger Williams observed: "Yet if I mistake not I observe in Miantonomo some sparks of true Friendship."[35]

To suggest that the allied Indians had nothing to do with the battle of Mystic is wrong-headed. Peter Vincent explained why the Pequot death toll there was so high: "For the Narragansetts beset the fort so close, that not one escaped." And Bradford insisted that the Narragansetts taunted their dying enemies by yelling "O brave Pequots!," a phrase which had been part of Pequot victory celebrations. Once the battle had been won, Vincent explained what followed next: "They now all went a-shipboard, and sailed to Seabrook fort, where the English feasted the Narragansetts three days, and then sent them home in a pinnace." Outraged Indians would not normally be expected to attend the victory party.[36]

What did Miantonomo believe about the killing of women and children in warfare? Granted, he had wanted to save women and children in his advice to Williams, but he soon changed his mind. By May 13, 1637, not long after his earlier advice, Miantonomo had learned that some Pequots, in order to obtain more food, had sown corn in unusual places in case the colonists targeted their traditional fields. Miantonomo explained to Williams, before Mystic, how he wanted to proceed against those Pequots:

> He will direct the pinnace to the places and in the night land his men, despoile them of their Canowes Cut of [off] the men he finds the greatest numb[er] being women and children, wch for the most of them he would Cut of as allso to spoile their fields.[37]

In order to disrupt Pequot agriculture, primarily done by women, he wanted to kill most of the women and children. Or rather, his men would do the killing while he stayed aboard the ship with any English who had come, a typical stance for Miantonomo.[38]

Did this massacre of Pequot women and children by Narragansett warriors ever take place? Although the Puritans sent some soldiers to assist, Williams suspected that the whole business was only a scam to encourage the Puritans to send more wampum. Miantonomo did set sail, but he went to the Mystic battle site. He arrived after all the fighting was over, also typical behavior for Miantonomo.[39]

While the surviving Pequots were dealt with, Miantonomo began to claim the fruits of victory. He wanted a gun and gunpowder as a gift, and asked Massachusetts to see to it that his people could hunt in former territory of the vanquished Pequots. Massachusetts did petition its fellow colony to allow such hunting privileges; Connecticut rejected the suggestion.[40]

Despite Miantonomo's belief that he deserved rewards, his ego soon took a pounding. He attempted to visit and talk with a Pequot sachem guarded by colonial militiamen, but the sentinels did not recognize him. "I was," Miantonomo complained, "thrust at with a pike many times, that I durst not come near the door." Furious, he tried to recall every Narragansett guide serving with colonial forces, but Canonicus vetoed Miantonomo's angry gesture. "Did ever friends deal so with friends?," Miantonomo asked Williams.[41]

Roger Williams was concerned about a growing problem between the English and the Narragansetts. "I saw them to [be] much disregarded by many" colonists, he informed Governor John Winthrop of Massachusetts Bay. Individual settlers had noticed that Miantonomo had, in reality, done very little against the Pequots. Also obvious to many of the English was that many Narragansett warriors had fled from the enemy rather than fight. Why, colonists no doubt thought, should we pay much regard to quivering allies? Uncas and the Mohegans were far more dependable than the Narragansetts, who had "seldome ingag[ed] in any fight," Edward Winslow wrote.[42]

Other colonists passed on disturbing reports that Miantonomo and the Narragansetts "keepe not the articles they subscribed." Instead of passing on wampum meant for the English, Miantonomo kept it for himself. "Yea the truth is they are so eagerly sett upon their owne ends, to gett booty, etc. . . . that . . . they use us as their stalking horse." Should not the remaining Pequots first be defeated before Miantonomo divided up the spoils, a colonist wondered. When Pequots "submitt to the Narragansett they say it is meerly for the English sake," again throwing doubt on the claims of Miantonomo for booty. In response, the Narragansett dual sachems insisted that although they "had paid many hundred fathom of wampom to their soldiers . . . yet" they "had not received one yard of beads nor a Pequot."[43]

Miantonomo's defense indicates what happened after Mystic. The new battle commenced over who would obtain most of the remaining Pequots. As one Englishman commented, "I perseave the Indians would be glad to make women of all the Pequots now." Uncas, Miantonomo's chief rival for the human booty, married a high-ranking Pequot; Miantonomo tried and, apparently, failed to consummate a suitable marriage. Try as he might, Miantonomo could not overcome a basic problem: the Pequots "seeme to feare the Narragansett men." On the other hand, the Pequots and Mohegans had some sort of family bond. The Pequots voted with their feet and went to Uncas. Williams had dismissed him as "a little Sachem," but that status rapidly changed. During September 1637 Uncas was seen with 300 warriors—over half of whom had been Pequots.[44]

In due course Uncas's victory was so complete that the frustrated Narragansett dual sachems actually suggested that all the Pequots should be sent far away to England. While that would deny the Narragansetts their Pequot booty, Uncas would lose far more. Uncas had a simpler solution to the ongoing dispute. He and Miantonomo should fight one-on-one; the winner won the Pequots. Miantonomo, of course, rejected the duel.[45]

During this squabbling, Miantonomo had to fend off negative stories about himself that Uncas had planted. But when Miantonomo made a deal at Boston on November 1, 1637, two other Indian leaders seemed to be more annoying than the Mohegan. The Puritans granted him permission to deal with his other foes; Uncas was not mentioned. In return, Miantonomo renounced any claim to both Block Island and the old territory of the Pequots. With no territorial gains from the Pequot War, Miantonomo's need to amass as many Pequots as possible became even more important. And the splendid reception Miantonomo received in Boston expanded his already large ego still more.[46]

Miantonomo, popular in Massachusetts, had no support in Connecticut. There, the Mohegans continued to spread stories about him, including one that he planned to kill Thomas Stanton, a trader from that colony, who was frequently employed to interpret Indian languages. Although untrue, Miantonomo did not trust Stanton's reliability. The sachem already distrusted the Connecticut settlers, suspecting that they were totally on Uncas's side. Miantonomo sized up the leaders of that colony correctly. Williams commented that Uncas had so "marvelously deluded" Connecticut "that Mr. [Thomas] Hooker writes no proof can be brought against [the Mohegans] for word or deed."[47]

As early as February 1638, Connecticut's leaders wanted to have a talk with Miantonomo. At the top of their agenda seems to have been some "proud speeches" he had given. But Miantonomo put them off because Canonicus was ill, and tradition specified that the other sachem not depart at such a time. Other colonists wanted a conference. The simmering dispute over the Pequots continued to escalate, and the settlers wanted to broker some kind of deal. Both Miantonomo and Canonicus were agreeable to an arrangement negotiated by the colonists.[48]

Before the conference, however, some colonists murdered an Indian, threatening the whole idea of a mediated settlement. Knowing that revenge was a real possibility, Miantonomo warned "the English [to] be carefull on the high ways." Furthermore, he sent word to the relatives of the dead man "that Mr. Govr. [John Winthrop] would see Justice done." Obviously, Miantonomo had learned about the English system of justice during his frequent talks with Roger Williams. Miantonomo's faith in the Massachusetts colony, which had treated him so royally, was confirmed; it executed the murderers.[49]

At last, in September 1638 Miantonomo journeyed to Hartford, site of the conference, through territory dominated by Uncas. Taking a guard of 150-200 warriors (plus his family and Williams to interpret), Miantonomo faced a constant risk of ambush. Rather than retreat and lose face, Miantonomo forged ahead. Constantly on alert, his warriors protected their sachem successfully; the main force avoided attack although others were less fortunate. Williams attributed his survival to a rumor that Miantonomo had a substantial colonial contingent with him, a disheartening factor to the Mohegans.[50]

Arriving at Hartford, Miantonomo and Uncas sparred over many things including who had which Pequots. Uncas denied directing his men to attack Narragansetts on their way to Hartford. On September 21, 1638 the attending parties signed the Treaty of Hartford, which declared that all old disputes between the Mohegans and Narragansetts were to be forgotten. The Pequot survivors were divided up equally; each sachem would obtain 80 men. In addition, if any future dispute arose, each sachem had to seek English permission before attacking his foe. The colonists convinced the two enemies to partake in the European custom of the handshake. Then Miantonomo actually invited Uncas to dinner—Williams had tutored his friend well. Although the colonial delegates pressured Uncas to partake of Miantonomo's venison, the Mohegan, obviously fearing poison, declined.[51]

Despite the treaty's terms, the bulk of the Pequots stayed with Uncas, who gained perhaps as many as 370 warriors. Miantonomo got far fewer.

Given that Uncas may have had only 50 warriors at the start of the war, the Mohegans profited greatly from the conflict.[52]

That result came about because Connecticut wanted it that way. Spurred on by John Mason, the colony believed Uncas was a true friend. "The reason that the English trusted Uncas was that he had always aided them," one colonist explained. Uncas's success in getting and keeping Pequots embittered Miantonomo, who then saw Uncas as his greatest enemy.[53]

Arguing over Pequots led to new troubles in 1640. The Eastern Niantics, tied to the Narragansetts, refused to hand over some captive Pequots, whom the English had branded as murderers, to Connecticut for punishment. Furious, that colony, during the summer of 1640, seemed ready to attack the Narragansetts. Connecticut showed no interest in a report that Uncas also had Pequot murderers. Miantonomo and Canonicus complained that Connecticut's "Partialitie to all the Pequots [among the] Mohegan is so great . . . that all their Arguments return back (which they use to the Niantic Sachems) as Arrows from a stone wall." A rumor that the Narragansetts had recruited, with wampum, the powerful Mohawks as allies did not calm English fears.[54]

Nonetheless, in August 1640 Miantonomo kept promising to come to Boston to talk about these matters. Massachusetts, less jumpy about the reports than either Plymouth or Connecticut, sent a Captain Jenyson with a few men and a Pequot interpreter to talk with the dual sachems who objected to the hostile interpreter. As a Pequot, he was an enemy (again demonstrating Uncas's success with them). The reasonable Captain Jenyson simply had someone else interpret. Miantonomo and Canonicus denied any deal with the Mohawks and promised peace with the colonists unless attacked.[55]

In November 1640 Miantonomo fulfilled his vow to journey to Massachusetts, which did not allow the banished Roger Williams to interpret for him. Unlike earlier ego-boosting forays there, this trip turned into a disaster. Thomas Dudley, now governor, lacked John Winthrop's finesse. Everything began to go wrong as soon as Miantonomo came to Dudley's home in Roxbury. The stubborn governor, knowing that Miantonomo had already rejected a Pequot interpreter, insisted that another Pequot be employed. Miantonomo soon left Roxbury "in a rude manner" without the usual civilities. At Boston, Dudley again insisted upon a Pequot interpreter. The colony's leaders suspected that Miantonomo was not very forthcoming. Since he distrusted the interpreter, such behavior was logical. Nor did the Puritans "admit him to dine at our table, as formerly he had done." The Puritans achieved little except insulting Miantonomo. Clearly, on his voyage back to his territory, Miantonomo realized that he needed a new strategy for dealing with the colonists. He required a way to intimidate them with superior numbers as had worked so well for his people in the past.[56]

The conspiracy of 1642 is what Miantonomo dreamed up. Although historians often claim that there is little evidence of what Connecticut branded the "mischevos plotte," there is in reality a great amount of information. Reports warning of Miantonomo's "horrid confederacy" reached Boston from New Haven, Connecticut, Plymouth, Maine and, most importantly, from Uncas.[57]

Miantonomo, it seems, went in person through a sizable area of New England seeking support. Lion Gardiner, a professional soldier in the service of Connecticut, wrote about what happened when Miantonomo, soliciting support from the Indians of Long Island, ran afoul of their leader, Wyandanch.[58]

According to Gardiner's source, Wyandanch, Miantonomo told sachems there that "we [are] all Indians" and were thus brothers. Without unity "we shall be all gone shortly." Furthermore, "you know our fathers had plenty of deer and skins," along with fish, turkeys and other birds. However, the English "having gotten our land" had destroyed grassland and trees and brought in cows, horses, and pigs. The English had to be destroyed. "When you see the three fires that will be made forty days hence . . . then do as we, and the next day fall on and kill men, women, and children, but no cows, for they will serve to eat till our deer be increased again." The plot fell apart quickly; Wyandanch warned his people not to attack the English, for "Then they will come and kill us all, as they did the Pequots."[59]

Meanwhile, a sachem briefed Roger Ludlow of the New Haven colony about the conspiracy and begged that his identity be kept secret. According to the cautious sachem, Miantonomo had told the Indians in New Haven that the Narragansetts plotted because they had killed John Oldham and the colonists would seek revenge for that and the killing of another settler by a Narragansett; the English had assumed the second man had committed suicide. Although Miantonomo mentioned "huntinge and fishinge," in New Haven he pushed land. He announced that "the english did get possession of all the best place in the countrey and did drive the Indians away and were likely to take awaye the countrye from them." So the Indians should "come unto the chief howses of the english . . . and soe should kill all in the howse and depart." Then, with their leaders dead, "the rest would be soe distracted that they would be easily vanquished."[60]

Connecticut learned of the conspiracy when an Indian hurt himself in a collision with an ox-cart. Because the plot included the killing of English animals too, the injured Indian assumed that the "Englishman's God" had ordered the ox to punish him for plotting. As Indians believed in animal spirits, logically the ox would willingly have sought to injure his potential murderer.[61]

Nothing ever happened to the English as a result of Miantonomo's conspiracy. And, by all accounts, the great majority of his prospective recruits realized that what he had been suggesting was doomed to failure. In New Haven, for example, his listeners told him bluntly that "these Massachusetts and that waye are full of people and [we] shall not be able to grapple with them." Miantonomo's bold response, "lett me alone with them," brought only more disbelief into the minds of his audience.[62]

Miantonomo made up details as he went along. Signal fires would announce the start of the rebellion to the Long Island Indians. When in New Haven, however, the signal was sending a colonist's "heade and handes" among the assorted conspirators.[63]

Bringing the Mohawks into the fight against the Puritans constituted an essential part of the conspiracy. Reports of Mohawks entering into local disputes were common. In 1644 the Mohawks were also supposed to be ready to swoop into action, but Benedict Arnold, an interpreter, discovered the truth. Indians admitted that, in living memory, the Mohawks had never "come into these parts to do as is reported." The Mohawks had little or no interest in southern New England—at least not enough to justify war.[64]

The military aspect of Miantonomo's plot makes no sense, because this Indian confederation was never supposed to actually make war. Going to war was not the Narragansett way—they won by intimidating their foes through their superior numbers. Because Massachusetts now had a substantial population, that tactic no longer worked. But if Miantonomo had united many Indians under his leadership, superior numbers would again come into play. No governor of Massachusetts Bay would ever dare treat Miantonomo as Dudley had. With the Puritans cowed, no war would be necessary.

Did Miantonomo really believe in the things he spoke about to potential confederates? Regarding land, Miantonomo would be selling more soon after all this talking. While hunting was not what it had been, the Narragansetts had been a definite winner due to English colonization. After the European arrival, the Narragansett control of wampum production brought them substantial wealth. The destruction of the Pequots greatly increased Narragansett dominance over wampum. They also had switched quickly to the new, imported tools to speed up the creation of wampum. Similarly, they eagerly used European metal axes to chop down trees; getting rid of trees was not just an English avocation.[65]

Miantonomo was hardly a leader against English ideas. Before Mystic, he wanted a set of European clothing to wear while his warriors killed Pequot women and their offspring. Roger Williams witnessed another of Miantonomo's conversations about European culture. Arguing with another Indian about the differences between their traditional religion and Christianity, the debate centered on where souls went after death. After hearing an attack on Williams's Christian beliefs, Miantonomo defended his friend: "He hath books and writings, and one which God himself made, concerning mens soules, and therefore may well know more then wee that have none, but take all upon trust from our forefathers." Miantonomo did value literacy. In 1641 he was using as his mark, shown in Table 1, an inverted M. All in all, Miantonomo does not seem like much of an advocate of the good old days before the English arrival.[66]

Even if Miantonomo had expounded to his confederates things he really believed, the nature of the dual sachem system has to be recalled. In order for the Narragansetts to have waged war on the English, Canonicus would have had to agree. He once told Williams, "I have never suffered any wrong to be offered to the English since they landed, nor never will." Given the knowledge about Canonicus's peaceable inclinations, there is no reason to doubt his statement. Canonicus had not approved an English war. The true object of the grand confederation Miantonomo had tried to create was the destruction of Uncas. Even Canonicus would have accepted war against the Mohegans.[67]

Wyandanch had warned the English that the Narragansetts "would let us alone 'till they had destroyed Uncas and him." In New Haven, Miantonomo asked his potential allies "howe they might compasse Uncas, for they feared he would not be gayned." Uncas had been invited to join the conspiracy, but he smelled the proverbial rat and informed the English. Uncas realized that he was Miantonomo's ultimate target. Uncas, who had a long memory, would deal with Miantonomo at the right time.[68]

By September 1642 Connecticut was hurriedly making preparations for a major war with the Indians. Meanwhile, Massachusetts summoned Miantonomo to Boston to talk about what had been reported. An emissary was dispatched to him with two interpreters (Winthrop was governor again) and Miantonomo gave satisfactory responses. When at Boston, he demonstrated "a good understanding in the principles of justice and equity"—talking with Williams had been a good education in English law. Miantonomo demanded that his anonymous accusers should suffer death "if they could not prove" their stories. Proving a conspiracy is, of course, very difficult. Overall, "his words were smoother than oil," according to one observer. Uncas, the Narragansett insisted, had been responsible for the silly stories; blaming Uncas for everything must have been Miantonomo's backup plan from the start. Although Massachusetts did not have sufficient evidence to convict Miantonomo, he was not believed completely. He did not dine at Winthrop's table; the sachem remained "discontented" until Winthrop "sent him meat from his table." Massachusetts Bay made a point of keeping its defenses ready.[69]

A few months after Miantonomo's conspiracy had shaken the colonists, in November 1642 Samuel Gorton and some supporters moved onto the land of two sachems, Pumham and Socononoco, near Providence, Rhode Island. Gorton, a religious radical, was on excellent terms with Miantonomo. When the two local sachems refused to sell the land to Gorton, Miantonomo intervened. Because the local sachems had few warriors, Miantonomo intimidated them, the usual technique of the Narragansetts. In January 1643 Pumham marked a deed to the property, as did Miantonomo. Pumham, however, refused to take payment for the land, "it being the Indians manner not to account any thing sold, till the party have received the thing it is sold for."[70]

Unable to stand up to the powerful Narragansett sachem—and still wanting to keep their land—Pumham and Socononoco decided to follow the example of Massasoit of the Wampanoags. He had placed himself "under [the] wings" of the Plymouth colony and so had escaped from the dominance of the Narragansetts. The local sachems appealed to Massachusetts Bay. Their act was not some sort of conspiracy hatched by the Puritans. Instead, the desperate Pumham and Socononoco sought the intervention of a power great enough that Miantonomo could not intimidate it.[71]

Massachusetts Bay, always eager to expand its territory, summoned Miantonomo to answer the two sachems' complaints. Miantonomo insisted that Pumham and Socononoco were subject to him and he could order them to sell land. But, of course, he had no documentation. In contrast, many witnesses willingly contradicted him. Joining Pumham and Socononoco was Cutshamakin, the sachem of the Massachusett, who stated that both were independent. Benedict Arnold added his belief that, from everything he had heard, Miantonomo had no authority over them. Even Roger Williams wrote that the two supplicants were "free Sachims." If these authorities had exaggerated the independence of the rebellious sachems, Miantonomo did not have the right to force the tributary sachems to sell land. Massachusetts Bay, therefore, extended its protection from "the oppressing tyranny of Miantonomo" to Pumham and Socononoco, who gave their allegiance to the colony. The furious Miantonomo "beat one of Pumham's men and took away his wampom, and then bid him go and complain to the Massachusetts."[72]

Meanwhile, Uncas had been planning his revenge against Miantonomo. During the early months of 1643 a Pequot allegedly "shott Uncas with an arrow through the arme but aiming at his life." This curious assassin, who seemed to think an arm wound would kill his prey, then ran away to tell the Narragansetts that Uncas was dead. Soon changing his tune, he then insisted "that Uncas had cut through his owne arme with a flint, and had hired" him as a pretended murderer, all to incriminate the Narragansetts. Miantonomo came to Boston with the curious assassin. The colony demanded that he be returned to Uncas; Miantonomo agreed. Despite the promise, soon after, Miantonomo "cutt of[f] the Pequot's head," thus suggesting to the colonists that the Narragansetts had tried to kill Uncas.[73]

Unfortunately, Williams remained silent on this alleged assassination and may have already left for England. He was on the scene, however, in 1649 when a remarkably similar event happened. Suddenly, "a gentle and peaceable Spirit," an Indian who had never fought "in their Wars," supposedly tried to kill Uncas in the midst of his supporters. Williams believed that the whole affair was merely a "plot" hatched by Uncas who "acting himself [put] a small stab on his breast in a safe place" to make the story look convincing. The accused Indian confessed after some of his fingers had been cut off.[74]

Either the Narragansetts were in the habit of hiring inept assassins, or Uncas was repeating a successful tactic. In 1643, one Puritan noticed,

Uncas's arm "wound cured in a short time after." Such rapid healing is more likely in a superficial, self-inflicted wound than one caused by an arrow's entrance and exit. Perhaps Uncas already realized how he could use the supposed assassination attempt of 1643 against Miantonomo; it would have a very significant effect. Why did Miantonomo kill the Pequot? The man was an admitted agent of Uncas. A sachem such as Miantonomo undertook executions "with his own hand," the traditional form of Indian justice.[75]

Miantonomo's own time was running out. One of his subject sachems attacked Uncas, and Miantonomo—after first getting permission from the English to obey the Hartford Treaty—supported his subject. For the first time in many decades, the Narragansetts would wage war. Surprising Uncas, Miantonomo appeared at "the Sachem's Plain" in Connecticut with a largely superior force of "able young men," twice the size of Uncas's group. Once again the Narragansetts depended on their superior numbers. Uncas, though, challenged Miantonomo to stake everything on a fight between them alone. As he had done before, Miantonomo refused: "My men came to fight and they shall fight." Why should he risk a duel with Uncas when the Narragansetts had a substantial advantage in manpower?[76]

Uncas knew that Miantonomo would never fight him. Immediately, Uncas fell down and the Mohegans unleashed a barrage of arrows at Miantonomo's warriors. Stunned, they ran away, which Uncas had also expected. Miantonomo ran too, but he had made a mistake. He had worn some English armor given to him by John Wicks, one of Gorton's allies. The heavy contraption slowed him down enough to enable his capture. Brought before Uncas, Miantonomo refused to speak, "choosing rather to die than make supplication for his life."[77]

Most sachems would have simply killed their mortal enemy without hesitation. Miantonomo had expected death when he fell into the hands of the Mohegans. When he did start speaking again, he asked "again and again" for execution. Perhaps his death would erase the shame of his defeat and capture. But Uncas had a clever plan in store. He had signed a treaty with the English where they had demanded that the Indian sachems receive their permission first before dealing with other Indians. Uncas followed the treaty to the letter, and turned Miantonomo over to the Puritans. Uncas hoped to ensnare them into protecting him from his Narragansett enemies.[78]

Uncas surrendered his foe to the commissioners of the Confederation of New England, a league of all the Puritan colonies except Rhode Island. These leaders came to a quick conclusion: "Uncas cannot be safe while Miantonomo lives." Indeed, the chief focus of the deliberations involved Uncas and his future. If the English did not advocate Miantonomo's death, then Uncas would see that as fear. Logically, Uncas would lose confidence in his fearful allies and decide it was safer "to make friendship with Miantonomo." Then, the two sachems, in a stronger version of the conspiracy of 1642, would unite "against the English."[79]

The commissioners authorized Uncas to execute Miantonomo but not in English territory. In addition, the execution had to demonstrate "all mercy and moderation" without "tortures and cruelty." To be certain, some colonists would witness the event. None of the Puritans wanted to see Uncas wearing "bracelets of the forejoints of [Miantonomo's] fingers, etc." To justify the Narragansett's death, the commissioners pointed to his alleged hiring of that Pequot in 1643 to kill Uncas, a violation of the Treaty of Hartford, which the Mohegan sachem probably had anticipated. Suspecting that the Narragansetts would seek vengeance against Uncas, the colonists vowed to defend him, a promise that was kept.[80]

Now, Uncas had only one thing left to do—eliminate Miantonomo. After entering Mohegan territory, Miantonomo was killed inside a building—probably a wigwam—by "one blow with an hatchet on the side of the heade as hee walked easily in the room." A secret execution was common among the Indians when they expected trouble. Uncas may have thought that some Narragansetts would try to rescue their sachem. Legend has it that, despite the English witnesses, after Miantonomo's death Uncas ate a chunk of his foe's shoulder and said: "It is the sweetest meat I ever ate. It makes my heart strong." Called "ritual cannibalism," the act was supposed to endow the eater with a dead man's traits, in this case Miantonomo's strength. This tale of cannibalism may be merely myth.[81]

What is certain is that Massachusetts moved against Samuel Gorton after Miantonomo's demise. Already having lost the dispute of the rebellious sachems' land, Gorton sealed his fate when, after Miantonomo's capture, he wrote Uncas demanding the Narragansett's freedom "and threatened him with the power of the English if he refused." The last thing Massachusetts Bay wanted was for someone like Gorton possibly alienating their loyal and vital ally, Uncas.[82]

In contrast to the dependable Uncas, some Puritans suspected Gorton and his men of treason. Gorton's "extraordinary familiarity" with the dead Narragansett caused suspicion that there existed "some combination between the Indians and them." As proof, Puritans could point to the armor Miantonomo had been wearing; Winslow informed Gorton that "you hold forth more familiarity" with Miantonomo "then becomes you." Gorton was soon lodging in a jail.[83]

By 1645 Canonicus feared a revolution among the Narragansetts. The young warriors wanted war, and seemed ready to "sett all the Country in Combustion," no matter what the elderly sachem wanted. Tradition survived, though, and Canonicus prevented a major war.[84]

Sporadic fighting between the Narragansetts and Mohegans went on for years because of the death of the People's Choice. In the 1670s the two tribes fought on different sides. Uncas stuck with the English; the Narragansetts joined the cause of King Philip. The long rivalry ended when the son of Uncas executed the son of Miantonomo. Uncas won that one too, just as he had triumphed over Miantonomo.[85]

Chapter 5

Samuel Maverick

Some years after the royalists returned to power in England, they decided to have a special commission investigate the situation in New England. One of the commissioners, Samuel Maverick, had become an enemy of the Bay colony. Because of Maverick's opposition to the Puritans, historians have branded him tactless, "grossly partisan," greedy, and a drunkard. He even allegedly "appalled his neighbors," a curious charge considering that in 1658 his neighbors elected him to what became known as The Ancient and Honorable Artillery Company of Massachusetts.[1]

Samuel Maverick was neither a drunken sot nor a greedy man. One of the first settlers of what became Massachusetts, he could remember when Boston was a swamp.[2] Yet he had also been an eyewitness to (or had learned about) many of the most controversial actions undertaken by the Bay colony. Such knowledge made him a very dangerous foe. This essay will delve into both his life and the royal commission he served on, which was not as prejudiced as historians have asserted.

After the Stuart monarchy was restored in 1660, Puritan Massachusetts petitioned Charles II for "kindness," as the colony's spokesmen called it. To assure the king of their loyalty to his Church and his Crown, the Puritans informed him: "wee are not . . . schismaticks as to the matters of religion; wee distinguish betweene churches and their impuritys, betweene a living man, tho not without sickness or infirmitie, or no man. Irregularities, either in ourselves or others, wee desire to be amended." Massachusetts knew that complaints about its conduct, especially involving its treatment of Quakers, had reached Stuart England. But, the Puritans insisted, they were "fearers of God and the king, not given to change, zealous of government and order. . . ."[3]

Some voices in England, nonetheless, asserted that Puritan Massachusetts was badly in need of reform by the triumphant royalists. If Edward Hyde, the first earl of Clarendon, had not been aware of the peculiarities of the Bay colony, Thomas Breedon, who lived in Boston, made sure to enlighten him. Equipped with a copy of the Massachusetts laws, Breedon demonstrated that the Puritans, instead of administering an oath of loyalty to the Crown, insisted upon such an oath "to themselves and their government." No one who refused this oath could fill any office. Furthermore, anyone who proposed a fundamental change in their government could be put to death. Breedon declared that backers of the king were assumed to be "Mutiners" against the Bay colony. In addition, Breedon pointed out that "The distinction of Freemen and Non-Freemen, [church] Members and Non Members is as famous as Cavalleeres and Roundheads was in England and will shortly become as odious, and I hope abandon'd."[4]

An associate of Breedon's, Samuel Maverick, the most persistent opponent of Massachusetts, became a thorn among the Puritan saints. But Maverick's relationship with at least some of the Puritans had once been different.

Maverick arrived in America during 1624. He came with agents of Sir Ferdinando Gorges, and Maverick was also connected with him. Later, Maverick was associated with Gorges's settlement of Agamenticus, Maine (the present-day York) and received land there which the Puritans eventually deprived him of. Maverick spent at least some of his first days in New England exploring the Maine countryside and he discovered the site of the failed Popham settlement of 1607-1608. By 1625 he may have left Gorges's employ as he built a home at Winnisimmet, now Chelsea, Massachusetts. Strongly built and equipped with guns, Maverick had designed his home there to frighten away potential Indian attackers. About 1628 some natives did consider an attack, but a barrage from Maverick's guns convinced them to leave him alone.[5]

In June 1630 John Winthrop and the other passengers aboard the *Arbella* met Maverick when the ship anchored near his home at Winnisimmet. Maverick, "a man of a very loving and curteous behaviour, very ready to entertaine strangers. . .," freely extended his hospitality to the newcomers and made them welcome. References by travellers such as John Josselyn to Maverick's almost proverbial hospitality are common. Sometimes, though, Maverick's befriending strangers did not work out to his benefit. When in 1645 the Frenchman Charles La Tour came to Boston, Maverick gave him shelter for months. Maverick and another New Englander, Edward Gibbons, even became business partners with La Tour, entrusting him with a cargo worth some £ 200. The Frenchman sailed away with the cargo and that was the last time his partners saw or heard from him.[6]

Despite such disappointments, Maverick prospered in early Massachusetts although his attempt to breed slaves seems to have failed. In April 1633 the Massachusetts legislature, the General Court, awarded him an island in Boston harbor named after an early settler, Noddle's Island, for only a small rent. Maverick also did well in his trade as a merchant. Once he swapped a ship with some pirates, who included a supply of otter and beaver skins for Maverick in the deal. During the earliest days of the colony, he sent a ship to Virginia and sometimes stayed there for months at a time.[7]

Still, Maverick had plenty of time to perform good deeds in New England. In 1633 during a smallpox epidemic, he tended to sick Indians every day. According to Winthrop, Maverick and his household "ministered to their necessities, and buried their dead, and took home many of their children." Because of this behavior, Winthrop was moved to write that Maverick was entitled to "a perpetual remembrance." On another occasion, Maverick aided the Puritan leaders in calming some offensive sailors.[8]

Nevertheless, Maverick still ran afoul of some Puritans because of one simple fact—he was an Anglican. As Johnson described him, he was "an enemy to the Reformation in hand, being strong for the Lordly Prelaticall power." Maverick realized that some Puritans were hostile to him. Writing in 1641, he observed: "I hope God will enable me in some measure to walke inoffencively, but [I find] by 10 yeares experience that I am [an] eye sore to diverse here." Even his fortified home at Winnisimmet may have frightened some of the political extremists among the Puritans. After he sold that property to Richard Bellingham in February 1635, Maverick moved to Noddle's Island. However, in March 1635 the General Court ordered Maverick and his family to move to Boston— where they could be watched—and not to entertain "any strangers for longer time then one night" unless permission had been obtained first. Yet suddenly, in September 1635, this order was revoked.[9]

Quite likely, this reversal occurred because Maverick had a protector among the Puritan leadership. He and John Winthrop appear to have been rather close for some time. As early as 1630, Winthrop and Thomas Dudley joined in a business venture with Maverick. And Winthrop enjoyed talking with Maverick. For example, in 1636 Maverick, just returned from Virginia, related to his Puritan friend that he had seen there "the bone of a whale," a fossil in reality, that had been removed from deep under the ground. At least once the Anglican Maverick sent some squabbling servants to the Puritan Winthrop when they deserved "a checke." Indeed, the Puritan governor and another friend, Edward Gibbons, were, Maverick informed Winthrop, "the only men which ever dealt plainely with me by way of reproofe and admonition, when you have heard of any thinge in which I have beene faultie . . . and by it you have much obliged me." In fact, both Winthrop and Maverick had something in common—relatives of different faiths. Winthrop had Catholic relatives he stayed on good terms with, and Maverick's father was a Puritan minister who settled in Massachusetts. Following divergent faiths did not stop them from forging a friendship.[10]

Maverick needed an influential friend in high places. In 1641 two men, John Morecroft and William Bell, were to be tried for "unfit carrige," and asked Maverick for his advice. He urged the men, who claimed to be innocent, to stay. Although both said they would, Bell fled the colony. The politically extreme Puritans then tried to prove that Maverick had known of Bell's plans by taking "an inquisition like course" in gathering "what they can from malcontented servants or the like." The incident disturbed Maverick so much that he told Winthrop he had "seriously resolved to remove hence" after a commercial transaction was completed. "My well wishes shall ever attend the Plantation," Maverick assured Winthrop, "and your selfe and yours in particular. . . ." However, Maverick remained in the Bay colony and was not charged in Bell's case.[11] Winthrop may well have urged his friend to stay.

A few months later, Maverick was again in trouble. In 1641 he entertained Thomas Owen and Mrs. Sara Hale as was his custom with strangers. It is highly unlikely that Maverick knew that they had escaped from prison after being jailed for "notorious suspicion of adultery." Eventually, the culprits were captured and punished—Owen was fined £ 20 or a whipping; Mrs. Hale was fined £ 13 1/3 or a whipping and banishment. Seven others who had aided or concealed them were fined up to £ 26 2/3. Yet Maverick was fined £ 100.[12]

Maverick petitioned the General Court for a remission of the excessive fine. A committee of the Court—no doubt after some prodding by Winthrop—suggested that the fine be lowered to £ 60. But Richard Bellingham, then governor, tried to alter the amount to £ 80 without the committee's knowledge. When detected, Bellingham claimed that he had only been joking. In reality, Bellingham, one of the political extremists, wanted to punish Maverick as severely as possible.[13]

Samuel Maverick remained safe until 1646, when he signed the remonstrance of Dr. Robert Child and five others. Comparing Massachusetts to a leaky ship, the petitioners urged that the leaks be plugged by such things as the Bay colony's government paying attention to English laws. Child, Maverick, and the rest called for the Puritan leaders to extend the right to vote to men qualified for it in England even if they had not undergone a conversion experience. Furthermore, the remonstrants suggested that the creation of both Anglican and Presbyterian churches be tolerated in Puritan Massachusetts.[14]

The petition of Child, Maverick, and the others presented a serious challenge to the Puritans. Governor Winthrop had hoped to downplay the problem by only having the Court issue a declaration of its "apprehensions" about the remonstrance. The deputies, however, insisted on questioning the signers. Although all of the petitioners (except for Maverick) came to the Court, Child was clearly the leading force and spokesman. The questioning turned into a free-for-all, with the members of the General Court jeering Child and the others. Rebuffed by the General Court, the six signers appealed to Parliament. But Winthrop

> told them, he would admit no appeal, nor was it allowed by our charter, but by this it appeared what their aim was in their petition; they complained of fear of perpetual slavery, etc., but their intent was, to make us slaves to them and such as themselves were, and that by the parliament and commissioners, (meaning, by threatening us with their authority, or calumniating us to them, etc.).[15]

Finally, the Court stated that the petitioners were wrong to believe "that the liberties and privileges in our charter belong to all freeborn Englishmen, inhabitants here." To the contrary, the charter liberties "are granted only to such as the governor and company shall think fit to receive into that fellowship."[16]

All of the signers were punished either with heavy fines or imprisonment. At first, Maverick was only fined £ 10 because he had not appealed to Parliament before the General Court. Unfortunately for Maverick, the Puritans intercepted another petition signed by him and the others which described what had happened. This petition also requested the English to appoint "a general governor or some honorable commissioners" who could settle the dispute. Because Maverick had been made a freeman before church membership was required, he had sworn an oath to support the government of Massachusetts. The Court, therefore, punished him harshly with a fine of £ 150. Before paying the fine, Maverick went to jail for a dozen days.[17]

Despite the furor, Maverick remained in Massachusetts. Near the end of 1647, Maverick petitioned the General Court for a remission of his fine, but his petition was rejected. Trying again in May 1649, Maverick pleaded with the Court:

> Whereas I have been formerly charged with conspiracy and perjury, which, to my understanding, hath not been sufficiently proved against me . . . which moved me to petition . . . for a review of my cause; yett I desire the Court to understand me, so as if I accounted myself altogether free of error, but have cause rather to suspect and judge myself and actions then your justice and proceedings; and being confident and experimentally assured of your clemency to others in the like kind, I am bold rather to crave your mercy in the favorable remittance of my fines then to stand either to justify myself or proceedings, which, as they have (contrary to my intentions) proved prejudiciall and very offencive, so it hath been, is, and will be, my griefe and trouble. I shall not trouble you with arguments respecting myself and family, though the burden lies heavy in that respect; the only motive lies in your owne breasts, your wonted charity, which will render you to the world mercifull, and refresh and fully satisfy your humble petitioner. . . .[18]

The deputies were moved by the petition, and recommended that Maverick's fine be lessened to £ 50. But Governor John Endicott, speaking for the magistrates, insisted that he had not sufficiently acknowledged his guilt. The fine remained at £ 150. There was no one among the magistrates to protect Maverick now as John Winthrop had died a few months before. Nevertheless, in June 1650 Maverick tried again with another—presumably more humble petition—and the fine was lessened to £ 75.[19]

Maverick's petition quoted above suggests that he was suffering financial troubles at that time, and the suggestion was not just a ploy for sympathy. These financial woes appear to stem from his dealings on the West Indian island of Barbados. Drawn away from Virginia's trade by the lure of sugar, Maverick had merely followed the lead of Governor Winthrop, who had pioneered trade with Barbados. Exactly what problem Maverick had is uncertain, but it was probably some sort of legal difficulty with a resident of Barbados. Whatever the problem was, Maverick needed money and there was a quick way to get it—selling Noddle's Island. On January 14, 1650, he sold the island to a Barbadian trader, George Briggs, for a substantial amount of sugar.[20]

But this sale did not end Maverick's distress. Briggs seemed unable to produce what he had promised, and so Maverick sent his son Nathaniel to Barbados to, quietly, look for another buyer. Hopefully, the elder Maverick mused, someone willing to pay more for Noddle's Island could be found. Nathaniel Maverick did find another purchaser, Lieutenant-Colonel John Birch, who was an important figure on Barbados; Briggs stepped aside. Yet Samuel Maverick became infuriated when he learned the facts behind Birch's purchase. Nathaniel had gotten himself heavily into debt with Birch and, to eliminate his own financial problem, Maverick's son sold Noddle's Island to Birch for much less than his father had wanted. The elder Maverick tried to repudiate his son's act, while Birch insisted that Nathaniel was simply disposing of his inheritance.[21]

Neither man wanted to give in and Birch sued Maverick in the Massachusetts courts. In 1653 the case was settled by the General Court, which ruled that the purchase of Noddle's Island was legal, but that Birch had to give Maverick an additional £ 700. Apparently, the extra cash satisfied Maverick. In 1656 he turned the island over to Birch, who the next year sold it for about what he had paid for it.[22]

Meanwhile, Maverick's generous nature got him into more legal trouble. In 1650 Maverick became a surety for a Barbadian merchant, John Parris, who was indebted to a prominent New England Puritan, Thomas Savage, for £ 300. By becoming Parris's surety, Maverick had obligated himself to pay the debt to Savage if Parris reneged. Parris was a careless debtor and he let the debt go unpaid past the due date, which greatly upset Maverick. Presumably, Savage was paid by Parris, if a bit late. Despite such a record, near the end of the decade the generous Maverick again became Parris's surety for another £ 300 debt owed to Savage. This time, however, Savage acted in a peculiar fashion. When Parris paid Savage's agent in Barbados, the Puritan was notified. Although he knew that he had been paid in Barbados, Savage sued Maverick in the Suffolk County Court for Parris's already paid debt. Maverick himself had evidence of the payment, but this proof had no effect on the jury or his judges, one of whom was Major William Hawthorn. Maverick was found liable and was ordered to pay Savage for the already paid debt. Furthermore, Maverick was fined about £ 150 by the county court. Not surprisingly, Maverick refused to pay anything and stayed in jail for six months until he finally gave in.[23]

After Maverick paid, he went to Barbados where he almost immediately became ill, perhaps because of his six months in jail. Calling the jailing "Unjust," Maverick in 1658 petitioned the Massachusetts government for redress. There is no record of what was done, but the government's action can be reconstructed from later evidence. In 1678 after Maverick's death, Savage was greatly interested in Maverick's estate. Apparently, the General Court had returned to Maverick his share of the twice-paid debt and Savage, twenty years later, still felt he was entitled to it. In 1668 Maverick petitioned the General Court about a fine; the Court passed the petition along to the Suffolk County Court. This petition had to refer to the fine levied by that court because of the Savage case. Seemingly, the government had not returned the fine to Maverick although it had recognized the injustice of Savage's legal action.[24]

The government of Massachusetts had done what it considered fair, but its logic was strained. Maverick was fined for not paying a debt that had already been paid. Such a result was not in accord with English law, which Maverick and Child had urged Massachusetts to pay heed to. Besides, the government's logic contradicted its reasoning in an earlier case. In 1657 Maverick had petitioned the General Court over a bond he had generously given for a drunkard, who had pledged his good conduct. But the man failed to live up to his promise, and Maverick lost his £ 20 bond. Yet when Maverick petitioned the legislature, reminding its members that he had paid substantial taxes over the years, he got the bond back. In that case, Maverick had no legal justification for his petition but was reimbursed anyway. On the other hand, when he had solid legal justification for having the Savage case fine returned, he had been refused. Justice in Massachusetts Bay seemed to be both uncertain and arbitrary.[25]

The Savage lawsuit and its illogical results had to be the last straw for Samuel Maverick, who had "Deeply Suffered" because of what had happened with the lawsuit. This time, he could soon do something about it. Earlier, reform of the Bay colony could not have been had in an England still controlled by Oliver Cromwell. Cromwell, however, died in 1658, and elements of the army restored Charles II to the throne in 1660.[26] After the Stuart restoration, the long-exiled royalists could be expected to be sympathetic to complaints against the Puritan colony of Massachusetts.

Maverick, wisely, gave no hint of his plans while he remained in Massachusetts. He remembered that Child had been arrested by the Puritans when he had tried to go to England to complain about the Bay colony. Instead of staying in New England, Maverick journeyed to the Dutch town of New Amsterdam by 1661 and began writing to Lord Clarendon, a close advisor of the new king. During that year, Maverick probably sailed to England in the company of the son of his deceased friend, the "ingenious" John Winthrop, Jr., who had left for the mother country from New Amsterdam. Maverick was on good terms with the younger Winthrop (as can be seen from their correspondence) and a comrade of theirs in England linked them together in a letter written in October 1661. Both Maverick and Winthrop were then in touch with each other, and an assumption that they traveled together is reasonable.[27]

In England Maverick could make his case in person as well as by the written word. He urged Lord Clarendon to conquer the Dutch colony of New Netherland and to force obedience from Massachusetts. This opponent of the New England Puritans assured the chancellor that the Bay colony's leaders were isolated from the common people who still accepted the king. "To the best of my observation," Maverick asserted, "3 quarter parts of the inhabitants in the whole Country are loyall subjects to his Majeste in theire harts" although their leaders had favored Cromwell. These quiet royalists would happily obey a government loyal to the king. Maverick was wrong to assume that anything more than a small minority of the residents of Massachusetts were opposed to their leaders.[28]

After Maverick questioned the support of the Puritan leadership, he attacked their excesses. They had hung Quakers, he pointed out. They had killed two people for adultery. They had punished those who had asked for laws similar to English laws. They had prevented freeholders from having the right to vote. They had refused to permit appeals to England. They had refused holy communion to "inoffencive" people. They had refused "libertye of Conscience" to everyone who deviated even in small matters from Puritan orthodoxy. They had refused baptism to thousands of children of non-church members. They had fined those who did not attend Puritan services. Surely, Maverick believed, the inhabitants would welcome salvation from such "bondage."[29]

Maverick even suggested to Clarendon that the English should resort to military force, if necessary, to subdue the Bay colony. A few small, armed ships would be enough to "awe them" into submission. If more persuasion was needed, a blockade of Massachusetts for a few weeks or months would do the trick. Not surprisingly, Maverick learned that some English officials were very reluctant to use force against the Puritans so soon after the Stuart restoration. He insisted that he was not advising such extreme actions merely for personal revenge but had "only a desire . . . that as I saw the first settellment of those parts so that I may see the reducement of them under his Majesties obedience." Nor could the zealous Maverick forget his "affection" towards the loyal people of the Bay colony and his own friends there.[30]

Samuel Maverick's charges against the Puritans did not long escape their attention. Captain John Scott, an adventurer who sided with the Puritans, attended one of the relevant council sessions. Later, in Boston the Puritans regaled Scott "as their Saviour." In addition, John Leverett, the colony's agent, had quietly left for Massachusetts, presumably to warn them. Leverett, Maverick declared, had stated "that before New England should admitt of appeales to England, they would deliver it up to the Spaniard."[31]

Massachusetts Bay had already planned to defend itself against its enemies. As early as December 1660, Governor Endicott sent secret instructions to Leverett. He was to influence potential friends of the Puritans to support them, and to get as much information as possible about both the king's and Parliament's opinion of Massachusetts. Leverett was also to present a petition to the king, which pleaded with him not to judge the colony until it could explain itself. As for the Quakers, those "open and capitall blasphemers, open seducers from the glorious Trinity, . . . the blessed gospell, and from the Holy Scriptures as the rule of life, open enemies to government itself as established in the hands of any but men of theire owne principles . . .", Massachusetts had little choice but to banish them. The Puritans continued:

> The Quakers died, not because of theire other crimes, how capitoll
> soever, but upon theire superadded presumptuous and incorrigible con-

tempt of authority; breaking in upon us, notwithstanding theire sentence of banishment made knowne to them. Had they not been restreined, so farr as appeared, there was too much cause to feare that wee ourselves must quickly have died, or worse; and such was theire insolency, that they would not be restreined but by death; nay, had they at last but promised to depart the jurisdiction, and not to returne without leave from authority, wee should have been glad of such an opportunity to have said they should not die.[32]

The Puritans did learn about the activities of their enemies in England and took action. On December 31, 1661, the General Court chose John Norton and Simon Bradstreet to represent them in England and to answer all complaints against them that had reached the mother country.[33]

When the agents arrived in England, they sought the assistance of various influential sympathizers of Massachusetts. According to Maverick, the agents thought they had succeeded in blocking any move against the Bay colony. Maverick realized that his cause was in danger. He repeated his charges and again reminded Clarendon that two regicides who had escaped to New England had been secreted by the Puritans. As evidence of their "Disloyaltie," Maverick mentioned Endicott's brash act of 1634 when he cut the red cross from the English flag "terminge it a badge of the whore of Babell." At the time this defacing of the flag had worried many of the Puritan leaders themselves. The subject of Anne Hutchinson's banishment in 1637 also came up as an example of Puritan "Injustice." She was forced to go to New Netherland, Maverick related, and was there "murdered by the Indians." Her only "Crime was . . . difference in Judgement." He could have added that Baptists as well had been forced to flee to the Dutch.[34]

Samuel Maverick's persistence surely helped to keep the anti-Massachusetts crusade alive. He had attacked the Puritans anywhere he found an audience, even in an inn. During September 1662 Clarendon declared that a special commission would investigate the problems in New England. But the Puritan supporters shifted their tactics. If they could not prevent an investigation, they could at least stop Maverick from having a role in it. He had dredged up long-forgotten embarrassments. In return, the Puritans tried their best to spread news of "secret scandalls" involving him. He was a "debauched" and "idle" man, the rumors claimed. The only basis for such a charge was thirty years old. In August 1631 Edward Gibbons and two other men in Massachusetts had been fined for being "disorderly with drinking." One of their offenses had occurred at Maverick's home at Winnisimmet, but he himself was not fined.[35]

Nevertheless, Maverick was concerned enough about the rumors to seek a statement endorsing his character. In March 1663 eighteen men who had either resided in Massachusetts or traded with it certified that most people there were on good terms with him. The only possible "objection" against him, the signers testified, was "that (for conscience sake) hee could not subject to bee a Church member." Aside from that, Maverick was held "in greate esteeme as a person whose desires and endeavours have allwayes been for the generall good of the Cuntry. . . ."[36]

The Puritans' attack on Maverick's character failed—he was named to the commission. First of all, his knowledge of New Netherland could be of some assistance when it was attacked by the commission's forces. But he was not the only one then in England who knew something about the Dutch colony. His membership on the commission probably had another benefit for Clarendon. Naming Maverick a commissioner could reassure critics of the Bay colony that their complaints would have a sympathetic ear among the investigators. Similarly, Clarendon may have intended to name someone to the commission whose presence would reassure the Puritans. In fact, the commission's instructions asserted: "Wee had once a thought of inserting the names" of "some principall persons" of Massachusetts onto the commission. But "few of the very names of any of our subjects" there were "knowne to Us." Although John Winthrop, Jr., was highly regarded in England, he was too closely identified with the interests of Connecticut.[37]

Along with Maverick, the English government sent three soldiers who were to conquer New Netherland. Colonel Richard Nicolls, the chairman of the commission, Sir Robert Carr, and Colonel George Cartwright were Maverick's colleagues. The English have been criticized for sending three soldiers, but the commission's military mission made such a selection logical.[38]

The members have also been criticized for being greedy. Without a doubt, Carr was a grasping and greedy man. His toughest critic was Colonel Nicolls, who accused him of seizing anything worth taking from the Dutch while his own men went hungry. Maverick, however, is a very different case. There is no reason to believe that he profited financially because of his service. He and the other commissioners did each receive a horse as a personal gift from John Winthrop, Jr. In addition, the Crown sent money to the commissioners, which Maverick insisted only covered their expenses.[39] Later, in 1669 Maverick did receive a house in New York City as a royal gift, which Nicolls's influence obtained for him. This was a small payment for a man who could no longer safely live in Massachusetts. Maverick had learned that the Puritans planned to punish the commission members "severely," that is, if any of them could be seized, and he was not foolish enough to hand himself over. As Thomas Morton had learned, an enemy of the Bay colony who went back to Massachusetts might regret it.[40]

Indeed, the commissioners' work brought them the hate of the Puritans. Their public instructions required major changes in the Puritan commonwealth. The commissioners should see to it, the king instructed them, that freedom of conscience be established in Massachusetts, "it being very scandalous that any man should be debarred the exercise of his religion" by people who had been given the "liberty . . . to be of what profession in religion they please." After all, religious differences should "not lessen their charity to each other, since charity is a fundamental in all religion."[41] While such instructions were just what Samuel Maverick wanted, the Puritans of Massachusetts resisted them.

The private instructions again reminded the commissioners that religious toleration "and the observation and preservation thereof is our very hearty purpose and determination." Therefore,

> You are to bee very carefull amongst yourselves . . . that nothing be said or done, from or by which the people there may thinke or imagine that there is any purpose in us to make any alteration in the Church Government or to introduce any other forme of worshipp among them then what they have chosen: all our exception in that particular being that they do in truth deny that liberty of conscience to each other, which is equally provided for and granted to every one of them by their charter. . . .[42]

These secret instructions also told the commissioners to privately urge "peaceably inclined" men to run for the General Court to help bring about the changes called for in the public instructions. The English even hoped that these men would bring about the selection of Nicolls as governor of Massachusetts. (This idea hinted at the future Dominion of New England, in which the governor of Massachusetts was at the same time governor of New York.) The major goal of the commission, the English believed, was "to unite and reconcile persons of very different judgments and practice in all things, at least which concerne the peace and prosperity of those people and their joint submission and obedience" to the king.[43]

On the surface, these instructions seem incredibly naive, especially since Maverick had recommended that military force be used against the Puritans. But the instructions should be seen in the light of the English Civil War and the Stuart restoration. The Roundheads had dethroned and executed a king. Nevertheless, his son had been invited back to the throne and England had submitted to him. In 1661 a Parliament dominated by cavaliers had been elected.[44] The English royalists may be excused then, if they expected the Puritans of Massachusetts to submit to the Stuarts as the English had. A logical assumption, perhaps, but a wrong one. Maverick knew the Puritans of the Bay colony much better.

The commission's investigation of New England started slowly. Although both Maverick and Cartwright were in New England in January 1665, they could not act officially without a third commission member; Nicolls and Carr were still busy in the conquered Dutch colony. Maverick spent the time visiting old friends. As it turned out, these visits proved worthwhile. He learned about rumors current in Massachusetts that the commissioners planned to end freedom of religion and to force the baptism of all children. Meanwhile, Puritan leaders made a slight change in the colony's franchise requirements, but a voter still had to be "orthodox in matters of faith." Quietly, the leaders encouraged the submission of petitions to themselves which requested that no changes be made in the governmental structure of the Bay colony.[45]

Colonel Cartwright soon realized that there was little point in trying to influence any elections. Because only Puritans could vote, change was unlikely to be generated by the voters. In addition, Cartwright learned that Puritan leaders had, with impunity, given some "publick mutinous speeches" against the commissioners. Apparently, Cartwright believed, there was "some ground to fear that the fancy of a commonwealth is yet in some of their brains." In such an atmosphere, the commissioners decided to examine the other New England colonies first and hope that Massachusetts was more agreeable later.[46]

With Carr's arrival in New England, the commission was finally able to begin its work. In Plymouth, Rhode Island, and Connecticut the commissioners were received quite warmly and respectfully. All three colonies willingly submitted to the commission, and each made any changes required by it.[47]

Yet Massachusetts continued to resist Maverick and the others. After arriving there in April 1665, Cartwright urged Nicolls to leave New York and join them in the Bay colony. Because Nicolls was the conqueror of New Amsterdam, he was respected among the Puritans—unlike the other commissioners. Cartwright hoped that this respect would work to the commission's advantage and lessen the hostility of the Puritans. Colonel Cartwright also revealed that a Quaker woman—a servant of his—had overheard some Puritans call him a Catholic "and that Sir Robert Carr kept a naughty woman." If true, such information could help to destroy the commission's credibility. Hoping to discover proof of such scandals, some Puritans "examined her if I had not kept one too, or if she knew me not to be a papist," As for Maverick, the Puritans thought him to be "their profest enemy." Cartwright added that "Many factious speeches fly up and down."[48]

Meanwhile, the Puritans had turned to England in an attempt to destroy the commission. Writing to the king in October 1664, the General Court warned that the settlers might all have to leave New England or else suffer under heavy burdens imposed by the royal commission that would destroy their colony and so deprive the king of valuable customs. The Bay leaders insisted that if the king knew what the commissioners were doing, he would stop them. A puzzled Lord Clarendon responded to the Puritans and told them of his surprise. They demanded an end to the mission of the commissioners "without laying the least matter to their charge of crimes or exorbitances." After receiving the colony's complaint, Clarendon cautioned Maverick that the Puritans were "most offended" that he, "whom they looke upon as their enemy," was on the commission. However, Clarendon was confident that knowing about the Puritans' "prejudice" would make Maverick "the more carefull . . . , that they may have no just exception against anything you do, and that they may plainly discerne that you are quite another man in a publick trust then they tooke you to be as a neighbour." On the other hand, if Maverick sought to use his official position to seek revenge against the Puritans, the Crown would "take it very ill" and administer "justice." But Clarendon doubted that such a possibility would arise. "I am confident," the chancellor wrote, that "I have not beene so much mistaken in the observation I could make of your nature and disposition that you can bee liable" to such criticism. Finally, Clarendon observed that his advice "can do you no harme, and proceeds from much kindness."[49] In spite of the Puritans' complaints, Clarendon had not lost faith in Samuel Maverick.

Continued opposition by the Puritans notwithstanding, the royal commission tried to examine some of the charges against the Bay colony. Thomas Deane, a royalist merchant, had charged that, in violation of English trade laws, French merchandise had been brought into Boston. Deane later wished that his complaint had not received so much attention. Worried about his "security," Deane wished to "temporize." When summoned before the General Court, Deane denied that he had informed English authorities about the case.[50]

Another case brought before the commissioners presented them with a curious story of claimed injustice. While they were in Warwick, Rhode Island, a young man, John Porter, Jr., protested "that he had been unjustly imprisoned at Boston . . . for being undutifull to his parents." This accusation was "only pretended," Porter claimed. Still, he was found guilty and was to be subjected to either banishment or a fine of £ 200. Refusing to accept the verdict, he frequently asked the legislature for relief. But his petitions were never heard because Major William Hawthorn, who had made the original charge against him, blocked any action. Hawthorn's alleged motive was devious. According to Porter, Hawthorn "had married his daughter to [Porter's] younger brother, and now endeavoured to disinherit, or banish" him. Porter's petition then took on a more ominous turn: "by word of mouth [he learned] that Mr. Endicot the then Governor who had stayed the sentence from being wholly executed upon him, whilst he lay very weak, charged him that he should be sure to escape to the Commission as soon as he was dead." Maverick was surely intrigued by Porter's charge against Hawthorn, who had been a judge of the Savage lawsuit that had propelled Maverick into undertaking his anti-Massachusetts campaign.[51]

Porter's stunning charges could have caused serious problems for the Puritan leaders. The commissioners, having been warned in their instructions to be cautious with charges against government officials, checked Porter's story with unstated sources. The commissioners learned that Hawthorn "was the same man against whom they had had so many informations for making a seditious speech at the head of his [militia] company, and that the late governor had really befriended Porter." Therefore, the commissioners gave Porter a safe conduct to Boston, where he would have to prove his charges. But they advised him to wait for a message from them before entering Massachusetts, fearing that their safe conduct might be ignored.[52]

The Puritans bitterly attacked the commissioners for listening to Porter. The commissioners, the Puritans declared,

> presumed to plead that he had sustained great wrong by the proceedings of the Court against him; and in case such breach should be made in the wall of our government, it would be an inlett of much trouble to us, and all sorts of persons formerly punished . . . now would hope for some reparation to be made to them, even such as suffered twenty, yea, thirty years and more since, now resolving to trample upon the authority that sentenced them, when those gentlemen that had the cognisance of their causes were removed by death. . . .[53]

Colonel Cartwright defended the commission: "The Commissioners were not so senceless . . . to plead that John Porter had sustayned great wrong by the court, when they had not heard the cause, and had only seen the petition which he gave them. They took that petition to be no more gospell then what the court said." Cartwright also declared that the commissioners would have turned Porter over to justice if their investigation had found him to be guilty as charged.[54]

The leaders of the Bay colony gave Maverick and the others little opportunity to examine Porter's or Deane's cases. In May 1665 the commissioners assembled in Boston when the General Court was due to meet. The commission summoned Governor Bellingham as well as other Puritan leaders to answer questions about their conduct, but they refused to appear. Then, on May 24 at 8:00 AM, the commissioners woke to trumpet blasts and were presented with a declaration of the General Court. The Court refused to accept their activities in the province, and claimed that their involvement with Porter had violated their instructions from the king. Colonel Nicolls saw the Court's action as a threat to the commissioners' personal safety.

> This Manifesto of theirs might have drawne ill Consequences upon us for t'was ordered to bee read at the doore of the house where wee were mett together, and so it was accordingly performed, with a great Rabble of people attending, but the people were more civill then their great men imagined they would have proov'd after such a publicke Invective against us, however wee were sufficiently exposed to danger.[55]

On the other hand, Nicolls's colleagues seem to have been most annoyed that they had been disturbed before their breakfast. All four commissioners agreed that remaining in Boston would be a waste of time and effort.[56]

The commissioners had one important item left on their agenda, a planned visit to New Hampshire and Maine. These two areas had been taken over by Massachusetts despite a weak claim. Of special interest to the commission was the mouth of the Piscataqua River near Portsmouth, from which came a plentiful supply of ship masts of great importance to the English navy.[57]

In Maine the commissioners, acting upon the wishes of the inhabitants, appointed new local officials who were to govern until the wishes of the king concerning the Massachusetts claim became known. At the same time, agents of the Gorges family were prohibited from taking over Maine. Furthermore, some residents of New Hampshire complained to the commissioners about being governed by Massachusetts, but the commissioners left them under the authority of the Bay colony. Shortly after, a letter from the king ordered the commissioners to fortify the Piscataqua's mouth. In July 1665 they called public meetings in Portsmouth and three other towns to start the fortification of the area. But the government of the Bay colony learned of the announced meetings and ordered Portsmouth's constable to prevent them. According to a Puritan account, when the constable arrived and encountered the commissioners, "some words and carriages that were distasteful to the people . . . fell from some of them, and in particular from Mr. Samuel Maverick." Carr and Cartwright, who had remained calmer than Maverick, decided not to continue with the meetings and the commission abandoned its efforts to fortify the river's mouth.[58]

The dispute did not end there. The Puritan leaders informed the commissioners that they had, once again, violated the king's instructions. The infuriated commissioners responded with an attack on the government of the Bay colony:

> The duty which we owe to God, to the King, and to all his subjects, constrains us to persuade you not to suffer yourselves to be so much mislead by the spirit of independency. The King did not grant away his Soveraigntie over you when he made you a Corporation. . . . 'Tis possible that the Charter which you so much idolize may be forfeited, and it may probably be supposed that it hath been many ways forfeited; untill you have cleared yourselves of those many injustices, oppressions, violences, and blood for which you are complained against, to which complaints you have refused to answer; or untill you have His Majesties pardon, which can neither be obtained by nor bee effectuall to those who deny the King's supremacy.[59]

Nevertheless, Massachusetts continued to defy the commissioners. The Puritans jailed Abraham Corbett of Portsmouth, who had been responsible for petitioning the commission and also jailed those men who had been appointed by the commission in Maine.[60]

The battle moved to a different front—winning support in England. The Puritans hoped that the king would see that, despite all the complaints voiced by the commissioners, the Bay colony was innocent. To enlighten the king, the Puritans sent a written defense, totalling 195 pages, which argued that the commission's behavior showed that their earlier concern was not groundless. But the sheer size of the defense was a serious error. Cartwright sarcastically suggested that it would take several years to answer it. A potential reader, put off by the magnitude of his task, would have probably been willing to accept Cartwright's opinion that the defense worked "very well to the end they designed it, that is to tire his Majesty, the Councell, the Lord Chancellor, and the Secretaries too." He added: "there are so many falsities, and repetitions, that they are not worth the answering in particular."[61]

Colonel Cartwright would present the commission's side to English officials. When his ship was captured by the Dutch, the Massachusetts government declared a special day of thanksgiving, or so Maverick insisted. However, the Puritans' joy was premature—Cartwright was released by the Dutch and reached England safely. Although he had had to dispose of the documents he had brought with him, copies of many of them were sent by his colleagues.[62]

Cartwright attacked the Puritan lines of defense. Admitting that the voting law had been modified, he insisted that the change meant little. Earlier, he had estimated that only a handful of non-church members had gained the vote. While the Puritans had resumed using the king's name in legal proceedings, Cartwright pointed out that Massachusetts was the last colony to conform.[63]

One of the Puritans' chief defenses was to blame everything that had happened on Maverick's membership on the commission. But Cartwright observed: "if they had cause to suspect Mr. Maverick, who had (as many others relate) received great affronts, and high injustice from them, they had no cause to suspect the other 3 at that time, or to accuse them for expecting great matters there." The Puritans had refused to deal with any of the commissioners, not just Maverick. From America, Maverick defended himself to Clarendon:

Your Lordship knows I informed nothing but what was true, and as I
said there, all things have come to pass hitherto here, I did prognostik
the rebellion of the Massachusetts governour, and councell; and now
they have made good what I said. I am the man they looke on to be
their chiefe enemy, and on that account make no conscience of abusing
me: yet I praise God for it, they have nothing justly to say against
me. . . .[64]

Both Maverick and Cartwright made suggestions as to how England
should handle the defiance of Massachusetts. Maverick suggested a seizure of the Puritan leaders' English property or a limitation of the colony's
trade. Cartwright reminded the English that the fastest solution to the
problem of the troublesome colony was to take away its charter. Maverick and Cartwright agreed that Bellingham, Hawthorn, and other Puritan
leaders should be summoned to England to explain themselves. But Maverick urged that something be done quickly or else loyal New Englanders
would lose heart.[65]

In April 1666 Charles II wrote to the government of Massachusetts.
The king was angered by the Puritans' treatment of his commission and
demanded that Bellingham, Hawthorn, and at least two others come to
England so that he personally could "hear all the allegations, suggestions, or pretences to right or favour that can be made on the behalf of
the said colony." In addition, Massachusetts was not to alter the government the commissioners had established in Maine and anyone jailed "only
for petitioning or applying themselves" to the commission had to be
released "immediately."[66]

On September 6, 1666, Maverick delivered the king's letter to the
General Court. After ignoring the letter for a few days, the Court refused to send anyone to England despite the king's "expresse command."
The Court also claimed that the letter's authorship was not certain; rumors claimed that Maverick had forged it. But some residents of Massachusetts dissented from the General Court's arrogant dismissal of the
king's commands. Petitions of some Boston merchants and "the
considerablest" of some other places were sent to the court. Most of the
residents of Hingham also drafted a petition, but the town's deputy refused to deliver it. The petitioners were investigated for sedition, and
received "a sharp reproofe for their presumption." In 1667 an elected
deputy of Ipswich was removed from the General Court for having signed
one of the petitions.[67]

The Court's continued arrogance pushed the commissioners still in America into approving Maverick's earlier tough advice on how to deal with the Puritans. To quell the "rebellious" leaders of Massachusetts, Carr joined Maverick in urging an embargo on the colony's trade, to be enforced by naval forces. From New York, Colonel Nicolls also called for a trade embargo until the Bay colony handed over the "Ringleaders" for "Justice." But he urged that force not be used as it "might frighten the innocent" along with the guilty.[68]

Though Lord Clarendon was surprised by the Bay colony's continued defiance, he informed Nicolls that the commission was officially recalled because its members "have in truth done all they ought to do, at least as much as they are suffered to do. . . ." The recall was not meant to include Maverick, who, Clarendon wrote, could stay in America if he chose. Clarendon also promised that if the Bay leaders remained obstinate, "wee shall give them cause to repent it." Although Maverick volunteered to take part in any action against Massachusetts, nothing was done.[69]

The Bay colony was able to avoid any punishment because of England's war with the Dutch, which had been started by the commission's seizure of New Netherland. By the end of 1666, the royal navy was in desperate need of masts. Three times a fleet had tried to reach New England to obtain more masts, but had been driven back by bad weather. Then, suddenly, seven ships from Massachusetts—loaded with masts for the royal navy—arrived safely. This unexpected news was a godsend to Samuel Pepys. Without these masts, Pepys thought, "we must have failed the next year." The grateful royalists could not punish a colony that had provided such timely aid against a foreign foe. The leaders of the Bay colony had cleverly blunted the royal commission's impact. In New York, a saddened Maverick related how the Puritans boasted "of the gracious letters they have received from His Majestie. . . ." The "loyall party, which groans under the burthen of the Massachusetts government, now despaire of reliefe. . . ."[70]

For the rest of Maverick's life, he lived in New York, where freedom of conscience was a right as long as a worshiper did not cause a disturbance of the peace. He kept suggesting that something be done to help loyal New Englanders. But he had to endure a personal agony. "It grieves mee exceedingly," he wrote Nicolls, "that I should live to see His Majesties loyall subjects and my ancient friends enslaved, as now they are." Maverick insisted that his "whole aime was . . . only to have procured for them some freedome; but now they are left in a farr worse condition then wee found them." Sometime during the 1670s, Maverick died with this agony unresolved.[71]

Chapter 6

King Philip

Perhaps the greatest enemy of colonial New England was King Philip, the sachem (or leader) of the Wampanoag tribe. The war named after him is still the bloodiest—in proportion to the numbers involved—ever fought in America.[1]

Any study of the Indians of that time encounters numerous problems such as the almost total lack of documents written by the natives themselves, most of whom were illiterate. Along with the scarcity of Indian-produced sources, a historian must deal with sharply contrasting scholarship. Earlier accounts often gave the English settlers too much credit, but the turbulent 1960s and 1970s brought forth the "new wisdom," pushed by radical scholars of the New Left. Eager to display their ideological superiority over their predecessors, they found nothing good about the colonists. Francis Jennings became the dominant voice of these extremists. By the end of the 1980s Jennings's version of events had been toppled by revisionist historians, and the 1990s saw further revisions through the work of Jill Lepore and James D. Drake.[2]

Although Jennings himself is dead, two of his worst legacies—his extreme tone and blatant dislike of the English colonists—have survived him. Buttressed by the hostility generated by the multicultural movement of the 1990s, Jennings's old radicalism has been picked up by a new generation. A good example is the fascination with the work of a nineteenth century Indian, William Apess.

Apess, a Pequot, in his "Eulogy on King Philip," bitterly attacked the colonists. Apess declared that "It does not appear" that Philip's grandfather, Massasoit, and his heirs "were respected because they were human beings but because they feared him; and we are led to believe that if it had been in the power of the Pilgrims, they would have butchered them out and out, notwithstanding all the piety they professed." The "Eulogy" branded as traitors those Indians who sided with the settlers.[3]

Whatever Apess's "powerful writing" is, it is not history. The Indian never bothered to mention that his own people, the Pequots, allied themselves with those who destroyed Philip. Nor does Apess mention that the Mashpee, who took him in, were Christian Indians who also clearly sided with the English (despite a recent assertion to the contrary). Apess's work is excellent evidence of what one scholar has called "selective amnesia," which continues among some modern day Indians.[4]

Historians, however, have not been put off by Apess's bending of the truth. "Exaggerated, one-sided, propagandistic?," a scholar asked. "Certainly," he added, "but no more so than" accounts by descendants of the Puritans, and "for Apess the point was not so much to prove which angle of vision . . . was more accurate but to employ" his vision "in the service of a larger truth." The facts be damned; ideology is of overwhelming importance to some historians, so Apess's twisted vision is accepted and praised even though not all Indians of his time agreed with him.[5]

Given the ahistorical reasoning moving so many scholars, extremism is as rampant in the twenty-first century as it was during Jennings's glory days. "The very act of translation" of Indian texts, Joshua David Bellin asserted, "was an act of colonialism, even of colonial violence." Strange as that seems, Michael Leroy Oberg used the word "Cutthroats" as a synonym for the colonists six different times—the last five without quotation marks. A similar word used to describe Indians would be called racist immediately. To top it off, he implied that only Christian Indians in New England rejected a non-existent "unified Indian resistance" forged by King Philip. Fantasy has seemingly replaced reality.[6]

Perhaps, though, the oddest example of extremism occurred when one New Englander felt compelled to express his "liberal guilt" over his ancestor's participation "in the Great Swamp Fight, one of the most notorious massacres of King Philip's War." How pleased Jennings would have been. He showed great reluctance to use the word "massacre" when Indians were those responsible for numerous deaths. With the colonists, however, he had no such hesitation.[7]

Such bizarre analyses make another look at King Philip necessary. This chapter delves into New England's relations with Philip and his

Wampanoag tribe from the start of settlement in Plymouth and Massachusetts Bay. Special attention will be paid to John Eliot, who sought to convert the sachem of the Wampanoags.

Some years before the English colonized Massachusetts, Indians of New England saw a comet in the sky and believed it to be an omen of unusual events in the future. In this instance, their concern was justified. From 1616 through 1619, a terrible epidemic disease, which peaked in 1617, decimated the various tribes. So many people died at once that Indian society was stunned, and remains of the unburied died were still visible years later.[8]

When the Pilgrims on the *Mayflower* arrived in 1620, the Wampanoags had barely gotten over the shock of the epidemic. Luckily for the English colonists, the Indians' war-making ability had been weakened by the disaster—many of their most experienced warriors had been killed. Their chief sachem, Massasoit, soon made peace with the Pilgrims, and promised that no harm would come to any of the English. Furthermore, he agreed that any violator of his pledge would be submitted for punishment at their hands. Most important to Massasoit was the colonists' pledge to aid him if any of his enemies should "unjustly warre against him," and he vowed to aid the newcomers were the situation reversed. The first Thanksgiving resulted from this peace between Plymouth and the Wampanoags.[9]

In 1623 the Pilgrims learned that Massasoit was near death. Because the colonists had claimed to be his friends, they sent Edward Winslow to visit him. By doing so, the Pilgrims followed an Indian custom of visiting the seriously ill. As Winslow approached Massasoit's camp, he heard disturbing news that the sachem was already dead. Although he was still alive, Massasoit was very sick. Winslow ministered to the sachem, and, despite a brief setback, he managed to restore the chief's health. Impressed by the Englishman's skill, Massasoit had him take care of the other sick Indians in the village. Winslow's success was in sharp contrast to the failure of the powwows, the natives' religious leaders, who had been unable to do anything about the disease.[10]

Winslow's triumph had great importance for the English. Massasoit had been restraining his counsellors who were very hostile towards the settlers, and his return to health convinced him that peace with the newcomers should be maintained. As Massasoit said: "Now I see the English are my friends, and love me: and whilst I live, I will never forget this kindness they have shewed me."[11]

Massasoit's pledge had immediate benefits for the Pilgrims. He informed them that the Massachusett Indians planned to kill the settlers at Thomas Weston's troubled colony at Wessagusset. The Indians there believed that Weston's men had mistreated them. A successful attack on Wessagusset would likely have brought forth similar consequences for the Pilgrims, but they were reluctant to do anything because there had, as yet, been no attack. Massasoit, however, recommended a preemptive strike against the plotters. By killing them first, Massasoit explained, the Pilgrims could prevent any attack. Despite their qualms, they sent Miles Standish with sufficient force for the mission. As a professional soldier, Standish had no qualms. His disposal of the principal plotters was quick, brutal, and effective. [12]

After Standish's success, the Pilgrims had little trouble with the area's Indians for the rest of Massasoit's life. He stayed at peace with them and with the Puritan settlers of Massachusetts Bay, who arrived later. In 1632 both colonies protected and aided him in a dispute between the Wampanoags and their old rivals, the Narragansetts. With the exception of the Pequot War, the Puritan authors of *First Fruits* wrote, "we never found any hurt from [the Indians], nor could ever prove any reall intentions of evill against us" An early visitor commented that the Indians were "a loving people." [13]

During this period of general peace, both cultures interacted with each other and changed. The Indians accepted some European items that were more efficient than traditional goods. European cloth was especially prized. But some products did serious harm to the natives—alcohol, for instance. Liquor very soon was in great demand among them. [14]

To the great concern of the English, the Indians were also interested in European firearms. Far superior to the bow and arrow, guns became a major trading item almost immediately. The English tried to ban the sale of guns to the natives, but many English traders ignored such prohibitions. Nor were other Europeans very concerned about the matter. Both the Dutch and, especially, the French supplied these weapons in return for furs. Finally, in 1667 Massachusetts legalized the swap of guns for beaver by authorized traders. By King Philip's War, a musket was in the hands of any Indian who wanted one. [15]

Despite the continuing peace during Massasoit's lifetime, he seems to have been concerned about the future. He expressed the hope that relations between his grandsons, Wamsutta and Metacom, and the English would be as amicable after he died as when he lived. His concern was well-placed. After his death in 1660, the two societies seemed to be on a collision course.[16]

Wamsutta, Massasoit's eldest grandson, succeeded him as chief sachem of the Wampanoags. In 1659 as well as in 1660 Wamsutta, apparently being primed to assume his grandfather's authority, had been selected to complain to the English about damage done to Indian crops by stray horses and ravenous pigs. He also brought an Indian land dispute to the attention of the Pilgrim leaders, and asked their advice on the matter.[17]

In June 1660 Wamsutta, because he had become chief sachem, decided to change his name. He asked the Plymouth leaders for an English name, and they dubbed him Alexander Pokanokett. Alexander also asked that they do the same for his brother, Metacom. The Plymouth officials, again drawing upon classical Greek history, called him Philip. Both the Indians and Plymouth were seemingly pleased with each other. Having an English name was then popular among the Indians, who saw "renaming" as a way to cement ties between the two allied peoples. As for the colonists, they were likely honored by Alexander's gesture. They selected very regal names for the two sachems, suggesting the great importance they had to the settlers. Still, Plymouth's leaders were reluctant to grant another of Alexander's requests—he wanted permission to buy some gunpowder. Preferring to avoid a precedent, Plymouth gave him the small amount he wanted as a gift.[18]

Alexander's cordial relations with the English ended abruptly. In 1662 Plymouth learned of rumors that Alexander was plotting against the colony. When requested to explain the reports, he did not appear and Josiah Winslow was sent to bring him to Plymouth. When Winslow found Alexander, he explained why he had been delayed and then came with Winslow to Plymouth. While there, the sachem explained his conduct to the Englishmen and that ended the matter. However, as Alexander was returning to his territory, he became ill. Suddenly, a few days later he died.[19]

Alexander's death made his youthful brother, Philip, the chief sachem of the Wampanoags. Many Indians flocked to Mount Hope, the tribe's most favored area, to welcome his accession. As John Cotton later wrote, there was "great feasting and rejoicing" among the assembled natives.[20]

Because a new sachem now led the Wampanoags, Plymouth decided to investigate various rumors that the Indians planned to make war against the colony. The rumors were groundless. On August 6, 1662, Philip and

Plymouth agreed upon the terms of a new pact. Philip accepted that he was subject to the English Crown, and he promised not to break any treaty signed by his predecessors. Nor would he sell land to "strangers"—English settlers not acceptable to the colony. (Alexander had sold land to whom he pleased.) King Philip also vowed that he would "not att any time needlesly or unjustly provoake or raise warr with any other of the natives." On Plymouth's part, the colony promised that all settlers would treat the Indians as friends. In addition, the colony promised to advise the sachem and aid him—presumably with military force.[21]

About this time, Philip and Plymouth came to another understanding. Philip wanted to stop selling land for seven years, and Governor Thomas Prence promised to discourage any potential buyers, either Indian or English. The sachem was not moved by a fear that the Wampanoags were being cheated out of their land. To the contrary, King Philip had tired of the legal problems land sales had caused. In 1662, for example, an Indian accused Alexander of selling land that was not his to sell. Alexander and Philip were also involved in a land dispute with the Narragansetts, which in 1663 the colonists decided in the Wampanoags' favor. However, in 1665 Philip made an exception involving the sale of more land to the town of Rehoboth, a deal that had the full approval of Plymouth's General Court.[22]

During the 1660s, Philip and his tribe came into increasing contact with the Reverend John Eliot, of Roxbury, Massachusetts, who sought to convert them to Christianity. Because of Eliot's life-long mission of spreading Protestantism, he has been called the Apostle to the Indians.

In order to preach extensively to the Indians, Eliot had to learn the Indian language, Massachusett. He started that task with the aid of a "witty" bilingual Indian in the 1640s. Cotton Mather could not contain his astonishment at the difficulty of the tongue:

> For instance, if my reader will count how many letters there are in this one word, Nummatchekodtantamooonganunnonash, when he has done, for his reward, I'll tell them it signifies no more in English than *our lusts*; and if I were to translate, *our loves*, it must be nothing shorter than Noowomantammooonkanunonnash. Or, to give my reader a longer word than either of these, Kummogkodomattoottummooetiteaon-gannunnonash, is in English *our question*.[23]

Despite Eliot's determined missionary efforts, starting in 1646, the Indians were very slow in accepting Christianity. In 1657 he wrote that the natives "so disliked" the Christian faith "that if any began to speake of God and heaven and hell and religion unto them they would presently be gone." This distaste of the Indians soon became a "knowne thing to all English that if they were burdensome, and you would have them gone, speake of religion and you were . . . rid of them. . . ." Some Indians feared that their sachems would kill them if they became Christians, and the powwows' blatant hostility to converts added to their anxieties. By 1668 the Praying Indians—those who accepted Christ—remained few in number.[24]

The English settlers themselves gave the Indians little encouragement. When Eliot established new towns, called "Praying Towns," for the converts, many colonists near the sites reacted with great hostility. To make Eliot's task even more difficult, in 1652 wild charges spread that the Praying Indians were conspiring with the pagan natives and the Dutch against New England. Although colonial leaders tried to encourage the spread of Christianity, the common people had little regard for Indian converts.[25]

Still, with all these discouragements, Eliot got converts. As he related, "I have traveled many miles and among many Indians and never came yet unto that place where I found not some, ready and glad to hear the word of God preached unto them." These receptive Indians who accepted Eliot's teachings had to leave the society of the unconverted and dwell in a Praying Town, because Eliot believed that the natives had to accept Western culture as well as Christianity. Choosing to abandon one's heritage was a difficult step. But Eliot may have wanted them to emulate the example of Christ's apostles, who also had to abandon their former lives to follow Christ. The Praying Indians, like the apostles, were expected to try to bring non-believers into the faith.[26]

During the 1670s the Indian Church at Natick had "sundry young men, who were when I first began children and youths, whom I did cathechise and so train up ever since." Eliot realized that "these now are sundry of them of good parts able to teach." After additional training, the neophyte ministers went out "to call in their countrymen to pray unto God." Eliot had simplified his Christian message for his acolytes who no doubt did the same with their prospective converts. A strong believer in the millennium, Eliot surely taught his charges about the fast approaching end of the world. Some of the pagan Indians who listened to the native preachers believed that they were threatened with war if they did not convert. John Eliot had not equipped the Praying Indians with guns to intimidate the other natives. The pagans had misunderstood the preaching about the millennium when, during the world's last war, believers in Christ would be protected while pagans were doomed.[27]

Although the efforts of individual Praying Indians would be useful, Eliot understood Indian society well enough to realize the importance of converting sachems. If an important sachem embraced Christianity, others could be expected to follow his example. Christianity had used that path to expand centuries before in Europe. In 1652 Eliot had no hope of converting sachems such as Uncas or Ninigret. When they died, Eliot predicted, "there will be a door open for the preaching of the Gospel in those parts where they live."[28]

King Philip seemed to be a more promising target. At first he rebuffed Eliot's efforts. As Cotton Mather later wrote, Philip treated the offer of "everlasting salvation . . . with contempt and anger, and, after the Indian mode of joining signs with words, he took a button upon the coat of the reverend man, adding, 'That he cared for his gospel, just as much as he cared for that button.'" But if Eliot was anything, he was persistent. According to his *Indian Dialogues*, written in 1671, Philip gradually became interested in Christianity although he still had objections to converting.[29]

Of course a wary reader, knowing that Eliot stated that the *Indian Dialogues* were "partly historical, of some things that were done and said, and partly instructive, to show what might or should have been said," would tend to discount that record of events. Indeed, if the *Dialogues* were the only evidence for Philip's interest in Eliot's teachings, then little stock could be placed in it. But more evidence exists. As late as 1674, Daniel Gookin, a civil magistrate who assisted Eliot, wrote:

> There are some that have high hopes of their greatest and chiefest sachem, named Philip. . . . Some of his chief men, as I hear, stand well inclined to hear the gospel: and himself is a person of good understanding and knowledge in the best things. I have heard him speak very good words, arguing that his conscience is convicted: but yet, though his will is bowed to embrace Jesus Christ, his sensual and carnal lusts are strong bands to hold him fast under Satan's dominions.[30]

Eliot himself gave still further witness to Philip's interest. In 1664 he observed that "Phillip and his people of Sowamset [Mount Hope] . . . did this winter past, upon solicitations and means used, send to me for books to learne to read, in order to praying unto God. . . ."[31]

In the end, Eliot failed to bring Philip and his tribe into the fold. The Wampanoags as a whole rejected the Christian faith. As for Philip's own motives, his distaste for the Christian practice of monogamy—as Gookin suggested—may have been a factor. More significant deterrents, however, were the political consequences of his conversion. Philip may have feared losing authority over any Praying Indian from his tribe, and he may have rejected becoming "a common man among them;" in addition, those Indians who rejected Christianity would certainly reject the authority of a Christian sachem. As King Philip reportedly said, according to the *Indian Dialogues*, if he became "a praying sachem, I shall be a poor and weak one, and easily be trod upon by others . . . and I shall be a great loser by praying to God."[32]

But in the early 1660s Eliot could, with good reason, be hopeful about the religious future of the Wampanoags. He surely placed great importance upon the Indian missionary who, by teaching Philip to read, would help him move forward towards conversion. For this important task, Eliot selected John Sassamon, whose Indian parents had also been Christians. He had been living at the Praying Town of Natick as early as 1651. Sassamon, whom Eliot thought to be a sincere believer and "a man of eminent parts and wit," had been educated at the Indian school at Harvard. Despite Sassamon's Christianity, he attained a position of influence among the Wampanoags. In 1662, for example, he witnessed the treaty between Philip and Plymouth. He also served as Philip's secretary and was an advisor. Yet Sassamon eventually left the tribe, probably in the late 1660s, when Philip finally decided against becoming a praying sachem. Sassamon then settled at Middleborough, in Plymouth colony, where he served as an Indian minister.[33]

Sassamon's departure is indicative of a steady deterioration of the once friendly relations between the two different cultures. By the late 1660s many of the natives had undoubtedly experienced the growing hostility of the English settlers. As early as 1645, Roger Williams complained that he had often heard scurrilous comments, such as:

These Heathen Dogges, better kill a thousand of them then that we Christians should be indangered or troubled with them; Better they were all cut off, and then we shall be no more troubled with them: They have spilt our Christian bloud, the best way to make riddance of them, cut them all off, and so make way for Christians.[34]

Slowly but surely this hostility grew, and not surprisingly, it hurt the spread of Christianity among the Indians.[35] Men of good will such as Eliot, Gookin, and Williams became increasingly isolated as the original settlers died, for the next generation of Puritans cared little for the Indians.

Other problems surfaced during the 1660s. The royal commission of 1664-1667 found evidence that some English colonists had obtained Indian land by devious means. The natives also had to endure annoying incidents in which the colonists' animals—left untended—wandered onto the Indians' planted fields and destroyed their crops. To make relations still more strained, the colonists sometimes hurt the Indians' animals.[36]

By May and June 1667, the Wampanoags' growing hostility towards the English forced Philip to distance himself from his earlier interest in English culture. In May of that year, Philip's actions led Rhode Islanders to believe he had "treacherous designes." Just a few weeks later, in June, Plymouth's leaders received information that stirred their own suspicions. According to a Wampanoag source, Philip and the French were plotting against the New Englanders. In front of some of his warriors, he had reportedly announced that he wished to regain the Indians' old lands as well as seize the colonists' property. Some settlers at Rehoboth brought Philip's accuser to the sachem, and the informer "freely and boldly did avouch it to his face, and soe to particularise time [and] place. . . ."[37]

The General Court insisted that King Philip explain his actions, and in July he did so. Realizing that he was in a difficult position, Philip insisted that the whole report was just a plot of Ninigret, a Narragansett sachem, to discredit him. To prove his innocence, Philip presented a letter from another Narragansett sachem that supported his story, but that sachem soon denied having sent any such letter. Finally, Philip asserted that his joining with the Dutch or French made little sense as they had killed or kidnapped eighteen of his tribe in 1666. Having sifted through the evidence, the Plymouth leaders decided that "there was great probabillitie that his tongue had been runing out," but there was no sound proof of a real plot. Still, the Court fined him £ 40 as partial reimbursement for expenses incurred in investigating the affair.[38] Quite likely, Philip had been boasting to his tribesmen and had never thought his words would be carried to the English. This incident was surely both an insult and an embarrassment for the sachem.

In June and July 1669 the colonists had another scare. Some of Philip's chief advisors spent over a week visiting Ninigret. An Indian from Long Island spread a rumor that the two Indian leaders were planning an attack against the English. Ninigret, however, rejected the charge: ever since he had met with the royal commissioners of 1664-1667 a few years before, he had considered himself a loyal subject of Charles II. Ninigret insisted that he had sent one of his followers to the Wampanoags simply because Philip had asked "for an old man to teach or informe his men in a certaine dance." Although not satisfied with this explanation, the Rhode Islanders took no further action.[39]

Since Ninigret stayed friendly with the colonists during King Philip's War, it is unlikely that he was conspiring with the Wampanoags. A more reasonable explanation would involve the border dispute that the Narragansetts and the Wampanoags had brought to the royal commissioners. Relying upon the testimony of Roger Williams, Colonel Nichols and the other commissioners settled the dispute in Philip's favor.[40] Perhaps the two tribes were engaging in some form of ceremonial acceptance of the decision and were trying to establish peace among themselves. If so, they wanted no further participation by their English neighbors.

By 1671 the Wampanoags' hostility to the English had grown markedly. In that year Eliot wrote that he could not recall "such violent opposition" among the Indians to the preaching of Christianity. At this time, as well, damage to Indian property by stray farm animals may have reached a high point, for on June 5, 1671, the Plymouth General Court appointed people in eleven different towns to examine such cases.[41]

Undoubtedly, Philip was being pressured by a number of elements within the Wampanoags. The powwows had always resented Eliot's preaching—especially when he was successful—and they can be assumed to have been eager for a confrontation with the English colonists and their missionaries. Although Philip had calmed their agitation before, by 1671 he had another problem—his younger brother, Takamunna, had come of age. This young sachem, who was to take an active military role in the upcoming war (and died fighting), probably wanted to battle the English, as did the other youthful Wampanoag warriors.[42]

Whatever the cause of worsening relations, Philip was clearly persuaded to prepare for war. During the early months of 1671, the natives were spotted sharpening their tomahawks and repairing their firearms. In March 1671 Philip made a gesture that probably signaled his intention to fight. Assembling a group of fully-armed warriors, he and his men marched to the town of Swansea in Plymouth colony, but did not attack.[43]

The Plymouth General Court summoned Philip to explain his actions. Instead of following through on his threat, he came to Plymouth in peace and, incredibly, admitted that his tribe had been preparing for war against the colonists. He gave no reason why except that the Indians' desire for war came from within "theire owne naughty harts." Suddenly, despite their avowed aim, the Wampanoags lost interest in war. On April 10, 1671, they signed a peace treaty at Taunton, by which Philip pledged to surrender to the colonists "all my English Armes to be kept by them for their security, as long as they shall see reason."[44]

Peace seemed to have been restored. In May, when an Indian murdered an Englishman in Massachusetts, Philip was "industriously active" in bringing the culprit to justice. Relations soon soured again, however, over a difference in the interpretation of the new agreement. Apparently, Philip had assumed that only the guns he and his men had carried to Taunton were to be surrendered. Plymouth, on the other hand, insisted upon a literal interpretation: all guns meant every single firearm the Wampanoags possessed.[45] With this attempt to disarm Philip's tribe totally, the Plymouth leaders began blundering their way into a bloody war.

The Wampanoags refused to comply with Plymouth's interpretation. In retaliation, on June 5 the colony announced that it would confiscate all the guns that had been surrendered at Taunton. Furthermore, the colonists insisted that other Indians, including the Saconetts, who were associated with the Wampanoags, also had to surrender their guns. To back up these demands, on July 8 the Plymouth General Court made plans for a military expedition that would "proceed by force to reduce [the Saconetts] to reason." The Saconetts quickly backed down and surrendered their six guns, which satisfied the colony's leaders.[46]

Before Plymouth could turn its attention to Philip, John Eliot intervened, in a role that has been neglected by historians. The Praying Indians, under Eliot's guidance, sent three former missionaries—Anthony, William, and John Sassamon—back to the Wampanoags. Despite the Wampanoags' failure to accept Christ, the Natick Indians wanted to try to head off war. They believed that the best way to settle the disagreement was to ask Massachusetts Bay to arbitrate it. The missionaries were also to remind Governor Thomas Prence of Plymouth that arbitration was far superior "to kill or be killed, when no capital sin hath been committed or defended by them, (that we hear of)."[47]

On August 23, 1671, Plymouth's council of war charged Philip with trying to mislead Massachusetts about its conduct. The "insolent" sachem also had entertained hostile Saconetts and "many strange Indians which might p[or]tend danger towards us." These mysterious strangers were Narragansett sachems, probably enlisted for aid. John Sassamon, who had seen the Narragansetts while on his mission with the Indian missionaries, had reported their presence to the English colonists.[48]

Although Plymouth's leaders believed that Philip had to be subdued by force, their resolve had been weakened by Eliot's intercession. They decided to ask the advice of both Rhode Island and Massachusetts, a small concession to Eliot's arbitration scheme. But Plymouth still reserved the right to go to war against Philip on September 20 if the other two colonies disapproved of the use of arms. Meanwhile, Philip was again summoned to Plymouth to explain himself. The colony's order was in a letter to be conveyed by James Brown of Swansea and others.[49]

The messengers arrived at a bad time: Philip and his advisors had been drinking. After "some words" passed between the sachem and Brown, Philip knocked off the Englishman's hat. When Philip sobered the next day, he was more courteous but refused to indicate whether or not he would obey. He also expressed his anger at John Sassamon for informing the English about the visit of the Narragansetts.[50]

King Philip had been deliberately evasive with Plymouth's messengers because Eliot had invited him to Boston to talk with the Bay colony's leaders. Eliot still hoped for arbitration. Philip decided to go to Boston since he had been unable to muster the help of other Indians necessary to wage war against Plymouth. The Narragansetts had apparently decided not to get involved, and the Saconetts could not be depended upon. Although the sons and brother of Awasuncks, the queen of the Saconetts, were hostile to the English, both she and her husband wanted peace, and she had enough support among her warriors to keep her tribe off the warpath. Other smaller groups, such as the Dartmouth Indians, also favored peace.[51]

When Philip came to Boston, he talked not only with the Bay colony's leaders but also with John Winthrop, Jr., Connecticut's governor, who happened to be in the city. Philip stated his side of the dispute and the prominent Englishmen seemed sympathetic. Offering their aid in arranging a peaceful settlement, they wrote to Governor Prence that "they resented not his offence soe deeply" as did Plymouth and that no previous agreement had made the Wampanoags subject to Plymouth. Faced with this stand, Plymouth accepted arbitration by John Leverett of Massachusetts, Winthrop of Connecticut, and other prominent men from both colonies, including some who were not delegates to the Confederation of New England, a league of all the Puritan colonies except Rhode Island. No one from Rhode Island—a colony not on good terms with the others—was invited.[52]

On September 24, 1671, the arbitrators met at Plymouth and were joined by Philip and a host of interpreters. Disinterested inquiry soon gave way. The leaders of Plymouth made no secret of their fury that Philip had sought the intercession of the other colonies. Unfortunately for Philip, the arbitrators were simply too close to the Plymouth colonists, who called the arbitrators "our good friends and neighbors." Deciding that Philip was totally at fault, the arbitrators ordered him "to amend his wayes, if hee expected peace, and that if hee went on in his refractory way, he must expect to smart for it." The hapless Philip now faced three united foes.[53]

King Philip had little choice but to accept the imposed Treaty of September 29, 1671, which made him subject to Plymouth. He could not sell land or go to war against another tribe without the approval of Plymouth's governor. The sachem also had to do some service for the colony—each year five wolves had to be killed. But the harshest part of the treaty involved a fine. For his various offenses, Philip had to pay the colony £ 100 within three years. In November 1671 Takamunna signed a similar agreement which made him subject to Plymouth and required him to kill one wolf every year.[54]

Seemingly, Plymouth had triumphed. Philip had to endure the taunt of one of his advisors, who called him "a white-liver'd Cur" because he had not made war. Most galling, however, was the heavy fine. As late as June 1675, Philip mentioned his resentment about it to John Easton of Rhode Island. Despite his anger, Philip did pay up, with money he received from, reluctantly, selling land. After paying the fine, Philip still had cash left.[55] The surplus was probably used to replace the guns lost at Taunton and to buy more gunpowder. Such strategy was logical for a leader who thought that, some day, war would break out. Plymouth's victory in 1671 was clearly Pyrrhic.

In the midst of "these stormy times," Eliot believed that the conversion of the Indians had to continue. And he felt optimistic. Natick's native preachers were being sent out, and the *Indian Dialogues* had been printed along with an "Indian ABC." (In 1663 Eliot, with the aid of John

Sassamon, had produced a Bible written in Massachusett.) Still more good news came to the Puritan cleric—Uncas and his heir had agreed to listen to preaching by a Puritan minister in Connecticut. This was truly "a great matter." If the Mohegans converted, Eliot hoped that the Mohawks might be next. He dreamed of preaching to the Mohawks himself. Although Eliot had fallen into debt because of his missionary work, "I will never give over the work so long as I have legs to go." He would happily incur still more debt. Only God knew the future, "but this I do see, that the work doth enlarge and multiply."[56]

Uncas, however, did not convert. The situation in New England remained outwardly calm until March 1674, when the Indians reacted against land sales. Even though one of her tribesmen had cleared his title, Awasuncks and her husband had him tied up, and threatened for intending to sell land to the English. Among the Wampanoags, concern over land surely increased in July 1674, when Philip was sued for £ 800 in the Plymouth courts by a Rhode Islander who produced a bond from Alexander, dated 1661, which entitled him to a large amount of the natives' land. Although land was still plentiful in New England,[57] such events surely set disturbing precedents. Yet anxieties about future land loss did not provoke the outbreak of King Philip's War. Instead, the conflict was ignited by the death of John Sassamon.

At the end of 1674, Philip and his tribe were near Middleborough, and Sassamon went to the campsite. Exactly why is not known but perhaps he had continued to hope that the sachem could be converted. While there, the Indian minister somehow determined that Philip was planning a war against the colonists. Sassamon, fearing for his life, then journeyed to Plymouth and told the English about his suspicions, but he failed to convince them. Other Christian Indians had recently given similar warnings and had also been ignored.[58]

On January 29, 1675, soon after Sassamon left Plymouth, he was killed by three Wampanoags, one of whom, Tobias, was an important advisor to Philip. Sassamon's murder was made to look accidental: his body was found in a pond, where he had presumably fallen while fishing. Eliot eulogized him as having "the esteeme of a good Christian, and his death was much bewailed." Sassamon was buried and, at first, the authorities paid little attention to his death. But Tobias and the others did not know that another Indian, Patuckson, had seen the murder and could not resist talking about it. When William Nahauton, a Praying Indian, heard the story, he informed the English. Only then did they credit Sassamon's warnings.[59]

Tobias and the others were tried for Sassamon's murder in June 1675. There would be two juries in this case: one composed of Englishmen and a "Jury *de medietate linguae*" made up of Indians. This type of jury, an old English procedure to try someone whose native language was not English, is known to have been used in Massachusetts—both before and after the murder of Sassamon—whenever a crime's punishment could be death.[60]

In 1682, for example, Daniel Gookin summoned Indian jurors from Natick for a Jury *de medietate linguae* in a rape case where the accused man was an Indian. The jurors had to be "able and understanding men" who could "speake and understand the english toung." An unstated requirement was that the prospective jurors had to be Christian—Natick was a Praying Town. English law specified that jurors had to swear on a Bible, a meaningless act for a pagan Indian. If Joseph Dudley's memory was correct, Massachusetts had been using Juries *de medietate linguae* since the 1640s. Therefore, its utilization in the trial of the accused murderers of John Sassamon followed what had become standard procedure in at least two New England colonies.[61]

Although both juries found the three defendants guilty, some scholars have seen a conspiracy. Supposedly, Christian Indians had plotted to destroy Tobias and the others or that Patuckson, who owed the three suspects money, had merely been trying to escape from his financial burden.[62]

William Nahauton was a Christian, but was Patuckson? Francis Jennings declared he was. The only evidence Jennings had was John Easton's account of what unidentified Indians told him—and they did not even mention Patuckson's name. These Indian sources also smeared John Sassamon by saying that he tried to rig King Philip's will in his favor. But what will? No such will exists today and almost certainly it never existed at all. In sharp contrast to Easton's account, Increase Mather called Nahauton a Christian, but merely referred to Patuckson as "the other Indian" with no suggestion that he was a Praying Indian. Perhaps Patuckson was a Christian, perhaps he was not. Such skimpy evidence can not sustain the conspiracy charge. While Patuckson might have been in debt, the reported sum was not large enough to compensate for the great risk he took. His testimony made him a target for revenge by the kin of the convicted murderers. Why would Patuckson place himself in such danger unless he had witnessed the murder of John Sassamon? Clearly, Nahauton and Patuckson were not conspirators.[63]

Plymouth's leaders had no doubts about who had killed Sassamon, but they could not determine if Philip had known about or ordered the murder. In March 1675 he came to the General Court, without being summoned, and denied any role in Sassamon's death. The colonists, although suspicious, had no proof that implicated Philip, so he was allowed to leave.[64]

It is unlikely that Philip ordered Sassamon's death. There is no evidence that any of the Wampanoags knew that Sassamon had recently given information to the English. If Philip had wanted him dead, he could have so ordered in 1671—when the sachem was bitterly angry at Sassamon. Or Philip could have had him killed when he entered the Indian encampment in December 1674.

Instead, Sassamon's death was probably planned solely by Tobias and his confederates. The killing may have been motivated purely by hatred. Sassamon was everything that some Indians detested—he was a Christian, a minister, and a loyal follower of the English. He had been close to King Philip, and this closeness had surely earned him the envy of many. His role in the events of 1671 added to such ill feelings. After that incident, Tobias and the others may have been waiting for the right time to kill Sassamon. For some reason, January 1675 was the right time. Although a wait of four years to exact revenge may seem unbelievable, an Indian revenge killing once took place after a delay of thirteen years. The attempt to conceal Sassamon's murder—an act unusual for Indians[65]—may have been intended to protect the perpetrators not only from the English but also from the wrath of Philip.

Shortly before Tobias's trial, the Wampanoags appeared armed in public. The Englishmen assumed that Philip felt guilty about Sassamon's death. From the great interest the colonists were suddenly showing in Sassamon's demise, Philip may have guessed that Sassamon had told them about his plans. The Wampanoags may therefore have been armed out of suspicion that a preemptive strike, like that once urged upon the Pilgrims by Massasoit, might be used against them. But Plymouth's leaders were not planning an attack, nor was Philip questioned again about Sassamon's death. In fact, the colony's leaders later claimed that they had hoped "the cloud might blow over." As late as June 13, 1675, Roger Williams also believed that "the storme is over."[66]

The storm, though, had not yet gathered strength. Plymouth Governor Josiah Winslow knew of no *causus belli* committed by his colony, except possibly in having executed Tobias and his accomplices. Philip reportedly claimed that the executions had started the war. Without doubt, the executions inflamed the young warriors of the Wampanoags and other tribes. Much evidence suggests that the young braves pressured other sachems, who preferred peace, into fighting the English. King Philip, also pressured by militant young Wampanoags, probably had another, more compelling reason for deciding upon war. He realized that the power of the Indians was fast declining, that New England was becoming the domain of the English. If there was to be war, it had to be fought before the odds got worse and while there was still a chance for an Indian victory.[67]

Without the support of the other Indians, the Wampanoags had no chance at all against the colonists. Various emissaries were sent to neighboring tribes to urge them to join with the Wampanoags. Those sachems, such as Awasuncks, who were still reluctant to join them were threatened. In another effort to gain support, the Wampanoags held special dances for the young warriors of other tribes. The enthusiasm of the youthful Wampanoags infected their peers.[68]

Despite all these efforts and the dedication of the young men, Philip's decision for war seems to have been grudging. He tried to give special protection to certain colonists who had been friendly or kind to him. Even as late as June 17, 1675, he invited certain colonists to retrieve their stray horses—a long standing grievance of the Indians. Although Philip himself had been responsible for the settlers' presence at the Indian camp, some of the Wampanoags pointed guns at them; the Englishmen were clearly not welcome. Perhaps Philip was moved by memories of his grandfather's good feelings towards the colonists. William Harris, for one, had reminded Philip about the help "the plimoth old planters" had given to Massasoit in 1632. Whatever the reason, Philip was once more willing to consider peace.[69]

About June 13, a week or so before the war erupted, John Easton, the deputy governor of Rhode Island, and some others from that colony approached the Wampanoags to urge Philip to accept arbitration of his complaints against the English. At first, the Indians rejected the suggestion, having already been through an arbitration in 1671. Because all the arbitrators would be English, the natives insisted, the procedure would be unfair. But Easton and the others suggested that there be only two arbitrators: an Indian sachem to be chosen by the Wampanoags, and Edmund Andros, then the governor of New York. Judging from Andros's later career, he would not have hesitated to find against the New Englanders if he felt that the natives' grievances were valid. The Wampanoags were surprised by the suggestion, and Easton thought the idea was agreeable to them.[70]

Some Wampanoags wanted war, and had no intention of waiting for arbitration to be tried first. They were also mindful, however, of the powwows' prediction that if they began the war, they would be beaten. Both to prevent arbitration and to avoid fulfilling the prophecy, those Indians who wanted war had a simple plan—let the English start the war. Ironically, Easton and the Rhode Islanders may have inspired that strategy when they told the Wampanoags: "when in war against [the] English[,] blud was spilt that ingadged all Englishmen for we wear to be all under one king." Arbitration was impossible after fighting had begun. As for the prediction, having the colonists fire the first shot avoided that problem.[71]

A few days after the Rhode Island conference, some Wampanoags approached the town of Swansea in Plymouth colony and looted some abandoned homes. A young Englishman fired at the Indians and killed one. With that shot, King Philip's War had begun. On June 20 the Indians attacked Swansea and produced English casualties. A delegation from Massachusetts, which had also planned to propose arbitration, returned home, its mission hopeless. There could now be no turning back for either Philip or the English.[72]

Some circumstances suggest that the timing of the war was not Philip's, First of all, the Indians had not yet amassed enough guns and ammunition. Nor had the other tribes been firmly recruited into a general alliance against the colonists. At the very least, Philip may have hoped to use arbitration as a delaying tactic to prevent a surprise attack until these important matters had been accomplished. In fact, the sachem seems to have been unable to control the ardor of his warriors, not only in June 1675, but earlier as well. During the spring of 1675, some of them decided to settle some old scores with Ninigret's men and killed eleven of his followers. After that attack, Philip could not even ask for Ninigret's aid, aid he sorely needed. The Mohegans and the surviving Pequots, among others, supported the English. Not surprisingly, Ninigret made clear that he did not support Philip.[73]

With the war begun, the Wampanoags were in a poor strategic position. Mount Hope was on a peninsula, and they could not risk being trapped on that neck of land. Colonial forces were sent to attack, but the soldiers were so noisy that they alerted the Indians of their approach. The natives easily slipped around the soldiers and found refuge in Pocasset swamp, a typical Indian military strategy. But during July 1675 King Philip and his vastly outnumbered men were again endangered there. The colonial force attacked them and reportedly got near Philip himself. Suddenly changing their strategy, the colonists decided to starve the Indians out. While the Englishmen built a single fort to create a siege of the large swamp, the Indians constructed rafts. Using the craft to escape across the Taunton River, the Wampanoags could then bring the war to other parts of New England. That same month, the Nipmucs of Massachusetts, "well-wishers to Philip's design, began to Philippize in barbarous murders."[74]

By August 1 Philip's forces were at Nipsachuck Hill, about twelve miles from Providence. A combined group of Englishmen and friendly Indians discovered them and prepared to attack. However, they encountered a Wampanoag scout whom they shot and killed. The gunshot spoiled the surprise and Philip immediately started a hurried retreat as the combined force hit his men. The Wampanoags lost about fifty warriors at Nipsachuck. King Philip fled so quickly that his gunpowder supply was forgotten. Nevertheless, the surprise attack did not succeed in stopping him and the war went on.[75]

On August 7, 1675 John Pynchon, in hard-pressed Springfield, Massachusetts, received a report from friendly Indians that Philip was about twenty miles away. The sachem, "faint and weary," had come to seek food in the cornfields of the area. His battered party had but "40 men who are fled with Philip have but 30 guns and the other 10 bows and arrows." Concerned by Philip's presence, Pynchon commented: "I do most sadly fear he will first do some great mischief upon us if he be let rest." However, one Wampanoag warrior who had been with Philip but had gotten separated from the main group had been captured by Indians allied with the English. At the urging of these Indian allies, Pynchon had him shot. "The Lord grant that so all our enemies may perish," Pynchon prayed.[76]

So far, Philip had displayed some good martial sense since leaving Mount Hope. Because of the attacks upon his warriors, his force had been very weakened. By December 1675 he was near Brookfield,

Massachusetts. Instead of continuing the attack on New England, he chose to enter the colony of New York to rest his depleted band.[77] The war continued without him.

New York did not long remain a safe haven for the hostile Indians. Governor Andros had assured Pynchon that no guns or powder would be sold in New York to those Indians warring against the New Englanders. Visiting Mohawks informed Pynchon that such supplies had been cut off in Albany. Pynchon, however, likely wanted much more than that. When Francis Lovelace had been governor of New York a few years before the present war, some Indian fugitives had fled from that colony to Massachusetts. The fugitives had been turned over to New York. Now, Pynchon must have wanted Indian "murderers"—such as Philip—turned over to the Puritans. Although Andros surely would have liked to do so, his influence with the Iroquois at this time was not great. The Five Nations of the Iroquois had their own agenda which did not include surrendering Philip. Only in March 1676 did the Iroquois—for some grounds of their own—attack Philip and his band, driving them from their domain.[78]

Meanwhile, the "great flame" of war had engulfed New England. In October 1675 one observer commented that "a most bitter Spirit is entered both English and Indians, in which they greatly endeavour the utter destruction one of another."[79]

In the early months of 1676 many colonists in Massachusetts thought that victory against their Indian foes seemed impossible. To protect themselves, the idea of erecting a giant barricade to preserve the easternmost parts of the colony was suggested but it came to nought. (Later, in 1677 after Philip's death, a minister recommended expelling Indians to places "remote from the English pale," a reference to Ireland where, under Oliver Cromwell, the native Irish were expelled from territory settled by the English. That idea also failed to be adopted.)[80]

Prospects for victory were not as bleak as some colonists thought. Despite claims that Philip went to New York to inflame the Mohawks, he actually left New England to recover from the battering his men had already taken. King Philip and others had become sick as well. Soon after the war's start, epidemics of smallpox and influenza hit the colonists and the Indians. Philip's warriors, having been weakened by attacks from both man and nature, were no longer a very determined force. The older warriors were already tired of the fighting. Only the young warriors, who had pushed for war in the first place, were still interested in it.[81]

Although Philip could not stay in New York, he had another potential sanctuary. French Canada had been an important source of ammunition for the warring Indians—the French did not care what happened to their Protestant English enemies. Aside from replenishing his supplies, Philip could have waged a long guerrilla war with Canada as a sanctuary from which to launch attacks. Indeed, going to Canada seemed to be his original plan.[82]

King Philip, however, changed his strategy. While he had rested near Albany, those Indians not associated with him had treated him with "little Esteem." He had fought the English rather effectively in his retreat to New York, but it was still a retreat. An Indian who retreated from his foes lost face among other tribesmen. As related earlier, Miantonomo, when escorting Roger Williams, had been willing to die rather than retreat. Similarly, Philip abandoned the safer destination of Canada to return to Mount Hope, thereby regaining the prestige lost by his earlier retreat. Philip may have suspected that returning to New England would endanger his life. He cut his hair to help conceal his identity from the English and even some embittered allies. One angry sachem of western Massachusetts had threatened to kill him because "he has brought all this trouble on them."[83]

On the way back to Mount Hope, Philip met Mary Rowlandson, the most famous English captive of the Indians during the war. In March 1676 Rowlandson knit a shirt and cap for Philip's young son. Later, Philip told her of her eventual ransoming, and expected a reward for giving her the news. Nevertheless, he absented himself when the Indians finally agreed to release her.[84]

The English had their own prisoners, and these Indians painted a melancholy picture of King Philip and his supporters. Around June 1676, the captured Indians revealed, Philip "had of his own proper Company not any great number left." And defeatism had infested them. "Were it not for him and one Sachem more," the prisoners related, "the Indians would gladly yield to any terms of Peace with the English."[85]

Indeed, the war had been going poorly for the Indians. Gradually, the English discovered and destroyed the natives' hidden stockpiles of food. Starvation then became still another weapon used against Philip and his remaining supporters. A report reached the English that some Indians had killed their children because of food shortages. By August 1676 William Harris asserted: "There have [been] more Indeans died since the war began by sicknes and hunger then by the sword."[86]

Philip himself soon met his match in Captain Benjamin Church, who had mastered Indian techniques of fighting. Unlike most of the colonists, Church was familiar with the swampy places surrounding Mount Hope. When Philip returned there, he would not be able to escape from Church's grasp. And Church, along with John Pynchon, was an early advocate of using Indians against the hostile tribes.[87]

In July 1676 Church, at great personal risk to himself, decided to try to detach Awasuncks and the Saconett Indians from Philip's side. Despite Church's old closeness to Awasuncks, the early contacts were very tense. At one point, a Saconett Indian wanted to revenge himself upon Church because he had killed a relative. The angry warrior was restrained by others and Church succeeded in his task. In return for permission to return unharmed to their old lands, the Saconetts joined the colonists and fought against their former allies.[88]

With the Saconetts' assistance, Captain Church was able to make things very difficult for Philip. When warriors loyal to him were captured, Church tried to get them to join with the English. As he wrote many years later, he would pat a disgruntled native on the back, and then say: "Come, come, you look wild and surly, and mutter, but that signifies nothing." Pointing to his Indian allies, Church could explain that they had been recently "as wild and surly as you are now; by that time you have been but one day along with me, you'l love me too, and be as brisk as any of them." Whether or not the captured Indians actually enjoyed helping Church, they soon were ready to track down even their close relatives to turn them over to the English.[89]

King Philip, perhaps realizing Church's effectiveness, tried to ambush him near the end of July. But the Englishman proved too wily for the sachem. Church never left a place by the same route he had gotten there. The planned ambush went for nought. Church, however, was able to surprise Philip's forces, and came close to shooting him. Although the sachem managed to escape, his wife, Wootonekanuske, and young son were captured. The next day, Church's force again tracked Philip into a swamp. One of the sachem's scouts was shot, so the surprise was lost. King Philip again fled with what remained of his band.[90]

Now trapped on the Mount Hope peninsula, Philip was near his end. Church's allied Indians told him: "Sir, You have now made Philip ready to die . . . for you have now killed or taken all his Relations." Losing his family made him irrational. When an Indian gave advice he did not like, Philip killed him. The dead warrior's brother, fearful of his own life, offered to lead Church to the sachem. Seizing the opportunity, Church surrounded Philip's swampy hideout on Mount Hope. When firing began, the sachem tried to flee, but he ran into two of Church's men, one of whom was Alderman, an Indian. Alderman fired and killed King Philip. Because the war had left so many colonists unburied, Church ordered that Philip should share the same fate. His body was beheaded, then quartered; his head, sent to Plymouth, was displayed there on a pole until at least 1700. After the sachem's death, as he had been practically the last prop of the Wampanoag resistance, the "War of Sachem Philip" slowly sputtered to a conclusion. Some Indians betrayed their former comrades in return for lenient treatment.[91]

The harsh effects of the war were visited upon both the pagan and Christian Indians. A number of defenseless Indians who had surrendered, including women and children, were murdered by some colonists. These murderers were hung. Other once hostile Indians were sold as slaves. Plymouth was uncertain about what to do with Philip's son. Only a young boy, he had not taken part in any of the war's brutalities. The Bible commanded that such a child should not be killed because of his father's offenses. Therefore, the colonists sold him into slavery.[92]

Yet some colonists opposed the sale of the captives. Benjamin Church believed that Plymouth's ignoring promises to Indians who had surrendered early in the war only lengthened the conflict. Undoubtedly, many of the Indians preferred death in war than a life of slavery. Church was joined in his opposition by John Eliot. In August 1675 Eliot reminded Massachusetts Bay that the Puritans had once declared "that the indeavour of the Indians conversion, not their exstirpation, was one great end of our enterprize, in coming to these ends of the earth." Turning the Indians into slaves was similar to what the Protestants had once condemned Catholic Spain for doing. Besides, Eliot insisted, "the Country is large enough, here is land enough for them and us too." But he could not sway the Puritan leaders. In 1683 Eliot received a forlorn message from some Indians who had been sold in Africa begging him to try to have them brought back to New England. He could do little to help them. Nonetheless, as a historian has commented, "the English felt a sense of moral obligation to avoid wholesale slaughter or enslavement of the Indian peoples."[93]

During the war, as Eliot observed, "the profane Indians prove a sharp rod to the English, and the English prove a very sharp rod to the praying Indians." Indeed, much hostility was directed against them. Although only a handful backed Philip, all of the Christian natives suffered anyway. One "ungodly and unruly youth" shot at some defenseless Christian Indians, "killed a child of godly parents" and wounded five others including the child's mother. She prayed: "Lord thou seest that we have neither done or said any thing against the English, yet they thus deal with us."[94]

Some 350 "poore soules in terror," given only a notice of thirty minutes, had to leave "their goods, books [and] bibles" and settle upon "a bleak, bare island" in Boston harbor. Both provisions and fuel were in short supply there. At least the isolated locale helped make them safe from crazed colonists seeking revenge.[95]

Eliot noted that once New Englanders decided to use Praying Indians to defeat the hostile natives "from that forward we always prospered." The Christian Indians served well, convincing many colonists to change their former harsh opinion of them. Nevertheless, hatred of all Indians continued to flame. When enemy Indians were captured, some tried to implicate Christian natives. Those settlers who wanted to hate were very willing to believe their enemies' word, with or without proof.[96]

Hatred was also shown towards Eliot and Gookin because of their concern for the Praying Indians. These two relics of an earlier time were threatened with mob violence. Gookin said "that he was afraid to go along the streets," and he was told that "he ought . . . to be confined among his Indians." Nor did the voters of Massachusetts forget Gookin's sympathy for the Christian Indians. The voters ("in their distemper" Eliot complained) dropped Gookin as a magistrate for the first time in decades.[97]

What may have been the most serious retaliation upon the two advocates of the Indians happened in April 1676. Eliot and Gookin, in company with others, were travelling on some official duties in a small boat in Boston harbor. Suddenly, "a great boat of about 14 ton" veered into their vessel "whether willfully or by negligence, God he knoweth," Eliot commented. The small craft was pushed underwater. "I so sunke that I drank in salt water twice and could not help it," the minister related. His fellow passengers rescued him. "Some thanked God, and some wished we had been drowned," he admitted.[98]

The Praying Indians who had fought alongside the Puritans became endangered in a much more subtle way. The Englishmen they had soldiered with greatly appreciated their military assistance and happily greeted their former colleagues in arms. They brought the Indians to the local tavern and "made them drink, and bred thereby such a habit to love strong drink . . . that they would spend all their wages and pawne any [thing] they had for rum or any strong drink." Naturally, "drunkenesse increased and quarreling [and] fighting . . . were the sad effects." Eliot bemoaned that "Praying to God was quenched, the younger generation being debauched."[99]

Eliot was disturbed about what had happened to his converts. He wrote that "The work . . . is killed (in words, wishes and expression) but not in deeds as yet. It is (as it were) dead, but not buried, nor (I believe) shall be." Eliot's optimism was justified. As he later wrote, "the work is on foot to this day."[100]

As Eliot aged he became concerned by changes in Massachusetts including the increasing number of "drinking houses." To Eliot, "Quakers [being] openly tolerated" in the Bay colony was not good either. Age also slowed him down. He had once preached before Indians every two weeks, but when he became 84 he could only manage the task every eight weeks. Eliot died in 1690.[101]

During Eliot's last years, New England tried to recover from King Philip's War. Aside from the sale of Indian captives, the only "profits" the Puritans gained came from land. Plymouth and Rhode Island avidly sought the big prize, Mount Hope, Philip's favorite territory, both needing it to pay their heavy war debts. Rhode Island's eastern border with Massachusetts was finally established only in 1747.[102]

The Praying Indians at Natick continued to aid the Puritans in eighteenth century warfare. During Queen Anne's War, for example, royal governor Joseph Dudley made an effort to keep their friendship. "Be kind to your Indians," he urged a New Hampshire official, and asked that they be paid for their military service before leaving that colony. But this was not done, and the governor in December 1711 had to again request that all such Indians be paid. Finally, in March 1712 Governor Dudley had to complain: "I shall never get an Indian to serve for your province again if they want a Shilling of their due, besides the Continued trouble I have with them." And other Indians made worthwhile military contributions in the 1730s.[103]

During the first quarter of the nineteenth century, Washington Irving, while casually looking through a history of King Philip's War, was struck by the "great bitterness" over "the outrages of the Indians." After writing his own essay on the conflict, Irving observed:

Such is the scanty story of the brave, but unfortunate King Philip; persecuted while living, slandered and dishonoured when dead. If, however, we consider even the prejudiced anecdotes furnished us by his enemies, we may perceive in them traces of amiable and lofty character, sufficient to awaken sympathy for his fate, and respect for his memory.[104]

Some of today's scholars should contemplate Washington Irving's sensible analysis of the historical sources relating to Philip and the brutal war named after him. Philip's memory is not served by presenting a twisted version of what happened. The facts speak for themselves. John Easton put the blame for the war in perspective. Peace was "best" for everyone, Easton declared, "but the English dare not trust the indians promises nether the indians to the Englishes promises and each have great Case therfore."[105]

Chapter 7

Sir Edmund Andros

No study of the enemies of Puritan Massachusetts could be complete without Sir Edmund Andros, the first royal governor of the Bay colony. Until the twentieth century, historians depicted him as a fiend who robbed Americans of basic liberties. But, in 1911, Charles M. Andrews called for an end to the "unqualified denunciation" of the Stuart governor. Viola F. Barnes responded to Andrews by writing an overly sympathetic account. After Barnes, Andros has been treated by J. M. Sosin, Richard R. Johnson, and Stephen Saunders Webb, whose absurdly favorable version of the governor has been seconded by Mary Lou Lustig. Webb's exaggerated portrait has won acceptance. Clearly, "Sir Edmund Andros—a name never to be forgotten" in New England, needs a fair and balanced examination.[1]

Edmund Andros was born in 1637 to a family that had served the Stuarts for many years. When the dynasty was forced from the throne, the Andros family went into exile on the continent. As a young man, Andros fought in the Dutch army and gained practical military experience. A favorite of the exiled Stuarts, he became one of their household servants. Upon the Restoration, the Andros clan regained their ancestral rights on the island of Guernsey. Once reestablished there, they deprived Puritan Increase Mather of his ministerial position on the island.[2]

Andros soon received a prestigious military commission in the English army and fought in the West Indies. In 1671 the brother of Charles II, James, the Duke of York, picked the now Major Andros for a diplomatic mission to Sweden to investigate the prospects of a dynastic union with its royal house. Although nothing came of Andros's trek there,

James, impressed, served as his patron. In 1672 Andros further strengthened his ties to the nobility by marrying a niece of the earl of Craven. By
1674 the major succeeded to his father's hereditary role on Guernsey,
but Andros was called away for a difficult job in America. The Duke of
York had appointed him governor of his proprietary colony of New York.[3]

The duke's colony, although reconquered by the Dutch, had been
restored to the English. Upon arrival in New York, Andros immediately
began to ruffle feathers—a common event throughout his career. His
very firm treatment of Dutch colonists who had remained in New York
brought a complaint from Holland's ambassador to England. But Andros
did his best to quiet the grumbles of the Dutch, allowed their churches to
operate without interference, and won their loyalty. A New Englander
commented on the latest gossip about New York's governor: "The report at Albany is that he is a little man but of brave spirits and will not
hearken to reports against the Dutch."[4]

Still more feathers flew when Andros reasserted the Duke's authority on eastern Long Island, which had originally been settled by Connecticut. When the Dutch retook New York City, Connecticut moved to
protect its former outposts on Long Island. Because of that colony's
assistance, the Dutch could not seize the towns of eastern Long Island,
which accepted Connecticut's jurisdiction. But Major Andros had no
intention of permitting such a crimping of the duke's property. The blunt
governor ordered the towns to accept their status as part of New York.
Andros, with some military force, coerced the reluctant communities
and punished individuals who had resisted his demand. Connecticut's
expansion onto Long Island had finally been crushed.[5]

Andros planned to regain other parts of the duke's claimed domain
that had been taken by Massachusetts. The duke's governor repossessed
Nantucket and Martha's Vineyard—then part of James's proprietary. On
the other hand, the Bay colony still had too firm a grasp upon the Pemaquid
area of Maine for Andros to undo it.[6]

The governor of New York also riled Puritan Massachusetts about
trade. Because the Bay colony disobeyed the English Navigation Acts,
Andros stopped Boston merchants from bringing foreign imports into
New York that lacked documented proof of having gone through England first. Such a stand did not endear him to the Puritans.[7]

Nor did Andros display any reluctance in disturbing land titles in
New York. Those New Yorkers holding land in the colony granted by
one of the Puritan colonies had to obtain an official approval of the grant

from New York's government. In addition, Andros insisted that quitrents—a token payment acknowledging the feudal rights of the proprietor, James—be paid. The quitrents themselves, according to Andros's successor as governor, Thomas Dongan, "were very inconsiderable."[8]

Andros was even willing to disturb his proprietor over having an assembly for New York. The people of the duke's province wanted an assembly just as the New Englanders had. Although Andros did not permit the calling of such an assembly, he clearly urged the duke to permit one. James, however, refused such an innovation in his colony, because "such Assemblyes . . . would be of dangerous consequence, nothing being more knowne then the aptness of such bodyes to assume to themselves many priviledges which prove destructive to, or very oft disturbe, the peace of the government wherein they are allowed." Besides, James believed, New York City had a governing body called the court of "General Assizes" (later called the common council) which could deal with any complaints of the residents. Despite his resistance to an assembly, the duke informed Andros that the subject would be considered again if the governor continued to urge the creation of such a political body.[9]

The governor, however, had other worries. In Andros's commission, the duke claimed all of Connecticut west of the Connecticut River as part of his proprietary. In May and June 1675 Andros bluntly demanded that Connecticut surrender the territory to him. Not surprisingly, the Puritan colony, just as bluntly, refused. Then, in June 1675 King Philip's War broke out.[10]

On July 1, 1675, Connecticut's government received a call for help from two of its eastern towns. To alert Andros to what had happened, the leaders of the colony sent him copies of letters, which reached him at 3:00 AM on July 4, giving news of the Indian war. Andros realized this was no minor Indian problem and summoned his council the same day. The councillors believed that Connecticut had not asked for assistance from the duke's governor, but they agreed with Andros's idea of aiding Connecticut anyway. After all, they believed that western Connecticut belonged to the Duke of York, and his territory had to be protected. Andros promptly notified his opposite in Connecticut, John Winthrop, Jr., about his plans to bring military aid. "I am very much troubled," Andros declared, "at the Christians' misfortunes and hard disasters" in Plymouth and Rhode Island, "being so over-powered by such Heathen" and added that he would leave soon for the "Connecticutt River, his Royall Highnesse bounds there." He had already planned to journey there to lay claim to the supposed boundary. Rumors about his intentions had been circulating in New England at the end of 1674. Although Edmund Andros's offer of help was sincere, at the same time he could demonstrate to the people of western Connecticut that they would be safer as New Yorkers.[11]

On July 8 Andros's expeditionary force appeared by the western side of the Connecticut River, off the fortified town of Saybrook. Seeing no evidence of hostile Indians, the governor sent one of his ships to look for trouble eastward. As it turned out, Andros had enough trouble from the frightened leaders of Connecticut. The duke's governor had his offer of assistance rejected by Connecticut although its officials at the scene were ordered not to give Andros "any just provocation." Connecticut militia were ordered to Saybrook in case Andros planned to attack it. On July 10 Connecticut's General Court sent thundering answers to letters from Andros—who was still on board his ship. The Court called Andros's appearance off Saybrook "illegall proceedings" which would "tend to the incouraging of the heathen to proceed in the effusion of Christian blood." His "arrivall with men and armes and provisions for warr into one of our ports" was something the king should be told about. Finally, the legislators warned Andros that they would "defend ourselves against such intrusions as well as we can."[12]

Andros remained on his ship. As one Connecticut official informed the General Court: "The Govr. Androsse still speakes of his purposes of defence and protection of us here against the Indians, and wonders much at our jealousy of him, and seems ready to be in action upon that account."[13] Andros—ever the good soldier—was eager to face the heathen enemy. But on July 12 he received the General Court's critical letter of July 10 and took it as an insult. Never one to let an insult go unanswered, Andros landed early on the 13th with a few of his officers to talk with the Connecticut clergy and officials on the scene. He refused to talk about a treaty with Connecticut and instead had the duke's charter—with its claim to western Connecticut—proclaimed before his audience. In retaliation, they read aloud a resolve of the General Court that criticized him. Andros called the resolve "a slander, and so an ill requitall for his kindnesse," and asked for a copy of the resolve. His request was refused. Despite this confrontation, the two sides parted without violence, and Andros returned to New York.[14]

Sometime later, Andros learned that his letters laying claim to western Connecticut had gone too far. As Sir John Werden, the duke's secre-

tary, explained to Andros, Connecticut's claim to its western territory
was far stronger than the duke's, which was of a later date. The Duke of
York himself wrote to his governor, thanking him for his dedication but
also ordering him to accept the New York-Connecticut border as it then
stood, at least for the immediate future.[15]

Andros's reaction to this rebuff from his proprietor is unknown. The
governor had enough to occupy himself with the still-raging King Philip's
War, which appeared to be approaching the duke's domain. Andros had
prohibited the sale of gunpowder to the warring tribes; penalties for this
offense ranged from a fine to death. And he donated some gunpowder to
the hard-pressed—and grateful—colony of Rhode Island. According to
Werden, the New England Puritans "deserve small courtesy from us, yet
still theire being Christians makes it charity for us not to furnish their
enemyes with the opportunityes or meanes to hurt them."[16]

But Andros intervened in still more ways during New England's
bloodiest war. When Philip and some of his warriors entered New York,
Andros ordered them to leave the colony; the Iroquois (for their own
mysterious reasons) drove Philip out. Then, in 1677, Andros saw a chance
to both regain Pemaquid for the duke and end the fighting there. Andros
learned that the Indians of Maine, who had seized Pemaquid, had left it.
Furthermore, the Bay colony had paid no attention to it during the fighting. In June 1677 a force sent by Andros reoccupied Pemaquid and stayed
there. Troops from Massachusetts arrived too late to prevent Andros's
coup. Soon after, the Maine Indians agreed to a peace with the duke's
men, which the Indians grudgingly extended to the Puritans as well.
With the return of peace, Andros saw to it that the Indians released all
their prisoners. Edward Randolph noted that "the Governour of New
York hath proved very friendly and serviceable to the Massachusetts in
this warr."[17]

Despite the war's end, Andros still resented how the Puritans had
treated him. Especially upsetting were charges in various Puritan histories that New Yorkers had supplied the hostile Indians with gunpowder.
No one had accused Andros of laxness: some violations of his ban were
inevitable. But he could never accept any sort of criticism of his record,
either then or in the future. In 1678, while on a trip to England, the
duke's governor complained to the Privy Council about the histories
being sold in New England. He blasted both Massachusetts and Connecticut for refusing "proffered Supplys and Assistances" from him during the war. (Earlier, he had declared that the two colonies had "slighted"

his aid.) Andros added that the division of New England into separate colonies weakened them, and that this weakness could be eliminated if the king controlled all of their military forces.[18]

The Privy Council, faced with the charges from the furious soldier, asked the agents of Massachusetts to explain New England's side of the dispute. The flustered agents were puzzled how Andros could have been insulted by Massachusetts' declaration of war against the Indians (as the sensitive soldier had been) or the accounts of the war. Surely, no New Englander had suggested that the government of New York had supported the Wampanoags; only "evill minded persons, who will easily venture all for gaine" had been responsible for the sale of powder to the hostile warriors. But the agents did not know the names of these culprits. Realizing the reasonable attitude of the agents, the Privy Council decided upon a safe bureaucratic response to Andros's complaint. The Council declared that, as no evidence of the reported dealings had been discovered, no one could be punished for the alleged offenses without a proper trial.[19] As no one was ever tried, the problem disappeared, and, apparently, Andros felt that his good reputation had been restored.

Some months later, the new knight, Sir Edmund Andros, returned to his governorship. The New Englanders, who wanted his help with the Iroquois, were very careful with the touchy soldier. The Mohawks had recently attacked the Christian Indians of Massachusetts and had taken captives. Assuming that Andros had influence with the Iroquois, the Confederation of New England asked him—in a very respectful tone—to intercede. Andros—seeing that the Puritans treated him with the respect due his person—responded favorably. His "freindly Lines" delighted the New Englanders. However, most of the captive Indians had already been killed by the Mohawks.[20]

But Andros had not mellowed. In 1680 he stirred up the colonial scene again. While in England, he thought that the Duke of York had wanted to regain political control of the Jersies, which he had granted to the Carteret family and other proprietors. Andros had Philip Carteret, the governor of New Jersey, dragged to New York and tried for various offenses, but a jury found him not guilty (despite being ordered by Andros to reconsider the verdict). To make Andros's embarrassment more acute, the duke—in political trouble at home—had no desire to be burdened with a colonial dispute and disowned the actions of his governor of New York.[21]

By 1680 many complaints about Andros had reached England. The sheer number of complaints is impressive, but the one that disturbed the duke was the charge that Andros and those under him had sent only half the customs fees to England. These fees were the duke's chief income from his proprietary. Because New York was a financial drain upon James, this allegation forced him to examine the conduct of his governor; he recalled Andros. As Werden explained the situation to him: "I verily believe it is best for you to be here . . . that you may vindicate your selfe from these chardges. . . ." Werden assured Andros that he fully expected the loyal soldier to be exonerated.[22]

The duke believed that the investigation should be conducted "by a person wholly unconcerned." John Lewin, a merchant familiar with the northern colonies, was James's selection. However, Lewin was not as uninvolved as James imagined. A business partner of Lewin's in New York was one of Andros's toughest critics.[23] Perhaps, though, James should not be faulted too much on this point, for it was undoubtedly very difficult to find anyone totally neutral where Sir Edmund Andros was concerned.

When Lewin and Andros met in New York, Andros ordered full cooperation with Lewin and soon after left for England. Lewin's investigation centered upon William Dyre, the collector of customs for New York, who was at the same time mayor of the city and a councillor of the colony. What Lewin saw in the customs records disturbed him. Pages had very clearly been torn out of the records; numbers had been changed. And Lewin also got the impression that he had been denied access to port records. Later, Lewin compared English records with those of New York and found that they did not agree. The investigator had little choice but to declare "that there hath not been just or honest dealing" in the New York customs office. He added: "I cannot find that any fraud hath been or could be committed in the Customs but by Connivance or Knowledge of Mr. Dyre . . . there hath been noe Checke upon Dyre."[24]

Lewin intended to investigate not only the customs office, but the land and financial records of New York City as well. When he tried to examine them, he was stymied by the shadowy figure of John West, who was then the "Deputy Clarke of the Court of Mayor and Aldermen," and so served under Mayor Dyre. In the 1680s West became a prominent official of the Dominion of New England. Lewin asked to see the various records listing land grants; West replied: "hee could not deliver them without order." Then, Lewin wished to see the records detailing city fines; West responded "hee was butt a Servant to [the] Citty and could not deliver them without the Mayor's order," that is, Dyre's order. Naturally, the investigator next asked the mayor, who stalled him as long as possible. The exasperated Lewin went back to West who then commented that

> hee had asked advice or consent of the Alderman severally who answered That if any such fines . . . were on Record, they were imployed for the use and behoofe of the Citty and noe way related to his Royall Highness soe they conceived I [Lewin] had nothing to doe with them, which was West's reply, and I doubt not to be his own sence who plainly refused to deliver the Records to my perusall.[25]

Lewin had to declare: "Mr. West and Mr. Dyre and others used all their cunning practices to give mee all the trouble they could." Not surprisingly, while Lewin was busily trying to examine what had been going on in New York City, West was promoted to city clerk in his own right. Without a doubt, this promotion was either his reward or a bribe for bedeviling the investigator.[26]

Nor is it surprising that New York City's officials tried to smear the investigator. Lewin's commission from the duke did not empower him to take testimony of witnesses under oath. Yet he had done so. The aldermen condemned these "Clandestine and private Oaths . . . which the partyes Concerned Cann have noe Knowlidge of." Lewin had not asked them for their help. Such secret oaths were "Extrajudiciall and Illeagall."[27]

Sir Edmund Andros was also angered by Lewin's "confused" findings. Andros thoroughly defended himself against various charges levelled at him by Lewin. Andros was not involved in any shady dealings performed by Dyre and West while governor. But Andros's reaction demonstrated some flaws in his personality. He was just not interested in charges of "malecontents" who criticized men in whom he had placed his trust. Similarly, in the 1680s he placed little stock in complaints about officials of the Dominion of New England.[28]

At the end of 1681 English officials who handled the duke's finances looked into Lewin's charges and completely exonerated Andros. As for Dyre, they admitted that changes had been made in the customs books but no "gros[s] sum" was involved and Dyre seemed to be vindicated. The Duke's men also praised Lewin, who had "really been very industrious in gaining the best Information [that] could be had of what was objected" by the residents of New York. Everyone was vindicated. So long as the duke's revenues had not been greatly harmed, everyone seemed to prefer that the whole messy business be dropped and forgotten.[29]

Sir Edmund Andros's tenure as governor of New York was important in the history of the colony. Trade was increased, new towns built, and the city's harbor improved. This part of his record helps to explain the great regard some Englishmen, such as Henry Hyde, the second earl of Clarendon, had for him.[30] Nevertheless, Andros showed many of the traits that later helped doom the Dominion of New England. Stephen Saunders Webb is correct in pointing out that, in 1683, William Penn praised Andros: "tho he was not without objection he certainly did great things more than both his predecessors and if I had a Place worthy of his Care I would give him tenn thousand Acres of Land and the Comand of the Three Countys and use him always as my Friend." But in 1682 Penn was more specific in his criticism of the soldier: "I must needs say . . . that I find [Andros to be] over eager and too pressing [in] an execution of his powers, where provoakt especially." This last comment well sums up Andros's character.[31]

Events had already taken place in both England and New England that eventually led to Andros returning to America. In the early 1670s various complaints about Massachusetts Bay had pushed the Council for Foreign Plantations to consider ways to lessen that colony's troublesome behavior. By the end of 1675 the Privy Council had ruled out another fact-finding commission, but had decided to hear the New Englanders' side of the story before any major decisions were made. Copies of the complaints were to be sent to the Bay colony with an order that agents be sent to London. The man selected to bring these items to New England was Edward Randolph, who arrived there in June 1676. Randolph, more than anyone else, was responsible for the destruction of the Puritan commonwealth and the creation of royal government in Massachusetts.[32]

Randolph, related to Robert Mason, a claimant to New Hampshire, was then as now a controversial figure. To Cotton Mather, Randolph "was born to do mischief." Joseph Dudley referred to Randolph's "angry and fierce temper." In 1687 Dudley, who managed to both encourage and infuriate Randolph at different times, commented that he was then "as uneasy as ever, and that his temper will never Suffer him to bee very happy." Randolph's temper was not improved by the open hostility New England's Puritans displayed towards him and his family. He sometimes allowed his anger to affect his judgment, and was "often given to exaggeration and distortion" as J. M. Sosin has written. Nonetheless, sometimes Randolph was correct about the abuses of the Puritans and the royal officials who later ruled them.[33]

Over several years Randolph informed English officials of all the problems he could find in New England. Massachusetts, for example, coined money and committed obvious violations of the Navigation Acts. Anglicans were discriminated against and the Puritans had outlawed the celebration of Christmas. Already by 1678, a number of the members of the Committee for Trade and Plantations thought that New England needed a royal governor, but Charles II had many serious internal problems to deal with and colonial affairs seemed unimportant by comparison. British colonial policy remained erratic.[34]

Massachusetts did everything it could to stall the English government. Only in 1682 did the Bay colony send agents to England—agents whose presence had been ordered three years earlier. Meanwhile, Randolph had been ordered to enforce the Navigation Acts, but he encountered much resistance in the Puritan colonies. In one case, Randolph had tried to seize a cargo that seemed suspicious to him, only to have the General Court of Massachusetts interfere and restore the seized property. The continued resistance of Massachusetts pushed English officials into starting a *quo warranto* against the charter of the Bay colony. A delighted Randolph sent witnesses to England to help assure the desired verdict. The cherished charter of the Massachusetts Bay Company was voided in 1684.[35]

Another factor that helped to push the English bureaucrats into acting against Massachusetts was their concern over the potential military weakness of New England. Andros had already criticized New England's performance in King Philip's War, and in the 1680s the Indians on the frontier, with the probable aid of France, were still a serious threat. English officials thought that the disunited colonies of New England had to be strengthened by combining at least some of them to enable them to resist the French and their allied Indians.[36]

Yet the English government was very slow to change the political structure of New England. Only in 1686 was a temporary government, which had no elected assembly, created and headed by Joseph Dudley. Because of the lack of a popularly-elected assembly, Puritans complained that the new government had deprived them of a fundamental right possessed by all Englishmen. Ironically, the Puritans had, for all practical purposes, earlier denied non-Puritans the right to vote for deputies in the General Court. Now, no one could.[37]

Meanwhile, English bureaucrats argued over who should be governor of the new political entity in New England. An early candidate was Colonel Piercy Kirke, whose very name frightened the Puritan colonists. Kirke had been especially ruthless in suppressing a rebellion against the new king, the Catholic James II, by the Duke of Monmouth, a Protestant claimant to the throne. Even Randolph was opposed to Kirke. One of Randolph's choices was Sir Edmund Andros, who had retained the favor of James, and had recently been promoted to colonel by the new king. When James II learned that Kirke had been bribed to protect some rebels, Andros had the court connections plus the colonial and military experience that the post needed.[38]

At first, the Dominion of New England that Andros would govern consisted of Massachusetts, the charter-less colony of Plymouth, the disputed Narragansett country of Rhode Island, and the two sparsely-settled areas of Maine and New Hampshire.[39] Later, the Dominion was expanded to include the rest of Rhode Island, Connecticut, New York, and both sections of New Jersey.

Andros was given two commissions (one in 1686 and the other in 1688) as governor and special instructions. They gave much detail about his military powers and exclude an elected assembly. The functions of government were to be performed by the governor himself and an appointed council. Taxes common in the colonies could be "imposed upon the Inhabitants." Although "liberty of conscience" was specified, Andros had to promote the Anglican Church throughout the Dominion. The governor's instructions ordered a limitation on "liberty of printing"—all publications had to be approved by the governor.[40]

Certainly, James II did not establish a liberal government to administer the Dominion. But little attention has been paid to some rather startling innovations in Andros's instructions. Concerning both indentured servants and slaves, Andros was ordered to bring more humaneness into the bondage systems and the treatment of Indians:

> You shall pass a law for the restraining of inhuman severity which by ill masters or overseers may be used towards the christian servants or slaves; wherein provision is to be made that the wilfull killing of Indians and Negros be punished with death, and a fitt penalty imposed for the maiming of them.[41]

As for the restrictions on printing, such instructions are not very unusual for the period. The revolutionaries who overthrew the Dominion themselves suppressed publications critical of their government.[42]

In December 1686 Andros arrived in Boston and received "a good reception" from "the militia in armes and a great concourse of people." A new era seemed to have started. To mark the great change, some crew members of H. M. S. *Kingfisher*, the warship that brought Andros to Boston, erected a maypole in Charlestown on May 1, 1687. Soon chopped down, the sailors retaliated by building an even larger one. Royal government and its symbols seemed to be in New England to stay.[43]

Andros settled down to work and surveyed the military defenses of the Dominion. He was not pleased by what he discovered. Just about everything on Castle Island was badly in need of repair, Boston had no barracks for the small group of regular soldiers who had accompanied the governor, and the militia lacked enough weapons. A substantial sum was needed to correct these problems. Not surprisingly, the council imposed taxes on land and other property, a duty on imported wines, and a poll tax. On another important subject, a special committee of the council met to examine the various laws of the old colonies to create a body of laws suitable for the Dominion.[44]

Opposition to the Dominion soon appeared. The last governor under the Massachusetts charter, elderly Simon Bradstreet, refused to serve on the Dominion's council. Following his example, Bradstreet's son and Nathaniel Saltonstall also turned down the appointment. Nothing seems to have happened to the Bradstreets, but Saltonstall got into much trouble. Summoned by Andros to explain his refusing the appointment, Saltonstall apparently riled the always sensitive soldier. The governor had already been upset, Saltonstall wrote, because of his "folly in not formerly and in season paying my respects" to the sensitive Andros. When they met, Saltonstall "gave answers of truth" to the governor's questions. The Puritan was probably too blunt for the governor's taste and was jailed for fifteen days.[45]

Andros had more serious problems to deal with than Saltonstall's imagined disrespect. Specifically, the governmental structure of the Dominion of New England did not work well. Given the haphazard way it was created, the difficulties encountered by Andros are not surprising. By all appearances, the decision to exclude an assembly was not very carefully thought out. During 1684-1685 some English bureaucrats and even Edward Randolph assumed the new Dominion government would have a popular legislative branch. But such a body was denied to the New England Puritans. This denial probably represented merely another erratic shift in the quagmire of royal colonial policy, which then quickly shifted again. Various colonies in the West Indies were permitted assemblies after the New Englanders were left without one. Neither Andros nor the Puritans liked the situation the Dominion had been placed in. Randolph was not hesitant to report to London the continuing dissatisfaction of the population on this subject.[46]

With no popular branch, Andros's council had an expanded role. But the very vastness of the Dominion made the council ineffective. Along with the difficulty of travelling long distances in the 1680s, there were financial problems as well. Councillors did not receive any compensation for travel expenses or, for that matter, any salary at all. A councillor who did not live near the meeting site—which was usually Boston—had to spend much time away from home, family, and livelihood. Council meetings, therefore, tended to be dominated by members who lived around Boston and other areas tended to have sporadic representation at best. The quorum for the council was only five (seven was preferred except "upon extraordinary emergencies"). In July 1687 Andros explained to English bureaucrat William Blathwayt that it was "hard (the Council living far distant) to get a quoram together."[47]

To further weaken support for Andros and the Dominion, the government's attempts to tax New Englanders roused resentment. Plymouth, for example, had never before experienced a poll tax. Even the people of Massachusetts were discontented by the Dominion's desire to raise money. Despite the taxes being based on old laws of that colony, people complained about innovations in the Dominion's tax laws. First of all, the Dominion had mistakenly set excessively high valuation rates for farm animals. Secondly, Massachusetts had permitted payment in produce or in money; a cash payment was especially welcome and was rewarded by a cut of 1/3 of the tax owed. Under the Dominion, however, the advantage obtained by paying with cash was eliminated. Those non-farmers who had long benefitted from the cash loophole now had to pay the full amount they owed. The tax on wine also caused grumbles. The Dominion's excise collectors were very industrious in finding violators. Their industry paid off in money for the financially-strapped Dominion. In August 1687 Andros reported that revenue from the wine tax "proves to be better than expected."[48]

Although Andros's excisemen were enthusiastic in their duties, the selectmen of the towns were not. The selectmen were ultimately responsible for raising the tax on land and other property. To begin with, the lack of an assembly proved a stumbling block because the Massachusetts General Court had itself ordered the collection of the taxes each year. Some of the Dominion's councillors themselves did not believe that they had the power to follow the old General Court's example. Furthermore, Andros discovered that town officials made sure they undervalued the worth of each resident's estate, thus lowering the tax bill at the same time. The old charter government had tolerated such tactics, which seemingly had become customary. When the old government had needed more funds, it simply requested another levy of the artificially low assessments. But Andros did not approve of the practice, which probably explains why he recommended that a quota of revenue for each town be established. Early in 1687 the Dominion government tried to push town officials into producing the revenue they were supposed to. On August 31, 1687, Andros had to admit defeat. "I find that notwithstanding all endeavors," the governor declared, "the rate of 1 d per pound will nott be assessed to its value being of the inclination of everybody." In September, though, Andros did have the satisfaction of learning that most towns had raised more money for his levy than they had been accustomed to.[49]

Nevertheless, there had been a serious tax revolt centered in the town of Ipswich. Near the end of August 1687 at its town meeting—and spurred on by its minister, John Wise—the residents refused to elect an official to assess them for the Dominion's taxes. Wise insisted that, without an assembly, such taxes were a violation of "the liberty of freeborne English men." Other towns in Essex county followed Ipswich's example.[50]

Andros had no choice but to deal swiftly with the "chief actors" of the tax revolt. Some thirty people faced a trial for their part in the resistance. At an extraordinary court session, the culprits received a trial during which John West, now a judge of the Dominion, taunted them, saying "that the people in New-England were all Slaves, and the only difference between them and Slaves is their not being bought and sold." Wise, found guilty, was prohibited from preaching and ordered to jail until he paid a fine. The others received similar penalties although those "who were nott so salty" were spared imprisonment. Meanwhile, the taxes were collected from the rebellious towns. Soon afterward, Wise was allowed to return to his pulpit and the crisis was over. But Wise was not the only Puritan minister who had opposed the Dominion. Others were being critical of the administration of Governor Andros. In November he insisted; "I do not abridge them of their liberty but shall take Care of them as I ought."[51]

Bringing such men as the Ipswich tax resisters to justice was a very important matter for both Andros and the very financial survival of the Dominion. Taxes had to be obtained and obtained quickly. In 1686 the Massachusetts Bay colony had been all but bankrupt—its coffers were "wholy empty." Besides which, both Massachusetts and Plymouth colonies had huge debts left over from King Philip's War. Andros painted a very sad picture of New England as conditions were in March 1687:

> This country has sustained lately very great losses by the Indian war, two great fevers in this town of Boston, some disasters at sea, and all their wheat blasted many years together, and are generally but poor; their fishery and lumber, their chiefest trade and support, and that wholly supplied by Connecticut, from whence all their wheat and much other grain and provisions, and without it cannot maintain their fishery and trade.[52]

By August 1687 the situation was still bad and Andros's government was spending more money than it was taking in. Back in March the governor had believed that Connecticut's addition to the Dominion was absolutely essential to enable it to pay "the ordinary charge of the government." Randolph was of the same opinion. Connecticut, which had escaped most of the ravages of King Philip's War, seemed like a juicy plum and was avidly sought by both the Dominion and New York.[53]

With the government in such desperate straits, Andros was always happy to increase the income of the Dominion. Its treasury was ever hungry and in need of more revenue. The trade in beaver furs with the Indians was made a government monopoly. The blubber of beached whales also belonged to the Dominion. Its councillors were ordered to think of items that could have new excise taxes slapped on them. And fees could seemingly get in the way of justice. In one case a man was found innocent of a crime he was accused of. Despite his acquittal, he had to stay jailed because he could not pay his court fees.[54]

Fees for government services became a very serious grievance of the colonists. Randolph, who had been secretary of the Dominion, had tired of the office. Having decided he was actually losing income because of the job, he wanted to sell it. Unable to find an "able man to discharge it," he sold it to John West. As secretary, West used his position to delay any Dominion action in settling an official list of fees that the secretary could charge. With no restrictions upon him, West practically had a free hand. According to Randolph, West "extorts what fees he pleases, to the great oppression of the people, and renders the present government grievous."[55]

The taxes and fees of Andros's administration seemed intolerable to the New Englanders. Of course, Dominion officials had different motives—West wanted personal profit, Andros sought revenue for the government. Nonetheless, the Dominion seemed to be very grasping in its pursuit of the wealth of the colonists. This apparent lusting after the peoples' money came at a time when the economy was still poor. By 1687 the fur trade in New England had seen better days. Even the lumber-rum trade with the Caribbean colonies was weak at that time. Only whaling seemed to be prospering in the 1680s. There was a shortage of coin as well. In 1688 trade was still depressed. Certainly, the careful enforcement of the Navigation Acts did not help New England's commerce. But, in the temper of the times, most people preferred to blame the economic difficulties upon the Dominion's taxes and fees rather than upon the more abstract English mercantile policies. In fact, one of the charges voiced against Joseph Dudley in 1689 was "his extream covetousnes, getting to himself so many bags of money, to the ruinating of trade."[56] The Dominion's eagerness to bring in more revenue could not have helped the battered economy of New England.

To make New England even more hostile to the Dominion, it appeared to threaten the security of practically every land grant in the area. Because Plymouth had always lacked a royal charter, it probably had no legal right to grant land in the first place. Although Massachusetts did have that power, the colony's officials had paid almost no attention to the correct legal forms. Furthermore, some New Englanders had no real proof of ownership. Still worse, the New England towns had granted land to their residents, yet none of the settlements had ever been properly incorporated as towns. In the English legal system, such unincorporated communities had no right to give out land to anyone. Not surprisingly, Andros insisted that there were no towns in New England.[57] Andros appeared ready to threaten the very social fabric which had been established among the Puritans.

Sir Edmund Andros had a number of reasons for taking such an extreme view. While governor of New York, he had granted to some petitioners unfenced land which had been held by others. According to

Jasper Danckaerts, Andros had believed that the land was being wasted because it was not then being cultivated. The original owners had purchased this supposedly wasted land for their descendants. Colonial farmers had to have an eye to the future and keep some land in reserve for their children. But Andros believed that all land should be used without delay. Why let land go unused by one man when someone else was willing to farm it? Andros knew a great deal about war, forts, and the like. He knew next to nothing about farming. He probably assumed that New England's smaller farmers were misusing their land by not getting the maximum use out of every square inch. Considering Andros's record in New York, Randolph's petitioning for large tracts in both Lynn and Cambridge is understandable. These tracts, which Randolph claimed to be unfenced or unoccupied, seemed to fit with Andros's ideas about misused land.[58]

There was another basic reason why Governor Andros was willing to disturb New England's land system. By forcing the Puritans to obtain new land deeds, he hoped that they would realize that they were not independent but merely subjects of the king. And here the governor saw a chance to create another revenue source for the Dominion—quitrents. The charter of Massachusetts Bay had specified that land in New England be held in the style of an English manor. Therefore, quitrents were to be paid to the crown. This point had been ignored by the Puritans of the Bay colony, but Andros intended to change that. To provide an example to others, the Dominion government began legal proceedings against Samuel Sewall and some other prominent men who held land around Boston. Sewall discovered that his legal problems ended when he agreed to ask for a land title with a quitrent.[59]

Quitrents were an annoyance to a well-off landowner such as Sewall. For Andros, they were just another way to build up the Dominion's treasury. But to poorer New Englanders, quitrents were one more burden in bad times. Aside from that expense, a poorer man had to be concerned with other expenses involved in getting a solid deed from the Dominion government. First, he had to pay a surveyor and then the fees of various Dominion functionaries. Such charges would likely have been a very severe imposition to many small farmers of New England. All this had to be done even for land held by the same family since the 1630s. Oddly enough, Governor Andros apparently had forgotten a statement of James II himself. In 1676, while still only the Duke of York, James had insisted that no assembly was needed in New York as long as the government obeyed the laws "thereby preserving every man's property inviolate." By threatening the property of New Englanders, Andros appeared to demonstrate that there was, indeed, need for a popular assembly in the Dominion.[60]

Sir Edmund Andros would never have considered using the confused land system in New England for his personal gain. But West and two other New Yorkers, John Palmer and James Graham, were not so honest. West and Graham tried to finagle Robert Mason's land in New Hampshire away from him. Palmer and the obviously very busy West had threatened various people in Maine. Either they took new land grants or they would lose everything. Such a fate could be avoided by paying a hefty sum to them. Randolph was disturbed by the actions of these "ill men from New-York." West especially was "a great instrument in imposing upon this people." In 1688 these New Yorkers were Dominion officials and very close to Governor Andros.[61] They appear to have been gifted at ingratiating themselves with Sir Edmund, who must be severely criticized for allowing such characters to serve him.

Andros and the Dominion of New England also infuriated many Puritans over religious matters. The governor had been ordered to allow the Puritans to have religious freedom. All marriages performed by magistrates, for example, were considered binding although such marriages were contrary to English law. On the other hand, Andros had to promote the Church of England, which had been practically non-existent in Puritan New England. This attempt to gain a following for the Anglican church infuriated some Puritan ministers, who thundered from their pulpits that Anglicans were certain to spend eternity in a fiery inferno.[62]

Governor Andros appears to have planned to restore the Congregational church as the established church at least in those areas where it had been before. Quakers, Anglicans, and Rhode Island would have been exempted from paying for the Puritan church. But there was much hostility to the plan from councillor Walter Clarke, a Quaker from Rhode Island. At the same time, Puritans on the council were just as determined to restore their faith to its privileged status. The bitter arguing convinced the governor to delay action. The establishment of the Puritan church appears to have been put into the Dominion's new law code, but then West prevented the new code from being acted on.[63]

Anglicanism aroused much controversy as well. Before Andros's arrival, Robert Ratcliffe, the first Anglican cleric in Puritan Boston, had been performing the Church of England service in a small room in a public building. Too many wanted to attend to make such cramped quarters a viable option. The question of where exactly Ratcliffe would preach on a permanent basis rapidly became a very pressing issue. In England, some friends of the Puritans had made an incredible promise to the Archbishop of Canterbury. If the New Englanders were allowed to worship freely, then they would happily give one of their meetinghouses over for the use of the Church of England. This promise had to have been made without any input from the New Englanders themselves, but, clearly, the Lords of Trade and Plantations expected it to be done.[64]

In December 1686 Andros also expected a meetinghouse to be handed over to the Anglicans. His plan was for one meetinghouse to be used at different times by both Puritans and Anglicans. However, none of the three Puritan congregations in Boston was willing to allow the Church of England to use their facilities. Finally, in March 1687 the governor—with the approval of his council—demanded that the newest of the congregations, the Third (better known as the Old South) hand over the keys to its building. After a vigorous protest by the congregation, Andros got his wish. The Anglican service was performed in a Puritan meetinghouse.[65]

Andros's plan proved unworkable. Services of both groups tended to be long, which delayed the other group from starting its worship. Major holydays—when both religions wanted to distribute communion—made the delays even worse. A series of petty—almost childish—disputes broke out about the starting times of the different ceremonies and even who would ring the church bell. By 1688 the Anglicans decided the only solution was to build their own church and Andros tried to intimidate the Old South congregation into helping to pay for it. The attitude of the Puritan congregation towards the governor in June 1688 can be easily detected in its choice then of the 57th Psalm for singing. In this psalm the Israelites beg for mercy from their God until a powerful storm is over; those who oppressed God's people will themselves be shamed by the Almighty.[66] Without a doubt, the church-sharing plan only embittered both sides.

Building an Anglican church in Boston was no easy matter. In 1686 the Anglicans in the capital numbered about 400 people, but many of them were only temporary visitors to Boston; the Anglicans found it difficult to support Ratcliffe by their own contributions. His small salary from the church appears to have been supplemented by Andros, who appointed the clergyman chaplain to the regular soldiers. This additional job enabled Ratcliffe to continue in Boston. Despite the problems faced by the Anglicans, they managed to build King's Chapel, which was first used for services in June 1689.[67]

As if all of these difficulties were not enough, the Dominion of New England aroused still more complaints among its subjects. That famous trademark of New England, the town meeting, was restricted to only one a year. People therefore had practically no voice in any aspect of the Dominion government. Some colonists grumbled as well at their sudden increased distance from the center of power—many legal matters had to be settled in Boston, not the nearer capital of their former, smaller, colony.[68]

Much has also been made of an "Act against Emigration" that was created by the Dominion. This act required a ship captain to make public the names of the passengers who planned to leave New England on his ship. The law's intention was to prevent slaves and indentured servants from fleeing their masters. But it has been called a hinderance to trade and an attempt to stop critics of the government from going to England. However, the law did not have any devious motive behind it and any possible effect on trade had to be rather minor.[69]

Another area of conflict centered upon the governor's attempt to reconcile the Puritans to both English law forms and practices. Andros complained that New England was a "place where none do and few care to understand (if they could help it) the laws or methods of England." His task was made much more difficult by the scarcity of "honest atturneys (if any such thing [exists] in nature)," to quote Randolph. Nor did the Dominion have very many men who knew how to be judges. Randolph believed that there were only three New Englanders who could fill such a position. Some needy English lawyers, Randolph urged, should be encouraged to emigrate to help fill the great gap that existed in the Dominion's legal structure.[70]

The Puritans and the Dominion's legal system soon clashed over the method of swearing an oath in court. From the very beginning of settlement, the Puritans had refused to touch the Bible when taking an oath. Touching the book suggested to them that that particular object in itself was holy. Puritans followed the word of God; they did not wish to venerate a book by taking part in what they saw as a man-made Anglican religious ceremony. Instead of touching a Bible, they raised "up their Hands to heaven," which seemed more appropriate to them. Nevertheless, English law specified that oaths had to be taken while touching the

Bible. If a jury in a court case did not take the oath properly, all action taken was in error and so invalid. Anyone who refused to swear upon the Bible was subject to a fine. The Puritans feared that this procedure was instituted to stop them from serving on juries. With juries composed only of men willing to touch the Bible—that is, Anglicans—juries would decide whatever way the Dominion's government wanted. The fears of the Puritans were unfounded.[71]

Getting the Puritans to accept the English legal system was difficult enough for Andros without having an uneducated man in an important legal position. Andros, though, was saddled with Sir William Phips, a prime example of a poor boy who made good. Born into poverty in Maine, Phips made his fortune by excavating a sunken Spanish galleon loaded with wealth. A grateful James II, flushed with his share of the booty, knighted Phips. As another sign of favor, Sir William received a royal commission as the Dominion's provost-marshal-general. The last thing Andros needed was a barely literate treasure hunter in that important post, and Andros acted as if Phips's royal commission did not exist. An infuriated Phips then returned to England to protest to the king. While in England, Phips joined with Increase Mather and other foes of the Dominion of New England.[72]

Increase Mather, New England's most important Puritan minister of his generation, had opposed in 1683 any attempt to come to some sort of arrangement with English demands. By March 1684 he had himself become a target of the English bureaucracy. William Wharton, whose father sought support for his land speculation, gave some of Mather's letters into the hands of the bureaucrats. These letters were to a prominent English minister in Holland, Abraham Kick, who had sheltered some conspirators against Charles II.[73]

Yet there was much worse in store for Mather. George Ross, a friend of Randolph's, claimed to have read another of Mather's missives while in Holland. Ross wrote that he copied the letter and then sent it to Randolph. The alleged letter, dated December 3, 1683, was incredible. Aside from insulting the Crown, Mather supposedly wrote that New Englanders had protected Whaley and Goffe, two Englishmen who had been among those responsible for the death of Charles I, and that Randolph was an arsonist. Not surprisingly, Mather staunchly insisted that the letter was a blatant forgery. Indeed, internal evidence in the letter strongly suggests that Mather did not write it. Simon Bradstreet aptly remarked that "I cannot think him soe foolish and absurd to write all that is contained in that letter."[74]

Nonetheless, Randolph believed that Mather, "the Bellowes of Sedition and Treason," had written the letter. Meanwhile, Mather informed Joseph Dudley that Randolph had been the forger. According to the outraged minister, Randolph was skillful in mimicking the handwriting of others. Randolph and Mather detested each other and legal proceedings would ensue. A libel suit by Randolph led Mather eventually to flee to England.[75]

After the preacher wrote his letter accusing Randolph, Mather made no secret of it around Boston. Infuriated, Randolph planned his revenge and sued Mather for libel. Randolph expected to demonstrate that the Puritan had slandered him and had damaged his reputation to the value of £ 500. Unknown to Randolph, however, the preacher had gotten some clever legal advice. Knock Randolph's own character, Mather was urged. Had not he claimed that the minister had written the forged letter? By the laws expounded in Deuteronomy, Randolph deserved to be executed for such an offense. But most clever of all, Mather was advised to deny having written that accusing letter to Dudley. Although Mather had signed it, the letter itself had been penned by someone else. Armed with this legalistic defense, in January 1688 Mather faced Randolph in a court of law and before a jury. To Randolph's undoubted surprise, he lost the case.[76]

Mather had already been planning in December 1687 to go to England, but Randolph's suit had delayed him. In March 1688 he announced his intention to leave for England and, appropriately enough, preached a sermon based on Exodus. But Randolph had no intention of allowing Mather to escape from his revenge. Randolph was trying to give to Mather some of the harassment the royal servant felt he had been given. In England Randolph had twice been hit with law suits—for old debts—by men he thought were friendly to New England.[77]

Mather's version of what Randolph did is well-known. According to the preacher, Randolph and his colleagues in villainy wanted to stop Mather from complaining to English authorities. So the scoundrels sent a sheriff to "arrest" him again for Randolph's old libel suit. Luckily for the Puritan, he had taken a "physick," which caused him not to speak to the sheriff. Fearful of arrest, Mather stayed in his house to avoid being caught and detained by Andros's minions. Then, late one night, Mather disguised himself and slipped out. A man assigned to watch the preacher's house simply lacked the courage to stop him. In early April 1688 Mather sailed for England, having escaped from the clutches of his foes.[78]

Heroic as Mather's story is, it probably does not quite explain what happened. To begin with, the word "arrest" had other meanings than "to imprison." During 1641 in Maine, for example, there is a record of a man being "arrested" in a slander case. But there is no hint of the arrested man being jailed and the action was solved by arbitration. Here, "arrest" seems to have the meaning of "indict" or perhaps "notify." By 1660 "arrest" could mean that a court decision had been halted because the verdict had "manifest error."[79] That is, a case had been overturned and the whole matter could be tried again.

There was no legal way that Increase Mather could have been jailed by Randolph. Nor does it seem likely that the reopening of the suit could have delayed Mather's trip for very long. Clearly, though, the sheriff had no intention of making sure that the preacher was behind bars. After all, the lawman did not drag the indisposed minister out of his house. As long as the message was delivered, the sheriff did not even need to see Mather. Nor did the sheriff have to return another day. Furthermore, Mather had to have known this. When Randolph first started his libel suit in December 1687, the sheriff was then ordered to "Arest" the Puritan, a task that was performed on December 24, 1687. Although Samuel Sewall noted the event in his diary, he did not write that the preacher spent any time in jail. All Mather had to do was to produce bail, money that would be forfeited if he did not appear to answer the charge against him.[80]

Mather was indeed frightened by Randolph's resuming the libel action. To Cotton Mather, the first verdict was "Miraculous," and Increase felt he had been very lucky in the composition of the jury. If a second trial took place, the legalistic defense used by Increase Mather might not be successful again. What he truly feared was expressed in the Declaration issued by the Boston rebels in April 1689. Andros and his underlings sought "not only to interrupt his Voyage, but to ruin his Person too."[81] Mather fled to avoid a second trial that might force him to pay £ 500 to Randolph.

Even Mather's encounter with one of Randolph's "creatures"—supposedly watching him—seems like a bit of wishful thinking. The minister's description of the encounter with the villain, a Thurton, has him declaring: "Hee had no power (notwithstanding his being empowred by the marshall) to lay his hands on me." Everything seems to point to one conclusion—the parenthetical expression was an assumption by Mather and not something actually said by Thurton, who may have been near the preacher's house only through a coincidence. Moreover, if Mather was really concerned about being seized, the last thing he should have done was to wear "a white cloke" as a disguise.[82] Wearing white at night only made him more visible. But wearing white was really a symbolic act for Increase Mather. White was the color of angels, the heavenly messengers of God. Mather believed himself to be embarking on a divine mission—the destruction of Sir Edmund Andros and the Dominion of New England.

Governor Andros had little time to worry about what Increase Mather was planning to do. During 1688 relations with the French in Canada and Indians under their influence had become of great importance. Earlier, James II and Louis XIV of France had come to an agreement about their American territories. By treaty in 1686 the kings decreed that their colonies would remain neutral if their mother countries went to war; the American colonists were not to help the Indians attack the other empire's possessions. This treaty was especially aimed at the fighting between the French in Canada and the English Hudson's Bay Company. In 1688 a trade agreement was also signed by the two monarchs. On that agreement, Randolph wrote that it "has been duly observed, both by our Indians and English, but not generally by the French."[83]

The Iroquois Confederacy was of great concern to the French too. The Iroquois were seen as a very great threat, and the French did everything possible to win their favor. Catholic missionaries of the Jesuit order went among the Iroquois and, according to Randolph, "strangely allure them with their beades crucifixes and little painted Images, gaining many converts." Where the Jesuits traveled, French influence grew. Randolph's solution to the success of the Jesuits was to send English Catholic priests among the Indians at such places as Penobscot (the present-day Castine) in Maine. By having English Catholics minister to the Indians there, Randolph felt that their loyalty to England would be secured.[84]

Sir Edmund Andros had no intention of allowing the French to encroach upon the Dominion of New England. He was as concerned as Randolph about the growing French influence at Penobscot, particularly the effect a Jean-Vincent D'Abbadie de Saint-Castin had there. This Frenchman, an Indian trader, had married a sachem's daughter and so had much influence with the Indians. During May 1688 Andros traveled in force to Penobscot to try to get Saint-Castin to renounce Louis XIV and support the English. The Frenchman fled upon the governor's approach. With Saint-Castin gone, Andros was stymied. He therefore ordered "some small matters of indian trade"—guns, ammunition, kettles, cloth, and some sleighs—taken out of Saint-Castin's house and brought to Pemaquid. All Saint-Castin or a comrade of his had to do to reclaim these items was to go to Pemaquid. Naturally enough, the Frenchman or his messenger would then be pressured to come under the protection of the English Crown. While Andros was on this trek to Maine, he also met with the local sachems to ply them with liquor and the usual presents. Governor Andros promised protection to the assembled Indians against the French.[85]

Saint-Castin, surely angry at Andros's seizure of his property, complained to the French governors of Acadia and Canada about it. In fact, the Canadian governor branded the seizure "an act of hostility." The Puritans quickly blamed this action of Andros for the Indian troubles that occurred both before and after his overthrow. Exactly what effect the removal of Saint-Castin's goods had on the future turmoil can not be determined. Quite likely, however, there would have been Indian warfare even without Andros's mission to Maine, only one of the areas hit by Indians.[86]

What is certain is that hostile natives soon threatened all of northern New England. In August 1688 some pro-English Indians were attacked and killed near Springfield, Massachusetts, reportedly by enemy Indians who had fled to Canada upon the failure of King Philip's War. Soon after that attack, some colonists were killed at Northfield on the Connecticut River by Indians, again, identified as having come from Canada. Francis Nicholson, the Dominion's lieutenant governor, observed that "the news from Northfield" sent a shiver of fear throughout the people of Massachusetts "for they have nott yett forgott the cruelties of the Indians" during King Philip's War.[87]

While the Indian troubles were erupting, Andros was in Albany in northern New York and so far away from the endangered areas. The councillors in Boston were in charge there. The settlers near the Saco River in Maine, greatly concerned about the resumption of Indian problems, feared devastation like that in King Philip's War. To prevent that possibility, the settlers seized some twenty Indians who had been active during that war. In retaliation, other Indians seized some colonists and vowed to keep them as long as the natives were held. Frightened by the turn of events, the settlers of remote places in Maine began to flee.

Meanwhile, Dudley and the other councillors at Boston sent to Casco an armed force which Indians attacked, resulting in reinforcements being sent from Massachusetts. As Andros wrote in October 1688, "a Pannick" had arisen in Maine and Massachusetts.[88]

When news of the problems reached Andros, he was furious at the "rash" seizure of innocent Indian hostages. He was "displeased with" English Army lieutenant Thomas Treffry for agreeing with the councillors' actions, which were "grievous" to the governor. A regretful Joseph Dudley assured Andros "that what was done by the Gentlemen here, was what we truly thought your Excellency would Expect of us that the province might not be Lost in your absence." From Maine, Edward Tyng wrote to Andros: "I pray god make your Excellency a happy instrument to Settle the disturbances that we are att present under and feares of more."[89]

Andros felt he had to calm the situation before things got even worse. First of all, he journeyed to Springfield and Northfield to reassure the inhabitants there and then returned to Boston. Once back in the capital, he learned that hostile Indians who killed colonists in Maine "bragg of further encouragement and assistance from Canada." The governor decided on a two-prong plan of action. Since the Indians seized originally had done nothing, the governor (with the council's approval) ordered their release and then ordered all Indians to release their captives. Those Indians who complied would not be harmed. On the other hand, Indians who had already killed settlers could not be forgiven. Andros intended to send enough force to capture the hostile natives and to protect Maine.[90]

In October 1688 the governor himself went into Maine and received those Indians who said they would submit. However, Andros concluded that, of the sachems, "none [were] to be trusted." The governor, taking no chances, garrisoned strong points in the interior of Maine. In order to protect Maine's coastal settlements, Andros dispatched an armed vessel to each exposed port. Yet hostile natives still attacked some smaller settlements. By November 1688 there seemed no alternative except a military expedition against the warring Indians. The only question was who would command the force. Andros recommended that Fitz-John Winthrop, the commanding officer of the Dominion's militia, be in charge, but Winthrop declined due to ill health. The governor accepted his excuse. Because no one else on the council was able or had the skills to command in a dangerous situation, Andros decided to lead the expedition himself.[91]

A winter campaign against Indians was very difficult to carry out. Luckily for Andros, the winter of 1688-89 was mild, so he and his fewer than 200 soldiers could march deeply into the "desart" of Maine. When Andros and his men on their long march into the backcountry reached an abandoned Indian village, they burned it and took all canoes, corn, gunpowder, and other essential items. By destroying Indian food supplies and canoes, Andros demonstrated that he had learned one of the great lessons of King Philip's War: starvation was an effective weapon against the natives. Driving the Indians deep into the countryside moved them far away from their traditional fishing and hunting grounds. When threatened by starvation, Indians had to be more concerned with their own survival than with making war.[92]

Andros, thinking that the situation in Maine had stabilized, left for Boston about March 16, 1689. His armed force remained behind and, with additional militiamen, garrisoned the various forts he had built. Unknown to the governor, a number of Boston merchants—John Foster, David Waterhouse, and perhaps John Nelson—came to Maine after he had left. Knowing what the Indians lacked, the merchants came well-prepared. They sold food, cloth, and ammunition to the natives thus nullifying Andros's efforts. The merchants, though, reportedly made an excellent profit.[93]

Back in Massachusetts, Puritan critics of the Dominion scoffed at what Andros had done in Maine. The Puritans determined success by counting the bodies of dead Indians. Rather than trying to kill Indians with bullets, the governor had chosen to drive them away and starve them. Andros's strategy had pleased many of the people of Maine, some of whom later petitioned William III to tell him so. Unlike the critics in untouched Boston, these Maine residents believed that Governor Andros's efforts would have defeated the Indians (if those who overthrew him had not interfered).[94]

Although those on the scene appreciated the diligent actions of Sir Edmund Andros, the people of Massachusetts became disgruntled over the Maine campaign. Strange rumors spread that Andros had actually paid the natives to war upon the colonists. Still other stories had Andros encouraging the Indians to venerate the Blessed Virgin; he had to be a Roman Catholic. These bizarre accounts added fuel to the discontent about the casualties incurred by the campaign in Maine. A "great cry" was also raised in the towns of Massachusetts about the welfare of ill militiamen in Maine. In January 1689 some people were clearly incensed at the Maine campaign and the various controversial aspects of the Dominion of New England. At that time a broadside was distributed in the countryside that was entitled: "New England alarmd to rise and be armed, let not Papist you charme. . . ."[95] These grumblings came at a very bad time for the governor, because events in England had already greatly changed the political landscape.

James II had infuriated so many important groups in England that his overthrow became possible. William of Orange and his wife, Mary, had been invited by prominent Englishmen to come to England and undo the work of the Catholic king. After William and his army arrived in November 1688, James's support crumbled away and he fled to France and the protection of Louis XIV. This "Glorious Revolution" had taken place without a serious fight and resulted in the Protestants William and Mary becoming joint rulers of England. Increase Mather and his allies, who had been trying to undermine Andros with James, now switched their tactics and lobbied the new king.[96]

Mather and Phips tried their best to have the old charter of the Massachusetts Bay Company restored to the colony. On that issue, the Prince of Orange refused to give in, but the lobbyists managed to defeat Andros, who had long been connected with the deposed monarch. Although the Lords of Trade planned to remove Andros, another royal governor would eventually replace him under a new charter. Despite Mather's last-ditch lobbying of William in March 1689, the old charter was dead.[97]

Yet Increase Mather was probably scheming to restore the old charter, one way or the other. In January 1689 William III had ordered that a circular letter be sent to all Protestant colonial governors that would keep them in their positions until further notice. Andros, as a Protestant, would receive the authorization, and that was the very last thing Mather wanted. Without question, Mather had a fair idea of what some of the anti-Andros Puritans in New England had been thinking about—overthrowing Sir Edmund Andros. The logical source of this information was Cotton Mather, but his letters had to have been vaguely-worded in case they came before unfriendly eyes. Such letters do not now exist; they would have been consigned to flames immediately after being read. To protect the colonial plotters, Increase Mather lobbied to prevent Andros from getting the authorization and the Puritan minister succeeded. A revolt in New England could now be undertaken against a governor with no authority from William and Mary.[98]

But Increase Mather could not have known for certain what had been happening in New England. Quite likely, he hoped that Massachusetts Bay would revolt and take up its old charter. Perhaps the king and the bureaucrats would bend on the charter if they were confronted with a *fait accompli.* Sir William Phips did arrive in New England in May 1689. En route, he made no secret of his intention of leading a revolt against Andros. Mather had to have suggested to the treasure hunter that he do so. Of course, Phips learned that he was already too late. If Mather was, indeed, behind Phips's planned revolt, the minister would learn that nothing could save the old charter. However, the Rebellion of 1689 did put an end to the Dominion of New England.[99]

By February 1689 New England was abuzz with news that William of Orange had landed in England the previous November. That was all the colonists then knew. With all the rumors about Andros "flying like Wild-Fire about the Country," the inhabitants were very suspicious about their colonial government. Later on, even Cotton Mather admitted that "the Suspicious People . . . were doubtless more extream in some of their Suspicions, than there was any real Occasion for. . . ." Nevertheless, revolt did not seem to be in the air. On February 23, 1689, John West reported from Boston: "All is well here, save that some ill spiritts appear in scattering and publishing seditious and rebellious libells, for which some are in custody."[100]

The situation changed drastically in early April. On April 4 John Winslow, a young New Englander who had been in the West Indies, came to Boston with two broadsides concerning the monarchical crisis in England: the "Declaration of the Nobility, Gentry, and Commonalty . . . at Nottingham," which was dated November 22, 1688; and "The Declaration of the Lords Spiritual and Temporal . . . Assembled at Guildhall" of December 11, 1688. Winslow revealed that the Prince of Orange had been warmly received by many Englishmen, and that at least some prominent people in England supported a forced removal of James II. When Andros—starved for information about what had happened in England—learned that Winslow had "Declarations" about events there, he immediately wanted to see the young Puritan. But Winslow refused to give the governor the broadsides "because he would not let the people know any news." Irritated by this "Saucy fellow," the sensitive governor had him jailed for a day. Andros was not trying to suppress Winslow's intelligence; the knight just could not abide a slight from anyone.[101]

Winslow's news triggered immediate planning for a revolt against Andros. A meeting took place at Cotton Mather's home soon after Winslow arrived. Of course, the participants insisted that rebellion was not planned there—they were simply preparing to prevent bloodshed. Nonetheless, they clearly planned a coup d'etat for April 18, 1689, when the Dominion's council was to meet. A rebellion on that day would be likely to net most of the principal figures of the Dominion, who would be in Boston to attend the council. The plotters' decision for revolt is easily understood. They could not foresee that Prince William would gain control over all of England as easily as he did. Although the plotters may have received additional news from the Caribbean suggesting the victory of the Prince of Orange in England, they could not be absolutely certain about the truthfulness of these positive reports. Erroneous stories about the situation were common even near to the scene of events. Nor could the New Englanders discount that a sudden reversal might have occurred. For example, a few days after the pro-William meeting at the Guildhall in London, that city warmly welcomed the arrival of James II there. As far as the conspirators knew, England was on the verge of another bloody civil war. And they knew what side they wanted to be on—that of the Protestants William and Mary. Logically, the conspirators assumed that Andros, a servant of the legitimate king James II, would support his old master in a civil war. Therefore the governor and his minions had to be made harmless to ensure that New England opposed the Catholic monarch. To protect the plotters in case the revolt failed, they created the illusion of a spontaneous rebellion by the oppressed people of Massachusetts, a fictitious story also useful in case James won in England. But claims of spontaneity do not fit with the planning that made the coup a success.[102]

The identity of the leading light behind the conspirators is unknown, but Cotton Mather is a good guess. The young minister, very influential with the rebels, was later asked to preach before the revolutionary government. Randolph identified him as one of the "chief promoters of the rebellion," and Andros had commanded that Mather be arrested on the very day of the revolt. The Declaration issued by the rebels is often attributed to him as well. While, again, no real proof exists, Mather is the probable author of the Declaration. Kenneth Silverman questioned this attribution of authorship. No draft of the Declaration still exists, but an important document relating to it does remain. Silverman, noting that this item is in a different hand, suggested that the lack of Mather's penmanship weakened the chance that he was the true composer. Given Increase Mather's defense in the Randolph libel suit—that the offensive letter was not in his hand—Silverman's theory is not convincing. The need for personal safety if the revolt failed was reason enough for Cotton Mather to have had someone else with a less identifiable handwriting pen a possibly incriminating document.[103]

Whoever the chief leader against Andros was, the rebellion or, as Ian K. Steele called it, the "well-prepared coup," took place as scheduled. Captain John George of H. M. S. *Rose*, which was stationed at Boston, became the first man seized. His capture occurred about 8:00 AM, probably ahead of schedule. A deserter from the *Rose* had spread the rumor that George planned to use his ship's guns against Boston, and so a group seized him as soon as possible. Only at 9:00 AM did the rebellion really get started. According to Nathaniel Byfield, who was hostile to the rebels, at that time "the Drums beat through the Town" to summon the militia "and an Ensign was set up upon the Beacon."[104]

Meanwhile, Andros, Randolph, and some other Dominion officials, in a small bastion in Boston called Fort Hill, were ordered by the plotters to surrender. Sir Edmund had little idea about what was really happening. He could tell that some 2000 militiamen were in Boston. To counter them he had a total of 14 regular soldiers in Fort Hill—the bulk of his regular troops were in Maine. Andros later explained what happened next:

> . . . understanding that severall of the Councill were at the Councill Chamber where . . . they were to meet, and some particularly by him sent for from distant parts also there, he and those with him went thither. And tho' (as he passed) the streets were full of armed men, yett none offered him or those that were with him the least rudeness or incivillity, but on the contrary usuall respect; but when he came to the Councill Chamber he found severall of the . . . former popular Majestrates and other chiefe persons then present, with those of the Councill, who had noe suitable regard to him, nor the peace and quiet of the Countrey, but instead of giveing any assistance to support the Goverment, made him a prisoner. . . .[105]

After the seizure of the governor, the so-called "Committee for the Conservation of the Peace" mopped up what little possible resistance remained. Both the small garrison in Fort Hill and that of Castle Island soon surrendered. All of the important pro-Andros figures in Boston were seized. Joseph Dudley, who had been on Long Island, was taken a few days later in Newport. The Committee also propagated its Declaration, which gave their version of the reasons for their rebellion. Among the charges were: very high fees, the enforcement of the Navigation Acts, and packed juries. This Declaration seemed to pave the way for a resumption of the old charter. The revocation of the charter, the Committee suggested, was illegal.[106]

When Andros, Randolph, and their comrades were taken at the council chambers, Randolph noticed Cotton Mather and other ministers there as well. Some preachers seemed to be playing a very large role in the rebellion. In 1689 John Palmer insisted that the clerics "had a great share in the late Revolution. . . ." But the ministers and the Committee soon discovered that the rebellion seemed to be out of control as more and more people from outside Boston flocked in to the city. As one anonymous critic pointed out, the new people coming into Boston frightened the Committee, "for they were like young conjurers, who had raised a Devil they could not govern."[107]

Probably the most serious problem the revolutionary leaders faced involved Maine. The forts built by Andros there were abandoned and even Pemaquid was left with a garrison that was much too small. The armed vessels that Andros had stationed in Maine were recalled. A complete collapse in Maine followed quickly. Pemaquid was lost to the French and huge sections of Maine and New Hampshire were devastated by the Indians.[108]

What little legitimacy the revolutionaries had was destroyed when the old charter was taken up again. William III had authorized the junta to run the colony until further notice. But the new king did not give his approval for the resurrection of the Massachusetts Bay Company. The argument that the charter had been wrongly voided was not convincing to many of the inhabitants. As one anonymous critic observed: "if a man be killed though never so unjustly it wil not bring him to life again though he be taken up and upon his legs with great complaints how basely and unmanly he was killed." With no real legitimacy, the old charter government was in a very weak position. In order to pay for expeditions against the French, the Bay government raised taxes "over thirty times their prewar level" according to one historian. Even the unpaid taxes left over from the Dominion were collected. These heavy taxes were greeted with much resistance.[109]

The government faced many other grumbles. Militiamen fumed that they had received no pay for their military service. Other men resisted being drafted to fight the French and Indians. Seeing little choice, the revolutionaries used much "harshnesse and violence" against such men. From jail, Randolph insisted that some people hoped that Sir Edmund Andros would be released to run things again until the king had decided what to do with New England. Cuthbert Potter, a hostile visitor from Virginia, declared "that many who had been for, were now inveterate enemies to the present Government." About a year after the revolt, Benjamin Bullivant (who had been an official under Andros) reported that people were yelling in the streets: "God blesse King William, God blesse Sir Edmund Andros, and Damn all pumpkin states."[110] Public opinion is a very fickle thing.

However, the jailed former governor, who had been held upon Castle Island, had other concerns. When in August 1689 a guard became careless and drank too much, Andros took the opportunity to escape. He reached Newport but dallied too long there, perhaps because he hoped to meet with some followers of Thomas Dongan, the former governor of New York. Dongan had helped Francis Nicholson to escape and may have wanted to help Andros too. Or, possibly, Andros stayed in Newport because he was ill. Whatever the case, he was recaptured and promptly returned to Boston. Rhode Island was not a safe place to hold the soldier, because his captors feared that the Quakers there wanted to have him set free.[111]

All told, Andros spent some ten months under confinement in Boston. After his escape, his captors were sometimes very petty as when he was denied milk. (Befitting someone from Guernsey, Andros greatly relished milk.) Other complaints, such as lack of heat and a leaky roof, were much more life-threatening. Such treatment greatly angered Andros's ally in the English bureaucracy, William Blathwayt. Knowing of Blathwayt's support, Andros could confide in him his hope that "I shall not be censured unheard. . . ." Finally, William III ordered that the former governor and those others held with him be sent to England for trial.[112]

Andros's judges were to be the Lords of Trade, and a more sympathetic group could not be found. And Blathwayt was on the scene to smooth out any potential rough spots. The soldier also discovered that many of his other contacts were now servants of William and Mary.[113]

The trial itself was more a comedy of errors than a real threat to Andros and his fellow defendants. The Bay colony had sent additional agents to England to assist Increase Mather. These new agents brought what evidence had been assembled against Andros and his comrades. Yet neither Mather nor the other agents was willing to sign the charges presented against the deposed royal officials. Signing the charges could have made them vulnerable to a law suit by Andros and his colleagues. An anonymous critic back in New England observed that Mather and his partners "found ther was a difference between talking high at home and doing businesse at white[h]all." Because no one would sign the charges, all the defendants were freed in April 1690 and they were honored with a meeting with William III.[114]

King William, who remembered Andros from his years in Holland, wanted to find a suitable position for the displaced soldier. Rumor around official circles in England had Andros going back to New England as a governor there. A triumphal return to Boston was not in store for him although by the early months of 1691 the king still wanted to "gratify" Andros. At last in 1692 the soldier was rewarded with the governorship of Virginia. Not surprisingly, his administration there was just as stormy as his earlier ones.[115]

Meanwhile, New England had to adjust to the consequences of its own version of the Glorious Revolution. The possibility of a French attack upon New England had been commented upon by both Randolph and the rebels themselves. Logically, the chaos in New England and New York after the Glorious Revolution seemed like an obvious invitation for a French and Indian invasion. Although Maine and northern New York were attacked, the French paid little attention to the disrupted colonies.[116]

The French had had their own fears, which centered upon Sir Edmund Andros. In January 1689, having learned that William and Mary were on the English throne, the French in Canada had no doubt that Andros would repudiate James II. The change in England greatly endangered Canada, one French official believed. According to the Frenchman:

> Chevalier Andros, as well as the whole English Colony, is protestant . . . and we must expect that he will not only urge the Iroquois to continue the war against us but he will even furnish them with Englishmen to lead them and to seize Niagara. . . . and other posts. . . . It is to be expected then, that they are about to endeavor to invest the entire of Canada and raise all the Savages against us. . . .[117]

Nor could the French hope that the Dutch in New York would be disloyal to the English. After all, William was Dutch himself. To defend Canada, the French came up with a bold and risky gamble to neutralize the Iroquois by seizing Albany and New York City. In June 1689 Louis XIV gave his approval to the project.[118]

Nevertheless, when Andros was overthrown, the entire military picture changed. The revolutionaries did not seem to have the martial abilities of Andros. Canada did not appear to be in as much danger with the English soldier in jail. Instead of gambling on a major invasion of the Dominion, the French spent their time attacking the posts of the Hudson's Bay Company.[119] Ironically, the revolutionaries may have prevented a major invasion of New York by overthrowing an able soldier.

J. M. Sosin has commented: "The burdens imposed upon Edmund Andros when he went out to preside over New England would have tested the patience and wisdom of a Solomon."[120] Andros was no Solomon. Attacked by critics when governor of New York, Andros seemed to pay little attention to what others thought were his mistakes. As governor of the Dominion of New England, he was expected to administer without an assembly where the inhabitants had grown accustomed to one. Andros's faults and those of his officials created more discontent. Although he was not the epitome of a colonial governor, Andros did have one important trait. He was a good soldier.

Chapter 8

Satan

Every Puritan child knew that God had thrown Satan, a fallen angel, out of heaven into the fiery depths of hell. This chapter is not meant as an up close and personal look at the legions of hell. Rather, it discusses the episode when the devil allegedly injected himself into the history of New England—"the horrible Enchantments and Possessions" that erupted in Salem Village during 1692. Better known as the Salem witchcraft trials, they demonstrated, at least to Cotton Mather, that Satan was an enemy of the Bay colony.[1]

Hardly originating in 1692, witchcraft—or at least a belief in it—had existed in Christian Europe far into the distant past. Before the Salem debacle, the last major outbreak of reputed witchcraft occurred on the European continent in Sweden during the 1660s and 1670s.[2]

English folk wisdom that travelled to America had devised ways to protect against the malevolent designs of a witch. A bay leaf kept evil away as did a horseshoe hung in a prominent place by a door. People also knew that women predominately practiced witchcraft because they more easily fell for Satan's lures just as Eve had in the Garden of Eden. Men, in Salem as elsewhere, sometimes indulged in satanic service too. (Technically, a male witch was a wizard but the Salem records usually ignore the distinction.)[3]

Folk wisdom also knew ways of detecting witches and such ideas entered the English legal system. Servants of Satan such as witches inflicted what became known as *maleficium* upon individuals who aroused their ire. Sudden disease, death, or ill fortune had to be the evil handiwork of witches. One victim not only suffered bizarre pain and sores, but also "strange, extraordinary and unaccountable Calamities befell his cattle." When an accused witch predicted that a cow would not do a person "any more good," it died despite being "a stout Lusty Cow." Although that cow had died over two decades before the Salem outbreak, it still seemed to be a sign suggesting *maleficium* had struck a sufferer due to sorcery.[4]

Sometimes a witch utilized props called "poppets," often referred to as puppets today although the seventeenth century version looked nothing like the modern toys. According to testimony at Salem, an ally of the devil, having used sorcery against a pig and killing a child as well, then "tied a knot in a Rag and threw it into the fire to hurt" a victim. Others "complained of her [that] by squeezing popets like them . . . [she] almost choked them." Pins or thorns might also be inserted into the devilish devices to torment a target.[5]

Because witches had associated themselves with the denizens of hell, Satan gave them great powers such as, for example, superhuman strength or speed. But dealing with the devil had its drawbacks too. One such weakness could help to expose the identity of a witch. As a magistrate at Salem related, "it is no strange thing that God will not suffer a wizard to pray to him." An ally of Satan could not recite a prayer properly, so an accused witch would be asked to say aloud a Christian prayer, the Lord's Prayer, often called the Our Father. A suspected wizard stumbled over the words five times in a row. Still another failed the test "after Many Trialls." Guilt could be established if only one word was added or mispronounced.[6]

An even more medieval method of smoking out a witch, a touch test, received much use at Salem. The theory of the touch test seemed simple. If a witch touched someone she had bewitched, the evil would rush from the harassed victim into the witch, thus curing the now relieved victim. At Salem, an accuser "was made well after said Reed had grasped her arm." Five accused people wrote afterward: "[we] were laid upon the afflicted persons, they being in their fits. . . ." When the bedeviled victims reported their recovery, all five fearful suspects were arrested.[7]

Just as medieval as the touch test—and possibly even more so—was the search for "devil's marks." Satan supposedly sucked nourishment from a witch through this mark, which could be almost anything thought unusual, even a spot. Finding such a "witch's tit" on a body made the searchers very suspicious. The lack of such curious oddities, however, would not prevent a suspect's execution.[8]

At least devil's marks could be seen even though their supernatural aspect might be debatable in seventeenth century Massachusetts. On the other hand, spectral evidence was other-worldly by any standard. Theoretically, a servant of Satan allowed his master to use his image to perform evil. Seeing a spectre or ghost of an individual seemed clear proof to some that that person was in cahoots with the devil, especially when the spectre hurt someone. Despite Mary Bradbury reposing in jail, accuser Elizabeth Hubbard insisted "she or her Appearance has come to me and most grievously tormented me which if she were not a witch she could not do."9

Spectres could do anything. The obviously careless Mary Bradbury was also once seen "as a blue boar." Another flew by a witness and an odd spectre boasted "that she had ridden a man with an enchanted bridle." Most spectres, though, tried to strangle or otherwise cause pain to a victim, often to recruit her to Satan's cause.10

Or did they? Could the devil appropriate the image of one of his earthly foes? Scripture suggested that scenario might be true. An image of the Hebrew judge Samuel was conjured up to talk with King Saul. Even Cotton Mather related that witches had admitted they had used the images of innocents. Nonetheless, spectral evidence became vital in the prosecution of alleged witches at Salem. Abigail Faulkner, Sr., insisted she was tried merely because of the "Spectral Sight" of the witnesses against her.11

Given the disputed status of spectral evidence, a confession by a witch was avidly sought. In Sweden mock executions were staged to trick witches into confessing; only those who then confessed died at the now real execution. At Salem things worked out differently. When George Jacobs, Sr., learned that Margaret Jacobs, his granddaughter, had admitted practicing witchcraft he was shocked and said "that if she were Innocent and yet Confest she would be accessary to her own death." Surprisingly, George Jacobs, Sr., was hanged and Margaret survived.12

During the Salem witchcraft trials, only those who refused to confess were hanged. Those who confessed, even if scheduled for death the next day, were allowed to live. No one who admitted doing witchcraft died with the sole exception of Samuel Wardwell, who had changed his mind and repudiated his confession. He died as a warning to others not to follow his example. This circumstance of only hanging non-confessors might have changed if the trials had gone on longer.13

Not executing a person who admitted practicing sorcery flew in the face of English legal tradition, but the Puritans, at Salem, saw a confession as a sign of repentance, a willingness to reject Satan and all his works. Confessors had, once again, joined God's side. This curious situation came about because of advice that Cotton Mather gave to a Salem judge. Rather than kill everyone recruited by Satan, the Puritan minister suggested, spare some "lesser criminals" who provided a "solemn, open, public, and explicit renunciation of the devil." Furthermore, he urged that an execution be "either diverted or inflicted, according to the success of such their renunciation." A confessed witch should be spared.[14]

The authorities at Salem wanted confessions—and they got them. Although Cotton Mather did not recommend torture—it was "un-English"—some suspects did suffer various types of torture, some more brutal than others, John Proctor insisted. When two sons of a suspected witch refused to confess—and implicate their mother at the same time—the authorities "tied them Neck and Heels till the Blood was ready to come out of their Noses." Both sons confessed. Proctor's own son was similarly tortured "till the Blood gushed out at his Nose." If not for a kindly individual, young Proctor would have been subjected to such "Popish Cruelties" for "24 Hours."[15]

Massachusetts officials subjected others to sleep deprivation. The examinations of witches were very, very, long—as long as "eighteen hours"—and were conducted by different shifts of questioners. Worn out by "tedious" questions and promised both "freedom from hardships and Irons," many people surrendered and said they had engaged in nefarious practices. Then they were released.[16]

Women and girls do not seem to have been brutally tortured. Instead, they encountered a more psychological approach. Shocked by the behavior of their accusers, some women were "affrighted even out of our reason." Sarah Wilson, Sr., became "fearful of herself." Margaret Jacobs later wrote that "persons at the sight of me fell down, which did very much startle and affright me." Then the questioning began and she was threatened with "the dungeon" and hanging if she did not admit her guilt. Martha Tyler was warned in private that by not confessing she was "undone body and soul for ever." Even her brother had insisted "that she must . . . be a witch, since the afflicted accused her." Finally, he told her "that God would not suffer so many good men to be in such an error about it." Now "terrified" she agreed to "almost any thing that they propounded to her." Mary Bridges revealed "that she was brought to her confession by being told she certainly was a witch, and so made to belive it." Nor should it be forgotten that most women knew little about the legal system and accused witches were not allowed lawyers. Margaret Jacobs, for one, willingly swore she was a witch because she had no idea what swearing meant.[17]

An important part of these so painfully extracted confessions was what Paul Boyer and Stephen Nissenbaum called "corroborating detail." This "minutiae" of witchcraft confirmed to observers that the proceedings against the suspects had legitimacy, that these exposed witches were truly dangerous. When a confessor said she had tormented a victim "with a spear," the examiner immediately wanted to know what the spear was made of. When the slave Tituba confessed, the question arose about what she had ridden. Tituba responded as a witch should: "I Rid upon a stick or poale and Good and Osburne behind me we Ride takeing hold of one another." Indeed, flying on a broomstick was dangerous before the invention of seat belts as demonstrated when, in flight, a broomstick broke while still "above the tops of trees." A lucky witch managed to "hang fast about the neck of Goody Carrier." Wisely, the maximum capacity of a broomstick was set at four witches. Even servants of Satan had to be concerned about in-flight safety.[18]

Safe was not how many New Englanders felt in 1692; Massachusetts, its collective confidence shattered, was distraught. As related earlier, Sir Edmund Andros and the Dominion of New England had been toppled in 1689. Soon after, the resurrected corpse of the Massachusetts Bay Company had taken over complete with its venerable governor, Simon Bradstreet. The old government had not done well in the ongoing conflict with the Indians in Maine, eventually called King William's War. By 1692 every town there north of Wells had been either destroyed or abandoned and many refugees had fled to Massachusetts. A surprising number of refugees became ensnarled, one way or another, with the Salem witchcraft trials. The witchcraft frenzy took place during very troubled times.[19]

The times became even more troubled because of the extreme behavior of the magistrates and judges who took part in the witch trials. Urged to "be a terror to evil-doers," they certainly were. John Proctor, who declared that "nothing but our Innocent Blood will serve their turn, having Condemned us already before our Tryals," did not exaggerate at all. When Mary Laccy, Jr., entered her place of examination, one of her accusers had "a violent fit." Immediately, a magistrate snarled at Lacey:

"how dare you come in here and bring the devil with you to afflict these poor creatures." And William Stoughton, the "very zealous" chief judge, did not want to bother with evidence that suggested something was wrong with the trials. Such rash behavior sharply contrasted with customary procedure in dealing with charges of witchcraft. Normally, judges, very skeptical about such accusations, rarely found a person guilty. Salem witnessed rash judges and hosts of convictions. What caused such drastic differences?[20]

The answer lies in a basic fact: the Puritans were evangelical Protestants who took the biblical book, Revelation, very seriously. An eventual judge at Salem, Samuel Sewall, had taken notice when the number 666, associated with the beast of Revelation, popped up in an earlier election—Joseph Dudley, who had joined the forces in favor of royal government, received that number of votes. But Sewall was not the prime mover regarding the apocalypse and Salem. Cotton Mather earned that distinction.[21]

Cotton Mather, in his *Midnight Cry*, all but shouted from the rooftops: "I am verily perswaded, we are now Entred into those Earthquakes, which are to attend and assist The Resurrection of our Lords Witnesses," the end of the world, "the Coming of our Lord." Or, as Mather also dubbed it, the "Glorious Revolution."[22]

There had already been two political Glorious Revolutions—one in England, another in New England. These events suggested to Mather the chaos before the apocalypse. But other signs of that chaos had appeared—"the very Indians which are now preying upon our East" and their killing of young children. "Plagues of War and Smallpox, and Fever" all afflicted New England. Yet more was to come. Revelation foretold how at the millennium Satan would escape from hell and convince many to join him—his forces would swell for the great battle of Armageddon. What was happening in 1692? "While you are Sleeping, the Devil is Busy; even to throw his Nets over you; and you are Hagridden by the most ugly things Imaginable."[23]

Not surprisingly, Mather announced in another work that "I have indeed set my self to Countermine the whole Plot of the Devil against New England, in every Branch of it." His determination was vital because "An Army of Devils is horribly broke in upon the place which is the Center, and after a sort, the First-born of our English Settlements"—Salem. The revealed witches there were soldiers of Satan; their ranks had to be decimated before Armageddon. Confessed witches had seen

the light and switched sides. Those who did not confess had to be dealt
with promptly. The judges surely shared Mather's apocalyptic view. When
Mather's calmer side emerged, he could advise the judges to be cautious.
He did not want innocents executed because that would diminish the
forces of the righteous at Armageddon. When his millennial side came to
the forefront, he cheered the judges on and defended them.[24]

While learned ministers and judges contemplated the end of the world,
the more humble farmers around Salem were distressed by a more down
to earth concern about the fate of their livestock, a very important matter
in a rural area. Indeed, strange things were happening to animals. As one
disturbed farmer observed: "I had a cow well [healthy] in the morning as
far as we knew. This cow was taken strangely running about like a mad
thing a little while and then ran into a great Pond and drowned herself."[25]

Witchcraft seemed the logical explanation to many when their animals died unexpectedly. One witness complained that after "differences"
with an accused witch "Evil occurrences" happened and he suffered "some
strange losses . . . amongst our cattle."[26] Witchcraft was not behind
these mysterious deaths.

A better explanation involves ergotism, a fungal infection that sometimes has the hallucinogen LSD in it, which has been suggested as a
possible reason for the strange behavior of people during the Salem episode. No evidence exists, however, that the fungus entered the human
population and significant reasons why it probably did not affect people
at Salem. Bread made from grain infected with the fungus can be very
discolored and few would eat bread that was pink or purple. For that
matter, ergot in a crop of rye is very visible and most individuals, again,
would not consume it. Experts even disagree if a child can receive ergotism by breast-feeding.[27]

Animals, though, can be infected with ergotism by grazing on grass
that has the fungus. More pertinent is the practice of farmers, even in
modern times, of feeding obviously infected grain to their animals. The
various mad cows running about and other oddly acting animals can be
easily explained by ergotism and not by satanic actions.[28]

Ergotism can not explain every curious ailment among the livestock
in Salem. Take the fate of Isaac Cummings's horse, which looked "burnt
with a Red Hot Bridle" where it rubbed against the horse. The horse's
"soft inner hooves" were also badly "bruised as if she had been running
over the rocks." And it refused to eat. Suddenly, the mare died.[29]

The culprit in that case is a fungal infection far more obscure and deadlier than ergot. Named in the Soviet Union during the twentieth century, alimentary toxic aleikiia is caused by a mold called Fusarium that can infect rye. The condition is marked by a variety of symptoms. Skin can be seriously discolored "with the least scratch or trauma"; blood can appear in urine; and glands (even in the groin) can get swollen. Most serious is swelling in the "oral cavity" leading to "difficulty in swallowing." If this swelling becomes too extensive, an animal's or human's air supply is cut off bringing about "strangulation." The unfortunate mare mentioned above clearly had alimentary toxic aleikiia (often abbreviated ATA). The horse's skin appeared seriously disrupted whenever there was any rubbing or contact around the bridle and the inner hoofs which touched the ground. Nor could the animal eat and it seems to have died when air could no longer reach its lungs.[30]

Unlike the case with ergotism, there is strong evidence that ATA affected the human population of Salem, not just its livestock. A man accused of witchcraft, John Willard, was blamed for the health problems of his in-laws, the Wilkins family. Seventeen year old Daniel Wilkins, Rev. Samuel Parris of Salem Village asserted, was "bewitched to death." Wilkins's skin was seriously damaged—a sign of ATA. At his end "he appeared to be choking shortly before he died"—an indication that swelling caused by ATA had strangled him.[31]

Young Wilkins's elderly grandfather, Bray Wilkins, also displayed symptoms of ATA. Bray Wilkins, whose ordeal is well known, insisted that his health problems started after a disagreement with his son-in-law John Willard. Almost immediately afterward, Wilkins discovered that he could not urinate and "could not dine, nor eat." His inability to urinate soon caused excruciating pain, as if he was "on a Rack." His condition suddenly cleared up after "Willard was in chains" although now, making up for lost time, his urine kept flowing out. A short time later, during a conversation with "friends," Willard was mentioned. Very promptly, the old pain returned and his urine "turned into real blood" but this reappearance lasted only about a day and he survived.[32]

Bray Wilkins's suffering has been attributed to a urinary disorder such as stones, which were common in New England, or an inflamed prostate. But Wilkins never mentioned seeing stones. In addition, an inflamed prostate is a long-lasting condition that will not go away quickly and certainly not in the seventeenth century. None of these other problems prevents an individual from eating. Recall that Wilkins said he could not eat—not that he had lost his appetite. Just like the horse, Wilkins ATA-induced swollen oral cavity stopped him from eating. ATA probably caused his prostate gland to swell, preventing urination, the likely cause of the great pain. This fungal infection is notorious for "relapses, especially if [the victims] are reexposed to the toxin." Since the relapse occurred right after a gathering of friends (presumably male) it is important to note here that ATA can survive in beer that has been made from bad grain. Perhaps Wilkins, being a good host, drank the last of an old batch of beer and gave his friends a new brew made from uninfected grain. Certainly, his bloody urine can be caused by ATA. John Willard was hanged for witchcraft because of what was caused by this fungal infection. Whether or not ATA affected anyone else in Salem is unknown.[33]

Whatever the impact of ailments upon the witchcraft trials, the death of Willard and all those executed in 1692 ultimately happened because of the actions of some young girls in Salem Village. An agricultural settlement some miles away from the port city itself, Salem Village still was within the town of Salem's borders. The two girls in question, Betty Parris and Abigail Williams, lived with their father and uncle respectively, Rev. Samuel Parris. He had been ordained only a few years before, in 1689. As an ordained minister, Parris was empowered to baptize and give out communion.[34]

Exactly how the witchcraft frenzy started has always been a bit vague. In January 1692 Parris gave a sermon that dwelled on the devil. This talk may have inspired the two bored girls living in his home. Apparently, though, the traditional version of events has validity. Betty and Abigail appear to have been trying to use one of "the Devils tools," an old English custom of fortune-telling called a "Venus glass." This curious practice involved a glass and an egg. And what did they want to know? According to Rev. John Hale of a neighboring town, the girls were curious about their eventual husbands thus "one door was opened to Satan to play those pranks; Anno 1692."[35]

Although Mary Beth Norton disputed that such fortune-telling occurred, the practice is mentioned in the Salem witchcraft records and beyond. In 1702 Parris's successor, Joseph Green, had to twice rail against divination from his pulpit, and the custom still existed in Salem Village as late as 1746. Children seem to have been very intrigued about divination. Folk traditions take a long time to die out, if they ever do.[36]

Tituba, Parris's Indian slave from a Spanish colony, may have told the girls about such fortune-telling. Though not born in English territory herself, Tituba could have learned about it either in Barbados or Boston, wherever Parris bought her. A Venus glass was in the same league as colonial Spanish customs. Magic in the domains of Spain centered on what has been called "love magic," which focused on what husbands might be doing and controlling their behavior. Although Tituba did not mention fortune-telling when she confessed, that omission is easily explained. She confessed because Parris whipped her. The minister had every reason to convince his slave not to mention what his family members had been doing. Instead, Tituba presented the girls as victims, not children who had dabbled with "the Devils weapons."[37]

In fact, both of Tituba's confessions are filled with supposed threats of killing Betty, Abigail, and others. Imagery from northern Europe such as broomstick flight, which Spanish culture thought absurd, were detailed by Tituba, suggesting as well that Parris had given some specific orders about what to say. Tituba willingly related anything else her interrogators wanted to hear.[38]

Whatever folk wisdom the girls tried, both started acting weirdly. There is no clear reason for this behavior. Abigail, as the older child at 12, likely was the ringleader. Little is known about Abigail Williams except her age and her blondish hair. Aside from her age, Abigail's aggressive words with a minister in the church suggests she was behind what happened.[39]

Another hint exists about why she acted as she did. In a conversation with an adult, Abigail named "the black man" she had seen: "She told me it was the devil. I asked her if she was not afraid to see the devil. She said at the first she was and did go from him but now she was not afraid but could talk with him as well as she could with me."[40] At the age of 12 Abigail had a weak hold on reality. The young girl may have been suffering from some psychiatric disorder.

Abigail Williams had a continuing role during the witch trials, a role she enjoyed. Young Betty, however, was sent by her father to stay elsewhere which removed her from Abigail's influence. Away from Abigail, Betty Parris calmed down and soon disappeared from the witch frenzy.[41]

But that was still in the future. Concerned about the girls in his household, Rev. Parris summoned a doctor. His diagnosis, that witchcraft was involved, stirred up Salem Village. The girls identified as witches Tituba and two other women who looked or acted like witches, Sarah Osborne and the poor and hostile Sarah Good. Good stated that Osborne was responsible for the girls' condition, which seemed to prove the presence of witchcraft. Tituba's confession about odd, devilish creatures and the sinister "tall man of Boston" greatly interested the authorities. Testing her, they questioned her a second time. When the second confession "agreed exactly," the examiners, "encouraged," moved on. More and more suspects were accused as the frenzy continued.[42]

Rapidly, what Norton has christened the "core group" of accusers formed. This victim chorus expanded beyond Abigail to include teenagers, some married women, and an occasional male. Among these new recruits was Ann Putnam, Jr., another young girl. She was joined occasionally by her mother and another woman, Sarah Bibber, who was in her thirties. Teenagers (and some in their twenties) who enlisted in the victim chorus were, among others, Elizabeth Hubbard, Mary Warren, Mary Walcott, Mercy Lewis, Elizabeth Booth, Susannah Sheldon, and Sarah Churchwell (or Churchill). Additional victims joined in from time to time especially John Indian, another Parris slave and the reputed mate of Tituba. Seeing the turn of events, John Indian became an active accuser. The role of the young and older women was essential because girls such as Abigail younger than 14 were too youthful to be considered reliable witnesses by themselves. With such an assortment of victims, the witch frenzy became a very substantial affair. All of them, especially the female servants among the chorus, surely relished the attention and power their accusations gave them.[43]

Whatever can be said about the motives of the victim chorus, they put on a good show that astounded their audience. Watching as a spectator, Samuel Sewall was full of awe over the apparent sufferings of the victim chorus. The writer of an official transcript asserted that they were "almost killed." The numerous fits that they seemed to experience sometimes affected the very people they were accusing of witchcraft. Rebecca Eames, who was spat at during her questioning, later related that she was "hurried out of my Senses by the afflicted persons." A number of times the show appeared incredibly real. Mary Walcott managed to cut her "arm till the blood came." However, Mary Warren topped that when, during one fit, she "was brought neare having a pin run through her hand and blood running out of her mouth." After the show had concluded and the "scores of strange fits in a day" had stopped, Thomas Brattle noticed that the victim chorus was "hale and hearty, robust and lusty, as tho' nothing had afflicted them."[44]

On other occasions the show seemed more like a pantomime. Abigail Faulkner, Sr., supposedly possessed of an "evil eye," only had to look at the victim chorus and they all had fits. When John Alden was ordered to look at them, "he did and then they fell down." When Alden asked a magistrate how could he look at him but "not strike him down as well," no answer was forthcoming.[45]

Evil eyes notwithstanding, almost anything an accused witch did could result in a coordinated response. When Mary Easty grasped her own hands, the chorus did the same; when she lowered her head, they lowered theirs. Whenever Bridget Bishop moved at all, the chorus had fits; when she looked up, they looked up. "Why you seem to act witchcraft before us," the magistrates insisted, "by the motion of your body, which seems to have influence upon the afflicted." Both Easty and Bishop were hanged.[46]

What defense could be mounted against what Bernard Rosenthal has called "calculated . . . behavior"? A member of the victim chorus only had to say, "Oh she is upon the beam," and an accused witch was in serious trouble.[47]

Not surprisingly, anyone undergoing a witchcraft examination in Salem faced an extremely stressful—and sometimes physically danger-ous—situation. In one case a chorus member tossed "her muff" at Martha Corey, "but that flying not home, she got off her Shoe, and hit Goodwife C[orey] on the head with it." Sarah Cloyse fainted during the question-ing (and some of the chorus, seizing an opportunity, had fits). Elizabeth Cary, under questioning, cried and sweated and came close to fainting. Asking if she could lean on Nathaniel Cary, her husband, a magistrate responded "she had strength enough to torment those persons, and she should have strength enough to stand." Her courageous husband's com-plaints—he risked drawing attention to himself—brought an official de-mand "to be silent or else I should be turned out of the Room." With him silenced and decorum restored, the proceedings continued. Soon John Indian "fell down and tumbled about like a Hog." A touch test proved that Mrs. Cary was responsible. Jailed, she was forced to wear iron chains and had "convulsions." Nathaniel Cary broke his wife out of jail. As a seaman, he had a means of escape. The couple fled from Massachu-setts.[48]

Nathaniel Cary's bold public declaration that he "desired that God would deliver us out of the hands of unmerciful men" had been asking for trouble. Those individuals who confronted the victim chorus usually did not do well. George Jacobs, Sr., who said "You tax me for a wizard, you may as well tax me for a buzzard I have done no harm," was executed. "We must not believe all that these distracted children say," Martha Corey insisted; she was hanged. When Ann Putnam, Jr., "threw her Glove in a fit" at Susannah Martin, she laughed. Asked why, she remarked: "Well I may at such folly." After another similar display, she "laughed again." Susannah Martin was hanged. Laughing had not helped Jacobs either. Elizabeth Proctor, after being accused by Abigail Williams, said "Dear Child, it is not so. There is another judgement, dear child." It was not wise to call attention to Abigail's age. Both she and young Ann Putnam then "had fits." Elizabeth Proctor, convicted of witchcraft, escaped death because of her pregnancy.[49]

Trying to defend oneself was not what either the magistrates or the victim chorus desired. What they wanted is demonstrated by Mary Lacey, Jr.'s behavior during her examination. After she confessed about being a servant of Satan "not above a week," she "did Ernestly ask Mary Warren Forgiveness for afflicting of her and both fell a weeping Together etc." Another penitent, Hannah Post, said "She would go Shake hands and beg pardon of the afflicted persons and not afflict them." Her relative, Susannah Post, joined in her sentiments. William Barker, Sr., also repentant, not only renounced Satan "and all his works" but added that the victim chorus did "God good service. And that he has not known or heard of one innocent person taken up and put in prison."[50]

What happiness the magistrates must have felt during such joyous occasions which proved quite a contrast to how Dorcas Hoar reacted to the chorus on May 2, 1692: "Oh! you are liars, and God will stop the mouth of liars. You are not to speak after this manner in the Court[, a magistrate ordered]. I will speak the Truth as long as I live." Wisely, she changed her mind right before her execution, confessed, and survived.[51]

Sometimes, however, the victim chorus split. One lucky man, Nehemiah Abbott, Jr., was accused by Ann Putnam, Jr., of being "upon the beam." But, for the only time, that did not seal an accused witch's fate. For some reason, Mercy Lewis seemed fond of him. The other chorus members decided Abbott was not hurting them. He became the only individual vindicated before a trial.[52]

The most bizarre example of a division in the victim chorus involved Mary Warren. Elizabeth Hubbard, furious that Warren had commented "that the afflicted persons did but dissemble," accused Warren of tormenting her; the others had the standard fits. So did Warren, who became incoherent. Some witnesses came forward and told the magistrates that Warren publicly had implied the victim chorus was crazy. She had stated as well that "her head was distempered" and that she probably had not seen any spectres. Despite all that, the magistrates, whose professed motto had become—"We came to be a Terror to evil doers"—continued to accept Mary Warren as a credible witness against others. Servants of Satan had to be uncovered.[53]

Authorities who took a self-admitted crazy woman seriously had no trouble going after church members. This was an odd affair, as Nathaniel Cary would emphasize, "considering what a People for Religion, I mean the profession of it, we have been." Especially amazing to Cary was that "most" of the accused witches had been "unspotted" in their lives "till their Adversary the Devil took up this Method for accusing them."[54]

In spite of Martha Corey being a church member—a "Gospel Woman" in her words—she was not totally unspotted. She had given birth to a child of mixed race. However, what endangered Mrs. Corey was a spectral vision experienced by Ann Putnam, Sr. According to Mrs. Putnam, Corey's spectre tried to kill her. Giles Corey, the accused's husband, all but finished her off with odd stories such as their dispute about killing a family cat. He also did not support her story about clothing supposedly seen on her spectre. However, Giles Corey, who was 80, may have had a mild stroke. He had wanted to pray, he revealed, but "could not utter my desires with any sense" or "open my mouth to speak." Memory loss after a stroke is common. Perhaps that explained his not remembering a conversation with his wife about the clothes.[55]

Given Giles Corey's history in the community, he should have been suspected of witchcraft before his wife. In 1647 and 1648 he fell asleep during guard duty with the militia and did personal business while on duty. Charged with theft a number of times, Giles Corey was accused in 1678 by John Proctor of having set fire to his house. Although cleared of that charge, another neighbor insisted that Corey, "a very quarellsome and contentious bad neighbor," had stolen many things from him.[56]

Despite Corey's church membership, a husband of a suspected witch was thought to be a possible partner in her evil designs. A spectre of Giles Corey was spotted trying to kill. Both Coreys joined the ranks of the accused.[57]

Another Puritan church member, Rebecca Nurse, became one of the 46 people fingered by the Putnam family. (Another Putnam target, Sarah Osborne, died before she could be tried.) Nurse's parental family had

had run-ins with the Putnam clan over land. Ann Putnam, Jr., no doubt egged on by her mother, claimed to have seen a spectre of Nurse. Nurse's own mother had been called a witch in the past, making it easier for this new accusation to stick. Mrs. Putnam chimed in with a horrific tale of being visited by spectres of a host of dead people, all claiming that Rebecca Nurse had killed them; Nurse's spectre admitted killing others. Either Mrs. Putnam had a mental disorder or she was consumed by hatred of Rebecca Nurse.[58]

Nurse's own religious temperament made her fatalistic about what was to come. Ill and in bed when she learned about the charge against her, Nurse "sat still awhile being as it were amazed and then she said . . . I am Innocent as the child unborn but . . . what sin hath God found out in me unrepented of that He should Lay such an Affliction upon me in my old age."[59]

In spite of the insistence of neighbors of John and Elizabeth Proctor that "they lived [a] christian life in their family and were ever ready to help such as stood in need of their help," such sentiments did not save them from charges of witchcraft. Elizabeth Proctor had a family history of witchcraft charges and the misfortune of having the crazed Mary Warren as a servant. She denounced both her master and mistress as servants of Satan. Abigail Williams claimed that spectres of both Proctors pinched her. Spectral evidence put the Proctors in jail.[60]

Notoriety, not Christianity, appeared most prominent in two other cases. According to neighbors, Sarah Good's hostility resulted in the deaths of cows, pigs, and sheep. Her threats did not help her reputation, and her denials of witchcraft did not convince anyone. Even her husband, William Good, suspected her. Authorities talked her daughter Dorcas—at most five years old—into calling her mother a witch. Dorcas confessed to performing witchcraft herself, resulting in her being in jail, enchained, for months. (An eight year old agreed to say that her mother, Martha Carrier, turned into a talkative cat—black of course.)[61]

Another notorious case, that of Bridget Bishop, may have been one of the few that would have resulted in a conviction in normal circumstances. Bishop had been falsely accused of witchcraft two decades before, but such charges tended to live on even if they had been retracted. There was more old baggage. About 1685 a neighbor complained about Bishop's late night shuffleboard parties. Soon, the neighbor, apparently bewitched, killed herself. Another neighbor, who complained about Bishop's straying chickens, was nearly killed by her spectre. Workmen found poppets—complete with pins—on her property. Still another person blamed her for the death of his child in 1690. When accused again in 1692, her guilt seemed obvious when a devil's mark was found on her body.[62]

Nonetheless, the importance of Sarah Good and Bridget Bishop paled in comparison to the "very Puny man" who became the focus of the witchcraft frenzy. Rev. George Burroughs had for a time preached in Salem Village but had moved to Maine, now devastated by the Indians. Wisely, Burroughs had finally settled in Wells and so had escaped the destruction of more northerly Maine communities. In April 1692 Abigail Hobbs, a refugee from Maine, admitted having surrendered to the devil there and had bragged about it. Soon the victim chorus identified Burroughs as her leader—which she then seconded. The examiners believed that they had uncovered a particularly dangerous ally of Satan, the "little black minister that lived at Casco Bay." Tituba's mysterious tall man in Boston had now become a short man in Maine.[63]

Unfortunately for Burroughs, one of the victim chorus, Mercy Lewis, had been his servant in Maine. Burroughs, Salem Village gossip asserted, had mistreated his first two wives, who had died. During his stay in Salem Village, Burroughs had run afoul of the Putnam clan. Not surprisingly, Ann Putnam, Jr., supplied with information from Lewis, first brought up Burroughs's name as a spectre she had seen. And what tales came from young Ann. Burroughs had recruited Hobbs, and had cast spells upon Sir Edmund Andros's forces in Maine—no wonder so many disasters had befallen that bewitched land. The minister's dead wives—now spectres—revealed he had killed them and these spectres even had a confrontation with a spectral Burroughs. Still more incriminating, the spectral minister insisted that, as a conjurer, he ranked higher than a mere witch. Salem and Maine were now united as fronts in the war against Satan, explaining why the witches said Satan "resembles an Indian."[64]

Burroughs was brought to Salem to answer the charges levelled against him. The victim chorus did its usual routine, which strongly hinted at "collusion." Despite the reputation of fluency Puritan ministers have, Burroughs was not verbally nimble. When asked during his eventual trial why his accusers were so afflicted they could not testify, Burroughs "supposed it was the Devil." Then came the crushing response: "How comes the Devil so loathe to have any Testimony . . . against you?" Stunned by the trap he had entered, Burroughs was "cast . . . into very great confusion." His acknowledgment that toads, often associated with witchcraft, were near his house hurt still more as did his failure to take communion recently. Furthermore, most of his children had not been baptized. Burroughs, unordained, could not baptize his own offspring.[65]

Even Burroughs's substantial physical strength turned into a weapon against him. Strong as a child, he had a long history of exaggerating his prowess. In Maine he kept saying, to many people, that he could lift a heavy barrel filled to the brim with molasses. Of course, nobody had actually seen him do it. He had also made a habit of supposedly clutching a "very heavy" gun equipped with a "seven foot barrell" with just "one hand." A witness could not hold it "with both hands." Such strength appeared to be a gift from Satan. In reality, Burroughs had used trickery, much like a modern day magician. Burroughs admitted that he leaned the stock of the weapon upon his chest; apparently, he also managed to distract onlookers who never realized they had been bamboozled. A nice trick, but it confirmed what the spectral evidence had made him out to be—a servant of Satan.[66]

One other factor helps to explain why so many people came forward to testify about Burroughs's superhuman strength. When Andros still governed the Dominion of New England, Burroughs in Maine had written to the governor supporting his belief that the town grant of land Burroughs had received was invalid—no towns had been created according to the norms of English law. Observing that he had actually farmed on the land, a fine point with Andros, Burroughs asked that the governor formally give him the land and agreed to pay a quitrent, another Andros innovation. Such an attitude, which likely became well known, would not have endeared the minister to some of his neighbors, making him a pariah among enemies of the now-defunct Dominion.[67]

Another link with Andros may have brought the Salem merchant Philip English to the attention of alleged victims of witchcraft. English had been born on one of the Channel Islands, Jersey. Andros also came from a Channel Island, Guernsey, a neighbor of Jersey. In the tense atmosphere of 1692, such small details could cause suspicion and bring forth a charge of witchcraft. Nor did it help that his wife, Mary, had a family history of witchcraft accusations.[68]

As the stories of Burroughs and English suggest, the witchcraft frenzy had escaped the confines of Salem Village and had reached to the port of Salem and as far away as Maine. Charges of witchcraft also spread to neighboring towns around Salem, causing Mary Beth Norton to comment that the whole episode might be better dubbed the "Essex County witchcraft crisis."[69]

Nearby Andover, swamped by witchcraft charges, is a good example of this geographic spread. A parent of an ill girl brought in two members of the victim chorus—probably Elizabeth Hubbard and Mercy Lewis—to determine if spectres were behind the sickness. Not surprisingly, they spotted spectres and accused witches were rounded up. After agreeing to arrest dozens of suspects, Justice of the Peace Dudley Bradstreet—a son of the old governor—decided to stop the arrests. Promptly accused of witchcraft himself, Bradstreet fled the Bay colony.[70]

On May 14, 1692 the new governor of Massachusetts, Sir William Phips, arrived, finally ending the uncertainty about the colony's future government. As Phips later commented, he discovered that the Bay colony had been "miserably harrassed with a most Horrible witchcraft . . . which had broke in upon severall Townes." Informed that it was "much like that of Sweden about thirty years ago," and that the jails were crowded because of this satanic crime wave, Governor Phips appointed a special court to deal with the crisis. This court moved quickly to try the suspects. It was Judge William Stoughton's fate, Cotton Mather believed, to be God's "instrument for the extinguishing of as wonderful a piece of devilism as has been seen in the world."[71]

Stoughton and his colleagues did their best to extinguish Satan's plot in Salem Village. Although Burroughs's trial attracted the most spectators, that of Rebecca Nurse is most noteworthy. At first, the jury found her innocent, but the judges refused to let her go. Twisting one of her comments out of context, the judges ordered the jury to treat it as a confession. The second time, the jury declared her guilty. This was a hanging court.[72]

On June 10 Bridget Bishop was hanged and the court briefly recessed. Nathaniel Saltonstall, one of the appointed judges, wanting no further connection with the trials, resigned. Then he was accused of witchcraft, a personal ordeal that did not end for months. In February 1693 Samuel Sewall noticed that Saltonstall had been drinking heavily.[73]

Saltonstall's departure from the court did not slow the pace of the executions. On July 19 Nurse, Sarah Good, Susannah Martin, and two others were hanged. Good's last words still ring out. Before her hanging, Rev. Nicholas Noyes of Salem called on her to admit her guilt, but she declared: "I am no more a Witch than you are a Wizard, and if you take away my Life, God will give you Blood to drink." Such defiant words might have caused some to doubt the justice of the hangings, but Cotton Mather was not among them. Instead, he soon rejoiced when some accused witches from Andover confessed and assured everyone that the five hanged people, along with Burroughs, had all been their colleagues in the service of Satan.[74]

Burroughs's own end came on August 19 along with John Proctor, George Jacobs, Sr., John Willard, and Martha Carrier. Margaret Jacobs, who had helped convict Burroughs, came to him beforehand to ask for forgiveness. Her wish was granted and he "prayed with and for her."[75]

Quite a crowd assembled to see the death of the ringleader of the witches. But Burroughs amazed his audience. He declared his innocence and, to top off his performance, he recited the Lord's Prayer perfectly. His correct rendition demonstrated that something was truly wrong—a witch could not say the prayer. In fact, Burroughs "drew tears from many so that it seemed to some that the spectators would hinder the execution." To prevent such a rescue, the authorities quickly hanged him. Cotton Mather, in attendance, rushed to the defense of the legal process, recalling "That the Devil has often been transformed into an Angel of Light." The crowd calmed "and the Executions went on." Nonetheless, both Willard and Proctor were "very affecting and melting to the hearts of some considerable Spectators."[76]

The executions of August 19 proved to be a serious blow to the witch trials. Sewall recorded that most of the ministers present—even Noyes— were now convinced that those five supposed witches were not witches. Cotton Mather dissented, Sewall revealed. "They all died by a righteous sentence," Mather insisted. Still, the eventual change in public opinion about the trials owed a great deal to those who witnessed this mass execution. Unnerved by Burroughs's performance, the authorities continued to collect evidence against him after his death.[77]

But more executions were to come, including a very medieval one. Giles Corey, despite declaring his innocence, refused to accept a jury trial and thus was "standing mute." The action taken in such a case was called pressing to death—stones were piled on the individual until he died. In 1710 a member of Corey's family called the procedure a "cruell and painfull . . . death." Why was Corey willing to die in such a way? Since 1840 it was believed that being pressed to death saved property from seizure by the government. However, that was clearly not the case.[78]

So why did Corey accept the idea of being crushed by stones? Perhaps he thought a trial was a waste of time, but there is always a chance that a surprise could happen; no uncertainty exists with pressing to death. The answer seems to lie in the medieval nature of the punishment. To a seventeenth century mind, hanging was a decidedly more humane form of execution than such a medieval relic as pressing to death. Even the authorities tried to talk him out of it. By preferring such a brutal end, Corey may have been making an appeal to public opinion. Could he have hoped that a public outcry would save him? If so, Corey did not reckon with the ever vigilant victim chorus.[79]

Ann Putnam, Jr., once again tortured by spectres, had gotten the news from a dead man that Corey had pressed him to death and so he should have the same fate. She suggested that hanging was "an easy Death," hinting that Corey was, indeed, playing for sympathy. Young Ann was just tossing a story out as she had done many times already. This time, however, she jogged the memory of adults, including her father Thomas Putnam. He recalled that in 1676 Corey had been involved in the death of his servant Jacob Goodale, "a Natural Fool." Presumably, Goodale was mentally retarded. Putnam insisted that the inquest jury wanted Corey tried for murder, but nothing happened "tho' it cost him a great deal of Money to get off."[80]

The Essex County court records have plenty of detail about Goodale's death, including the autopsy report. Two witnesses, one of whom was John Proctor, testified that Corey had savagely beaten his servant; Corey admitted it. But Corey's second wife insisted that Goodale's own brother had also savagely beaten him over some apples. Another witness said that Jacob Goodale, while he was dying, complained that one of Corey's sons-in-law, John Parker, had "struck him with the side of a bed."[81]

Given that Goodale had experienced three terrible beatings in a short time, death because of internal bleeding is a logical possibility. In fact, Putnam's mention of "clodders of Blood about his Heart" (which apparently refers to the jelly mentioned in the autopsy report) does indicate internal bleeding. Corey was not indicted because no one could be certain which of the beatings actually caused the death. No bribe was given— Corey had to pay a fine and compensate certain people for their time. So much for the Putnam family's version of local history. The report of Corey having pressed to death his servant cheered Samuel Sewall and became another justification for Corey's punishment, which occurred on September 19.[82]

A few days later, September 22, additional hangings took place. Martha Corey, Mary Easty, Ann Pudeator, Samuel Wardwell, and four others died at the gallows. Wardwell is known to have insisted that he was not a wizard, but Martha Corey upstaged him "with an Eminent Prayer upon the Ladder."[83]

During the Salem witchcraft frenzy, twenty people had been executed so far. Except for Giles Corey, all were hanged. Two dogs also suffered the ultimate punishment. One canine of Salem Village was supposedly bewitched and ridden by another son of Simon Bradstreet, John Bradstreet, who wisely fled. An Andover dog who afflicted everyone it looked at incurred the death penalty too. Any ally of Satan had to be dealt with severely.[84]

But would the witchcraft executions—both human and animal—continue? As things turned out, the executions of September 22 became the last. One factor lessening the death toll is that some prime targets decided to flee. Not trusting the "lying Spirit" of the victim chorus, John Alden escaped from imprisonment and so avoided a trial. Philip English and his wife both forfeited their bail and journeyed to the colony of New York where they found asylum as did the Carys.[85]

Another factor, other than fortuitous escape, ended the witchcraft frenzy. As early as May 31, 1692, Thomas Newton, the first prosecutor at the trials, wrote that he had been present at an examination of accused witches "where I have beheld most strange things scarce credible but to the spectators." Once away from the spell of the victim chorus, what happened in Salem was just not credible. That reality explains Newton's eventual resignation and also why Phips tried to suppress written accounts of the transactions. Written descriptions of events there made them seem dubious at best, a fact as true in 1692 as it is today. What happened on August 19 drove the truth of the mess at Salem home to many.[86]

How, for example, would educated people have reacted to a tale about a talking fly? Another story—John Westgate's testimony against an Andover suspect—should have raised eyebrows too. After a sojourn in a tavern, Westgate experienced a stunning encounter with what can only be called the Hog from Hell. Of course witchcraft was behind the satanic swine. In a different case, when some butter that an accused person sold spoiled quickly, sorcery was the explanation.[87]

Perhaps the most incredible tale involved testimony against Burroughs given by a leading member of the victim chorus, Mercy Lewis. She coopted a story from the Gospel of Matthew in which Satan tempted Christ. Lewis said that Burroughs told her "that the devil was his servant."

Burroughs then transported her to a mountain and offered her every country if she signed up with him. Anyone hearing her relate this story must have been shocked. Every Puritan in earshot would have known her account to be totally contrary to the scriptures. Satan's great pride had pushed him to try to place himself above God. Satan now would not be serving a Puritan minister (and one not ordained to boot). Most shocking to a Puritan audience in 1692 was a teenaged female servant putting herself in Christ's place. Such a corruption of scripture should have sowed much doubt, but not, of course, to Cotton Mather who noted the story with approval.[88]

Plenty of other evidence emerged that indicated that the victim chorus had been faking everything. On June 1, 1692 Sarah Ingersoll, a tavern employee, notified the authorities about what one accuser, Sarah Churchwell, had confessed to her. Churchwell admitted to lying and added that Rev. Noyes—and no doubt the others engaged in the investigation—simply "would not believe her" if she said "the truth . . . a hundred times." A different witness described how the accusers, for a laugh, pretended to see spectres in his presence. Seeing spectres, it appears, constituted "a jest." Still another concerned witness told of a supposed victim who, when he told her "she lied" about a spectral vision, got the response: "she did it for sport they must have some sport."[89]

With such reports spreading about, it should not surprise that opposition to the witchcraft trials appeared even before Burroughs's execution. On August 9, 1692, Robert Pike, one of the leaders of the Bay colony, complained to one of the judges. Noting the uncertainty of spectral evidence, Pike emphasized that it "cannot be known when they are real and when feigned, but by the Devil's report." Satan was "not to be believed, because he is the father of lies." And Satan "may tell these lies to murder an innocent person." Mentioning what happened to Samuel, Pike believed that Satan could appear in the "shape" of "innocent persons." Why, indeed, would Satan reveal the identity of true witches? After all, witches "are a considerable part of his kingdom, which would fall, if divided against itself."[90]

Finally, one person accused of witchcraft decided to use the legal system himself. A Boston "Gentleman" filed a defamation suit, asking for £ 1000 in damages against his accusers in Andover. Apparently, the gentleman had at least one friend in Andover with a good memory. In 1659 John Godfrey of Andover had filed a similar suit against those who had branded him a witch.[91]

October 1692 saw many more blows to the trials. A disturbed individual said that the wife of Rev. John Hale was a witch. Suddenly, Hale realized that Satan could assume the appearance of innocents. More important, in October Thomas Brattle wrote a devastating letter against the trials, which was clearly passed around to influential people. Brattle, a leading colonial astronomer, in a few years would help found a church that bore his name. Although not a member of the Royal Society, it regarded him highly.[92]

Written to an unidentified cleric, Brattle's letter may have been provoked by and written to Cotton Mather, whose own book, *Wonders of the Invisible World*, was being composed about the same time. Intending his tome in part for an English audience, Mather may have sent the manuscript to Brattle, a leading expert on the visible world and known abroad, to get his approval thus boosting its appeal there.[93]

If Cotton Mather had hoped for Brattle's endorsement, the minister would have been very surprised. Brattle attacked every aspect of the trials, calling a touch test "sorcery, and a superstitious method, and that which we have no rule for, either from reason or religion." Echoing Pike's attack on spectral evidence, Brattle dismissed listening to spectres which he called "testimony" directly from Satan. If such evidence was taken seriously, Brattle warned, "our liberty vanishes, and we are fools if we boast of our liberty." Most disturbing to Brattle, he observed, was "that ages will not wear off that reproach and those stains which these things will leave behind them upon our land."[94]

Brattle made a point of mentioning to his clerical correspondent that it was best to "retract" actions that were "amiss and irregular." Certainly, Increase Mather had written a book that attacked the liberal use of spectral evidence.[95]

In spite of Brattle's not very subtle hint, Mather did not back off. His *Wonders of the Invisible World* was a full blown defense of the Salem trials. Nor did the stand of Increase Mather and other ministers faze him. On October 20, 1692, the younger Mather, writing about criticism directed against himself, declared: "That I run against my own father and all the ministers in the country, merely because I run between them when they are like mad men running against one another, they can make me no reparation; however, my God will!"[96]

Despite Cotton Mather's apologia for the trials, Governor Phips had now gotten into a very difficult mess. Phips had encouraged Mather on with his book, but circumstances changed quickly. By October 1692 "many hot words" had been spoken about the Salem witchcraft trials which had become "a very great scandal and stumbling block to many good people." Phips knew how public opinion had shifted. The governor feared the "likelihood of kindling an inextinguishable flame." He could not have forgotten that the people of the Bay colony had overthrown Sir Edmund Andros. Furthermore, the trials were a threat to prominent people as Saltonstall had discovered. The trials could anger Massachusetts so much that another revolution might erupt.[97]

A witchcraft accusation even reached into the governor's own household when Lady Phips, his wife, was identified as a witch. But the governor himself was a potential target. Treasure hunters such as Phips were often suspected of using suspicious techniques such as divination. Phips also seems to have been interested in astrology. With his wife accused of witchcraft, he might be next.[98]

In addition, Phips may have learned more about what had happened in Sweden. The truth was far different from what Cotton Mather implied in his *Wonders of the Invisible World*—that there was only one false accusation in that witchcraft episode. In reality, hundreds of Swedish children eventually admitted that they had lied. Four accusers, including a teenager, received the death penalty there.[99]

Phips needed advice and he chose to go to a man who had been a political enemy, Joseph Dudley. Far from being surprising, consulting Dudley was very logical. As chief justice of the Dominion, Dudley had presided over the last witchcraft case in Boston that resulted in an execution. The accused witch had confessed and not under duress. Dudley had just returned from New York where he had served as chief justice. He obviously seemed to be an authority on laws about witchcraft. Most important to Phips, however, Dudley had not been associated with the Salem proceedings. Advice he gave would not be colored by a need to defend his earlier behavior during the trials.[100]

What Dudley suggested to Governor Phips is obvious. Acting for the governor, Dudley wrote in early October to ministers of different faiths in New York asking for their ideas about witchcraft, including spectral evidence. One of them, Church of England minister John Miller, specifically questioned the reliability of the victim chorus. After each fit, the chorus was "cheerful, healthful, and merry," not traits expected after satanic torture. The other New York ministers apparently agreed with Miller.[101]

Phips, now armed with the opinions of ministers in New York and New Englanders such as Increase Mather, shut down the special court that had condemned so many people. Bail was granted to some jailed suspects. When a new court met in January 1693, 52 cases were dismissed because the use of spectral evidence had been limited. Although three more were convicted, that was the last thing Phips wanted—he reprieved them and another five who had been condemned by the old court. "When this prosecution ceased," Rev. Hale later wrote, "the Lord so chained up Satan, that the afflicted grew presently well." The frenzy had ended.[102]

Stopping the Salem witchcraft trials turned out to be Phips's major achievement or, perhaps, his only achievement. One other strange event of Phips's period in office involved an English naval captain, Richard Short, who in 1692 decided to find some deserters in Boston. Short found no deserters, but did seize two members of the Massachusetts House of Representatives. When Phips learned what had happened, he attacked Short with his fists in front of some amazed onlookers. Viola F. Barnes aptly observed that Phips had "an excellent pair of fists."[103]

Phips, who often uttered profanities, became an embarrassment to the colony. In August 1693 Chidley Brooke, a New Yorker, tried to talk with him, but

> found his reason was Drown'd in passion and the Storm increasing, so thought it high time to leave him. The gentlemen of his Councill present, all the while seemed asham'd of his behavior, and desir'd me to blame his education for what I saw. I told him his Governor was very hott. he Returned; Sir you must pardon him 'tis dogg-days he cannot help it.[104]

As Rev. John Higginson noted sadly, Phips "had run himself into Inconveniences, which have disobliged his friends." Ordered to England "to answer complaints against him," Phips left the colony for the mother country in November 1694 and died there in 1695.[105]

Although Phips had departed, other Puritans who remained in Massachusetts had to deal with the consequences of the Salem witchcraft trials. In 1696 a critic taunted Samuel Sewall by saying if someone walked around Boston carrying Beacon Hill, it was no big deal. So much for superhuman strength proving witchcraft. Finally, in January 1697 Sewall, at a church service, asked for forgiveness for his role as a judge at Salem.[106]

In 1693 Cotton Mather, after conversing with a woman who saw "Spirits," believed that "a new Storm of witchcraft" was going to hit the Bay colony as punishment for "the Iniquity" of the authorities in 1692. Yet the witchcraft plague never materialized. Shortly after Sewall's public apology, the younger Mather dreaded "Divine Displeasure" because of his "not appearing with Vigor enough to stop the proceedings of the Judges" in the Salem "Storm" of 1692. Having learned from God that he would be spared that horrible fate, he became joyful over God's mercy.[107]

Only in 1711 did the Bay colony formally remove the stain of "attainder"—which took all rights from a person—from 22 individuals executed or found guilty at Salem. These people or their heirs received compensation, payment of which was ordered in that year by the then governor of the colony, Joseph Dudley. The compensation did not lift William Good out of poverty; in 1712 he still received alms from the Salem Village church. Nor did it help the youngest victim of the witchcraft frenzy, Dorcas Good. As her father related, having been "chained in the dungeon" for months, the girl had been so "terrifyed that she hath ever since been very chargeable having little or no reason to govern herself."[108]

What happened to the "Vile Varlets," the victim chorus? According to Robert Calef, they demonstrated "by their Manifest Lives, Whoredoms, Incest, etc." just how detestable they were. The authorities agreed that "some" of them "have since discovered themselves to be persons of profligate and vicious conversation." In 1706 Ann Putnam, Jr., one of the most active accusers, was admitted to the Salem Village church. She declared "that it was a great delusion of Satan that deceived me in that sad time." She accused people "whom now I have just grounds and good reason to believe they were innocent persons."[109]

How did the Parris household, where the frenzy started, fare? His enemies forced Parris out of his pulpit in 1696. Tituba, imprisoned for a year, was sold when her master did not pay the fees due to the jail. Betty Parris married, was a mother, and lived to 1760. Abigail Williams was not as fortunate. According to Hale, when the Salem trials ended, "she was afterward followed with diabolical molestation to her death; and so died a single person."[110]

England dropped witchcraft from its catalog of crimes in the 1730s. Yet witchcraft prosecutions are not something banished to the remote past. In the United States the last known legal prosecution for alleged witchcraft happened in 1950 in Delaware.[111]

Let us close this account of Salem witchcraft by focusing on two of the major participants. In 1711, when Massachusetts would begin disowning the trials' legacy, Cotton Mather visited Salem again. Concerned about the activities of Quakers there, he made an observation that may also be a distant echo of 1692. "Where People do by Indulged Wrath Give Place to the Devil," the minister proclaimed, "and if the Evil Spirits, of Strife, and Envy, and Clamour, infest the place, who can imagine that the Glorious Lord will have his Tabernacle there?" He continued: "If . . . there be any Silly Contentions, Variances, Animosities in a Town," then peace was needed. "Let the Maxims of Peace govern the Town."[112]

But Susannah Martin, hanged as a witch, deserves the last word. She had referred to the "Master" of her accusers, and the examiners demanded to know "who do you think is their Master?" Her answer seems definitive. "If they be dealing in the black art," the realm of Satan, "you may know [their master] as well as I."[113]

Chapter 9

Joseph Dudley

John Gorham Palfrey greatly disliked Joseph Dudley who, as an advocate of royal authority, became opposed to the old Puritan commonwealth. Calling Dudley "treacherous," "arrogant," and insolent, Palfrey gravely damaged his subject's reputation. This negative image remained strong until 1911, when Everett Kimball, mentioning Palfrey's "evident bias," defended Dudley's public career. Kimball wrote a useful scholarly work but absorbed some of that bias. Although he rehabilitated Dudley's public life, Kimball complained about Dudley's personality and claimed, falsely, that "the hatred that attached to his name was deeper and more consistent than fell to the lot of any other man."[1]

Other scholars continued this assault upon Dudley. Richard R. Johnson, for example, criticized the "depravities of his nature" although he did have some good points. To Kenneth Silverman, Dudley was "divisive, and largely unpopular" as governor of Massachusetts.[2] Such comments are, at best, exaggerations. Merely because Dudley helped run the Dominion of New England does not make him a scoundrel. This essay will attempt to escape from distorted images of Dudley and to treat fairly this opponent of the old ways of the Bay colony.

Joseph Dudley was born on September 23, 1647. Puritan Thomas Dudley, a frequent governor of Massachusetts and his father, was then in his seventies making young Joseph truly "the Son of his Old Age." This fact explains the choice of Joseph as his name. The Puritans rarely doled out that name and usually allotted it to babies who fit its biblical usage. The Joseph of the Bible was born to an old patriarch, and Joseph Dudley fit the bill perfectly.[3]

Like any good Puritan lad, Joseph carefully studied the Bible and learned it well. He attended Harvard and seemed slated for the ministry. Increase Mather, whom Dudley later called his "spiritual father," was impressed enough by the young man to recommend that the Old North Church select Dudley to assist him in God's calling. But Joseph Dudley's future would be devoted to the secular world, not the ministry.[4]

After serving in the militia during King Philip's War, Dudley began to follow in his father's footsteps. In 1676 the voters of Massachusetts Bay wanted to punish long-time magistrate Daniel Gookin because of his sympathy for the Praying Indians. Throwing him out of office, they picked Dudley in his stead. The selection of Dudley suggested that a new era had begun, because he was the first native-born New Englander elected as an assistant.[5]

Dudley received his basic political education as a magistrate. He served on committees that delved into the coinage of the colony, an excommunication in a troubled church, and whether to raise ministerial salaries to encourage the clergy. And he also saw to it that people paid their taxes.[6]

Another unpopular task helped to point Dudley in the direction of his future career. Appointed to a committee to examine the colony's compliance with England's mercantile regulations, in 1679 Dudley and his fellow committeemen urged that the colony watch trade more closely so that no "lapse be Committed whereby the Countryes Creditt and peace be Indangered." Dudley and others came to feel that ignoring English complaints about the colony's conduct was foolish and threatened the charter. When the English government placed Edward Randolph in charge of the customs of Massachusetts Bay, the political extremists among the Puritans obstructed him. Along with some colleagues, Dudley opposed such interference with a royal official.[7]

In 1682 the General Court selected Dudley and John Richards to serve as the colony's agents in England. By any standard, theirs was to be a difficult task. They had to fend off attacks upon the charter with little ammunition of their own. When they got into a tight spot, the two agents were ordered to say that they had "received no instruction in that matter." The General Court had successfully obstructed the king's officials for so long that such strategy seemed sensible. This time, however, it would not work.[8]

During June 1682 the agents sailed for England. The ill Dudley appears to have been lucky to have survived the trip. When the agents

reached England, they tried to defend their colony with the English bureaucrats. Not surprisingly, the agents failed and were ordered to get
real authorization. The agents' new instructions of March 1683, rather
desperate in tone, suggest that Massachusetts was in great trouble and
could even lose the Puritans' religious freedom. Grasping for a solution,
the General Court appeared willing to bribe the king by surrendering
Maine if no substantial changes were made in the Massachusetts charter.[9] Such concessions were too late to do any good.

As of December 1682 Dudley was still willing to work with Richards
in an attempt to stall action. Richards wanted both of them to be dismissed by the colony. If there were no agents, Richards assumed, the
English bureaucrats would be stymied. But Dudley had little faith in such
tactics. He later wrote that if the Puritan political extremists "had not
. . . utterly refused any submission" the charter would have been saved.
His stay in England convinced him that revocation of the charter had
become a certainty.[10] What was the point of battling the inevitable?

Edward Randolph hoped that Dudley could be converted into a servant of the king. Randolph expected that when Dudley discovered that
the English government insisted upon change, he would go along with it
because, as Randolph wrote, "he hath his fortune to make in the world."
Even a minor office would be enough to bring him over to the king's
side.[11] Indeed, Dudley had no immediate prospect of advancement from
the voters of Massachusetts; they usually elected elderly men to serve as
governor. Dudley, then in his mid-thirties, faced a wait of perhaps thirty
years—too long for an ambitious man—before he could be raised to the
governorship.

Dudley talked with Randolph and William Blathwayt and received
assurances that quieted any lingering doubts he may have had. From
Blathwayt, Dudley got an important, if vague, promise. According to his
letter to Blathwayt in 1683 from Massachusetts: "I am very Glad of your
Assurance that I have that you will no[t] forward any thing that may
discourage this plantation which . . . is very capable to serve his Majesty. . . ."[12] Joseph Dudley was surely convinced that he had chosen the
right path.

While in England, Dudley and Randolph drew up a list of councillors for the new government that was to replace the Puritan commonwealth. Dudley strongly favored having a temporary government for
Massachusetts until the English decided what they wanted to do with
New England. An interim government would help to lessen the impact of

future changes. It was also essential, he felt, "that persons Improved in the Government may be acceptable [to the people] and such as they may have some Confidence in." Naturally, Dudley was to be one of those "Improved" men. Randolph did everything he could to get Dudley appointed as governor of the future Dominion of New England, but that was beyond Randolph's power. Instead, Dudley received the presidency of the interim government.[13]

On October 27, 1683, Randolph brought the *quo warranto*, which ended the life of the Massachusetts Bay Company, to the General Court. With defeat in front of them, the Court argued over what should be done. Dudley and others urged obedience; Richards and his allies advised a legal battle. When, in 1684, the election of magistrates took place, the voters retaliated upon Dudley and some others by denying them re-election. Dudley informed Blathwayt that "Severall of the Magistrates but especially my Self have in a great Measure Lost our reputation with the people which yet I am not concerned for, for that I am sure I have persued nothing more than their own best Interest."[14]

The people of Massachusetts, though, did not see things that way. The legal form of the *quo warranto* frightened some, because it seemed to suggest that some individuals had been declared to be outlaws. Dudley learned to his sorrow that he had truly burned his bridges. "Since my return," he wrote in November 1684, his advocacy of surrender "hath procured me the Hatred of factious and ill Minded Men." He and an ally, William Stoughton, met with hostility from their political enemies and from some of the enraged common people.[15]

Dudley became concerned by this "strange Spirit in some of the people." Although hostility was also shown to Stoughton and others, Dudley believed that it was directed mostly against him. He lamented to Randolph that "if the New Settlement should take no notice" of him and his allies, the people "will fling up their caps for joy." The delay in creating the interim government had made him nervous that he and other "Loyall persons" had been forgotten by the bureaucrats in London. Despite his fears, he continued to condemn "the false and absurd Suggestions of Men whose hopes are built upon Confusions and Mischeifes." And he rejoiced that "the expectations of some evil minded persons" of the overthrow of the new king, James II, had been disappointed. By 1686 Dudley was pretending not to notice that the doomed Massachusetts Bay Company was starting its election process.[16]

At last, in May 1686, Randolph returned from England with Dudley's commission as president of the interim government. Some of the ministers tried to talk Dudley into refusing the job. After having endured so much hostility, there was no chance at all that he would refuse the honor. Nor did taunts about another Dudley's fate stop him. The Puritans remembered what had happened to Edmund Dudley, who had been a faithful servant of Henry VII; when the tide of public opinion went against this Dudley, Henry VIII had him executed. Working for a king could have unforeseen consequences. This history lesson did not frighten the new president.[17]

On May 17, 1686, Dudley appeared before the General Court to notify it about his commission. Or more precisely, he informed it that "we may not deal with you as a Governour and Company any more." The former Court members were now merely "considerable gentlemen of this place and Inhabitants of all parts of the countrey." Dudley vowed to do his best to forget "the unkindness of this good people and the many injuries they have done me." The president also promised to use his influence to secure freedom of religion for the colonists. Those complaints he learned about would be transmitted to London, President Dudley pledged. Some days later, the General Court adjourned itself out of existence.[18]

By May 25 the interim government of all New England, except Connecticut and part of Rhode Island, began its operations. The councillors took their places and the president addressed the assembled spectators:

> If there be any so ill minded as to suppose that we are now escaped from under a strict and severe Government, and think to allow themselves in debauchery and ill-living, (which hath hitherto happily been prevented from overrunning these Plantations, and which hath been the true cause of their being so much more considerable than their neighbours) . . . [the king's] commands . . . to us are expressly to the contrary, and most agreable to our own inclinations; and we . . . intend the suppression of all vice and ill-manners. . . .[19]

James II had no intention of turning Boston into an American Babylon. President Dudley hoped to convince the Puritans that a change in government did not mean a change in morals.

This approach was part of Dudley's plan to win the approval of the general population. In the first few weeks of his administration, Dudley sensed that his plan was working with some of the people. Although he realized that "a discontented faction" still opposed royal government, the president observed "no hazard but that the Government will be in all things Obeyed." The Council, though, made sure to place the militia under the control of "well affected" men.[20]

Dudley and his Council of New England especially wanted to reconcile the Congregational ministers to the new state of affairs. The Council ordered that all contracts that towns had made with ministers and school teachers remained valid. When Malden, Massachusetts, tried to cut the salary of its minister, Michael Wigglesworth, the Council prevented it. Ministers had their tax exemptions continued and were empowered to perform marriages. The Council also provided "for the strict observation of the Lords day." However, in November 1686 the councillors did urge one preacher "to hasten his Sermon because of the short dayes." Apparently, royal councillors did not relish long sermons.[21]

New England's legal system came under scrutiny as well. Courts were created, amateur lawyers were forbidden to charge for their services, and the jury system was brought into line with English practices. Dudley reminded Judge Samuel Sewall not to interfere in matters under the jurisdiction of an admiralty court. As for the potentially lucrative probate office, it was placed in the hands of President Dudley.[22]

Although Dudley's administration was much more sensitive than that of Sir Edmund Andros, the future governor of the Dominion of New England, the interim government was afflicted with many of the eventual problems of the Dominion. Dudley found it difficult to reach the Council's quorum, and his administration was "loaden with debts and no money to be found." Old taxes were continued, but the councillors agreed upon the "necessity of an Assembly." The Council of New England asked the king for "a well regulated Assembly to represent the people in making needfull lawes and levyes." But the request fell upon deaf ears. Moreover, the Council of New England saw the start of Anglican services in Boston. What was done was just not enough for Randolph. On the other hand, the appearance of the Church of England surely disgruntled the Puritan ministers, who were being carefully courted by the interim government.[23]

President Dudley also had to confront the depressed economy of New England, which had the added burden of a "poor, distressed people," the Huguenots. These French Protestants had fled from the persecution of Louis XIV, who in 1685 had ended religious toleration in his realm. Despite the bad economy in New England, the extremely generous Puritans helped the refugees. Joseph Dudley and his government coordinated relief efforts for the newcomers. Dudley's administration of an oath made the swearers English citizens. The Huguenots blended in well, becoming the first ethnic group in America to assimilate completely and disappear.[24]

Despite all of President Dudley's efforts, some open opposition to royal government existed. A number of men spoke "Seditious" and "treasonable words" for which they were prosecuted. Some others refused to obey a fast that Dudley's government had proclaimed. Perhaps the most telling example came in September 1686 when an English naval captain suggested that a bonfire be lit to encourage "Loyalty," an idea that the Council promptly rejected. Such a fire might accidently cause a disaster in largely wooden Boston and, the Council informed the captain, "the spiritts of some people are so royled and disturbed that inconveniency beyond your expectation may happen. . . ." Such comments boded ill for the success of the Dominion of New England.[25]

Oddly enough, even Edward Randolph became opposed to Dudley and the interim government. Randolph accused the president of being a "wind miller," who "has turned to Every Gale." Attempts to win over the Puritans to royal administration had disappointed Randolph, but he and Dudley split over another matter. Randolph and John George, the captain of H. M. S. *Rose*, feuded over who had the right to seize illegal traders inside New England's harbors. At one point, George threatened Randolph with a whipping. When Dudley supported George in the dispute, Randolph was unforgiving to his former friend and became his bitter critic. And Randolph pounced on Dudley's land speculation, a practice established in the president's own town of Roxbury well before his birth.[26]

By the time Dudley became president, he had already amassed a considerable amount of land. He and some partners owned two New England towns. Their settlers, lacking enough money to get started by themselves, had turned to speculators like Dudley who, in return for the land, willingly supplied the start-up funds. Dudley, though, had speculated in another way. In 1681 he and Stoughton made a deal with the Puritan government. They would serve as the colony's agents in the buying of some Indian land and would survey the property. As a reward, each agent received 1000 acres and both were allowed to buy some of the remaining land for themselves, a privilege they were not shy in using.[27]

During 1685 Dudley joined in with Richard Wharton, Stoughton, and others in the "Million Purchase," a huge land speculation gambit in New Hampshire and neighboring sections of Massachusetts. After the land was purchased from the Indians, the speculators compensated Robert Mason, who had claims to New Hampshire. The speculators gave shares in the Million Purchase to such men as William Blathwayt, who could get confirmation of the deal in England. When the interim government was established, the speculators of the Million Purchase and those with other land deals dominated the Council of New England. They soon used their authority to strengthen their land claims.[28]

A snag developed with the Million Purchase, however. The land deal had to be officially recorded by Randolph, who handled such matters. Randolph seems to have been shocked by the magnitude of the Million Purchase. He complained that the interim government seemed interested only in procuring land for its members. In July 1686 he observed: "I found [the Council] twas still but the Govr and Company with this alteration onely: they goodmen were most of them old and infirm and had lands enough." During May 1686 the speculators had given Randolph a share of his own in the land deal. Gradually, this action softened his resistance and he recorded the Million Purchase.[29]

Dudley's role as president ended when Sir Edmund Andros arrived in December 1686. Although no longer in charge, Dudley became chief justice of the Dominion, a very important post for a man in his early forties. As both a large landowner and a Dominion official, he could be "a good Example to others" about quitrents, which Andros wanted to institute in New England. Dudley obtained new deeds for his lands received from the old Puritan government—and the new deeds had quitrents written into them.[30]

If this acceptance of quitrents was a calculated move to influence Andros on the Million Purchase, Dudley greatly misjudged the new governor. Andros totally opposed such speculative schemes. Asked by the English government to look into the land claims, Andros declared that the speculators did not have a "clear" right to the land in question except for one area that Wharton had improved in the Narragansett country. Dudley and the other partners in the Million Purchase had their hopes dashed. Many of the speculators became foes of the governor and aided in his overthrow. But Dudley, a notable exception among the speculators, remained faithful to Andros.[31]

Dudley's service as the Dominion's chief justice brought him little but trouble. He presided over, for example, the trial of John Wise and the other Ipswich tax-resisters. Although Dudley's political enemies later accused him of having declared that the people were slaves, the charge was false. In another case, some citizens of Charlestown made a scene by bringing a duplicate copy of the old revoked charter into his courtroom.[32]

During the fateful days of April 1689, Dudley, hearing court cases in New York, was not in Boston. On April 21 the chief justice came to Newport and learned of the downfall of Andros. Letters warned Dudley not to return to Massachusetts. Quietly, he left Newport for a place of supposed safety, but some people tracked him down, seized him, brought him back to Boston, and jailed him.[33]

The chief charge against Dudley seemed to be his "Perfidiously under-minding the well-faire of his Native Countrey." A son of a Puritan governor, he had nonetheless joined forces with opponents of the Puritan commonwealth. From prison, Dudley defended his agency and denied the charge of his foes that he had turned Catholic. He denied ever having kissed James II's hand. He denied having been paid to destroy the charter or having purchased the presidency. The imprisoned Dudley also attempted to distance himself from Andros's more controversial actions such his handling of the Maine Indians and his demand that new deeds be issued to prove land ownership.[34]

Dudley's defense did not calm some of the more extreme foes of the Dominion. Due to Dudley's ill health, the revolutionary government on July 13, 1689, allowed him to post a bond, leave jail and return to Roxbury (where he lived) under a modified form of house arrest. Except for trips to church escorted by guards, he had to stay in his house and its immediate environs. But late in the evening of July 13, a "Rabble" appeared at his home and "Brought him like a dog" back to the jail. Soon after, he was allowed to leave and took refuge with a friend. Then on July 15 John Winslow, whom Andros had jailed, stirred up another mob by declaring "that Mr. Dudley would or should be in Prison again before night." The enraged mob pursued the ex-president. Seeing no alternative, Dudley went back into prison. Although Winslow was briefly jailed on account of his "sudden unadvised Speech," he was soon released. The revolutionaries did not condemn the "tumultuous disorder" involving Dudley, probably because the town representatives of the resurrected charter government had originally opposed allowing bail in his case. Dudley complained to people of note in England "how sadly the mobile [i.e., mob] use him."[35]

After several more months of confinement, Dudley complained in September 1689 to Governor Simon Bradstreet of the "many barbarous usages offered" him in that "horrible Jayle." To Dudley, being denied a chance to listen to a sermon was a major grievance. He felt "oppressed to death and death . . . as an Infidel . . . shut out from the worship of god. . . ." The following month, his fortunes sank still further. John Wise sued him for £ 500 because Dudley had denied him the use of the writ of habeus corpus during his tax-resistance trial. This incident was ironic—a jailed man denied habeus corpus was sued for denying it to someone else. The outcome of the case is unknown.[36]

Joseph Dudley remained in jail until January 7, 1690, when he was allowed to return to Roxbury; the representatives, once again, had at first resisted releasing him. Still not really free, he was required to be guarded by sentinels he had to pay. Finally, on February 10, 1690, the former president, Andros, and others were sent to England to be tried. What there was of a trial resulted in the prompt release of Dudley and the rest. Granted an audience with the new king, William III, Dudley urged the monarch to "thinke of New England to settle them againe." The king's measured response was gratifying but unspecific: William said "he would take Care of them."[37]

Instead of Dudley's unrealistic hope of an immediate royal appointment back in New England, Andros and Blathwayt used their influence to make him New York's chief justice. And Dudley accepted the job. Although not in Massachusetts, of course, it was better than nothing. On January 24, 1691, Dudley returned to Boston to visit his wife, family, and friends before going to his post. The chief justice of New York could not have guessed that while he enjoyed his reunion, a major crisis was brewing in New York that would greatly involve him.[38]

The ship bringing New York's new governor, Henry Sloughter, was diverted to Bermuda while the commander of its garrison, Richard Ingoldsby, sailed directly to New York City with his troops. When Major Ingoldsby arrived at the end of January 1691, Jacob Leisler, a militant Protestant then in charge in New York, refused to give the fort over to Ingoldsby. Leisler, with no proof whatsoever, seems to have believed that Ingoldsby and his soldiers were Catholic supporters of the deposed James II. Leisler, lost in fantasy, assumed that the Dutch William III would place New York's Dutch settlers in charge of the former Dutch colony; Leisler and his followers named themselves "Williamites" not "Leislerians." The dispute between Leisler and Ingoldsby became increasingly nasty. By the time Dudley reached New York, February 26, 1691, the situation was already on the road to tragedy.[39]

On March 17, 1691, Dudley wrote Blathwayt about Leisler's actions in New York. "We are forced to bear his Insolence and Intolerable reflections every day," the chief justice complained. Leisler's forces and Ingoldsby's men soon fired on each other causing some deaths. Some firing continued until Governor Sloughter arrived on March 19. The next day the crisis ended when Sloughter gained entrance into the fort.[40]

Leisler and some other Williamites were tried for treason. As chief justice, Dudley presided over the controversial trial. On the one hand, the Williamites objected to him, claiming "he was not a Competent Judge" because he had been with Ingoldsby. Later, Leisler's followers complained that "the Judges and particularly Mr. Dudley" stated "that Leisler had no legall authority at all" to take over New York. Leisler's opponents were just as furious at the chief justice. The New Yorkers deeply hated what Dudley called Leisler's "Intolerable Methods" and wanted their enemies executed. When two defendants were cleared of all charges, one anti-Leislerian blamed "the strange favourable charge given by Mr. Dudley" to the jury.[41]

Despite Leisler and the other defendants being found guilty, they were not immediately executed. Leisler's foes, again, blamed Dudley for the slowness in getting their vengeance. "President Dudley," insisted one critic, "demonstrate[s] on all Occasions, his affection and assiduous care for those of Leislers Faction, which tho he has not the Courage to own bare fact, yet itts manifest and apparent to all that are not very dimsighted. . . ." On May 14, 1691, New York's Council, with Dudley conspicuously absent, decided to execute only Leisler and Jacob Milbourne.[42] Apparently, Dudley, who had been victimized by mobs in Massachusetts, had no desire to participate in a sentencing that had all the appearances of a legal lynch mob.

Overshadowed by the difficulties caused by Leisler, Dudley had a smaller quandary. He had been given a commission to be the deputy governor of the proprietary colony of West New Jersey. Dudley seems to have been interested in the job while still in England. But by May 1691 he was backing away from the office and never performed its duties. Dudley had soured on serving in New York because of the Leisler affair as had some "uneasy" army officers. Of course, Dudley had family concerns pulling him back to Massachusetts. Nevertheless, even the prospect of dealing with his enemies in Boston was more pleasant than the vicious political scene in post-Leisler New York. In May 1692 Dudley abandoned New York for Roxbury.[43]

The Bay colony of 1692, much different from the province Joseph Dudley had grown up in, had been enlarged with the addition of Plymouth; Maine had been returned to Massachusetts. As for the government of Massachusetts, it was now a royal colony with a charter. According to this new charter, the Crown appointed the governor, lieutenant governor, and secretary. The people elected the lower house of the General Court, the House of Representatives. The representatives and the outgoing governor's council elected the new council, the upper house of the General Court. The royal governor could veto the election of a councillor. Increase Mather picked the first governor under this system, Sir William Phips, who has been summed up nicely by William Pencak as "hopelessly incompetent" and "truly bizarre."[44]

Meanwhile, Dudley had lost his position in New York because he no longer lived there, and Massachusetts appeared uncongenial to him. Its leaders, he lamented, "Look upon Mee as a strange creature in their forests." Some of his English connections urged him to seek a royal position in Ireland, but the prospect did not appeal to him. Instead, Dudley hinted to Blathwayt that he be appointed an admiralty judge, a very modest ambition for the former president of New England and chief justice of New York.[45]

Dudley, however, had misread the situation in his native province. The Salem witchcraft trials had diverted attention away from the old Dominion. In 1693 the House of Representatives almost elected Dudley to the governor's council. With the old hatred caused by his service to Andros evaporating, the former president realized that, because of Phips's antics, the governorship of Massachusetts seemed suddenly obtainable. Dudley's old ally, William Stoughton, angered by Phips's backing away from trying witches, favored replacing the erratic treasure hunter with Dudley. Another foe of Phips, Nathaniel Byfield, came to the same conclusion. By August 1693 Dudley left for England to bring down Phips and obtain the governorship for himself.[46]

Soon after Dudley's arrival, he became the lieutenant governor of the Isle of Wight, a military garrison in the south of England. The governor of the Isle, Lord Cutts, an important general of the time, had extensive military duties that often kept him elsewhere. He needed an able man to take over its administration when he was away. The job had many advantages for Dudley. Cutts could introduce him to influential men of the day, such as the Duke of Marlborough. In addition, Cutts's connections—and no doubt some of Dudley's money—got the colonial an army commission, a logical thing for the second-in-command of an important garrison. Besides, having the title "Colonel" could only be an asset for a colonial seeking a governorship.[47]

When Cutts was in England, Dudley's duties resembled those of a steward or personal secretary rather than a lieutenant governor. And Cutts, a difficult man to work for, seemed to enjoy reminding Dudley of his subordinate position. One reason Dudley took the job was to provide himself with an income while in England. To keep up appearances, he seems to have employed five servants, surely stretching his resources. In 1698 Cutts, furious at not hearing from Dudley in a week, reminded him that he could cut off his lieutenant governor's salary any time he chose.[48]

Lord Cutts also reminded Dudley that he was his patron. "You shall find," Cutts wrote him, "(take my word and honour for it) that your pains is not lost in serving me." And again, Cutts promised Dudley: "serve but the King, and me, effectually in this present storm, and I'll be instrumentall to put you in such circumstances as you shall have reason to be more than easy in."[49] Such promises of aid from the influential Cutts, just what Dudley wanted to hear, made him put up with the general's quirky personality.

Dudley needed all possible help in order to succeed Phips. Rev. John Higginson of Salem, Massachusetts, endorsed Dudley's bid and hoped that he would be another Nehemiah. Writing to an English dissenting minister, John Howe, Higginson emphasized the superiority of Dudley to an Anglican, a "Huffing Hectoring Blade," or a "hungry Courtier." Higginson added that, "so far as I cann judge," Dudley would "be acceptable to the generality of this people," although the Mathers and some others had not forgiven him for throwing in with Andros. For that matter, Higginson had not completely forgiven Dudley for that either, but "he was too Severely punished, when in the time of the disorders of the Revolution he was numbered with . . . the Transgressors of that time. . . ."[50]

In 1695 Joseph Dudley wrote Blathwayt that he still wished to be one of his "Dependents" and would happily fill "any vacancy in America." Without question, though, Dudley wanted to be governor of Massachusetts. During May 1695 rumors reached Boston that suggested that Dudley had won the job he coveted.[51]

Dudley had some major roadblocks in his path, including the unremitting hostility of Sir Henry Ashurst, a friend of the Mathers and the Bay colony's agent. Ashurst did everything he could to stop Dudley then and in the future. The Englishman thought that Dudley endangered Protestantism in New England. Apparently, Ashurst really did believe that Dudley was a secret Catholic.[52]

To embarrass Dudley, Ashurst threw his support behind a parliamentary effort to overturn the conviction of Leisler. Dudley, called as a witness, demonstrated that he knew little about conditions in New York before his arrival there. With Ashurst's guidance, the bill sailed through Parliament and became law. Dudley was surely exasperated by the Leisler case being brought up.[53]

The prospective governor had a more serious roadblock. Another candidate for the office, Lord Bellomont, had better connections than he did—Bellomont had the king's support. Bellomont became the new governor of Massachusetts. It all boiled down to some basic facts—Bellomont was an influential nobleman and Dudley was a colonial.[54]

Most men would probably have abandoned the quest after such a disappointment. Dudley's letters to his wife do express a yearning to be back with her in Massachusetts. When Benjamin Colman was in England, Dudley told him "that of temporal things he most desired to be with his Family and to be buried in the Grave of his Father." A mysterious back pain constantly reminded him of death, and a death far from his native land. By 1700 he worried that his debts incurred in England would force him to sell his New England property.[55]

Despite such concerns, Dudley remained in England in pursuit of his dream of becoming governor of Massachusetts. He could not give up. "If I now fayle of his Majestys favour after so Many Stepps of Advance toward it I shall account My Self undone," he confided to Blathwayt. If he had done something "injurious or unjust" towards New England he could understand the hatred of people such as Ashurst. What infuriated Dudley was being told that he was stymied "for standing up for the dependance of the plantations upon the Crown." How could he possibly give in when he felt justified in his actions? Joseph Dudley was just too stubborn to allow his enemies to defeat him.[56]

Dudley continued with his quest and made additional connections in English society. His efforts to cultivate the rich and powerful may have been easier for him than for most colonials. After all, he had been the target of "the foaming but impotent billows and surges of tumultuous anarchy and republican fanaticism."[57] Having been the victim of mobs surely earned him the sympathy of the English aristocracy.

Dudley's careful cultivation of helpful people was not in vain. During 1701 both Lord Bellomont and his lieutenant governor, Stoughton, died making the governorship of Massachusetts vacant once again. By 1701 Dudley's political assets had grown considerably as Cutts had secured him a seat in Parliament for the Isle of Wight. Dudley could support his desire for the governorship by pointing to his years as the Isle's lieutenant governor and his familiarity with the potentially troubling Indians of Maine.[58]

Everything seemed to be going well for Dudley. Even the Mathers supported him. Their former foe assured Cotton Mather that his long "absence has given Mee a New Value of My Country and the Religion and Virtue that dwells in it." Cotton Mather declared that Massachusetts would be fortunate to be governed by Dudley, "a gentleman that is our own countryman and perfectly understands how to serve the King, as well as how to ease the people." The younger Mather even promised to help reconcile Dudley with Sir Henry Ashurst, an impossible task. The Mathers' embrace of Dudley is logical: all three shared a common enemy, Elisha Cooke. By endorsing Dudley the Mathers hoped to regain some of their lost influence in Massachusetts.[59]

Dudley did everything he could to neutralize the continued opposition of Ashurst. A talk with the Archbishop of Canterbury about the Leisler trial convinced the cleric that Dudley was blameless in that matter. Everyone, the Archbishop assured Dudley, knew about Ashurst's "Violent way." Bringing up Leisler seemed strange after Dudley's "seven years Service on the Isle of Wight with reputation." Some prominent dissenting ministers also ignored Ashurst and wrote favorably to New England about Dudley. The powerful Sidney Godolphin favored him as well. General Cutts added his support and equated Leisler's Rebellion with Virginia's Bacon's Rebellion. And Blathwayt lobbied the king in Dudley's behalf. To give Blathwayt some interesting arguments, Dudley reminded him that New Yorkers involved in Leisler's execution were still in office in that province. Why should he alone be banned from office because of Jacob Leisler? Although Ashurst might claim that he opposed Dudley because of that affair, Dudley insisted that "the true articles against mee are My Long declared Resolution to keep that

Goverment in a strict dependance upon the Crown." Also angering
Ashurst, Dudley declared, was his intention to enforce the Navigation
Acts and so bring the colony fully into England's mercantile system.
Ashurst could not prevail against Dudley's forces.[60]

Meanwhile, in Massachusetts Dudley's supporters such as Nathaniel
Byfield had Ashurst removed as agent for the colony because of his
opposition to Dudley. Elisha Cooke and Wait Winthrop tried to obtain
Winthrop's selection as an agent. A thinly-concealed stratagem to boost
his own ambitions, the plan got nowhere. Byfield assured Dudley that
Ashurst's activity against him would "Receive the thanks but of about
half a dozen, Angry Ill Tempered men."[61]

Ashurst proved to be as stubborn as Dudley. Even while Dudley's
commission as governor was being prepared, Ashurst intervened again
and won a delay. Only after the English elections were over did Dudley's
appointment finally get through the bureaucracy. In February 1702 Dudley
at last had his long-sought office. Ironically, the king's death the next
month invalidated it, but the new sovereign, Queen Anne, reappointed
him in April.[62] Dudley could now return home triumphant.

On June 11, 1702, Governor Joseph Dudley arrived in Massachusetts. The bewigged governor swore his oath of allegiance while touching a Bible and then kissed it, a traditional Anglican ceremony. Five
days later, Governor Dudley addressed the House of Representatives for
the first time. He tried to stir his listeners' patriotism by reminding them
that, for the first time since the great Queen Elizabeth, England had a
queen as sole ruler. Just as Elizabeth had defeated Spain's dream of
world dominion, Dudley predicted, Queen Anne would defeat the ambitions of France's Louis XIV and so preserve "the Ballance of Europe."
Such stirring thoughts helped prepare his audience for the governor's
comments on the place of Massachusetts in the empire. He complained
that his province did not bring England the sort of financial rewards that
the more southerly colonies did. To redress this problem, the English
"Justly Expected of Us that We Use all methods . . . to Supply . . .
England With navall Stores, and other Comodityes there wanted. . . ."
Dudley also insisted that the Navigation Acts be carefully enforced.[63]
The governor soon discovered that the House had a different vision about
its duties than he did.

As for Dudley's reception by the colony's inhabitants, there were
some grumbles. In July 1702 some Charlestown residents appear to have
discussed assassinating him. Whether this was a real plot, a rumor, or

only some loose talk is difficult to say. Such feelings seem to have been created, not by Dudley's presence, but by the extreme use of impressment by a naval ship, H.M.S. *Swift*.[64]

On the other hand, the Mathers' reaction to Dudley is quite clear. Increase Mather tried to be gracious, praying that Dudley "may be such a Governour to this people as your Eminent Father was in the former Generation." Cotton Mather, however, fell out with the new governor in 1702. According to the minister's version, he merely advised Dudley not to join in with any particular party, whether that of the Mathers or the group headed by Byfield and John Leverett. Dudley, that "Wretch" (to use Mather's word), apparently assumed that Mather wanted some reward for his support—the governor should ignore Byfield and Leverett. When Dudley told the two men what Mather had said, they were "inflamed . . . into an implacable Rage against" the younger Mather.[65]

Once the Mathers discovered that the governor had no intention of turning Harvard over to them, both ministers resumed their old opposition to him. "The Generality of People throughout the Province have not the Love for . . . Mr. Dudley that were to be desired," Increase insisted in 1703. He added: "The old prejudices occasioned by his former mismanagements are revived." Years later, the elder Mather still wished "that the country were in other hands." Privately, Cotton Mather rejoiced in 1709 when "Ahab" (Dudley) snubbed him by not inviting him to a social gathering with other ministers. Rather than waste time "eating of his Dainties," Cotton could fast and so please God instead of his palate.[66]

The man best suited to governing Massachusetts, the Mathers thought, was Sir Charles Hobby, a Boston Anglican. Cotton Mather believed that Hobby, "Beloved" by everybody, possessed numerous virtues such as militia experience and a respectful attitude toward "conscientious Christians." Thomas Hutchinson was amazed that the Mathers could have detested Dudley so much that they supported Hobby, "a free liver." In spite of a voyage to England by Hobby, his campaign for the governorship failed.[67]

While the Mathers fumed, Dudley settled into his new job. The governor may have noticed how Massachusetts had changed from the days of his youth. He later estimated that in 1702 Massachusetts Bay had a population of about 50,000 people, calculated from militia totals. Despite the troubles caused by Queen Anne's War, the population grew by about a thousand a year. The increase came almost completely from natural causes as Dudley insisted that there was almost no immigration into the colony. Natural increase took place because Massachusetts Bay was generally much healthier than the other colonies.[68]

London had instructed Dudley to obtain a regular salary, a standard practice in almost every colony except Massachusetts. The House of Representatives had refused a salary to both Phips and Bellomont who had to be content with what were called presents or gifts. By giving out these presents twice a year, the House of Representatives kept the governor as dependent as possible upon itself. The House was trying to emulate the English House of Commons, which by its control of finances had greatly increased its role in government.[69]

When New Hampshire (of which Dudley had also been named governor) gave him a salary, Massachusetts became the sole holdout among the American colonies. The best he could get from the assembly was two gifts totaling £ 500. Another request from London, that the colony create an official residence for the governor, was also rejected. Try as he might, Dudley could never budge the House of Representatives on these issues.[70]

Nor were the assembly's gifts really adequate. Dudley estimated that a governor of the Bay colony needed, at the very least, £ 1000, because his expenses far exceeded the £ 500 he usually received. But, of course, Dudley was wealthy and had not wanted the job for financial gain; his home in Roxbury was close enough to Boston for him to go back and forth frequently. Nevertheless, the assembly's stance on his salary exasperated him when, for example, in 1708 the representatives gave the colonial treasurer a larger present than the governor. Not surprisingly, the governor became very insistent upon his right to the blubber of beached whales. The little money gained from such whales helped to partially make up for the tightfisted ways of the House of Representatives. And the small gifts led to a curious practice of private individuals giving presents of money to Governor Dudley.[71]

Another battle between Governor Dudley and the House of Representatives erupted over the ruined fort at Pemaquid in Maine. Pemaquid had been destroyed after Andros's overthrow. Although William III had ordered it reestablished, he had been ignored. When Queen Anne renewed the order, Dudley tried his best. In October 1702 the governor addressed the assembly and explained why the fort should be restored— "all the Stones necessary are in place, the foundation yet good, and Lime to be had very near and easy." These fortunate circumstances lessened the cost, Dudley explained, and added that the Indians of Maine had requested a trading post north of Casco. A committee from the assembly examined the site and agreed with the above assessment of it.[72]

Despite such positive reports, the House refused to restore the old fort, insisting that it had little real military worth and was too expensive. After Queen Anne's War broke out, they suggested that the colony could not afford Pemaquid because of the heavy expenses of the war. By 1705 Dudley informed the assemblymen that the queen had complained of "their great neglect of their Duty to Her Majesty and their own security. . . ." No matter what the Crown thought, Pemaquid stayed in ruins.[73]

Dudley had no chance of beating the House of Representatives on any financial matter. But he did gain some victories for the Crown by using the veto which the charter had given the governor. Before Dudley, the veto of councillors had only been used once—Phips had rejected Elisha Cooke—and the assembly imposed whomever it wanted on the governor. In 1703, however, Dudley vetoed five of the House's picks, including Cooke. The assemblymen did not like Dudley's strong use of the veto, but they had no choice except to accept it. After this purge, the governor only vetoed "One or two . . . to maintain Her Majestys Prerogative." The yearly reminder was usually exercised upon Cooke.[74]

Having resurrected the veto, Dudley sought to expand it. In 1705 the House chose Thomas Oakes as its speaker. The governor had previously vetoed him for the Council and now did the same with his election as speaker, claiming that the charter gave a governor the right to do so. Totally unprecedented, Dudley's veto created a donnybrook in both the House and Council. The governor eventually allowed Oakes to serve as speaker, because the dispute could have interfered with pressing business relating to Queen Anne's War. On this issue, however, London backed him and in the future the power to veto the speaker was added to the governor's small arsenal of weapons.[75]

Such victories as Dudley managed to eke out against the House of Representatives did not obscure the major defeat he suffered on salaries. Dudley insisted that the salary problem would never be over while the representatives had the power to block a salary. The Crown should see to it that a governor's salary was automatically taken out of a province's funds. Nor did the governor approve of the selection of councillors by the House, which had made a point of removing councillors who had supported repairing Pemaquid. "Those priviledges of Election of Councilours," he continued, "are no manner of benefit to these provinces, but are scandalously used to support partyes against the Honour of the Crowne and Government. . . ." Suggesting another reform, the governor urged the creation of a court of chancery, a weapon of the Crown in England, which did not use juries. The governor would head such a court, giving him some influence within the judicial system.[76]

If the Council of Trade and Plantations, the London bureaucrats who handled colonial affairs, had obtained Dudley's recommended changes, Massachusetts would have had a very different government. But Dudley's advice went unheeded by most of those with the power to act. The bureaucrats found it easier to send letters telling the assembly of Massachusetts to do its duty. Beyond that, the officials were not willing to go.[77]

In contrast to the sometimes frustrating job of governing Massachusetts, New Hampshire was comparatively a joy for Dudley. For example, he became the first governor of that colony ever granted a regular salary by its assembly. But he had some difficulties, especially because of John Usher, New Hampshire's lieutenant governor. Usher had a talent for stirring up trouble, which the governor had to quiet. Sometimes, though, New Hampshire felt neglected due to the fact that its governor lived in Massachusetts, despite his being only "ten hours" of travel away. During Queen Anne's War, New Hampshire's Council was especially edgy. As Dudley reminded them, when the queen appointed him governor of two colonies, she "well knew that I Could not be in two places at the Same time." All in all, New Hampshire had few complaints with Dudley.[78]

Although New Hampshire might be nearby, travelling there still was eventful for Dudley. In March 1705 he journeyed to the colony by sea, only to be battered by a dangerous storm. His ship managed to reach its destination safely. But even the land route had its perils. On December 7, 1705, he left his Roxbury home on an official trip to New Hampshire and Maine. Having sent his guards on ahead, the governor was driven by his son, William Dudley; one of the horses was difficult to control and the coach was loaded with much luggage. Soon after starting out on the trek, the party discovered that two wagons loaded with wood blocked the road. When Governor Dudley asked the carters to get out of the way, one responded: "I am as good flesh and blood as you; I will not give way; you may goe out of the way." In this the carters were wrong. Because the governor was on official business, he had every right to ask them to move. The incident got carried away, as both Dudleys drew their swords; one carter broke the governor's. The carters were jailed but soon released.[79]

Being governor of both New Hampshire and Massachusetts put Dudley in command of the entire northern frontier of New England from the border with New York to the farthest reaches of Maine. This extensive frontier was vulnerable to attack during war. And war was just what Dudley had on his hands. Soon after his return to New England, he learned that war had been declared in Europe between England and France. As in the past, Dudley realized, this European conflict would spread to the American colonies.[80] Called the War of the Spanish Succession in Europe, its North American aspect has been dubbed Queen Anne's War.

In Maine, the most endangered section of Dudley's governments, French Jesuits had converted the local Indians to Catholicism. The Jesuits, very influential with them, were not only men of God but also agents of the French empire who sought to turn the Indians against the English. In August 1702 Dudley visited the Indians of Maine in an attempt to keep them at peace. Fearful that the Indians might attack in the spring of 1703, the governor again visited Maine to talk with the sachems and was relieved at the result. According to Dudley, the sachems had left him "with good inclinations, I think to be sure, with all possible promises of friendship, and I believe the French will not easily get them out of my hands." Although some colonists had been shot at, only a "few straggling rouges" were responsible.[81]

Maine's Indians had some grievances against the New Englanders. Resentments from both the 1670s and King William's War still lingered. More recently (about June 1703) Dudley reported that some "Ill Men" had taken some Indian "goods" away from them. Judging from later evidence, these culprits may have been New England fishermen, whose relations with the Indians were not always cordial. The culprits were punished and the goods returned, the governor thought. The Indians were also concerned about a native boy whom Phips had taken to England. Without the return of this Indian, Governor Dudley saw no chance to redeem a handful of captive colonists who had been seized in King William's War. After an investigation, the Council of Trade discovered that the Indian still lived and was a servant to, of all people, Sir Henry Ashurst.[82] These grievances provided material for the Jesuits in Maine to use against the English.

During May 1703 Dudley received secret intelligence from New York about a French expedition that planned to hit Maine. To lessen the effect of such an attack, in July 1703 Dudley met with the Maine Indians, while the Jesuits stayed discreetly out of sight. The governor complained about the natives' "Sullen Temper," but he gave them expensive presents and they signed a treaty. Governor Dudley thought he had been successful once again and "left them in a better and treatable Temper." As evidence of his success, he noted that the Maine Indians had informed him about the enemy expedition on the move. On August 5, 1703, Dudley boasted that he had "concluded a better friendship with them than at any other meeting. . . ."[83]

Only a few days after the governor's boast, events proved that he had been very wrong. The French expedition, with allied Canadian Indians, arrived in Maine and promptly "debauched" the local Indians. Then on August 10 the French forces, aided by some local Indians, attacked isolated English colonists and led about a hundred settlers into captivity. Reported atrocities committed in the surprise attacks surely stunned Dudley, who had thought he had saved the peace with his treaty of the previous month. Before the initial shock had worn off, the enemy forces attacked the most exposed fortified areas in Maine. Casco endured the most serious attack but reinforcements from Boston came to its rescue. For about a month after the outbreak, the Indians moved in small groups throughout Maine "stealing and killing Like the Rapparees," who were Jacobite bandits in Ireland.[84]

On September 15, 1703, Dudley poured out his fury to the Council of Trade:

> The french and Indians have in this Occasion shewed a great deal of Cowardise and Cruelty, have not killed one man under his Arms, but by surprise, have scarcely saved any women or children but slayn many three dayes After they were prisoners and the Fryers make it all religion and say mass over Every thing publickly in the Camp Night and Morning. . . .[85]

The French denied that they had been involved with any of this and blamed it all on the Indians. However, Frenchmen captured by the English told a far different story.[86]

The death and destruction in Maine brought home to New Englanders what this new French and Indian war could mean for them. Without a careful defense, disaster loomed for the frontier. Dudley undertook to protect the frontier with 150 garrison houses. Formerly private homes, these strengthened fortifications provided bases for militiamen and a refuge for settlers under attack. Furthermore, Massachusetts prohibited frontier inhabitants from fleeing their homes under penalty of forfeiting their land. And Dudley vowed: "There shall be nothing wanting to the utmost expence to save the Frontiers here from depredations." Although the governor meant what he said, he acknowledged that there was no defense against small groups who could evade detection.[87]

Despite the great difficulties of defending an exposed frontier, the English colonists had a major advantage. Their friendly Indians served as an extremely effective spy network. Dudley and the governor of New York, Lord Cornbury (and his successor, Robert Hunter), all utilized Indian spies. In 1703, for example, Cornbury passed on to Dudley information gleaned from spies about the intended French attack on Maine. Dudley's own "faithfull Indians" kept him very well informed about French plans and even checked on the construction of Quebec's walls. In addition, not all Indians in Canada supported the French. A "Tatachquisero Sachim of Cachanuage neer Mont Royall" secretly supported the English. Such allies in Canada were very valuable to the English cause.[88]

One nugget of information that Cornbury sent to Boston was the French plan to attack Deerfield, Massachusetts. In May 1703 Dudley ordered the inhabitants there "to be in readiness." By the time the French and their allied Indians attacked Deerfield in February 1704, its people had received so many warnings that turned into false alarms that they grew careless. The garrison was caught unawares by the pre-dawn attack. Many of the town's citizens, including its minister, John Williams, became captives. Some of the inhabitants held out until help from surrounding areas appeared. But the enemy force escaped because the New Englanders lacked snowshoes. Luckily for the frontier, Deerfield was an isolated example of carelessness. The disaster there angered the colonists instead of frightening them.[89]

More typical than Deerfield was the attack on Haverhill in August 1708. Spies again provided information about the attack and this time the alert garrison repulsed the French and Indians. The price of safety, it seemed, was eternal vigilance. As Dudley commented in 1704, "nothing will prevent their Incursions so much as to let their own scouts find us in a readiness for them." The attackers were indeed discouraged when they found the frontier "Lined with men."[90]

In Maine, Dudley chose a more offensive defense, which was basically how Sir Edmund Andros had battled the Indians there—"Constant Marches, Especialy in the winter to dislodge and starve them." The settlements in Maine were too scattered to protect easily, so Dudley decided to prevent the Indians from growing crops and fishing. Frequent "hard marches" were needed to make certain that the natives could not use their old settlements. "I am assured," Dudley declared in 1704, "if wee Keep not the warr at a distance they will Employ us nearer home." The colonists succeeded in keeping the Indians three hundred miles from the endangered communities. On the whole, this policy worked. Concern about Dudley's strategy made the Jesuits quickly convince the Indians to leave their habitations in Maine. The Indians discovered that though the French could encourage them to go on the warpath, the French could not protect them except far from the English territories.[91]

This success was partly brought about by the English colonists' "snowshoe men." These soldiers, equipped with their snowshoes, could pursue the inevitable small groups of Indian raiders or undertake scouting parties during the winter. As Dudley noted: "the Indians are now sensible that we can walk upon rackets and carry our victuals as well as they." According to the governor, as soon as hostile natives saw "our Tracks" they became "sensible . . . of their Danger." Because snowshoes greatly increased the mobility of the New Englanders, the Indians had to camp much further away and by 1706 were "in a starving discontented condition among the French. . . ."[92]

Dudley took the war directly to the French as well. In 1704 Colonel Benjamin Church led New England troops, supported by English naval vessels, in an attack upon French settlements along the Bay of Fundy. Church's forces burned four enemy villages and devastated everything but the main base of Port Royal. At one point, the colonial army killed prisoners who had surrendered, an apparent retaliation for what the French had done in Maine. The harshness of this campaign appears to have been vengeance for that and the destruction of Deerfield. Governor Dudley believed that Church's foray prevented French attacks for some time after.[93]

By virtue of New England's geography, the colonies of Massachusetts Bay and New Hampshire bore the brunt of Queen Anne's War. Connecticut and Rhode Island, both shielded by Massachusetts, did not want to help in the war effort. In the early days of the fighting, Connecticut sent several hundred militiamen to some Massachusetts towns along the Connecticut River, a deployment that also protected Connecticut itself. These Connecticut soldiers refused any orders from Massachusetts and did just about what they pleased.[94]

Rhode Island served as a haven for young men of Massachusetts who wished to avoid fighting in the war. Sailors too used the colony as a safe refuge. Such behavior, which duplicated what had happened in King William's War, had a basic logic. Why stay in Massachusetts to fight and pay heavy war taxes, when in Rhode Island a man could avoid both the war and the taxes? The Rhode Islanders did send 48 soldiers to fight against the French, which was minimal aid compared to the burden Massachusetts had to shoulder. Although the Crown gave Dudley control of Rhode Island's militia, the colony simply refused to surrender the control to him.[95]

Dudley sent the Council of Trade a long list of charges against Rhode Island. He suggested that the problems with both Rhode Island and Connecticut would remain as long as they possessed charters that made them independent of royal government.[96]

The bureaucrats in London, stirred by the charges against Connecticut and Rhode Island, took some limited action against them. Taking advantage of a legal ruling in 1694, the bureaucrats suggested that a royal governor could be imposed upon the two colonies if they continued in their ways. However, Sir Henry Ashurst, then Connecticut's agent, prevented any chance of real action against either colony in Parliament. Before the Glorious Revolution, the Crown would probably have sought to nullify the colonial charters with a *quo warranto* court action, a major weapon of the throne against the holder of a charter who had abused it. In 1703, however, the will of Parliament had to be considered. The Council of Trade informed Dudley that nothing could be done without Parliament's approval. Some further gestures by Connecticut against the French later in the war helped remove what little pressure still remained.[97]

Dudley again became enmeshed with Connecticut because of its land dispute with the Mohegans. In 1703 the chief sachem of the Mohegans, Owaneco Uncas, complained to the Crown that Connecticut had taken some Indian land and distributed it to townships. Connecticut had refused to rectify the matter, and so the Indians appealed to their ruler for aid. London made Dudley the head of a commission to decide upon a settlement.[98]

In 1705 Dudley tried to investigate the dispute in Connecticut with the other commission members. However, Connecticut officials, insisting that Dudley's actions were illegal, prevented some persons from testifying and claimed, falsely, that Owaneco was not the ruler of his tribe. Dudley knew the truth about the status of Owaneco, who had just executed an Indian murderer of another Indian, a power that the sachems in Massachusetts had been denied for decades.[99]

Despite Connecticut's resistance, the commission continued to meet. With little more than the Indians presenting their position, the result was a foregone conclusion—the commission ruled in favor of the Mohegan claim. Contrasting Connecticut with Massachusetts, Dudley insisted that the Bay colony accepted "the Sachems' right to lands and purchased them justly, and have in every part strictly reserved lands sufficient for the Indians to dwell upon and manure."[100]

The decision for the Mohegans and Dudley's complaints against Rhode Island brought the governor much trouble. The Mathers and Sir Henry Ashurst depicted Dudley as a "Cunning" man seeking to destroy charter liberties. Allies of Connecticut and Rhode Island demanded his ouster. Judging from his letters, Dudley believed that his foes might have their way as opposition to him had swelled in the Bay colony. Supporting an Indian tribe at that time seems not to have been very popular in Massachusetts, a colony beset by hostile Indians. In a letter to Blathwayt Dudley suggested that if he lost his position in Massachusetts, he hoped he could remain in charge in New Hampshire, where, despite the Mohegans' case, his popularity was undamaged. Dudley's friends in England protected the too pessimistic governor from the barrage of criticism.[101]

Dudley fared better than his verdict. Connecticut appealed to England and Sir Henry Ashurst prevented the verdict from being approved. In the meantime, Connecticut returned some of the disputed land to the Mohegans. Years after Dudley's death, in 1743 another commission recommended that the old verdict be overturned and it was. Only in 1773, however, did Connecticut at last win the case.[102]

While the English colonists squabbled among themselves, the suffering of the captives taken by the French and Indians continued. Their captivities became longer because Dudley changed the traditional method of redeeming them. In previous wars, captives held by the enemy were bought back. The going rate for the captives was usually about £ 5 per person. Governor Dudley refused to engage in such "an Algier Trade"— the Barbary pirates of North Africa had made a profitable business from captives for many years. The governor believed that buying captives was counterproductive. Despite the "pitty" he felt for the captives, he had no intention of making "a market for our poor women and children in the frontiers." If the enemy Indians were seemingly rewarded for seizing captives, then the natives might decide "they would make better Imploy of hunting for Christians than ever they have done for Beaver."[103]

Dudley held to this policy in spite of all the terrifying things the captives endured. In one case, a hostile Maine sachem then in New-foundland sent a Maine militia officer a strange demand. Either he used all his influence to have Dudley removed as governor or all the English captives in Newfoundland would be executed. The threat was never car-ried out. More typical was the treatment of the captives in the heart of French Canada itself. The French tried to convert them to Catholicism and some women were put into convents. Some of the captives did con-vert and married their former enemies,[104] but such actions did not mean these people had discovered a better way of life. Wrenched from all they knew, some of the captives could not resist the psychological pressures put upon them. As a means of escaping from this terrifying situation, they completely identified with their captors and, in effect, joined in with them.

When word of the captives' sufferings drifted back to New England, their relatives and friends were very anxious to get them back. For that matter, so was Dudley. Instead of buying them back, he decided to seize enough French subjects and swap them for the New Englanders. Seizing captives was a goal of Church's expedition and it succeeded in that. Dudley then used these prisoners to redeem most of the captives held by the French, including John Williams of Deerfield. The minister returned to his town in December 1706, which brought joy to western Massachu-setts. Williams, thankful for his freedom, dedicated his famous captivity narrative to Dudley, "the prime instrument" in freeing them "from the tyranny and oppression of our captivity." Williams became a determined supporter of the governor and a critic of his foe, Cotton Mather. And the support of Williams and others on the embattled frontier became very important for Governor Dudley.[105]

The year 1706 was to see the greatest crisis of Dudley's administra-tion. This serious affair started innocently enough. Dudley authorized Captain William Rouse to sail to Port Royal to swap some French pris-oners for English captives. Unknown to the governor, Rouse arranged with another ship to meet him and they illegally traded with the enemy. Samuel Vetch, a friend of the governor, joined in the illegal activities. Rouse returned to Boston on June 10, 1706, and the secret trading did not stay secret long.[106]

When the crime was discovered, Vetch and his associates were jailed, but this was not enough to calm the fury of the inhabitants. The people had suffered much in the war—stiff taxation and frequent militia duty for the lucky ones, enemy attack for the more unfortunate. Taking advantage of an exchange of captives for personal profit caused, in Dudley's words, "an unusual heat in the people." The governor seemed to fear that mob vengeance might be meted out to the culprits.[107]

The question immediately arose as to how Vetch and his comrades could be legally punished. The regular courts did not appear to be a good alternative. The crime had been committed in Port Royal, a settlement not under the English flag. Technically, the charter considered Acadia (or "Nova Scotia") to be part of Massachusetts, but this assertion was about as real as the English monarchs' claim to the throne of France. Instead, the General Court wanted to delve into the affair and Dudley encouraged it. The governor, concerned that the popular fury would lead to injustice toward the culprits, warned that while bringing them to justice, the colonists should not "lose our own honor and the Honor of the Government upon which all depends." In line with this, he commented that he "was glad to see in the house of representatives a better and more steady temper in their proceedings" than that of the general population. Despite the General Court's weak charter justification for such a trial, the power "to impose Fines . . . Imprisonments and other Punishments," Governor Dudley supported its intention because the assemblymen were calm enough to try the defendants fairly.[108]

The General Court's trial of Vetch and the rest began in August 1706. Found guilty, they suffered very heavy fines. Rouse, for one, hit with a fine of £ 1,200 that he could not pay, was jailed. Dudley, writing to England, defended having the assembly take part in the process although he advised the Council of Trade that the fines should really be halved. In England, the Lords of Trade objected to the trial because of the very bad example it created for all of the American colonies. The last thing London wanted was to strengthen the powers of colonial assemblies, and the Privy Council overturned the convictions.[109]

Meanwhile, Dudley's enemies, including both Mathers and Ashurst, saw Vetch's gambit as a way to attack the governor. Dudley, after all, had authorized Rouse's trip and the governor was friendly with Vetch. Rumors that Dudley was involved with the illegal traders had already spread in New England. To capitalize on them, Nathaniel Higginson, who hoped to succeed Dudley, and others petitioned the Queen about his "corruptions." Cotton Mather added his venom in a bitter tirade about the *Present Deplorable State of New-England* that attacked both the governor and his son, Paul Dudley. Joseph Dudley's enemies suggested that he had been involved in the illegal trade and had permitted the General Court to try the traders, because he knew that the Crown would void the convictions.[110]

Dudley continued to deny that there was "one criminal Reflection upon me . . . with a Shadow of truth. . . ." The Council of Trade backed the governor; his foes had little proof to back up their rather wild charges. Dudley did permit Rouse to carry some nails and other items with him. Clearly, as Everett Kimball wrote, "the privilege was abused, and . . . this innocent permission was made to cover commerce of a more doubtful nature. . . ." The governor's foes also appear to have tampered with the document in which Dudley had given his permission. The number of nails was increased to try to hurt the governor's claim of innocence. Furthermore, as Dudley had been very unsuccessful with the assembly in the past, how could he have gotten that body to cover up any proof of his alleged guilt? And if Dudley did have knowledge of Vetch's illegal trading, then the governor had taken a tremendous gamble—Vetch could not keep a secret. When in 1705 Dudley had sent him to Quebec for talks with the French, Vetch boasted around the town about the intelligence he was gathering. Similarly, Vetch kept plenty of evidence that detailed his illegal activities at Port Royal. If Dudley had been guilty as his foes insisted, Vetch would somehow or other have given the governor away.[111]

This crisis gradually petered away as the charges against Governor Dudley could not be proven. In 1709 the General Court pardoned Vetch, who made amends by his activity against the French in Canada. As for the others, the year before their trials had been dropped.[112] They had already been punished enough.

Dudley and the Mathers also tangled over the fate of Harvard. The governor always tried to give Harvard men government positions, and he wanted to reward his ally, John Leverett, with the presidency of the college. Leverett, however, was seen as too radical by the Mathers and by a majority of the House of Representatives. With no other choice, Governor Dudley offered Leverett's opponents something else that they dearly wanted. If Leverett was named Harvard's president, Dudley suggested, he would allow Harvard's original charter to be in force. This offer contradicted his old stand that the first Harvard charter had died with the Massachusetts Bay Company. Jumping at the offer, the assembly accepted Leverett. Everyone but Dudley apparently forgot that the old charter had a much smaller governing board than that created by later, makeshift arrangements. Dudley used this opportunity to reappoint only allies of Leverett to run the school; supporters of the Mathers lost much of their influence over Harvard.[113]

When the Mathers realized that they had been beaten, they vented their anger at the governor. On January 20, 1708, they wrote Dudley and blasted him with everything they could think of, including the Leisler trial again. The governor soon wrote back to tell the ministers: "I must think you have extremely forgot your own station, as well as my character. . . ." Their letters were "insufferably rude towards one whom divine Providence has honoured with the character of your Governour." He informed the ministers that they had "gone out of your line." Finally, he taunted the Mathers with Paul "the Apostle's wholesome advice," that ministers should be quiet and mind their own business. Nevertheless, the Mathers continued to fume that a lawyer headed Harvard. Increase Mather even tried to lessen English contributions to the college. Their complaints were shared by Sir Henry Ashurst, who declared that Dudley was "perverting that Colledge" and was responsible for "bringing up a strange generation."[114]

Dudley's plans for Harvard pale in comparison with his plans for the future state of North America. He had an "imperial vision"—a New World dominated by England. If the French were driven away from Canada and Acadia, the situation in North America would be very different: "it would give Her Majesty a very great country, all the trade of furrs and fishery besides the Naval Stores, and for ever quiet the Indians, there being no body left on this side mexico to give them a Supply of armes or ammunition." The French could easily be driven from the north, the governor believed, with the assistance of the Royal Navy.[115]

Port Royal, the base of the French privateers that attacked New England shipping, was an important target. In 1707 an expedition of Massachusetts against Port Royal greatly disappointed Dudley. Soon after landing near Port Royal, the expedition abandoned the attempt but the governor ordered the forces not to return to Boston and to stay at Casco in Maine. While at Casco, the soldiers cried "Home, Home, Home." Ordered by Dudley to press the attack again, the troops, very grudgingly, obeyed. As one leader commented, "the Soldiers are generally come to resolutions to go forward no farther then they are driven." The army did go back to Acadia, made a token effort against Port Royal, and then returned home. Trying to make the best of this failure, Dudley consoled himself that the campaign had at least destroyed some houses and food-stuffs in Acadia while losing only a handful of troops.[116]

Dudley's desire to conquer the northern French colonies remained undiminished and in 1709 another attempt against Port Royal was set. The governor declared: "It is come to A plain Question who shall be masters of North America." But much of the available British naval strength refused to take part and the plan had to be abandoned. However, in 1710 the British navy did join with the colonists against Port Royal. Confronted by this vastly superior force, the French at Port Royal quickly surrendered.[117]

Conquering Quebec was the goal of a powerful British military expe-dition commanded by Admiral Hovenden Walker. This armada arrived at Boston in 1711, and Walker noted that Governor Dudley "appeared very zealous in promoting the Good of the Expedition." But Walker's expedition would end in disaster when some of his ships ran aground in the St. Lawrence River. Despite the disaster, Dudley and the General Court petitioned Queen Anne for another attack upon Quebec. London, however, was no longer interested. Dudley's imperial vision was no longer possible.[118]

Along with Dudley's encouragement of action against the French foe, he sought to regain the friendship of the Indians of Maine, who by 1710 had had enough of warfare. Eager to obtain provisions, they were willing to abandon the French to get them. Governor Dudley was just as eager to have them back in the fold. When some Abenakis, despite the peaceful suggestions flying about, assaulted two colonists, killing one, the governor did not seize the culprits. Instead, according to the con-cerned governor of French Canada, the Marquis de Vaudreuil, Dudley "made them presents, expressing to them the regret they felt at being at war with them, and giving them to understand that if they would live in peace, they would be far happier in consequence, and would have goods furnished at a much cheaper rate than we could supply them in Canada." To offset Dudley's peace initiative, the French dispatched a Jesuit to the scene and some still hostile Abenakis to attack the English colonists.[119]

However, Queen Anne's War was at last coming to an end. About November 1712 Dudley learned that the fighting had stopped in Europe and he spread the word to Canada. The governor believed that generos-ity was the best way to deal with the rebellious Indians of Maine, whose numbers had been greatly reduced because of the war. On July 13, 1713, the Indians of Maine agreed to a treaty that restored them to their land and rights as of 1693. In return, the Indians accepted the rule of Great Britain.[120]

On August 24, 1713, a relieved Dudley wrote that, because of the new treaty, he hoped for peace with the Indians "while the Peace of Europe Continues, and now our Poor People may again return to their business instead of standing under arms." But the New Englanders would still be troubled. Although Acadia had become a British colony, Nova Scotia, the French retained nearby Cape Breton Island. Because of French influence coming from there, in 1715 some Nova Scotian Indians attacked the New England fishing fleet. In addition, the Jesuits stayed in Maine and they inspired another Indian uprising in 1722.[121]

Massachusetts had been warring against the French for some years. Less obvious than this imperial struggle was another one between the old Puritan ways and different, often English, traits. In 1704, for example, Sewall complained about the festivities commemorating the queen's coronation, because the anniversary fell on a Sunday. "Down Sabbath, Up St. George," the diarist grumbled. Even the feast day of the mythical St. George, the patron saint of England, was celebrated in Boston itself. In such events, Dudley fully participated, as when he celebrated Christmas.[122]

These changes should not suggest that the Puritan religious establishment was falling apart. To the contrary, the establishment of the Congregational churches and schools had been restored in 1692. However, some towns in Massachusetts had refused to support a Congregational minister. Historic opponents of Puritanism such as the Quakers had learned how to circumvent the establishment. By concentrating themselves in certain towns, these opposers could elect as town officials men who were sympathetic with their views. These anti-establishment officers could then refuse to collect the special tax which would have gone to pay a Puritan minister's salary. During Dudley's administration, the House of Representatives tried to deal with two such anti-establishment towns, Tiverton and Dartmouth. The House increased the provincial "Publick Tax" of these towns to pay for a minister, but the Quaker tax assessors refused to collect the provincial taxes from the inhabitants. To have collected the taxes would have meant the appearance of an established church in their towns, and these assessors had no intention of allowing that to happen. In retaliation, the assessors were jailed, but the House was reluctant to press the matter. The assessors were soon freed and the assembly dropped its attempt to impose ministers on the two towns.[123]

Governor Dudley expected criticism from London over the assembly's action against the assessors. He insisted that excusing Quakers from the tax to maintain a minister was not realistic. Exempting "those that are strictly of their profession . . . would be no great loss," Dudley wrote, "but it is Expected that if such an Indulgence be given, a great many will profess themselves Quakers to quit themselves of this Charge. . . ." Other towns would soon also lack a minister. Earlier, the governor had defended the Congregational establishment in a letter to Blathwayt by suggesting that the government might someday be able to slip Anglican ministers into the establishment.[124]

Although the Congregational establishment could be breached and was, this fact does not mean that the towns that escaped it practiced toleration. Dudley related what ensued in Swansea, when its selectmen were Baptists: "there was a Sober Young Divine a Master of Art who preached to some of the People at their request; The Selectmen . . . Issued a Warrant to the Constable to Convent him as if he had been a Vagabond, and like to be Chargeable to the Town. . . ."[125]

Governor Dudley, almost accidentally, became involved in a dispute between Connecticut and the Quakers. That colony all but banned them from its territory and roused English Quakers to seek the repeal of that colonial law. As usual, Sir Henry Ashurst thought Dudley was behind the whole repeal campaign, but the governor's only role in it occurred in 1706 when he passed along to Connecticut official documents about the repeal.[126]

Notwithstanding the Quakers, the continued presence of the Church of England was the greatest annoyance to some New Englanders. Dudley had been instructed by London to promote the Anglican church and therefore had to walk a tightrope—if he aided the Anglicans he might infuriate the Puritans, if he did not he would infuriate his superiors in England. He tried to please everybody. He had been raised as a Puritan, and he worshiped in Congregational churches; he also conspicuously attended Anglican services in Boston. As early as the 1680s, he had acted similarly in London while hoping for preferment. Dudley's strategy had mixed results. Benjamin Colman, the minister of the Congregational Brattle Street Church, did not object because he knew where the governor's heart really lay. The Anglicans were more uncertain. In 1704 Samuel Myles, the senior Anglican cleric in Boston, wrote a testimonial for Sir

Charles Hobby, the Anglican who hoped to replace Dudley. On the other hand, in 1706 Myles praised Dudley's support of the Church of England. In 1714 Myles went back to urging that an Anglican be made governor.[127]

In England, Dudley had become a member of the Society for the Propagation of the Gospel, which had been created to foster the growth of the Church of England in the colonies. When he returned to Boston as governor, Dudley brought the Rev. George Keith with him. Keith, who had been a Pennsylvania Quaker, had converted to Anglicanism and was then an Anglican clergyman. Within a few weeks after his arrival, Keith had started a theological debate over predestination with the Puritan minister, Samuel Willard. Such a controversy was not to the governor's liking, and he did his best to ignore the contentious convert. Stirring up theological waters risked alienating the common people. Soon after Keith's provocation, a rumor spread that Dudley intended to have a Congregational church used for Anglican services as Andros had done. Not wanting that fear to spread, Dudley started legal action against one of the gossips.[128]

Dudley did his best to aid the Anglicans. He had Myles's salary raised and sometimes, when donations were too small, he himself made up the difference. As governor, he appointed Anglicans to provincial offices when possible. And the Church of England did grow. By 1711 King's Chapel was not large enough for its congregation and various Anglican visitors.[129]

But in the early years of the eighteenth century, Anglicanism began to increase outside of the capital. In Braintree some earlier interest in the Church of England finally became strong enough to create an Anglican congregation. Although Braintree Anglicans succeeded in launching their church, they endured much harassment and charges of insincerity. Forced to pay for a Puritan minister anyway, they continued to remain faithful to the Church of England. Calling them Catholics did not discourage them.[130]

The greatest controversy over Anglicanism during Dudley's administration concerned Newbury. At first the dispute involved something different. By 1709 the town had greatly grown in size. Residents on Newbury's outskirts, now very far from any meetinghouse, insisted that a meetinghouse be moved to make attending it easier for them. Such demands had been common in Massachusetts Bay as the various towns had expanded; the location of meetinghouses was one of the most hotly argued local issues. Everyone wanted to be near a church, but not everyone could be. In this case, the General Court decided which Newbury meetinghouse to shift to accommodate the more distant inhabitants. By 1711 a building was demolished and a new one erected far from the old site.[131]

While such an act may have been familiar in colonial New England, this time resistance appeared. Newbury residents nearest the destroyed church, which had been used for three decades, greatly resented what had happened. The new meetinghouse was too distant for them. Infuriated, these people decided to construct a new church at the old location, despite the General Court's order. Partly to spite and partly to circumvent the provincial government, these Newbury church builders announced that the new structure would be an Anglican church. In no other case had an entire Puritan congregation, complete with deacons, defected to the Church of England. But this defection was not known in Boston. As soon as the General Court learned that its will was being defied, it ordered that the insurgents stop rebuilding the meetinghouse. Governor Dudley, who also knew nothing about the sudden mass conversion to Anglicanism in Newbury, accepted the Court's action.[132]

Confronted by the new order, the insurgents might have given up if they had not then received the support of John Bridger, an Anglican royal official. Bridger, empowered to protect trees suitable for masts for the royal navy, had recently fallen out with Dudley. What better way to embarrass the governor than to aid Anglicans he had seemingly neglected? To Bridger's credit, he intended more than a gesture and provided much vital support. He helped them finish the building and wrote to Great Britain to alert the church authorities there about the need for an Anglican minister in Newbury. The insurgent Anglicans of the town became convinced that Bridger—not Dudley—was the only real ally of the Church of England in Massachusetts. And Bridger let London know his opinion that Anglicanism could not gain strength in the colony as long as a Congregationalist such as Dudley was governor.[133]

The Anglicans presented the governor with another difficulty. The Congregationalists of Braintree and Newbury continued to harass the Anglicans in their towns by forcing them to pay for the Puritan minister's salary. Members of the Church of England were supposed to be exempt from supporting a dissenting preacher. In Newbury's case, Dudley issued a statement declaring that the Anglicans (or the "factious crew" as Cotton Mather called them) were exempt from such taxes. Yet local officials, ignoring the governor, still harassed the Anglicans and made

Dudley look ineffectual. The situation at Braintree regarding the establishment taxes was similar to Newbury's. At last, in 1714, Governor Dudley could inform the Society for the Propagation of the Gospel that the harassment of Anglicans in both towns had finally ceased.[134]

During Dudley's final years as governor, he had to deal with another problem, that of a bank. For many years, the Bay colony had had a chronic shortage of money. Some private individuals proposed the creation of a land bank—currency would be issued with land as its backing. Governor Dudley, sounded out on this plan, had strongly supported the idea of a bank in the 1680s and reportedly was enthusiastic about the new project. But he soon changed his mind. The identity of the land bankers who talked with him is unknown, although they were probably men not active in politics. Most likely, Dudley opposed the private bank because he had determined that many of his most prominent political foes were associated with it. The governor succeeded in blocking this private bank, and a government-run bank replaced it.[135]

Among the people pushing for the private bank was Dudley's long-time supporter, Nathaniel Byfield, who had become opposed to the governor. Exactly how the two men split is not certain, but the reason may have involved a legal dispute over the disposition of a deceased person's estate. Whatever the cause, Byfield, angry at Dudley's "Devellish Ingratitude," journeyed to Great Britain to oppose him and to try to obtain a charter for the private bank. While in Britain, Byfield, according to Jeremiah Dummer, was "so excessively hot against Col. Dudley, that he cannot use any body civilly that is for him."[136]

Byfield's enmity was but one of the difficulties Dudley faced. After Queen Anne died in 1714, the new monarch, George I of the Hanoverian dynasty, removed the governor's allies in the British government. With Dudley's pillars of support in London toppled, his own downfall seemed imminent. Two allies of Dudley were still on the scene, however. Jeremiah Dummer supported him and the agent knew how to use his influence. In 1711, for example, Dummer succeeded in stopping a plan in Parliament to raise funds by imposing a stamp tax on New Englanders. A second ally was Sir William Ashurst, the brother of Dudley's nemesis. Meanwhile, in America Increase Mather lent his backing to the governor, because he suspected that a replacement might be even less to his liking than Dudley. On the other hand, Cotton Mather joined the forces against him. The governor would lose this battle.[137]

A soldier, Elizeus Burgess, named as Dudley's successor, never left for New England, so Dudley remained in charge for some time. In May 1715 he advised the House of Representatives not to delay paying debts from Queen Anne's War. Such a delay, he cautioned, would destroy the value of the colony's bills of credit "to the very great Injury of every Body that have taken them, or are in Possession of them. . . ." Also in May, Dudley, for the first time, did not veto the election of Elisha Cooke to the Council. Beginning with Thomas Hutchinson, historians have seen this as a reconciliation. More likely, Dudley hoped that Cooke would make trouble for the next governor. Another inconvenient act for his successor, sending the legislature home in October, shows that Dudley was not making a gracious exit. At last, in November 1715 Dudley surrendered the government to Lieutenant Governor William Tailer, who had been reappointed.[138]

After Dudley's forced retirement, he had to accept what had happened. His retirement became more joyful in 1716 when William Dummer, his son-in-law, replaced Tailer, a member of Byfield's faction. The former governor believed this "to be design'd as a mark of the King's favour for my thirteen Years successful services to the Crown here. . . ." In Dudley's last years, he watched the "unreasonable Contentions" (to use a phrase of Jeremiah Dummer) that took place during the administration of Samuel Shute. Dudley also suffered the embarrassment of his daughter Rebecca, who had married a son of Samuel Sewall, giving birth to a child not fathered by her husband.[139]

In the end, Joseph Dudley would be defeated by the New England winter. On a trip to Boston during November 1719, he caught a chill from the windy weather. He never recovered. Seriously ill by March 1720, he died on April 2.[140]

Dudley was buried with his father. A sizable number of soldiers attended the impressive funeral service. Boston's church bells rang out and the guns in the Castle fired a salute. As for the onlookers, the impressed Sewall compared their numbers with a flock of pigeons. The *Boston News-Letter*, in its obituary, called Joseph Dudley

a Man of rare Endowments and shining Accomplishments, a singular Honour to his Country, and in many Respects the Glory of it: He was early its Darling, always its Ornament, and in his Age its Crown: The Scholar, the Divine, the Philosopher and the Lawyer, all met with him: He was visibly form'd for Government, and under his Adminis-

tration (by God Almighty's Blessing) We enjoyed great quietness and
were safely steer'd thro' a long and difficult, Indian and French War.[141]

Of the preachers in Boston, Paul Dudley asked his own minister,
Benjamin Colman, to eulogize his father. Paul Dudley gave Colman a
text from the book of Hebrews, which involved the biblical Joseph making plans for his funeral. From the text, the deceased governor had probably, before his death, made his own funeral plans and had picked his
eulogist. Perhaps Dudley had expected Colman to compare him to Joseph, as Increase Mather had done years earlier. But Colman refused "to
run a parallel between the Joseph whose death puts us into Mourning at
this time" and the "glorious" Joseph of the Bible. The minister made a
point of not mentioning similarities between the two. Instead, Colman
chose to see the text from Hebrews as being about the "Resurrection of
the Body."[142]

With due respect to Colman, the governor almost certainly wished to
be compared to Joseph in at least two particulars. Joseph had been sold
into slavery in Egypt by his people. Had not Dudley suffered a similar
rejection? He had been expelled from Massachusetts and sent out unto
England. Despite such rejections, both of their lives ended with their
dreams fulfilled.

Chapter 10

Benjamin Colman

Benjamin Colman's ministry at Boston's upstart Brattle Street Church was a major factor in the weakening of the once dogmatic New England Way. During the heyday of the old Puritan commonwealth, the Brattle Street Church would never have been tolerated. Despite Colman's importance, he is not very well-known. Overshadowed by Cotton Mather and Jonathan Edwards, Colman's career has not attracted much attention.[1]

Part of Colman's problem is the existence of a eulogistic biography of him published in 1749. Written by his son-in-law, Ebenezer Turell, *The Life of the Reverend Benjamin Colman, D.D.* obscures the real man and creates instead a minister who was practically non-controversial. If Turell were to be believed, the founding of the Brattle Street Church was easily smoothed over. Nor did Turell mention the Great Awakening, which enmeshed Colman.[2] This essay will try to correct Turell's bland portrait of Colman, who was an important foe of the old Puritan way.

Born in 1673, Colman was indoctrinated into the Puritan faith by the two Mathers, and he became a full member of the Old North Church. The two ministers undoubtedly watched with pride as Colman gravitated towards the ministry and graduated from Harvard. Their old charge preached in Medford, Massachusetts, for a time but decided to journey to England. Before he ventured across the Atlantic, however, the Mathers had a task for him. Asked to preach one day in Newport, Colman did so with great success. The Mathers, whose church had underwritten the trip to Rhode Island, were delighted with the result.[3]

When Colman finally embarked for England in 1695, King William's War had made voyages risky. His ship was seized by French privateers.

Stripped of anything of value, Colman was briefly jailed in France. After his release, he made his way to England, where he preached in several Presbyterian churches, primarily at Bath.[4]

Unknown to Colman, plans were being made in Boston that would greatly affect his future. In 1698 John Leverett, Colman's tutor at Harvard, and others had decided to revolutionize the old Congregational forms, the "traditional rigidities" as Robert Middlekauff has called them. Leverett's allies included some Boston merchants who were tired of the old ways. Leverett had already greatly reformed Harvard, and one of his associates there, William Brattle, had only recently been named to the Cambridge church. Another ally, Simon Bradstreet, preached at Charlestown. But Boston was the intellectual as well as the political center of New England. Leverett and his supporters decided that their new church should be established there.[5]

Leverett knew that their plans would be opposed by the Mathers. Both Mathers had made a point of criticizing any innovations at Harvard; they were also on the watch for deviances from Congregational norms. Still, the Mathers' conservatism should not be overemphasized. The Old North Church was not the most old-fashioned in Boston. Increase Mather had finally—if grudgingly—accepted the Half-Way Covenant of 1662, which permitted the baptism of the children of those who—although baptized themselves—had not undergone a conversion experience. Cotton Mather had agreed with his father, and the doctrine was approved by their church in 1693. In contrast, the First Church of Boston did not accept the Half-Way Covenant until 1731. But Leverett had already battled the Mathers over the college, a fight he eventually won. Placing the new church in Boston was a direct challenge to his powerful antagonists—and an intensely personal one—which helps to explain the Mathers' reaction.[6]

Leverett and his allies had still other reasons for founding a new Boston church. There was little chance that any of the long-established Boston churches would suddenly change itself into something agreeable to Leverett and his friends. Besides, a new congregation seemed to be the only way that a merchant such as Thomas Brattle—who would donate the land for the new church—could ever become a full-fledged church member. Brattle had so far failed to produce an acceptable conversion experience. More important, though, were the province's laws that codified the establishment of a Congregational church. The law mandated that the strict forms be followed throughout Massachusetts. However, the law also exempted Boston churches, which were allowed to do as they pleased. This loophole was just what Leverett's group needed for its plans.[7]

Early in 1699, Colman received an invitation to return to Boston as the minister of the new church. Colman was a logical choice for several reasons. First of all, he was known to favor the changes that the Leverett group supported. He was also popular with Boston's ministers, which would hopefully help in the acceptance of the new congregation. Besides, Leverett insisted, "We want persons of your Character."[8]

Some of Colman's friends in Boston, Simon Bradstreet and Ebenezer Pemberton (who would soon also minister to a Boston church) encouraged him to accept the offer and return to America. The "men of repute and figure," as Pemberton called the new church's founders, would see that Colman was well provided for. According to Colman's friends, these "men of repute" had very sensible motives. They were "too much crowded together, for want of room in the meeting houses." Dr. Oliver Noyes added that another church was needed so as to add some more "convenient Seats."[9] Although the meetinghouses were quite likely crowded, Colman had not been away from Boston long enough to believe that that was the only reason.

Although one of Colman's friends insisted that "faction" was not involved in the founding of the new congregation, Dr. Noyes was more candid. He first tried to lessen the impact of his news by declaring that the entire government, from the governor down to the selectmen, had no objection to the new congregation. The ministers were another matter, however. Some of them were very "harsh" against the new church and feared that it would depart from "Customs." Noyes suspected that the other Boston ministers were likely to refuse to ordain him, and so he should be ordained by Presbyterian authorities before leaving England. "It may prevent Trouble," Noyes pointed out.[10]

Turell was deliberately evasive when he insisted that Colman did not realize why his friends urged him to get ordained in England. Colman knew that such an action was directly contrary to Congregational principles. Only the church considering a prospective candidate—with the assistance of some nearby ministers—had the power to ordain. Colman's decision to be ordained by English Presbyterians was, in the words of Perry Miller, an "affront to the old system." Colman knew very well what he was doing. And he was not foolish enough to be ordained by a bishop, as was also suggested to him.[11]

Colman was attracted to the offer to return to Boston where he had grown up. In August 1699 he was ordained by English Presbyterians. While Colman busily prepared for his new position, the founders of the new congregation constructed the new building, which was soon to be called the Brattle Street Church. Its architectural style was clearly English, not provincial. On November 1 Colman arrived in Boston and a storm of words began.[12]

On November 17, 1699, the Brattle Street Church founders published a *Manifesto*—presumably written at least in part by Colman—which declared its hope of preventing "all Misapprehensions and Jealousies." The *Manifesto* demonstrated their adherence to Calvinist theology, but there were to be important differences in church policies and services. To begin with, they believed that it was "most suitable and convenient, that in our Publick Worship some part of the Holy Scripture," including the Lord's Prayer, "be read by the Minister at his discretion," a major variation from the New England norm. The Puritans had avoided reciting standard prayers such as the Lord's Prayer, which were associated with Catholic liturgy. Although Puritan services had included scriptural texts, they had always been followed by "Exposition," in which the minister explained the meaning of the text. In the new church, the Bible readings were usually to stand on their own without exposition. Such a use of the Scriptures was, again, suggestive of Catholic practice.[13]

There were still other variances from the New England Way as, for example, in deciding who should be baptized:

> we allow of Baptism to those only who profess their Faith in Christ and Obedience to him, and to the Children of such; yet we dare not refuse it to *any* Child offered to us by *any* professed Christian, upon his engagement to see it Educated, if God give life and ability, in the Christian Religion. . . . We think it the Pastors Province to receive such Professions and Engagements; in whose prudence and conscience we acquiesce.[14]

The long fought over Half-Way Covenant was to be ignored.

The Brattle Street Church would allow all "persons of visible Sanctity" to receive communion, although these strangers were subject to examination by the minister who could "require the Renewal of their Baptismal Covenant." As for the regular members, they could publicly relate a conversion experience if they wished, but a prospective member was allowed to inform only the minister about it. If he was "satisfied," then so was the congregation as long as no one objected to the person's "life and conversation."[15]

Nor did the Brattle Street Church totally accept the Puritan idea of a church covenant. To the Puritans, the organization of a new church, a complex affair, had to be carefully supervised by ministers of older churches. The *Manifesto* agreed that "a particular Church, as such, is a Society of Christians by mutual agreement." But the new congregation's church covenant, not based on divinely-inspired biblical texts, instead came from "the Law of nature."[16]

The *Manifesto* had another shock in store for the Puritans. Traditionally, only "Male Communicants" had any voice in such matters as the selection of a minister. Women, although often in the majority among the visible saints, were not consulted about church business. However, the founders of the new church believed that female communicants as well as "every Baptized Adult Person who contributes to the Maintenance, should have a Vote in Electing" the minister. It was "just," the *Manifesto* insisted, "that persons of the greatest Piety, Gravity, Wisdom, Authority or other Endowments, should be leading and Influential to the Society in that Affair."[17]

On the other hand, the *Manifesto* emphasized that these disagreements did not cast doubt upon the trueness of the other Puritan churches. The new congregation differed in "particulars only."[18] This attempt to placate the other Boston churches had only mixed results.

Colman himself tried to answer the complaints of Judge Samuel Sewall, an orthodox Puritan, who had once written a recommendation for the young minister before his trip to England. With an explanation involving a typographical error in the *Manifesto,* Colman managed to calm one of the judge's theological concerns. In addition, Sewall also cautioned the young man to remain calm in the face of the harsh criticism that was certain to be directed at him.[19]

On December 24, 1699, the Brattle Street Church officially opened. The curious flocked to it to see what all the excitement was about. As Sewall had expected, a barrage of criticism greeted the new church and its minister. These "Innovators," Cotton Mather thought, were "Headstrong Men . . . full of malignity to the Holy Wayes of our Churches." They were tools of the devil himself, who was "beginning a terrible Shake unto the Churches of New England." Salem's ministers added their criticism of the *Manifesto*. Also eager to join the fray against the newcomers were Increase Mather and James Allen, a minister of the conservative First Church. If the innovators wished to be accepted, they only had to abandon their *Manifesto* and its tenets.[20]

But there was nothing the Mathers and their supporters could do to stop the new church. The time had long since passed when disturbers of the New England Way could be driven to Rhode Island. Massachusetts was now a royal colony and not a Puritan commonwealth. Sewall, lieutenant governor William Stoughton, and some moderate ministers helped to bring the two sides together. The innovators made some minor gestures concerning church covenants, and on January 31, 1700, the Mathers joined in a fast at the Brattle Street Church. For the moment, at least, the Mathers appeared to have accepted Colman and his congregation.[21]

Nevertheless, the Mathers believed that the new congregation was an "Infection," for which they had the "faithful Antidote." Increase Mather had written a book attacking the Brattle Street Church but had not published it because of the various attempts in January 1700 to reconcile the two sides. But the bad "Example" of Colman's ministry still existed. Perhaps, too, both Mathers still felt betrayed by the "young Man" who had once been of their congregation but had turned away from the New England Way. Therefore, in March 1700 Increase Mather ignored his earlier acceptance of the innovators and published *The Order of the Gospel*.[22]

Mather's *Order of the Gospel* attacked the "Relaxation of Discipline," the most obvious example of which was the Brattle Street Church. He complained about the innovators' "Presumption" in making changes in the New England Way without a synod. As for freely dispensing baptism, Mather declared that "Such Laxness in the Administration of Baptism . . . is Popish and Antichristian." In addition, if a prospective saint did not publicly relate his conversion experience, the elder Mather thought that the whole procedure would "degenerate into a meer Formality." Nor did Mather accept the increased authority of women in the Brattle Street Church. Such a female role was condemned both by the writings of Paul the Apostle and by the New England Synod of 1662. Mather also thought that the Lord's Prayer should not be used in a Congregational service; the Apostles Luke and Matthew had written that prayer using different words. Luckily, the Puritan minister asserted, "as yet the Declension is not gone so far but a Stop may be put thereunto, and the Interest of Religion be Retrieved."[23]

Soon after the publication of his father's book, Cotton Mather lamented that, though "lovingly penn'd," it had raised "violent and impetuous Lusts" against it.[24] Colman and his supporters were furious that Increase Mather had broken the truce established earlier in the year. Eager to defend the new church, they responded with their own book directed against Mather's attack upon themselves.

Colman and several others wrote in their *Gospel Order Revived* that Mather had quoted his sources out of their proper context. The innovators demanded that their own "Consciences be not imposed on by Men or their Traditions." Throughout the book, the authors defended the principles of their church. When Mather called the unexplained reading of biblical texts during a service mere "Dumb reading," the innovators took special offense. As they wrote, no one among them could "guess what Dumb reading should mean, unless when men sleep over their Books; and in Charity to the Author, we wish he had been a sleep when this unlucky word drops from his Pen." The innovators remained convinced that they were justified in this departure from Puritan tradition:

> we are more and more confirmed, that the reading Gods Word in the great Congregation, is so far from being offensive to God, that it is the greatest Reverence and Honour we can do it, and the most suitable acknowledgment we can make to him, who in mercy has given us his Word, and will judge the World by it at the great Day.[25]

The innovators started another tempest when they attacked Boston printer Bartholomew Green for refusing to print the *Gospel Order Revived*. Rejected by Green, they had it published in New York City. The "Press in Boston," they charged, "is so much under the aw of the Reverend Author, whom we answer, and his Friends that we could not obtain of the Printer there to print" it. Green immediately rushed to his own defense. At first, he insisted he had been willing to print the attack on Increase Mather, but became frightened when they insisted upon being anonymous. His suggestion that lieutenant governor Stoughton read it and give it his approval was flatly rejected by the innovators. Mather's critics had also rebuked Green by observing that "it was a shame so Worthy a Minister as Mr. Stoddard must send so far as England to have his Book printed, when young Mr. Mather had the Press at his pleasure." Green's defense and the depositions he published with it are debatable. But he was—probably—truly worried about printing an anonymous attack. After all, he had printed the *Manifesto* itself.[26]

Cotton Mather also felt obliged to write about that "Volumn of Invectives," the *Gospel Order Revived*, which broke three different com-

mandments (or so his father thought). In Increase Mather's preface to his
son's book, the elder Mather called the *Gospel Order Revived* a pitiful
product "of so little a thing as that Youth is, who is famed to be the
Author." This "Raw and . . . Unstudied Youth"—Benjamin Colman—
was "also of a very Unsanctified Temper and Spirit." The younger Mather
then stated:

> The Aged Master [Increase Mather], in whose School, the Young Man
> . . . had his Education, hath written upon his Book this Distich, (desir-
> ing it might be sent to him,) which when he Learnt Rhetorick occurr'd
> for him, in one of his Lessons:
>
> Young man, you don't more than your Neighbours see,
> No! But more Saucy, and more Shameless be.[27]

But Cotton Mather's comments had little effect—the Brattle Street
Church could not be destroyed by ridiculing its minister. The Mathers
slowly accepted the inevitable as they had no other choice. Colman soon
joined the local ministerial association and cooperated with the other
ministers. Even Samuel Sewall decided to attend a Brattle Street service
as a sign of his acceptance of the church, a gesture greatly appreciated by
Colman's congregation.[28]

Cotton Mather also became reconciled to the new church and to its
minister as well. Although their differences were resolved, Colman did
criticize the Mathers in public if rarely. Private criticism was probably
more frequent, however. And Colman seemed to relish Cotton Mather's
occasional public embarrassments. In 1717, for example, Colman could
not resist calling Mather's effusive speech praising Governor Samuel
Shute "too long and too large." Nor could he resist enjoying an ungram-
matical printer's error in the speech's printed version.[29]

Once the serious disputes with the Mathers were over, an undistracted
Colman began to develop his own ministry and his preaching style. In a
marked departure from the unadorned Puritan traditions, Colman pep-
pered his sermons with poetry and the secular writings of Addison and
other luminaries of the day. Such usage of popular authors had become
the style among English preachers, but he did not neglect the old Puritan
classics or the Bible. Nor did Colman try to scare the Brattle Street
congregation with fiery jeremiads. Instead, he appealed not only to their
emotions but to their reason as well, befitting the Enlightenment of which

he was a part. Colman had no difficulty reconciling the Bible with reason, a task often beyond preachers of a later day. He urged students to study the Scriptures because, he wrote, "our Bible, that now neglected and slighted Book by many, will be open'd by the enthron'd Jesus at the last Day; when he will magnify it by judging the World according to it." Furthermore, Colman paid much attention to the history in the Bible, and tried to broaden his hearers' understanding of the past.[30]

Colman was also a prolific author, with 84 publications of varying lengths. In this, he was surpassed in his day only by the two Mathers. Contemporary observers seem agreed in their praise of his writing style. Cotton Mather referred to "the pious, and acute, and cogent Pen of a Colman." Jonathan Belcher commented that he had "an easy, free stile." Even Timothy Cutler—an Anglican cleric not very impressed with Colman's character—admitted that he had a gift "for Easy Expression."[31]

In Colman's writings, he demonstrated both where he agreed with conventional Puritanism and where he differed. Concerning baptism, for example, he strongly accepted public baptism and believed it to be a necessity. Yet, in 1723, an anonymous writer insisted that Colman had been the first to criticize what the Puritan founders of New England had done with baptism. In Colman's *Practical Discourses upon the Parable of the Ten Virgins* of 1707, he declared:

> Some call themselves Christians, and yet seek not Baptism for themselves or their Families. . . . A shameful defect on us, so peculiarly our own in this Land, and one woful Effect of the narrow Principles our Fathers generally began upon in the founding of these Churches; that I believe no professing People under Heaven has the like to show and blush at.[32]

Nor was Colman pleased with the lack of interest adults demonstrated in repeating the vows that had been made for them at their baptism. The young people of New England, he complained, "having never taken their Baptismal Engagements on themselves since they are grown up, . . . are externally Christians no further than as their Parents made them. . . ."[33]

But Colman, not only interested in the power of the written word, also sought to improve the use of music in the Congregational service. The old forms of singing in New England churches had evolved as a Protestant reaction to the highly organized Gregorian chant of the Catho-

lic Church. In New England singing during a church service had become, in the words of Patricia Bonomi, "an anarchy of song." No one
paid any attention to what anyone else was singing or gave the slightest
regard to musical notes. In 1712 Colman had seen how beautiful a properly sung hymn could be when he observed some Catholic Indians as
they sang: "their Chanting was indeed the perfection of Music and har-
mony. Not a jarring note could I hear. . . . They rose and fell like one
single voice for time and measure, but a sweet variety of Voices was in
it. I cou'd have stood motionless like them for an hour to have heard
them. . . ." Not surprisingly, during the 1720s Colman's church would
lead the way in abandoning the old Puritan anarchy and adopting more
modern singing routines.[34]

Yet there were some musical items that Colman could not approve
of. The Brattle Street Church refused two organs donated to it by Thomas Brattle in his will. Organs smacked too much of Catholic liturgy. In
addition, Colman was very particular about what hymns should be used
in his service. As he wrote in 1707 in his *The Government and Improvement of Mirth:*

> . . . Sing Psalms. . . . For I am not for the freaks of some mens
> Fancies, who love rather to compose Hymns for themselves, (and very
> silly dull ones too sometimes to my knowledge;) and bring them into
> the Publick Worship instead of Davids: as tho' one shou'd prefer puddle
> Water to the pure and Christal River of the Water of Life, proceeding
> from the Throne on high. . . .[35]

Colman was willing to use hymns not in the Bible, but he insisted
that such new hymns had to be paraphrased from the Scriptures. He
applied this standard even to the compositions of his English friend Isaac
Watts, whose psalmbook, published in 1719, eventually won great popularity in America. Colman did not think all of Watts's hymns should be
ignored—just the original ones. Nevertheless, the ministers of New England were easily outdistanced on this point by their congregations. When
Jonathan Edwards, for example, was away briefly from his church, his
congregation took matters into its own hands. Upon his return, a surprised Edwards learned that his congregation had introduced Watts's
hymns into the service and had completely ignored the biblical psalms.
Colman, however, never gave in. Only after his death did the Brattle
Street congregation sing original songs.[36]

But Colman was not only interested in debating theological fine points or writing learned tomes. He spent much time performing various pastoral duties. As part of his ministry, he handed out Bibles and other books with religious themes to the poor and to others whom he thought might profit from them. He personally preached to slaves and to Indians, and did everything possible to aid the New England Company's efforts to bring the Protestant faith to the natives. Still, Colman, dissatisfied with the work of his fellow Protestants, knew that the Jesuits were far more determined missionaries. Upon observing the devoutness of some Catholic Indians, he lamented that "we must bear our Shame that we did not carry the Gospel to them our selves."[37]

Colman also tried to rescue those who had rejected the Calvinist message. In 1719 he related his travels to Freetown in southeastern Massachusetts, where he preached in an area reknowned for its "Incivility and Irreligion, Licentiousness and Ignorance, error and heresie, profaneness and malignity." During the early days of Massachusetts, their "libertine Ancestors" founded the settlement "to be far and free from the Discipline of our Churches." While "our Fathers slept," Freetown continued in its irreligious ways. Later, when the government of Massachusetts tried to tax them to establish Congregational churches in the area, the Freetowners reacted with such fury that Congregational ministers were afraid to settle there. The efforts of Colman and other visiting ministers failed to change these people until 1747 when supporters of the Great Awakening created a Congregational church.[38]

With so many duties, being a New England minister was a heavy burden. As a result of the work required of a clergyman, the practice developed of having more than one minister serve an individual congregation. From 1701 until 1703 Eliphalet Adams aided Colman. After Adams's departure to a better job, Colman handled all the duties by himself for a dozen years. Finally in 1715 William Cooper joined him in the ministry of the Brattle Street Church. As a boy of 7, Cooper had attended the first service there and the congregation almost totally agreed on his return as a minister. His ordination was, in itself, an innovation. Previously, the new minister himself preached at the ordination service, but the young ministers themselves saw it "as a Great Impropriety Imposed on them." One can imagine the dread of an inexperienced preacher who had to deliver a sermon on such a momentous occasion. Colman sympathized with such feelings and, for Cooper's ordination, gave the sermon himself.[39] The two men worked as a team for most of the remainder of Colman's life.

Because of Colman's great interest in preaching, writing, and pastoral duties, he might appear to be the typical Congregational minister. But he did not consider himself a Congregationalist. Believing that Congregationalism was "narrow and unreasonable," he accepted the Presbyterian form of church government. The Brattle Street Church itself blurred the distinctions between the two Protestant groups. In 1717 Colman pointed out that his church was "entirely upon the Presbyterian foot so far as our Lott among Congregational Churches will admit of it." A Presbyterian system, he thought, was needed to stem the many arguments and disputes in the New England churches.[40]

Soon after the forming of the Brattle Street Church, Colman sought to reform the New England churches into something closer to the Presbyterian model. His method was to attempt to strengthen the various ministerial associations. According to Colman's ideas, these informal groups should be empowered to discuss important matters. There had been numerous informal meetings of ministers in Massachusetts since the early days of settlement. However, even when synods met, the ministers had to carefully mask their actions to avoid any hint of Presbyterianism. But by the beginning of the eighteenth century, the ministers were less frightened about being branded as Presbyterians and very interested in having more formal ties with other congregations.[41]

By 1704 Colman, Cotton Mather, and many other ministers around Boston were united in wanting stronger ministerial associations. In June of that year, they notified other ministers of their opinion. Later, in November the Cambridge association informed other ministers that its members wanted to "more comfortably enjoy the assistance of one another" because of "the difficulty which in their ministry they often meet withall." The next year Colman introduced his idea of "standing councils" to the Cambridge association. Although each congregation remained independent, the standing councils would strengthen the authority of the clergymen. Finally, the same year delegations from several associations met and drafted the "Proposals of 1705," which established what were, in effect, Colman's standing councils. These groups were to be empowered to investigate charges "of Scandal or Heresie" against a minister, judge the merits of prospective preachers, and give recommendations about good candidates to churches seeking one.[42]

The Proposals of 1705 were stymied by the opposition of a handful of ministers. But this opposition was headed by Increase Mather and John Wise, who were against the Presbyterian structure the reforms would have created. Besides, Governor Joseph Dudley of Massachusetts opposed any strengthening of the power of the Congregational church. Nor would the General Court have accepted the changes. Despite this defeat, the reform movement continued. Gradually, more local ministerial associations were established. And just as gradually, they began to act remarkably like Colman's standing councils. Without the permission of the colonial government, the associations began to decide important church matters and ruled on the suitability of potential preachers. Colman had largely gotten his way.[43]

As time passed, Colman became still more influential even in such a non-religious subject as inoculation against smallpox. As early as 1718, he had noticed that smallpox was most dangerous when older people—already exposed to the dreaded disease—had passed on and were replaced by "a rising Generation" of young children that smallpox "might . . . sweep away."[44] A few years later, in 1721, Boston was hit by a new outbreak of smallpox.

On July 27, 1721, the Mathers, Colman, Cooper, and two other ministers, Thomas Prince and John Webb, signed a letter written by Colman endorsing in a Boston newspaper the still controversial inoculation remedy. Immediately, the ministers faced strong protests against them for their interference in a secular matter. Oddly enough, much of the criticism came from the Anglican clergymen in Boston, who seemingly sought to gain support among the people by opposing inoculation. Nevertheless, Colman continued to support the remedy and saw much of the "publick Resentment" directed against him. Indeed, many foes of inoculation believed that he had inspired the whole thing, which he denied. He was even blamed for *A Vindication of the Ministers of Boston*, which Cotton Mather was partly responsible for. Colman's own book about inoculation received its share of criticism. In it, he insisted that he had not gone "out of my Line" by writing it. His "plain intent" was "to serve unto the preserving of Life, and to minister unto the comfort of Families. This is a Care beseeming me, or any one else, if it be manag'd with modesty and decency." Despite the criticism, Colman was confident that when the uproar died down, the controversy would "be a testimony for the Inoculation, that by the favor of God" the inoculated people had "recovered under so many Circumstances of [potentially] killing treatment."[45]

Colman's prediction was fulfilled, and his reputation quickly recovered. When John Leverett died, Harvard would settle upon Colman for its new president. This honor turned into a "troublesome Affair" for the senior minister of the Brattle Street Church. That Harvard would turn to Colman was really very logical. As one of the fellows of Harvard since 1717, Colman had helped run the college. Furthermore, because of his many connections with English dissenters, he brought many sizable donations to his alma mater. During Leverett's presidency of Harvard, Colman was one of his valued allies in reforming the college.[46]

To succeed Leverett, the Harvard fellows eventually chose Colman. He was elected to the position in November 1724 at a corporation meeting he attended. There was no job Colman wanted less than the presidency of Harvard. He had not sought it and had tried to "avoid" it. Such "dry things" as "Academical Studies" had no appeal to him. Nor was he eager to relearn "the languages, and forms of the School." To disturb him still more, Cotton Mather—bitter over his rejection for the presidency—sent Colman a letter that can best be described as a tirade. Despite the passage of twenty-five years, Mather had not yet really accepted his rival.[47]

Colman knew, as well, that he had to resign from the Brattle Street Church to accept the presidency, and this he was reluctant to do. His congregation made it plain to him how much they appreciated his service. Besides, the House of Representatives acted oddly in twice refusing to say how much he would be paid before he resigned from his church. Colman realized that he was not very popular with the lower house because of his liberality. But Colman understood that there was another, more basic, reason for the Representatives' reluctance—the "straitness of our Congregational Principles." The Representatives did not want to seem to be luring a minister away from his church with a salary before the church had allowed him to leave. Not knowing his salary was another reason against leaving his church. But then, he had never wanted the presidency anyway. Using the unknown salary as a convenient excuse, he turned down the job offer in December.[48]

To Colman's distress, the job seemed to keep coming back to him. The Harvard fellows kept badgering him to change his mind and become president. In addition, the Rev. Thomas Cotton, an English friend of Colman, sent a special contribution of £ 100 to Harvard to increase the president's salary if he accepted the position. With the financial excuse eliminated, Colman had to find another reason to avoid being drafted as president. This time, he rejected it because of his poor health.[49]

Colman's weak constitution was well-known. In 1695 many people, judging from his outward appearance, had assumed him to be near death. Although he recovered, he continued to have an assortment of other health problems, the worst being asthma. Colman so often thought himself to be near death that he always had a will in draft form nearby just in case. Such uncertainty in health was not fitting for a Harvard president, Colman thought. A president should serve the college for a reasonable span of years, and Colman doubted that he could. Although the fellows were willing to take that chance, he had finally gotten them to consider someone else. Another Boston minister, Benjamin Wadsworth, became Harvard's president. Colman saw to it that Cotton's £ 100 contribution went to Wadsworth, though Cotton had still preferred that Colman keep the money for himself.[50]

Perhaps to make certain that he would not be offered the presidency again, Colman wanted to end his role as a fellow. When a friend pointed out that a sudden resignation would imply dissatisfaction with Wadsworth, Colman delayed until 1728. At that time, the fellows tried to convince him to stay. In September a meeting was held at his home before and after which they surely pressured him into staying with them. But, by the end of the year, he did resign.[51]

During the years Colman served Harvard, he noticed that Massachusetts was changing. As he observed in 1719, "Strangers crowd in upon us daily." These newcomers were Scots-Irish immigrants who left Ireland for several reasons, including the "unrighteous and Cruel Test-Act," as Colman called it. This law aimed at driving Scottish Presbyterians in Ireland from public office or else forcing them to conform to the Church of England.[52]

The Scots-Irish, having decided to leave their drought-stricken land, were encouraged by Massachusetts governor Samuel Shute to settle in his domain. Shute eagerly sought new settlers for sparsely populated Maine, which was very exposed to French attack. In 1718 the first Scots-Irish arrived in Boston, where some stayed while others spread throughout New England. Many, however, did go to Maine and were decimated during 1722 in yet another Indian war that hit the northern settlements.[53]

At first Colman was pleased with the newcomers, who (along with their ministers) had much to teach New Englanders, or so he believed in

1719. But he soon changed his mind as the Scots-Irish seemed to bring dissention in their wake. In 1722, for example, a prospective Scots-Irish minister, Robert Sturgeon, caused much trouble in Watertown. When the General Court divided the town to form two parishes, the residents in what had been the center of the single parish were very angry. Now they were farther away from both new churches than before, and they decided to start their own congregation in the old church building. No Congregational minister would consider serving a group that had rebelled against the General Court, so the rebels invited Sturgeon to serve them. He made a great show of asking the Boston ministers and others for advice. Every minister whom he asked urged him not to aid the rebel group. But Sturgeon had every intention of doing so anyway. In a move somewhat similar to Colman's actions in 1699, Sturgeon was ordained—secretly— by some Scots-Irish Presbyterians who had only recently come to Boston from Ireland. Sturgeon then went to Watertown and began his ministry there.[54]

The New Englanders were greatly upset by these events. Colman and other preachers met in a church council and criticized the ministers who had ordained Sturgeon; most of them soon left Massachusetts. As for Sturgeon, he refused to meet with the Congregational ministers and did not care what they thought. The General Court took more direct action—it had the old Watertown church building torn down. Some years later, Sturgeon finally accepted the verdict of a new church council and abandoned the rebel congregation.[55]

Other disputes erupted around Worcester. Then an exposed frontier, the Scots-Irish were encouraged to settle there. But the New Englanders and the immigrants soon had some misunderstandings. The newcomers were sometimes confused with the Catholics of southern Ireland. Nor did they appreciate having to pay for the support of a Congregational minister.[56]

When an agreement to sometimes have a Presbyterian share the church fell apart, the Scots-Irish in Worcester and nearby Rutland became rather rebellious. The Rev. John Moorhead of Boston and other Scots-Irish clerics began visiting these communities and in 1736 chaos broke out, according to Thomas Frink, the Congregational minister of Rutland, who informed Colman about what transpired. The visiting ministers, Frink charged, gave the sacraments to "scandalous livers," including drunk- ards and thieves, as long as they were Scots-Irish. To make matters worse, Frink added, "Some Parents have taught their Children to condemn me and my publick Ministrations and Young People now run into excess of riot, and regard not my warnings and rebukes." The Scots-Irish ministers "countenance and justify their Separating Spirit and irregular proceedings" in both Worcester and Rutland.[57]

Colman, disturbed by what had happened, was disappointed that "the Brethren from Ireland who have been received so courteously among us, and with Such Christian respect in our Churches" had chosen to snub the Congregational councils and had set up a presbytery. The established churches of Massachusetts were just not good enough for the newcomers. Condemning those who were "making breaches in our Churches," Colman saw no need for a presbytery when a church council, "Clothed with more humility," was sufficient.[58]

By 1740 the situation had not gotten any better. But in that year, the Scots-Irish decided to build their own church in Worcester and had started working on it. Suddenly one night, their neighbors came to the site, demolished what had been built, and destroyed the building materials. Because of this action, many of the Scots-Irish abandoned the area and tried their luck elsewhere.[59]

The New Englanders' attitude toward the Scots-Irish had changed in Boston as well. There the newcomers gradually came to be seen as poor people likely to want relief. Bostonians tried to prevent their entering the community and ordered many other Scots-Irish to leave it.[60]

Not only the Scots-Irish immigrants upset Colman's peace of mind. Although well-known for having "an Enlarged Catholic Spirit," that is, being tolerant, his toleration disappeared when he thought of Anglicans. The Church of England had been started in Massachusetts during the 1680s. Despite the great hostility of the Puritans to it, Anglicanism had survived the elimination of the Dominion of New England. When the Society for the Propagation of the Gospel (SPG) was created in 1701, the Anglican church in New England became one of its beneficiaries. The SPG supplemented the salaries of Anglican ministers and so enabled them to survive in spite of a small or a poor congregation. Because of this support of Anglican missionaries, the SPG was a special target of New England's Congregational divines.[61]

Colman was an especially harsh critic of New England's Anglicans and the aid they got from the SPG. Perhaps his criticism stemmed from his own position in the Brattle Street Church. In 1726 his friend Henry Newman discussed Colman in a letter to the Bishop of London. Colman's church was "midway between the Church of England and Dissenters." It was created, Newman wrote, because of "the Narrowness of some other congregations who denied the Sacrament to those who were of the Church of England. . . ." In fact, many of the original Brattle Street founders had also aided the building of Anglican King's Chapel.[62] By attacking the Church of England, Colman kept his distance from it. Although his quasi-Presbyterianism was acceptable at that time, any flirtation with Anglicanism would have been impossible for his fellow ministers to accept.

Whatever Colman's reasons, he conducted a very long-range campaign against the extreme Anglican clergymen he detested so much and the Society that aided them. To the Bishop of London, Colman grudgingly admitted the need for Anglican churches in the larger New England cities to provide for English travelers. Still, these churches did not need help from the SPG. And why must the Society help Anglicans in Newbury, Braintree, and elsewhere in New England when these towns already had godly preachers? Should not such assistance be directed to other colonies where ministers were very scarce?[63]

Colman, not limiting his campaign to the Bishop of London, contacted another important Anglican cleric, Bishop White Kennett of Peterborough. Railing against the "Jacobite Spirit" of certain Anglican ministers, Colman declared that they were "not . . . so well affected to King George as they should have been." What success the Church of England had had in Boston, Colman insisted, was because of moderate clergymen who were less antagonistic towards dissenters. Strangely enough, Kennett responded by admitting that the quality of SPG ministers was poor and that sometimes the Society acted upon faulty knowledge. Kennett's solution, though, did not please many New Englanders. Clearly, Kennett believed, the presence of an Anglican bishop in America could solve such difficulties. Starting in 1713, New England's Anglican ministers petitioned for such a solution, but their prayers went unanswered throughout the colonial period.[64]

Having a bishop in the colonies was a serious matter to dissenting Protestants of America. In New England, however, opposition was especially keen. For example, Samuel Sewall saw an American bishop almost as a reincarnation of Archbishop Laud, who might persecute dissenters as the bishops of old had done. The New England Anglican ministers were already aggressive enough. In 1725 they had succeeded in preventing the Congregational churches from having a synod. Yet far more threatening had been the Anglican coup at Yale a few years earlier. Timothy Cutler and some other dissenting ministers had suddenly embraced the Church of England and became Anglican priests. Colman and many other ministers "bewail'd" their apostacy. If leaderless Anglicans could cause such problems, what could they do with a bishop on the scene to guide them?[65]

Nevertheless, the Anglican ministers were more like a persecuted minority than a powerful force. Some Massachusetts towns, in defiance of both the law and royal officials, tried to tax Anglicans to support a Congregational preacher. Despite what Cutler called "sad Prejudices," the Anglican church continued to gain followers. And the Church of England clergymen did not hesitate to defend themselves against what they considered slurs. Rev. Samuel Myles called their supposed lack of loyalty to the Hanoverians as "a most abusive Insinuation." In 1739 Rev. Roger Price insisted that he could prove that various charges against himself—which he believed had been spread by Colman—were "notoriously false."[66]

As can be seen from Colman's campaign against the Anglicans, he had amassed influence in the mother country regarding religious matters. He was also influential in political affairs in both Massachusetts and England although his role is not always clear. Unfortunately, Colman did not save "Copies of transient Letters,"[67] which, seemingly, were often about secular affairs.

Only rarely did Colman use his pulpit for political purposes. In one case, for example, he urged the retention of Joseph Dudley as governor.[68] Colman's usual circumspection sets him apart from the Mathers, who almost flaunted their political influence (when they had it).

Colman's writings and sermons, however, displayed his great interest in the secular world. His book on inoculation has already been mentioned. In 1719 he called for the creation of public markets in order to end the "Oppression" caused by "Hucksters" in Boston, but he did so anonymously. Yet the preceeding year he had not hesitated to preach before Governor Samuel Shute about the declining value of the money of Massachusetts. As the money depreciated, the minister complained, "the small salaries you allow your poor Ministers and School-masters" got even smaller. Years later, in 1736, Colman returned to this subject of the colonial currency when he preached before Governor Jonathan Belcher and the legislature. The minister suggested what should be done about "our tatter'd Bills of Credit" although he acknowledged that "to advise" the government was not a minister's "Province." Apologizing for his

"Boldness of Speech," Colman told the rulers of Massachusetts: "It may be I have gone beyond my Line, but I am old and leaving You."[69]

Near the end of the reign of Queen Anne, colonial affairs almost dwindled into insignificance to Colman in contrast to the tempestuous sea of English politics. Queen Anne had brought two arch Tories into her government: Robert Harley and Henry St. John, the Viscount Bolingbroke. These two protagonists struggled for power between themselves. As part of the factional battles, Bolingbroke in 1714 pushed the Schism Act through Parliament. This "barbarous and cruel Act," in Colman's words, was intended to drive English dissenters out of the colleges and universities and so cripple the education of non-Anglican ministers. As Colman explained the Schism Act: "our Children may learn to read and write and the Art of Navigation. We may be slaves and . . . hewers of wood etc." The Tories had done this because of "Envy," Colman insisted, because the dissenters had "as many fine Scholars and Preachers as we could desire rise up from a private Education that shone as bright as any of their own Doctors." Although the Schism Act was passed, the dissenters were spared any problems from it. The law went into effect the day of the queen's death, and so was null and void.[70]

With Queen Anne's death, the throne passed to the elector of Hanover, who became George I. The claim of the Hanoverians to the English crown was rather weak—well over fifty other possible heirs had closer family ties to the Stuarts than they did. But to the dissenters on both sides of the Atlantic, George I was a godsend. Because of Hanover's role in European politics, the new dynasty was thought to be friendly to dissenters, which was true. Eager to please the new monarch, in 1715 Colman wrote an address to the king from the Congregational ministers of New England. Colman and the others linked themselves to the English dissenters, and warmly endorsed the Hanoverian claim to the throne.[71]

But, as Colman realized, Massachusetts had to be alert "against the Enemies of our Charter." Relieved that supporters of the Schism Act had been removed from office, the ministers of Massachusetts decided to head off any possible attack upon the charter which protected their liberties. To influence the king still further, Ebenezer Pemberton wrote *A Brief Account of the State of the Province of the Massachusetts-Bay*. The ministers had the forethought to have it "translated into High Dutch" for the English king who could not learn English.[72]

Pemberton's version of history explained how the settlers of Massachusetts were "not only of approved Piety to God, but of exemplary

Loyalty to the Throne and Government they belonged to. . . ." The infamous Stuart James II had really destroyed the first charter, and the beloved William and Mary had presented their colony with a new one. This present charter protected "in all points the Rights and Prerogatives of the Crown," or so Pemberton claimed. As for the Anglicans, he proclaimed that "Persons of that persuasion are under no Restraints, or Discouragements, but are ever Treated with all Christian Respect," which was certainly stretching the truth. However, Pemberton was more accurate when he declared that among New England's Congregational and Presbyterian churches, "there is not one Minister or one single Person known in their Communion" who did not strongly support the Hanoverian dynasty and just as strongly opposed the "Rebellious attempts" of the Catholic Stuart pretender against it. Whether or not the king actually believed Pemberton, Colman and his colleagues could rejoice in 1719 when Parliament formally revoked the Schism Act.[73]

During the early 1720s, English opponents of the Massachusetts charter tried but failed to have it recalled. When in 1727 George II became king, the ministers decided to honor him as they had his father in order to strengthen the political position of Massachusetts. At the ministers' convention, they first battled over what to call themselves—"Ministers of the Churches" or just "Teaching Elders." They compromised upon "Pastors, or Teaching Elders." The petition itself was written by Colman, and signed by him and Cotton Mather. In it, the ministers again warmly praised the Hanoverians and attacked "the Poverty and the Chains of Popery and Slavery in the Person of a Pretender to Your Majesties Crown." Dissenting New Englanders, they again insisted, were "Loyal and Dutiful Subjects."[74]

New Englanders felt free to praise the distant monarch and vow their loyalty. A succession of royal governors placed over Massachusetts discovered that the colony was difficult to govern. The Massachusetts assembly seemed to have its own prerogatives which it demanded. At times, the colony seemed to want independence, not only from its governor, but from Great Britain as well.[75]

Samuel Shute, the first governor to serve only under the Hanoverians, began his administration with much support from Colman and Cotton Mather. But the House of Representatives and Shute fought almost constantly. The assembly tried its best to insult him by lowering his salary and ignoring all directives from London. Colman thought Shute was "a good Governr. who heartily loves us" and feared that the battle was merely giving ammunition to those in England who wanted to destroy the colony's charter. Eventually, Shute gave up and left Massachusetts for good. The brief administration of William Burnet also revolved around the salary issue; the assembly refused to back down.[76]

Oddly enough, some of Colman's letters well demonstrate the growing pretensions of the Massachusetts House of Representatives. He sometimes referred to the assembly as "the Commons" or even as "Parliament." The assembly was trying to invest itself with similar powers and the stature of the British Parliament. These pretensions created still another stormy governorship—that of Colman's friend Jonathan Belcher.[77]

Belcher managed to prod the assembly a bit on his salary. Instead of two grants a year, he convinced the house to give him just one. But that was all he could do. His enemies made much of the conversion of Belcher's namesake son to Anglicanism in England. At last, Belcher's foes resorted to fakery to destroy his credibility. Samuel Holden, a prominent English dissenter and friend of Colman, received a letter—supposedly from Colman—which accused Belcher of secretly scheming with Anglicans to undermine the churches of New England. Colman never wrote any such letter—it was a blatant forgery perhaps enclosed within an outer covering that Colman had addressed. This "scurrilous, villainous" slander hurt Belcher's standing with English dissenters. Despite Colman's vigorous attempts to restore his friend's reputation, both in England and in Massachusetts, Belcher was removed. In 1743 Colman tried to console him: "When you came over governour, mine was the highest joy; and when you left the chair, none but your own family felt an equal grief."[78]

Colman's relations with William Shirley, the new governor, almost started out poorly. In 1741 a rumor spread that Colman had stated that Shirley's replacing Belcher "would have been destructive of the Rights and Interest of the New England Churches." But Colman strongly denied having said anything like that. He realized that the colony could not always have a Congregationalist or a Presbyterian as governor. Far from fearing the Anglican Shirley, Colman knew that even Belcher, his predecessor, spoke highly of him. The senior minister of the Brattle Street Church also welcomed Shirley's stand "against Bigottry and Violence."[79]

Having "truly reverenced all the governours" of Massachusetts, Colman was pleasantly surprised that Governor Shirley "seems to venerate me for my age, and does me the justice to number me among his friends." Shirley used his ties with Colman and William Pepperrell to strengthen his own position in the colony. As Shirley's administration was a time of war with the French, he further cemented his ties with the two men by giving some of their relatives lucrative military contracts.[80]

Nevertheless, Colman did not need a mercenary reason to support a war against the French. His distaste for the Catholic enemy of Great Britain was intense. In 1708 he had rejoiced over the effect the union of England and Scotland the previous year would have upon France. "What could be more formidable to France" than a united Great Britain, Colman asked. After all, France had "so much sought our Divisions, Triumph'd in 'em and grown Prodigious by 'em!" Later, the minister detailed French "outrages upon us" in the early years of the eighteenth century and castigated Britain's rival for its "instigating the Indians to . . . villainous robberies and murders, which they have so often committed without any provocation on our part."[81]

Colman and all of New England were overjoyed when the mighty French fortress on Cape Breton Island, Louisbourg, was seized by an expedition led by Pepperrell. To at least one New Englander, "The finger of God has been . . . conspicuous in every circumstance of this expedition." In a letter to Pepperrell, Colman himself was pleased "to read the pious ascriptions of all the glory to the most High God in your own and the worthy officers' letters to their friends and dear relatives!"[82]

Although Colman hoped that the conquered territories would form "a string of provinces down to ours," he was very concerned about the British military. Louisbourg was to be garrisoned by regular British regiments, some of which were to be raised in America. Two of these regiments were to be commanded by Shirley and Pepperrell, but they had no authority to choose the officers, unlike the situation in the colonial militia. Owing to the British system of commission purchase, a number of new officers for the Louisbourg garrison were "very raw Youths . . . and next to Children. But were they all men, no Body here will list under 'em." Colman warned that if "Govr Shirley and Sir William may not name their own Officers, they" would be unable "to raise any Regiments!" Colman lamented: "what Weakness and Carelessness is it to send children to maintain the acquisitions, which God has so marvelously given us." As Colman predicted, New Englanders did not eagerly enlist with the regulars.[83]

These troubled days of politics and war were matched by the stormy religious state of New England, Colman's chief concern. During the 1730s Arminianism started taking root in New England. Named after

Jacobus Arminius (c. 1559-1609), a Dutch theologian, Arminianism watered down such harsh Calvinist doctrines as predestination.[84]

When historians describe the founding of the Brattle Street Church, they sometimes suggest that Colman moderated Puritan theology and so imply—probably unwittingly—that he was an Arminian. Nothing could be further from the truth. Benjamin Colman believed in orthodox Calvinism and differed only in such points as church organization. He never questioned any doctrines of Congregationalism or Presbyterianism and criticized other ministers when they deviated in theological matters.[85]

In 1735 Colman and other ministers got involved in the divisive attempt of Robert Breck—who seemingly accepted Arminian ideas—to be ordained for the Springfield, Massachusetts, congregation. The church itself twice voiced its desire to have Breck as its minister, but the Hampshire ministerial association refused to ordain him because of his theological beliefs. When local ministers stymied Breck, he misled Boston clergymen, including Colman and Cooper, into saying that he was not an Arminian. The Hampshire ministers, resenting the intrusion of the Bostonians into their affairs, spread a report that Colman's mind had so deteriorated from old age that his "Thoughts and Judgment now was not to be regarded." Meanwhile, Cooper and a Hampshire minister engaged in a "paper-war." In the pages of the *Boston Gazette*, they debated the comparative intelligence and character of city and country ministers. By December 1735, Colman called for a ceasefire and asked Breck "to go into healing Measures" with his foes which resulted in his ordination the next year.[86]

The controversy over Breck, while disruptive, was a mere ripple compared to the religious turmoil of the Great Awakening. Even by the time of the Breck affair, Colman had become the most influential Boston minister. With the death of Cotton Mather, he no longer had a rival in the immediate Boston area. Despite Colman's "manifest decays" and his continuing feeling that his own death was near, he had become the eldest cleric in Boston. His prominence thrust him into the middle of the crises ahead.[87]

After Mather's death, a fellow minister noted changes in the former stronghold of Puritanism. There were "many awful Divisions in our Churches" and other "gloomy, melancholy circumstances" disturbed the congregations. Even the preachers no longer seemed to have the old dedication—for some years they had commonly read their sermons aloud to their flocks. Clearly, the old intensity of religious feeling possessed by the Puritans had, at last, evaporated.[88] Colman may have been partly responsible for this situation. The founding of the Brattle Street Church had damaged the old ways—perhaps the damage had been fatal.

Whether or not Colman felt any unease over what had happened, he responded eagerly to news that a revival of religious enthusiasm had happened in Northampton, Massachusetts. In 1735, under their minister, Jonathan Edwards, the Northampton congregation had taken on "an abiding gracious disposition and Conversation becoming the faith and Laws of the Gospel." When Edwards informed Colman of what had occurred, he notified his English contacts and urged that the news be published. Because of Colman's prestige, Edwards's account was believed and influenced many. But this first glimmer of the Great Awakening soon dimmed. In 1737 a saddened Edwards wrote Colman: "The work that went on so swiftly and wonderfully . . . has seemed to be very much at a Stop in these towns for a long Time, and we are swiftly by little and little, more and more declining. . . ."[89]

There was still hope for a revival, however. A young Anglican preacher, George Whitefield, was touring the American colonies. Despite his ties to the Church of England, he bitterly attacked Anglican ministers and preached Calvinist ideas. Without a doubt, Whitefield was a brilliant speaker with a flair for the dramatic, but, as a Harvard cynic commented in 1744, Whitefield "hath not any superior Talent at instructing the Mind." What Colman had read about Whitefield convinced him to invite this spellbinder to Boston and to offer him the Brattle Street Church to preach in.[90]

Some months before Whitefield was to arrive in Boston, Colman's English dissenter friend Isaac Watts informed him about a private conversation he had had with the Anglican clergyman. Whitefield, Watts wrote:

owns that he can give me no sufficient proof of his being called to any extraordinary ministrations, nor of the prophetical speeches that are sometimes found in his diarys, but he tells me that he has some inward sensations of particular impulses which have been so often fulfilled to him that he knows they are divine, but he owns these are such, evidences that will not convince another person.[91]

But this report of curious spiritual messages did not yet disturb Colman—he was convinced that God had inspired this Anglican.[92]

George Whitefield arrived in Boston in September 1740. He found a city that, at first glance, seemed very religious. It had fourteen churches—nine Congregational, two Anglican, plus one each for Baptists, French Protestants, and Scots-Irish Presbyterians. Nevertheless, he suspected that many of the churchgoers "rest in a Head Knowledge" and were "Pharisees." Such was the fate of any place "when the Power of Godliness is dwindled away, and the Form only of Religion is become fashionable amongst a People."[93]

Almost immediately, Whitefield tried to change matters. He never asked Boston's Anglican ministers to preach to their people. Instead, Colman invited him to come to the Brattle Street Church. "This was no sooner told at the Door," Colman reported, "but within an Hours time the House was full" with some 4000 listeners. During the following days, Whitefield preached numerous times to large gatherings and lived up to his advance billing. On September 21 the Anglican cleric honored Colman by attending the Brattle Street service and listening to Colman's sermon. Later that day, Whitefield preached to a huge crowd of perhaps 15,000 on Boston Common. Boston had never experienced a phenomenon like George Whitefield before.[94]

Unfortunately, one of Whitefield's huge gatherings turned into a tragedy. On September 22 a throng of 8000 people crowded into a meetinghouse. While waiting for Whitefield, the members of the audience may have thought that the Boston churches had not had such a large crowd in them for many years. Suddenly, panic spread among the people; someone wrongly thought that a gallery was collapsing. (A few years before, a Puritan church had collapsed.) As Whitefield recalled, "some threw themselves out of the Windows, others threw themselves out of the Galleries, and others trampled upon one another. . . ." When Whitefield arrived, he hurriedly announced that he would preach outside and the panic subsided but not before five persons had been killed.[95]

Despite this tragedy, still more crowds came to hear Whitefield. On September 24 he preached at Harvard, an institution that did not impress him. "Tutors neglect to pray with and examine the Hearts of their Pupils," he complained. Even worse, he continued, "Discipline is at too low an Ebb: Bad Books are become fashionable amongst them." Works of the Anglican Archbishop John Tillotson were perused instead of books by "evangelical Writers." Four days later, Whitefield returned to a more congenial place—the Brattle Street Church. After still another virtuoso performance, Colman told him that "it was the most pleasant Time he ever had enjoyed in that Meeting-House through the whole Course of his Life."[96]

In October Whitefield planned to leave the city. Before he did, on October 9 Governor Belcher told him about one Boston minister who had read his sermons to his congregation. After listening to the Anglican preacher, however, this Boston minister had begun "to preach extempore" which caused Belcher to rejoice that the Boston cleric was now trying to "save his Eyes." Three days later, Whitefield gave his last sermon on this trip to Boston. When he mentioned he was leaving, his huge audience began crying.[97]

Colman was greatly pleased with the results of Whitefield's work. The Brattle Street Church was just as filled after Whitefield's departure as before. Such a reaction was just what Colman and other ministers had been hoping for. To keep the enthusiasm going, Colman published his *Souls Flying to Jesus Christ.* In it he wrote of his joy to see the "Flocks flying to the Doors and Windows of our Places of Worship; and hovering about the same, those that could not get in." But where were the families of those who had been affected by Whitefield? They should come to the church services as well. "Your Ministers would lead you in the Way, and go before you! Come, our dear People, and fly with us!" Indeed, Whitefield was not the only one who could teach them God's truth. "Walk not your own Ministers in the same Spirit, in the same Truth, in the same Wisdom and Grace of God!"[98]

Whitefield's trek to Boston also gave birth to much trouble. The Old North Church became bitterly divided over the Great Awakening. "New Lights" who supported Whitefield's preaching were in the majority. Dissatisfied with their junior minister, Samuel Mather, they fired him from the pulpit of his father and grandfather. The "Old Lights"—foes of the new enthusiasm—continued to want Mather and formed a new congregation around him. Such bitter, divisive struggles within New England churches became common.[99]

Potentially more divisive was an old ghost resurrected by the always critical Timothy Cutler. Both Colman and Cooper, he charged, had praised Whitefield as "the Wonder of the Age," but the enthusiastic preacher had "greatly revived and spread" disruptive "Antinomian Principles." Cutler insisted that "our Pulpits and Presses are never free from such Doctrines." According to Cutler, Colman himself was infected with it. What convinced Cutler of Colman's supposed heresy was a seemingly innocent reference to "free Grace" in *Souls Flying to Christ.* Nevertheless, the inner-directed Antinomians inspired by Anne Hutchinson were moved by internal voices quite similar to Whitefield's. In 1744 a Harvard critic of Whitefield insisted that he had given the impression of being "under the Inspiration of the Holy Ghost."[100] Colman and other orthodox ministers were to get a close view of how such voices could lead enthusiastic believers astray.

Among the itinerant preachers inspired by Whitefield were James Davenport and Andrew Croswell, both of whom infuriated Colman and others. Davenport, for example, often declared that a settled minister was not really converted and encouraged his congregation to rebel. Colman wrote that these itinerants "have been too much under the Impressions of a heated Imagination, and no doubt often preached under actual Fevers, judging and censuring the spiritual State of Ministers and People. . . ." In his *The Great God has magnified his Word*, Colman urged his readers not to abandon their settled ministers:

> if we give Countenance and Encouragement to illiterate and half-learnt
> Persons to go about exhorting and drawing Hearers by their Shew of
> Affection to Souls for their spiritual Profit and saving Good, or from
> their sincere Desire thereof . . . it certainly tends in Time to run the
> Churches into Confusion, and to bring the Ministry of the Word into
> Contempt.[101]

The Brattle Street Church itself became the scene of an argument over the excesses of itinerants such as Davenport. In 1742 Rev. Jonathan Ashley of Deerfield, who had opposed William Cooper's stand on Breck, was invited to preach at the Brattle Street Church. During Ashley's sermon, he complained about the "Disorders in our Churches" and hoped to "reclaim" the Brattle Street congregation "from them." After the sermon was published, Cooper attacked him in the *Boston Gazette*. Cooper, objecting to the very publication of the sermon, declared: "The Church to which this Sermon was preach'd, is quite free from the greater Part of those Extravagancies . . . , while such Effects of the divine Grace appear in it and give Occasion for much Thanksgiving." He quoted Colman as writing: "We have seen little of the Extreams, or supposed Blemishes of this Work in Boston, but much of the blessed Fruits of it have fallen to our Share."[102]

When Ashley learned of Cooper's attack upon him, he sought a chance to reply in the *Boston Gazette*. But its publisher found a convoluted excuse for not printing it. Times had certainly changed. At one time the founders of the Brattle Street Church had difficulty getting into print. Now, their critics were the frustrated ones. Ashley had no other choice but to answer Cooper in a separate pamphlet. In it, Ashley admitted that some hearers of his sermon walked out in protest as he preached it. If those people were "Children of God," he hoped "they have given better Evidence of their Right to be so called, than" such "indecent Behaviour." In addition, he reminded Cooper that James Davenport had already caused "many Disorders" in Boston if not in the Brattle Street Church itself. Some good had come from the Great Awakening, Ashley admitted. On the other hand, the wildness of the itinerant preachers such as Davenport "cast . . . much Blemish upon it."[103]

Indeed, by 1742 Colman and thirteen other ministers, including Cooper, were especially concerned about Davenport. Although they realized he was "truly pious," Davenport was subject to "sudden Impulses" which controlled his behavior. The next year Davenport's impulses shocked many New Englanders. Davenport and his New London supporters decided to burn books of unconverted ministers. One of Colman's books was among those tossed into the fire. Then, suddenly, Davenport urged his audience to rebel against fine clothes and other "Idols" as well. Pulling off his breeches, Davenport threw them into the flames, to the dismay of at least one woman there. Even Davenport became shocked at what he had just done. Just as suddenly, he decided that he had been inspired by the devil, not God. The stunned Davenport made a full public retraction of his wild charges and behavior, and accepted Colman's suggested changes in a revised version of his published confession.[104]

After Davenport's retraction, Colman lost William Cooper, his longtime colleague. Cooper's sudden death in December 1743 at the age of 50 stunned Colman. Apparently, though, Cooper himself did not think he would outlive the senior minister of the Brattle Street Church. According to the *Boston Gazette* of December 20, Cooper had "very lately said to several at different Times that Dr. Colman would live to bury him." In Colman's eulogy of his friend, he sadly observed: "I have been ministring these forty-four Years in a poor and feeble manner; and have had the returning Sorrows, within this Course of Years, of burying a Congregation; and now my dear Colleague after them. . . ." Colman also lauded Cooper for being "fix'd and firm against the Spirit of Separation from the Churches of New-England. . . ." If he had lived "he would have been a most strenuous Opposer of this Defection. . . ." Nonetheless, Colman continued, Cooper believed that the Great Awakening was "a remarkable Work of God." In this he and Colman had agreed—both men merely objected to its excesses. As Colman stated, godly people had to

> be on our Guard against the Errors on the Antinomian Side, which by the Subtlety of Satan are insinuating themselves in too many Places thro' our Provinces, and in some Parts are threatning to break in like a Flood and Inundation. . . .[105]

By this time, Colman was not robust enough to do all the strenuous tasks expected of a minister. Indeed, because of his "growing Infirmities," William Cooper had recently been doing "the whole Pastoral Care" of the church. After a year's wait, Samuel Cooper, the youthful son of the deceased minister, was picked to assist Colman. Although young Cooper was a prominent man at the time of the American Revolution, during the Great Awakening he stayed in Colman's shadow.[106]

In August 1744 Colman was still concerned over the excesses of the "many poor and miserable Exhorters who have sprung up . . . like Mushrooms in a Night. . . ." Hoping that they would profit from Davenport's errors, Colman reminded everyone "of the Dishonours done by him to Religion." Stop "listening too much to Impulses" he advised the "Separating Brethren." Certainly, the sharp divisions within Congregational churches had to stop. Already, Colman noted, many churches in Long Island, Connecticut, and Massachusetts were "broken to pieces."[107]

In Colman's *Letter to Williams*, the senior pastor of the Brattle Street Church complained about the problems caused by "Ministers of low and ordinary Gifts," not George Whitefield. But by 1744 Colman and other ministers were also concerned about Whitefield. When he returned to Boston in November 1744, he had to calm their fears that he would encourage still more revolts within congregations. Yet the fears of Colman and the others were easily dissipated. They knew that Whitefield was no Davenport—no one thought that Whitefield would remove his breeches while preaching. Still, there were now many in Boston—especially Charles Chauncy—who opposed Whitefield as well as the extreme New Lights. Boston was flooded with tracts against the visiting Anglican clergyman.[108]

One of these anti-Whitefield pamphlets was the *Letter* written by Caleb Cushing and many other ministers in nearby Essex County. Disturbed by Whitefield's "hasty admission" into many of Boston's pulpits, they reminded the Bostonians such as Colman of the "dangerous Consequences" caused by less important revivalists than Whitefield. "Hath the visible Good of his former Visit, by any Means equalled the visible Mischiefs that followed?," these critics asked. Why, then, should the Boston ministers take the "unhappy Step of setting the Author of our Divisions to preach among us again?"[109]

The critics in the Boston newspapers were far more vicious to Whitefield and the ministers who still accepted him. "Rustico Clerus" hinted that money collected by the English preacher for a Georgia orphanage was really spent for his personal comfort. As with so many other anonymous attacks, this charge was a blatant falsehood. In another personal attack, the *Boston Evening Post* ridiculed the supposed lack of religious enthusiasm of Whitefield's wife, who, it claimed, had not been seen in church. The rival *Boston Gazette* pointed out that she had, in fact, been to a service, "contrary to the false and abusive Reflections . . . on that Gentlewoman, . . . an harmless Stranger among us."[110]

Other critics in the journals were just as severe, if not as abusive. A "Layman" linked Whitefield with Davenport as "Men filled with Zeal, but not of God, for the Tree is known by its Fruit." The author of "A Letter from the Country" puzzled over the "deep Infatuation" of those who had wished for the return of Whitefield, the man responsible for "the many Errors in Doctrine, and gross Disorders in Practice that have prevail'd so mightily in this Land." Another letter to the "Reverend Ministers" wondered why Colman and his comrades would "sit transported" during the Anglican cleric's "empty Harangues." On December 24, 1744, the *Post* printed another letter supposedly to Whitefield which labeled the divisions in the churches as "the Fruits of your Doctrine." The anti-Whitefield *Post* delighted in spreading the news of an embarrassing scene in the church of Thomas Prince, one of Whitefield's supporters. A false rumor had it that the Anglican itinerant would preach at Prince's church. When Prince began the lecture instead of Whitefield, "great Numbers" of the audience walked out.[111]

Colman himself came under attack in early December 1744. At the Brattle Street Church Whitefield listened to Colman preach, and then was invited by Colman to give out the eucharist. An outraged critic, "J.S.," fumed: "There has no such Thing been done since the Day that our Fathers came over into this Wilderness, to this very Time." Having an Anglican distribute communion struck "the most daring Blow at the Foundation of our Churches." Another critic, "A.X.," insisted that Colman's act "surpriz'd" the congregation. "The Dr.," "A.X." thought, "is at this Time, fully sensible that he had not the Consent of his Church, and that it was unadvised in him to desire Mr. Whitefield to officiate." There is no evidence that Colman ever tried that again. In his long years at the Brattle Street Church, this incident appears to be the only time his congregation disapproved of his conduct.[112]

Perhaps the sharp reaction forced home to Colman that even in his church there existed some dissension over Whitefield. On January 14, 1745, Colman told Whitefield about some of his own fears about the Anglican's enthusiasm. Colman reminded his friend "of what occurred . . . a Century past, I mean the Agitations Agonies and Outcries of the . . . well meaning Persons then under the Fervant preaching of the Gospel"—the Antinomians—from whom arose Quakers. "Women . . . as well as mean and illiterate Men, set out to preaching after a miserable manner and continue to do so unto this Day. . . ." Such a terrible precedent should "keep us upon our Watch and Guard, lest Satan gain an Advantage against us." The pastor warned his friend to be cautious in his preaching. The excesses of the revivals "are not the genuine Tokens . . . of a Work of God . . . but . . . that false Spirit" that infected Davenport. Despite Colman's fears about Whitefield, the pulpit of the Brattle Street Church remained open to him through April 1745.[113]

In the summer of 1747 Whitefield again decided to preach in New England. Hostility to him had stayed high among the Old Lights. The *Boston Evening Post* printed the details of a hanging of "one of Whitefield's Disciples" who had deserted to aid the Stuart Pretender. The implication was that such "Methodists" were disloyal. Did the *Post,* complained a defender of Whitefield, "imagine that Mr. Whitefield is any Ways responsible for the Political Principles . . . of those who . . . follow him as a Preacher of Religion?" Any such suggestion was "stupid." Clearly, the controversy had not abated.[114]

On July 21, 1747, Whitefield came near Boston again. He arrived quietly, "without the admiring Throngs, the loud Acclamations, and Hosannas of the Multitude, which he formerly gloried so much in," according to the hostile "A.C." in the *Post.* This same foe claimed that the Anglican itinerant's "Interest runs very low in Boston, and the Love of many of his former Followers is waxed cold." Colman and some other Boston ministers were still willing to have the great preacher address their congregations. But now not one of them wanted to be the first to invite him to Boston and receive the censure of the Old Lights. Colman wrote to a fellow minister: "I wish we would act in concert for our mutual Peace and the Edification of the Flocks to which we stand related. . . . " No invitation was forthcoming from Boston, and Whitefield left to preach elsewhere. The still friendly *Gazette* claimed that Whitefield thought that he could do more "Good" in New Hampshire than in Boston. This excuse seems very transparent—Whitefield would surely have accepted an invitation from Colman or someone else in Boston. But at the moment, the Boston ministers were reluctant to weather still another storm over George Whitefield.[115]

Time, though, was running out for Benjamin Colman. On August 26, 1747, he complained of strange "Humours" in his chest—perhaps a sign of an impending heart attack. Soon after, on August 29 he had "a fainting Fit, and died in a very little Time." His funeral was marked by "A vast procession" of mourners.[116]

The *Boston News-Letter* hoped for "a just Character of this great and good Man, drawn by some able Hand." A few weeks later, the *Boston Gazette* provided a long obituary of Colman. Judging from the detail of his early days, the obituary was probably written by Ebenezer Turell.[117] Some years had to pass before a longer biography was published. After all, Turell needed the time to wade through the extensive correspondence and writings of one of the most eminent ministers of the age.

Epilogue

The "unhappy excesses" caused by the Great Awakening did not destroy the importance of religion in New England. By 1761, Ezra Stiles wrote, "Our churches have now in some measure cooled and recovered themselves." Although "the spirit of enthusiasm is not altogether extinguished as yet," it "operates and influences under different pretexts, and in a different form." Despite the chaos of the Awakening, Stiles happily related, over 150 "new churches" had been created, "founded not on the separations, but natural increase into new towns and parishes."[1]

Benjamin Colman surely would have rejoiced over such progress, but he did not live to see it. Nor does it fall within the scope of this book because, with Colman's death in 1747, this study comes to its conclusion. The year 1747 seems like a strange place to end. Puritanism had dissipated sometime around 1730, and 1747 has none of the excitement of 1775, 1776, or 1787. Nor does 1747 have any of the logic of 1783 or 1789. Yet if 1747 was not quite the end of an era, a new period was on the verge of commencing. In 1747 Thomas Hutchinson was already a public figure of some importance and the youthful John Adams was on the brink of adolescence.[2]

New Englanders of this post-Puritan period have often been mislabeled by scholars. Both Samuel and John Adams, for example, have been referred to as Puritans: Samuel was "a kind of late Puritan fanatic"; John had a "puritanical imagination" and a "Puritan spirit."[3] Neither of these men were Puritans. No Puritan could have written from Worcester what John Adams did in 1755: "But now hope has left me, my organ's rust and my Faculty's decay. Every Week Day is sacrificed to [   ] sunday to the Frigid performances [   ] Frigid John Calvin."[4]

Thomas Hutchinson, himself a chronicler of early New England, would have at least understood John Adams's complaint. In the same year Hutchinson, after examining a document apparently about the Salem witchcraft trials, observed: "what is very tolerable in one age is very ridiculous in another."[5]

The Salem episode is a good example of the embarrassment felt by many about New England's Puritan past. Long after the deaths of the alleged witches, those who suffered during the witchcraft trials have been pardoned gradually until, in 2001, everybody had been vindicated. A few years later, however, the town of Salem suggested still another pardon. Only the two dogs executed during the trials have not been apologized to. Stranger still, a governor of Massachusetts, Michael Dukakis, actually insisted that Salem should have its own "official witch" and duly made the appointment. Perhaps the oddity of that stand explained why Dukakis lost so many states when he ran for president.[6]

Even Anne Hutchinson benefited from guilty feelings of later New Englanders. In 1989 one church revoked her excommunication and welcomed her, once again, into the fold, centuries after her expulsion.[7]

Embarrassment over unattractive aspects of the history of Puritan Massachusetts had already become strong during the nineteenth century. Historians of that time tended to glorify Plymouth instead of Massachusetts Bay. The Pilgrims did not have as infamous a reputation as the Puritans of the Bay colony, a "people whom many Americans would like to forget." However, twentieth century scholars became queasy about the Pilgrims too due to bloody Indian wars. When a historian wanted to sanctify Sir Edmund Andros, he did so by depicting Andros as close to the Indians in contrast to the supposedly racist Puritans. The facts really did not matter as academics quickly fell in lockstep. Chadwick Hansen once shrewdly observed that "it is abundantly evident that American historians sometimes pay more attention to each other, and even to dramatists, than they do to their primary sources. But that will hardly be news to anybody."[8]

My own viewpoint echoes William G. McLoughlin's comment "that the Puritans were not a very tolerant people."[9] My position is based on facts, not guilt about my forefathers. The various enemies of the Bay colony were not necessarily saints themselves. But their struggles with Massachusetts helped to end its status as the foe of tolerance. For that alone, they deserve our thanks.[10]

Appendix 1

Philip's Name: A Cottage Industry

When the Wampanoag Metacom assumed the European name Philip, he unintentionally triggered a future debate over what to call him. When the New Left arose during the 1960s, the name Philip was cast aside and their hero reverted back to his former identity, Metacom. Even King Philip's War suddenly became Metacom's War.[1]

Although, of course, the name Metacom did appear in records of the seventeenth century, its resurrection served no real purpose. This name, so favored by the New Left, actually was popularized by its use in some melodramatic literature of the 1800s.[2]

Reviving Metacom also made little sense. American Indians frequently adopted new names when their lives changed in some way. Metacom, no exception to this practice, took at least four different ones after accepting his European name. In 1664 he was "Pumetacom Allias Phillip," and only two years later he was "Eleise Pokonoahkit." During 1671 John Eliot referred to him as "Philip Keitasscot," but in three years Plymouth addressed him as "Phillip, allies Wewasowannett." Calling the conflict that soon erupted by the phrase "Wewasowannett's War" would likely be historically precise but very confusing. And that revision assumes that Philip did not change his name again. Given his history, still another name is a real possibility. Scholarly renaming of King Philip's War or Philip himself is of dubious value.[3]

James D. Drake has suggested that Philip never took the name Keitasscot, observing that, because of its similarity to a word for king in Massachusett, Keitasscot was only a title. In addition, Drake believed that Wewasowannett, similar to another kingly Indian title, *werowance*, was also a title, not a surname.[4]

Keitasscot could, indeed, mean king. Among New England's Indian tribes, a common word such as king had different pronunciations but there was some similarity (as Drake noticed with Keitasscot). Nonetheless, merely because it meant king does not rule out its use as a name. Languages are full of titles that became names. English has plenty of examples: King, Queen, Duke, Bishop, Prince, Marshal, and so on. The Spanish word for king, *rey*, can be found as a surname. The Hindi *raj*—or king—is also a common name. Even the Celtic word *rix*—king in the dialect in Gaul—has become a family name as well. Although all of these languages are Indo-European, there is no reason to think that New England's Indian languages were any different. Keitasscot was a name. What Keitasscot's meaning of king does demonstrate, however, is that Philip₁ enjoyed being called king.5

As for Wewasowannett, Drake's guess is wrong. The two words are not very similar. It is comparable to saying that "karat" and "katydid" are really synonyms. Caution is required when making theories about the Indian languages once spoken in New England. Little is known about them except for Massachusett (thanks to John Eliot) and Narragansett (thanks to Roger Williams). Many entered the realm of dead—that is, unspoken—languages in the nineteenth century; Narragansett survived to 1810 while Pequot made it to the next century.6

A Praying Indian of the 1670s provided solid evidence about the name of Philip in question. Jacob Muttamakoog wrote: "Consider of this I Intreat you, consider of this great business that is done; and my wonder concerning Philip, but his name is—Wewesawanit, he engageth all the people that were none of his Subjects." Wewesawanit is clearly a variant spelling of Wewasowannett. Note that Muttamakoog says that Wewasowannett was Philip's name, not his title.7

Finally, should the sachem be called King Philip? The issue of his "kingship" is moot. The English settlers believed that the Indians favored a monarchy and therefore treated the sachems at first as petty princes. Those few sachems who controlled larger territories were, hence, kings. In fact, before Philip became the leader of the Wampanoags, he was likely called "Prince Phillip," which is how John Josselyn referred to him. Metacom was named King Philip when the Indians and the colonists were on friendly terms. There is no reason to avoid using the name or the title.8

Appendix 2

Who Was Philip's Father?

For many years, the identity of King Philip's father seemed obvious. Massasoit fathered both Philip and his older brother Alexander, formerly called Wamsutta. Then in 1990 Betty Groff Schroeder published an essay pointing out that written accounts of two treaties named another Indian, Moanam (fl. 1639), as Philip's father. Apparently, the genealogy of the Wampanoags' rulers had been clarified. Massasoit was the father of Moanam, and so the sachem of the first Thanksgiving turned out to be the grandfather of Alexander and Philip.[1]

Historians, however, are a contentious group. In 1998 Jill Lepore rejected Schroeder's claim, insisting that she had been misled by the mistake of the anonymous author, "N. S." (usually assumed to be Nathaniel Saltonstall), who referred to the treaties Schroeder depended upon. Lepore's curt dismissal puzzled me. I assumed it came about because Schroeder was not a professional historian. Therefore, she never went to historical conventions and told everyone in her field how brilliant they were. (This is the true purpose of historical conventions.)[2]

Deciding to look into Philip's ancestry myself, I checked the relevant works of "N. S.," which were published in England and are now available on microfilm. "N. S." did say that Moanam was Philip's father. The matter seemed closed. Then I discovered that three articles had attacked Schroeder for something that appeared factual. These articles will now be summarized.

Archeologists, for some reason, had become dogged investigators into Philip's ancestry. George R. Horner went through the writings of assorted colonists who made no reference to a Moanam. The treaties in question were merely "confused and sometimes inaccurate allusions to actual events that can be documented in historical records." Moanam, he believed, was "an early name for Wamsutta," Philip's brother. Lepore also suggested that Moanam was Wamsutta.[3]

Another essay by Terence G. Byrne and Kathryn Fairbanks attacked "N. S." for stupidly suggesting that King Philip had a second brother, Sunconewhew. As evidence of this stupidity, the authors pointed to the assertion of "N. S." that "Sachem Phillip was the grandson of Massasoit, revealing a basic lack of common information and public record." How could anyone accept "the hearsay evidence of an anonymous narrator"?[4]

Dennis P. Walsh added still more broadsides in an article dedicated to demolishing the idea that Massasoit could be Philip's grandfather. Attacking Schroeder for depending upon a "single, questionable historical source," Walsh correctly mentioned that "N. S."—Saltonstall—counted on secondhand information. Instead of "N. S.," Walsh emphasized the "seminal" history written by Nathaniel Morton in 1669 which, Walsh believed, had notes written by William Bradford. One note stated that Moanam and Wamsutta were the same individual. Walsh also revealed the existence of deeds that declared Massasoit's paternity of Philip.[5]

The best place to start refuting such claims is with Morton's *New England's Memorial*. Bradford did not write any of its notes because he died long before it was written. However, Bradford was Morton's uncle, and he had access to the Plymouth governor's history, then still in manuscript. Those familiar with Bradford's book will immediately recognize passages from it in Morton's history. Such unannotated, often word-for-word usage was acceptable practice in his century and the next one too. Morton's account was an influential one.[6]

John Josselyn's narrative of his time in New England was just as influential. Displaying great interest in the Indians he encountered, Josselyn stated that "Philip alias Metacon" was "the Grandson of Massasoit." Dismissing Josselyn's information rather cavalierly as Walsh did is a mistake. Historians once dismissed Josselyn's statement that enemy of the Bay colony Samuel Maverick was the offspring of a Puritan minister, John Maverick. In the 1940s the discovery of some legal records proved that the Puritan cleric had fathered the Puritan critic thereby vindicating Josselyn.[7]

Since Josselyn lived in Maine, how could he have learned about the parentage of King Philip? Josselyn traveled to Massachusetts and knew Boston well. His account of buying some of the "much diminished" passenger pigeons there is certainly memorable. But Josselyn also knew Roxbury, a town near Boston, seemingly just as well as the capital of Massachusetts. He commented upon the size of Roxbury's streets, the gardens there, and even the name of a stream coursing through that "fair and handsome" community.[8]

A man such as Josselyn, deeply interested in New England's Indians, would be drawn to Roxbury because it housed John Eliot, the Apostle to the Indians. Some of the Indian lore Josselyn passed along to his readers, including the exact relationship of Massasoit and Philip, probably came from the minister. Josselyn is very complimentary to Eliot, a common way to treat someone who provided useful information.[9]

Another unnoticed fact about Josselyn's well-known book is his dependence upon Morton's history. Josselyn's list of New England's missionaries to the Indians is straight out of Morton. The chronological table in Morton's history likely inspired Josselyn's own chronological list of events. The significance of Josselyn's use of Morton is clear. Josselyn knew about Morton's belief in the traditional genealogy that Philip was the son of Massasoit and rejected it.[10]

Did "N. S." utilize Morton's book too? The anonymous author clearly did so. In fact, the treaty summaries printed by "N. S." are taken directly from Morton except in one way. "N. S." added references about Philip's paternity to Morton's text. Massasoit is called Philip's grandfather and Moanam is identified as his father. "N. S.," just as Josselyn did, rejected Morton's genealogy of King Philip.[11]

Where did "N. S." receive information that caused him to contradict Morton? Possibly "N. S." had read Josselyn's book as has been suggested, but there were other sources available to him. Assuming "N. S." was Saltonstall (who did use his initials in drafts of letters and also in correspondence with his family), he likely came into contact with two important sources of information. Saltonstall seems to have liked attending the graduation ceremony of his alma mater, Harvard. There he could have met John Eliot, Jr., who did missionary work along with his father. The younger Eliot had graduated from Harvard a few years before Saltonstall and soon ministered at a church in Cambridge. Nor should a connection with Eliot's helper Daniel Gookin, who lived in Cambridge, be ruled out. Perhaps the two men met each other at a Harvard commencement or while serving in the militia. Certainly, in 1684 Saltonstall knew how to get to Gookin's home. Saltonstall, as a frontier resident, had plenty of motive to learn as much as he could about the Indians.

Either John Eliot, Jr., or Gookin could have informed him about the ancestry of the Wampanoag sachem.[12]

However, the "oral tradition of the Wampanoag nation" contradicts the assertion that Philip was the grandson of Massasoit. This supposed tradition also insists that Philip had only one brother, Wamsutta. A reader will recall that Philip had another brother, called Takamunna in this book. On August 6, 1675, John Pynchon wrote: "Philip's Brother is with them at Brookfield. . . ." Was Pynchon delusional? Clearly, "Current day Wampanoag tradition" can not be taken seriously. It even claims to know the name of Philip's young boy, but Lepore, not surprisingly, remarked that "I have found no seventeenth-century evidence" in support of that belief. The anonymous "N. S." turns out to be more reliable than alleged oral tradition.[13]

At first glance, the existence of two deeds contradicting Schroeder's discovery seems to be a far bigger hurdle. In 1664 Philip signed a deed stating that "Osamequin" (Massasoit) was "my father." Four years later Philip signed another deed declaring: "I Philip Sachem [am] son heire and successor to the said Osamequen Sachem." The same deed also referred to "the said Osamequin my father deceased."[14]

The word "deceased" is key here. Indian culture prohibited mentioning a dead person's name. That is why Indians used euphemisms such as "He that was Prince here." The consequences of saying the name of a deceased individual were severe and could even lead to war. In 1665, for example, Philip tried to hunt down one Indian who had dared to utter "Massasoit."[15]

Philip of course would not have read the deeds but his interpreter, John Sassamon, would have. He would never have said aloud the mentions of Massasoit or the relationship stated in the deeds. Instead, Sassamon would have talked to Philip about the land in question. The deeds, part of English law, were written by, and intended for, the English colonists. These deeds, therefore, have no bearing on the ancestry of King Philip.[16]

One of the supposed mistakes committed by "N. S." actually is very enlightening. The anonymous author wrote about "Quononshot [Canonchet], otherwise called Myantonomy [Miantonomo]." Charles H. Lincoln, the editor of "N. S.," stated that he had confused a son with his father. In reality, the Narragansett Canonchet did take Miantonomo's name after his death. Apparently, the taboo about mentioning a dead man's name did not apply if a son wished to take his father's name and thus honor the dead parent's spirit. The suggestion that Wamsutta had the name Moanam may be true—this could be another case of a son taking his father's name. Perhaps such a renaming was permissible if the father had died young or under unusual circumstances comparable to what had happened to the elder Miantonomo.[17]

What appears to be the strongest evidence against Schroeder's suggestion also contains more than is readily apparent. John Eliot certainly knew the truth about the genealogy of King Philip. But in the minister's *Indian Dialogues*, he has one person talking to Philip about "the good people of Plymouth, who were ever good friends to your father Onsamequin."[18]

What should be remembered is that the word "father" can mean more than merely the man who begat a child. It also refers to a man "who adopts another as his child." Shakespeare used the word that way and so did Eliot and probably others as well. After Moanam died, Massasoit took the children under his protection and so became their father. Eventually, Moanam was forgotten by New Englanders.[19]

The evidence appears to support Schroeder's contention. Massasoit had a son, Moanam, who was the father of three boys. Massasoit was Philip's grandfather.

Appendix 3

The PC Indian

What became known in the 1990s as political correctness, often abbreviated as PC, had its roots years before in the 1960s. Part of the New Left's reinterpretation of events involved casting aspersions upon the term "American Indian;" using it was frowned upon. "Hip" people favored the phrase "Native American" instead. When the 1960s faded away, "Native American" submerged a bit. However, the multicultural movement resurrected the New Left's invention and usage of "Native American" became dogma on American college campuses.

Banning "American Indian" makes no sense whatsoever. Roger Williams explained how the term spread in colonial New England. He related that Indians "have often asked mee, why we call them Indians Natives, etc. And understanding the reason, they will call themselves Indians, in opposition to English, etc."[1]

Once Indians learned about Columbus, they started calling themselves Indians. If Indians of colonial times had no problem with this inoffensive name, why, then, should academics of the twenty-first century be so opposed to it? Especially relevant is the fact that many modern day Indians freely use the term themselves. Saying "Native American" is really a political statement.

Luckily, I began my study of colonial Indians during the 1980s, a comparatively rational period when scholarship could still triumph over ideology. When I thoroughly criticized Francis Jennings, I hoped that the destruction of his silly scenarios would open a path for others to write far superior monographs than Jennings had produced. That hope came to fruition with the publication of good books by Jill Lepore and James D. Drake.[2]

Both Lepore and Drake wrote during the 1990s when multiculturalism's iron grip on American colleges remained strong, and both
tried to seem to be in step. Lepore thanked some Indians "for beginning
to educate me about contemporary views of King Philip's War within the
New England Native American community." Drake, meanwhile, wrote
about "the circle of we" and his "inclusive spirit."[3]

Lepore escaped the wrath of the multiculturalists, but Drake was not
as fortunate. One reviewer castigated his book: "In its own, very distinct
way, it is similar to Leach's 1958 account insofar as it is filled with
stereotyped racial language." This attack needs to be translated for the
uninitiated. Douglas E. Leach has been called racist because his book
employed the word "savages" to refer to the Indians, common usage in
the 1950s when Leach wrote. Leach was no racist, and the quoted comment about Drake's book is absurd.[4]

Such character assassination seems rife. During the 1990s I was selected to write the biography of King Philip for a reference source, *American National Biography*. I resolved to produce a neutral bibliography for
the article and even made no negative comment about Jennings. To my
great surprise, when I received the manuscript back I discovered that
some anonymous copy editor had twisted my words to denounce Leach
as a racist. Needless to say, I made sure that distortion never saw the
light of day.

PC accounts of the American Indian keep appearing. In 2003 the
Colonial Society of Massachusetts published a collection of essays that
should have been entitled *PC on Parade*. Its editors trumpeted: "For the
indigenous peoples of New England . . . the colonial period has not yet
ended." Furthermore, "the legacies of colonial invasion—dispossession,
racism, and ethnocide—are inextricably linked to loss of land, loss of
political sovereignty, and loss of control over the telling of native histories." The foreword to the book noted that "native peoples" felt that
"their past had been appropriated" by historians "who showed insuffi-
cient respect for oral tradition," which constituted "a source of knowledge to which Native Americans alone held the key." Or, perhaps, it
would be more accurate to say that Indians could make up such alleged
oral tradition.[5]

Tribal societies without a written language depended upon oral tradition to pass on their history. The Celts scattered throughout Europe had
a special class of bards who practiced for decades to perform their task
of preserving history. Oral tradition, however, is subject to change over

the years, sometimes by error, sometimes by design. A number of Celtic stories that have survived were deliberately changed by Christians who sought to purge them of their pagan purposes.[6]

The Christian Celts had their own agenda and so did American Indians. Take, for example, Indians whose ancestors took part in the sack of Deerfield in the eighteenth century. During the next century, the story arose that the sacking occurred because the Puritans had stolen a bell originally intended for the Indians' church—the stolen bell was in Deerfield. An Indian, when questioned "How much of this legend is historically true," responded "But very little I fear." He was an honest man.[7]

Indian oral tradition in New England has been shown to be inaccurate. Appendix 2 demonstrated that supposed oral tradition was wrong about how many brothers King Philip had. And Indian activists have an agenda as obvious as that of the Celtic Christians. In other parts of the United States, Indians have been known to deliberately mislead academic investigators.[8]

Oral tradition about either Philip or Miantonomo is made suspect by a basic reality. The hostile Indians of their tribes were all but wiped out. On the other hand, the Mashpee became Christians, thus abandoning their old culture. They fought against Philip's loyal Wampanoags and so survived. Individuals who abandoned their roots and pagan identities are unlikely to preserve oral tradition.

As for the Narragansetts, the situation is more complex. A group of Indians in Rhode Island are, indeed, called Narragansetts. But they are actually descended from Ninigret's people, who are sometimes called Niantics. They were closely related to the main body of Narragansetts ruled by Miantonomo. The Niantics were sometimes referred to as Narragansetts (as they are in this book), but they were not under the direct rule of Miantonomo, whose tribe was destroyed during King Philip's War. Although some lucky individuals may have survived and joined Ninigret's forces, the possibility of an accurate oral tradition about Miantonomo also surviving is practically nil.[9]

Despite such factors making Indian oral tradition unreliable, one scholar has suggested that a statement by the equally unreliable William Apess might have come from "the oral histories of the New England tribes." This is equivalent to pulling facts out of thin air. When I submitted my Miantonomo chapter to a journal, I was faulted for not consulting "present-day Narragansett people who keep the traditions and history of the people." I will never accept that activists, who have no reliable proof, are authorities on events that took place centuries ago.[10]

Historians of colonial New England have truly gone onto a slippery slope. What will be the next step? Will books about Indians have to be submitted to a "tribal council during the editorial process"? Or will owners of Indian casinos be consulted? How far politically correct historians will go on the aforementioned slope is yet to be determined.[11]

Finally, the PC movement has caused one Indian contribution to become obscured. References to the Indian development of valuable food crops such as corn are easy to find. Missing from PC lists of Indian accomplishments is the only plant that is decidedly not politically correct—tobacco. Its banishment represents a considerable change from the past when wooden cigar store Indian statues were practically cultural icons.[12]

The health risks of tobacco make it no longer something to be proud about. That should not obscure tobacco's importance among Indians, even in New England. Roger Williams observed that New England's Indians

> generally all take Tobacco; and it is commonly the only plant which men labour in; the women managing all the rest: they say they take Tobacco for two causes: first, against the rheume, which causeth the toothake, which they are impatient of: secondly, to revive and refresh them, they drinking nothing but water.[13]

Tobacco, while not politically correct, was a significant part of Indian life.

Abbreviations for Notes

AAS	American Antiquarian Society, Worcester, Mass.
BPCW	Blathwayt Papers, Colonial Williamsburg, Williamsburg, Va.
Cal.	*Calendar*
Coll.	*Collections*
Conn.	Connecticut
CR	J. Hammond Trumbull, ed., *The Public Records of the Colony of Connecticut* (Hartford, 1850; rpt. New York, 1968).
CT	Council of Trade
DAB	*Dictionary of American Biography*
DHM	James Phinney Baxter, ed., *Documentary History of the State of Maine, 2nd ser., Vol. IX Containing The Baxter Manuscripts* (Portland, Me., 1907).
DNB	Sir Leslie Stephen and Sir Sidney Lee, eds., *The Dictionary of National Biography* (London, 1885-1890; rpt. 1921-1922).
EIHC	*Essex Institute Historical Collections*
JD	Joseph Dudley
JW	John Winthrop
LT	Lords of Trade
Mass.	Massachusetts
MHS	Massachusetts Historical Society, Boston
NEHGR	*New England Historical and Genealogical Register*
NEQ	*New England Quarterly*
NYCD	E. B. O'Callaghan, ed., *Documents Relative to the Colonial History of the State of New York* (Albany, 1856-1861).
NYHS	New-York Historical Society, New York City
PCR	Nathaniel B. Shurtleff and David Pulsifer, eds., *Records of the Colony of New Plymouth* (Boston, 1855-1861; rpt New York, 1968).

PCSM   Publications of the Colonial Society of Massachusetts
PRO   Public Record Office, Great Britain
Procs.   *Proceedings*
RP   Robert N. Toppan and Alfred T. S. Goodrick, eds., *Edward Randolph: Including His Letters and Official Papers . . . 1676-1703* (Boston, 1898-1909; rpt. New York, 1967).
RW   Roger Williams
SPG   Society for the Propagation of the Gospel
SW   Paul Boyer and Stephen Nissenbaum, eds., *The Salem Witchcraft Papers: Verbatim Transcripts of the Legal Documents of the Salem Witchcraft Outbreak of 1692* (New York, 1977).
WMQ   *William and Mary Quarterly,* 3d ser.

Endnotes

CHAPTER 1
THE RESURGENCE OF THE PURITANS

1. Perry Miller, preface to *Errand Into the Wilderness* (Cambridge, Mass., 1956), viii.

2. Richard Schlatter, "The Puritan Strain," in John Higham, ed., *The Reconstruction of American History* (New York, 1962), 30; Michael McGiffert, "American Puritan Studies in the 1960's," *WMQ*, XXVII (1970), 36; Gregory M. Pfitzer, *Samuel Eliot Morison's Historical World: In Quest of a New Parkman* (Boston, 1991), 133.

3. Miller, preface to *Errand*, viii-ix; Edmund S. Morgan, "The Historians of Early New England," in Ray Allen Billington, ed., *The Reinterpretation of Early American History: Essays in honor of John Edwin Pomfret* (San Marino, Calif., 1966), 54; Francis T. Butts, "The Myth of Perry Miller," *American Historical Review*, LXXXVII (1982), 665; Edmund S. Morgan, *The Genuine Article: A Historian Looks at Early America* (New York, 2004), ix-x; Philip Ranlet, *Richard B. Morris and American History in the Twentieth Century* (Lanham, Md., 2004), 76.

4. McGiffert, "Puritan Studies," 64.

5. George Selement, "Perry Miller: A Note on His Sources in *The New England Mind: The Seventeenth Century*," *WMQ*, XXXI (1974), 453; Miller, preface to *Errand*, ix.

6. George Selement, *Keepers of the Vineyard: The Puritan Ministry and Collective Culture in Colonial New England* (Lanham, Md., 1984), 1; Morgan, "Historians of Early New England," 41-42; David D. Hall, "On Common Ground: The Coherence of American Puritan Studies," *WMQ*, XLIV (1987), 195; Morgan, *Genuine Article*, 3.

7. McGiffert, "Puritan Studies," 38; Butts, "Myth of Miller," 694.

8. Morgan, "Historians of Early New England," 50; Schlatter, "Puritan Strain," 35-37.

9. Schlatter, "Puritan Strain," 36-37; David T. Courtwright, "Fifty Years of American History: An Interview with Edmund S. Morgan," *WMQ*, XLIV (1987), 350, 353. New Left historians are a major exception to the above statement, but their work is so extreme that it is not believable. On the New Left, see Ranlet, "Another Look at the Causes of King Philip's War," *NEQ*, LXI (1988), 79-80, 100.

10. Schlatter, "Puritan Strain," 45.

11. Bernard Bailyn, *The New England Merchants in the Seventeenth Century* (Cambridge, Mass., 1955; New York, 1964), 114-126.

12. Richard L. Bushman, *King and People in Provincial Massachusetts* (Chapel Hill, 1985), 66.

13. Samuel Eliot Morison, *Builders of the Bay Colony* (Boston, 1930), 244-268.

14. JD to Josiah Winslow, Dec. 30, 1678, John Davis Papers, vol. 1, MHS.

CHAPTER 2
THOMAS MORTON OF MERRY MOUNT

1. For some American literature on the subject, see Donald F. Connors, *Thomas Morton* (New York, 1969), 123-132, 164.

2. *Ibid.*, 17; Thomas Morton, *New English Canaan* (1637), ed. Charles Francis Adams, Jr. (Boston, 1883; rpt. New York, 1967), 286; John Frederick Woolverton, *Colonial Anglicanism in North America* (Detroit, 1984), 261n11.

3. "Will of Thomas Morton of Clifford's Inn, Gent.," Aug. 23, 1643, in Charles Edward Banks, ed., "Thomas Morton of Merrymount," MHS, *Procs.*, LVIII (1924-1925), 163.

4. For the confusion over this date, see Ranlet, "The Lord of Misrule: Thomas Morton of Merry Mount," *NEHGR*, CXXXIV (1980), 283n6.

5. "Abstract of John Phipps vs. George Miller *et al*," n. d., Banks, ed., "Morton," MHS, *Procs.*, LVIII, 155.

6. "To the Kings Most Excellent Majesty," July 6, 1622, *ibid.*, 180.

7. "Chancery Proceedings," May 24, 1622, *ibid.*, 165-170.

8. Banks believed Miller's charge that Morton sold his wife's clothes when he deserted her. Since Morton at one time accused Miller of selling his mother's clothes, the charge in both cases was probably a legal fiction and therefore untrue. *Ibid.*, 159-160; "Chancery Decrees and Orders: Miller v. Morton," June 8, 1623, *ibid.*, 187-188; "To the Kings Most Excellent Majesty," July 6, 1622, *ibid.*, 183.

9. "The Joynt and Severall Answeres . . . ," June 3, 1622, *ibid.*, 174.

10. Thomas Wiggin to Sir John Cooke, Nov. 19, 1632, in James Savage, ed., *Gleanings for New England History*, MHS, *Coll.*, 3rd ser., VIII (1843), 323. Alice Miller died before 1636. (See "Blagrave vs. Miller," May 27, 1636, Banks, ed., "Morton," MHS, *Procs.*, LVIII, 189.) A stepson was referred to as a son-in-law at this time.

11. "To the Kings Most Excellent Majesty," June 21, 1636, Banks, ed., "Morton," MHS, *Procs.*, LIX (1925-1926), 92; Henry Gardiner, *New England's Vindication* (1660), ed. Charles Edward Banks (Portland, Me., 1884), 23; Samuel Maverick, *A Briefe Discription of New England and the Severall Townes therein, together with the Present Government thereof* (1662?), MHS, *Procs.*, 2nd ser., I (1885), 238; Sir Ferdinando Gorges, *A Brief Narration of the Originall Undertakings of the Advancement of Plantations Into the parts of America* (1658), MHS, *Coll.*, 3rd ser., VI (1837), 80.

12. Worthington Chauncey Ford, "Captain Wollaston, Humphrey Rasdell and Thomas Weston," MHS, *Procs.*, LI (1917-1918), 223; H. Hobart Holly, "Wollaston of Mount Wollaston," *American Neptune*, XXXVII (1977), 14, 16, 19, 24-25.

13. Holly, "Wollaston," 6-7, 10, 15-16, 18, 22, 24.

14. *Ibid.*, 15-16; Ford, "Wollaston," 221, 223.

15. Donald Francis Connors, "Thomas Morton of Merry Mount: His First Arrival in New England," *American Literature*, XI (1939), 164; Holly, "Wollaston," 16; Ford, "Wollaston," 221-222.

16. Holly, "Wollaston," 15-18; Gardiner, *Vindication*, 23; Frances Rose-Troup, *John White: The Patriarch of Dorcester [Dorset] and the Founder of Massachusetts, 1575-1648* (New York, 1930), 91, 99-100; Lawrence Shaw Mayo, *John Endecott: A Biography* (Cambridge, Mass., 1936), 8; Worthington C. Ford, ed., "The second and farther joint and severall answeares of John White, Clerke, and John Watts . . . ," MHS, *Procs.*, XLIII (1909-1910), 496.

17. Holly, "Wollaston," 15-16.

18. William Bradford, *Of Plymouth Plantation, 1620-1647*, ed. Samuel Eliot Morison (New York, 1952), 205; Abbot Emerson Smith, *Colonists in Bondage: White Servitude and Convict Labor in America, 1607-1776* (Chapel Hill, 1947), 246-247; Ford, "Wollaston," 227-228.

19. Morton, *Canaan*, 276-280.

20. Bradford, *Plymouth*, 205-206.

21. *Ibid.*, 208; *Governour Bradford's Letter Book*, MHS, *Coll.*, 1st ser., III (1794), 61; Bradford and others to the Council for New England, June 9, 1628, *ibid.*, 62.

22. Bradford, *Plymouth*, 205; Morton, *Canaan*, 276-277; David Cressy, *Bonfires and Bells: National Memory and the Protestant Calendar in Elizabethan and Stuart England* (Berkeley, Calif., 1989), 21-22.

23. Cressy, *Bonfires*, 21-22; E. A. Wrigley and R. S. Schofield, *The Population History of England, 1541-1871: A Reconstruction* (Cambridge, Mass., 1981), 286, 290-291; Michael Zuckerman, "Pilgrims in the Wilderness: Community, Modernity, and the Maypole at Merry Mount," *NEQ*, L (1977), 264-265; John Seelye, *Prophetic Waters: The River in Early American Life and Literature* (New York, 1977), 170.

24. Zuckerman, "Maypole," 267.

25. Karen Ordahl Kupperman, *Settling With the Indians: The Meeting of English and Indian Cultures in America, 1580-1640* (London, 1980), 26; Christopher Hill, *Society and Puritanism in Pre-Revolutionary England* (New York, 1964), 184-186; David Underdown, *Revel, Riot, and Rebellion: Popular Politics and Culture in England, 1603-1660* (New York, 1985), 177, 273, 275, 283.

26. Kupperman, *Settling*, 31; Woolverton, *Anglicanism*, 109; Underdown, *Revel*, 67-68, 90; Morton, *Canaan*, 109. When immorality stood by itself, the New England Puritans might ignore it. See the story of Freetown in this book's chapter on Benjamin Colman.

27. Morton, *Canaan*, 282, 295; *Bradford's Letter Book*, 61; Bradford, *Plymouth*, 206-207.

28. Bradford, *Plymouth*, 208; Worthington C. Ford, ed., "Paid for Th: Morton" [and] "Goods in the House and at Natascock," MHS, *Procs.*, XLV (1911-1912), 643; Zuckerman, "Maypole," 259.

29. Morton, *Canaan*, 286; Bradford, *Plymouth*, 208-210.

30. Bradford, *Plymouth*, 206, 210.

31. *Ibid.*, 210, 216-217.

32. Morton, *Canaan*, 283.

33. Edward Johnson, *Johnson's Wonder-Working Providence, 1628-1651*, ed. J. Franklin Jameson (New York, 1910), 69.

34. Morton, *Canaan*, 306-307; Clifford K. Shipton, *Roger Conant: A Founder of Massachusetts* (Cambridge, Mass., 1945), 80-81; Thomas Lechford, *Plain Dealing or News from New England*, Ed. J. Hammond Trumbull (London, 1642; rpt. Boston, 1867), xvi-xx; Thomas G. Barnes, "Thomas Lechford and the Earliest Lawyering in

Massachusetts, 1638-1641," in Daniel R. Coquillette, ed., *Law in Colonial Massachusetts, 1630-1800* (Boston, 1984), 7-9.

35. *Notebook of cases before the Court of wards and liveries,* Nov. 21, 1627, *Winthrop Papers,* ed. Allyn B. Forbes (Boston, 1929-1947), II, 44.

36. Morton, *Canaan,* 311.

37. Samuel Maverick, the source for these statements, claimed that there was "no hurt donn." The Indian apparently was not seriously wounded. Maverick to Earl of Clarendon, n. d., *The Clarendon Papers,* NYHS, *Coll.,* II (1869), 40-41; Thomas Dudley to Countess of Lincoln, Mar. 12, 1630/1, in Alexander Young, ed., *Chronicles of the First Planters of the Colony of Massachusetts Bay, from 1623 to 1636* (Boston, 1846), 321-322.

38. *Ibid.*; John Noble, ed., *Records of the Court of Assistants of the Colony of the Massachusetts Bay, 1630-1692* (Boston, 1904), II, 3-4; JW, *Winthrop's Journal: "History of New England," 1630-1649,* ed. James Kendall Hosmer (New York, 1908), I, 53.

39. Dudley to Lincoln, Mar. 12, 1630/1, Young, ed., *Chronicles,* 321-322; Morton, *Canaan,* 312-313.

40. Richard Arthur Preston, *Gorges of Plymouth Fort* (Toronto, 1953), 282-283, 289, 435n71; "Records of the Council for New England," AAS, *Procs.,* XLVII (1867), 113; Charles Francis Adaams, Jr., "Sir Christopher Gardiner," MHS, *Procs.,* XX (1882-1883), 66-67, 69; Louis Dow Scisco, "Sir Christopher Gardyner," PCSM, *Transactions,* XXXVIII (1947-1951), 10; Hosmer, ed., *Winthrop's Journal,* I, 64.

41. Wiggin to Downing, Aug. 31, 1632, in Savage, ed., *Gleanings,* MHS, *Coll.,* 3rd ser., VIII (1843), 320-321; Wiggin to Cooke, Nov. 19, 1632, *ibid.,* 323; Hosmer, ed., *Winthrop's Journal,* I, 99-101; Preston, *Gorges,* 292; Francis J. Bremer, *John Winthrop: America's Forgotten Founding Father* (Oxford, 2003), 233, 238.

42. W. L. Grant and James Munroe, eds., *Acts of the Privy Council, Colonial Series, 1613-1783* (Hereford, England, 1908), I, 183-185.

43. Preston, *Gorges,* 292; Hosmer, ed., *Winthrop's Journal,* I, 101.

44. Preston, *Gorges,* 295-297, 306; Perry Miller, *Orthodoxy in Massachusetts, 1630-1650* (Boston, 1933; rpt. Gloucester, Mass., 1965), 216.

45. Preston, *Gorges,* 295-297; Bradford, *Plymouth,* 272-274; Robert M. Bartlett, *The Faith of the Pilgrims: An American Heritage* (New York, 1978), 177-178; "The Petition of Edward Winslow," MHS, *Procs.,* V (1860-1862), 131-133.

46. Morton to William Jeffreys, May 1, 1634, in Hosmer, ed., *Winthrop's Journal,* II, 194-196; *ibid.,* I, 130.

47. Morton to Jeffreys, May 1, 1634, *ibid.,* II, 194; Morton, *Canaan,* 344; Connors, *Morton,* 120-121; *Bradford's Letter Book,* 63; Richard Slotkin, *Regeneration Through Violence: The Mythology of the American Frontier, 1600-1860* (Middletown, Conn., 1973), 61; *Oxford English Dictionary,* s. v. "gossip."

48. "Records of the Council for New England," 129; Charles M. Andrews, *The Colonial Period of American History* (New Haven, 1934-1940), I, 420-421. The *quo warranto* is printed in Thomas Hutchinson, *A Collection of Original Papers Relative to the History of the Colony of Massachusetts-Bay* (1769), (New York, 1967), I, 114-118.

49. Morton, *Canaan,* 288, 306, 330-334; Connors, *Morton,* 102,106; Andrews, *Colonial Period,* I, 363n. For *New English Canaan,* see Edith Murphy, "'A Rich Widow, Now to Be Tane Up or Laid Downe': Solving the Riddle of Thomas Morton's 'Rise Oedipeus,'" WMQ, LIII (1996), 755-768.

50. Morton, *Canaan*, 121-123, 179-181; Kupperman, *Settling*, 169.

51. Morton, *Canaan*, 181. William Cronon, *Changes in the Land: Indians, Colonists, and the Ecology of New England* (New York, 1983), depicted the Puritans as despoilers of the environment, and John Demos, "The Maypole of Merry Mount," *American Heritage*, XXXVII (Oct.-Nov. 1986), 82-87, saw Morton as an ecological prophet. Peter Shaw raised disturbing questions about Cronon's book in Shaw, "The Demotion of Man," *Commentary*, LXXXII (Sept. 1986), 32. As for Demos, he is simply wrong.

52. Cradock did not identify what he had read, but from his reaction, the year, and the reference to Morton, the "writing" was a manuscript copy of *New English Canaan*. Matthew Cradock to JW, Mar. 15, 1636/7, Forbes, ed., *Winthrop Papers*, III, 379.

53. Bradford, *Plymouth*, 217; Maverick to Clarendon, n. d., *Clarendon Papers*, 40-41.

54. Gorges to Privy Council, c. 1634, in James Phinney Baxter, ed., *Sir Ferdinando Gorges and his Province of Maine* (Boston, 1890; rpt. New York, 1967), III, 271; Gorges to the king, May 12, 1634, *ibid.*, 260-262; "Considerations by Sir Ferdinando Gorges," Nov. 1634, *ibid.*, 265-268.

55. Gorges to Windebank, Mar. 21, 1634/5, *ibid.*, 273; Preston, *Gorges*, 307-308, 310-311; Leo Francis Stock, ed., *Proceedings and Debates of the British Parliaments respecting North America* (Washington, D.C., 1924-1941), I, 53; Robert E. Moody, "Thomas Gorges, Proprietary Governor of Maine, 1640-1643," MHS, *Procs.*, LXXV (1963), 11.

56. Gorges to Coke, Feb. 27, 1636, Baxter, ed., *Gorges Letters*, III, 278; Gorges to Windebank, Jan. 28, 1639/40, *ibid.*, 294-295; Gorges to JW, Mar. 26, 1640, *ibid.*, 295-296; Gorges's commission, July 23, 1637, Mary Frances Farnham, ed., *Documentary History of the State of Maine, 2nd ser., Vol. VII, Containing the Farnham Papers, 1603-1688* (Portland, Me., 1901), 219-221.

57. Gorges to Windebank, June 20, 1638, Baxter, ed., *Gorges Letters*, III, 288-290.

58. James Phinney Baxter, *George Cleeve of Casco Bay, 1630-1667* (Portland, Me., 1885), 57-59, 63-65; Connors, *Morton*, 26-27; Gorges to Vane, JW, and others, Aug. 23, 1637, Forbes, ed., *Winthrop Papers*, III, 493; Charles Edward Banks, *History of York, Maine* (Boston, 1931), I, 435-439; *York Deeds* (Portland, Me., 1887), I, fols. 94-95, II, fols. 85-86.

59. Baxter, *Cleeve*, 118, 120; Connors, *Morton*, 26-27; Baxter, ed., *Gorges Letters*, I, 189-190; Stock, ed., *Procs. of Parliaments*, I, 143-144; Anthony Fletcher, *The Outbreak of the English Civil War* (New York, 1981), 347.

60. George Lee Haskins, *Law and Authority in Early Massachusetts: A Study in Tradition and Design* (New York, 1960), 64, 115; Miller, *Orthodoxy*, 217; Preston, *Gorges*, 313-314.

61. Thomas Gorges to Sir F. Gorges, [Sept. (?) 1641], Robert E. Moody, ed., *The Letters of Thomas Gorges: Deputy Governor of the Province of Maine, 1640-1643* (Portland, Me., 1978), 55. On Thomas Gorges, see *ibid.*, ix, 6n.

62. Maverick to Clarendon, n. d., *Clarendon Papers*, 40-41; Morton's will, Aug. 23, 1643, Banks, ed., "Morton," LVIII, 163-164; Morton to General Court, May 1645, in Morton, *Canaan*, 89-90.

63. Winslow to JW, Jan. 7, 1643/4, Forbes, ed., *Winthrop Papers*, IV, 428-429.

64. *Ibid.*; Connors, *Morton*, 27; Lothrop Withington, "English Notes about Early Settlers in New England," *EIHC*, XLIX (1913), 256; Morton's will, Aug. 23, 1643, Banks, ed., "Morton," LVIII, 163-164.

65. Morton's will, Banks, ed., "Morton," LVIII, 163-164; William Coddington to JW, Aug. 5, 1644, Forbes, ed., *Winthrop Papers*, IV, 490-491; Nathaniel B. Shurtleff, ed., *Records of the Governor and Company of the Massachusetts Bay in New England* (Boston, 1853-1854), I, 119, 291 (cited hereafter as *Mass. Records*); Holly, "Wollaston," 5; Maverick to Clarendon, n. d., *Clarendon Papers*, 40-41.

66. Coddington to JW, Aug. 5, 1644, Forbes, ed., *Winthrop Papers*, IV, 490-491; Endicott to JW, June 23, 1644, *ibid.*, 464.

67. Endicott to JW, June 23, 1644, *ibid.*, 464; John Browne to JW, June 26, 1644, *ibid.*, 465; James M. O'Toole, "New England Reactions to the English Civil Wars," *NEHGR*, CXXIX (1975), 9-10.

68. Hosmer, ed., *Winthrop's Journal*, II, 194-196; Morton to General Court, May 1645, Morton, *Canaan*, 89-90; Maverick to Clarendon, n. d., *Clarendon Papers*, 40-41; Mayo, *Endecott*, 180-181; *Mass. Records*, II, 90, III, 15; Cleeve and others to governor of Massachusetts, Feb. 18, 1645/6, Forbes, ed., *Winthrop Papers*, V, 61; Banks, *York*, I, 159-160.

69. Hosmer, ed., *Winthrop's Journal*, II, 196; Maverick, *Briefe Discription*, 238-239.

CHAPTER 3
ANNE HUTCHINSON

1. JW, *A Short Story of the Rise, reign and ruine of the Antinomians, Familists and Libertines* (1644), in David D. Hall, ed., *The Antinomian Controversy, 1636-1638: A Documentary History* (Middletown, Conn., 1968), 307-308, 310; Rev 2: 20-23; James Fulton Maclear, "Anne Hutchinson and the Mortalist Heresy," *NEQ*, LIV (1981), 101, 101n; Lyle Koehler, "The Case of the American Jezebels: Anne Hutchinson and Female Agitation during the Years of Antinomian Turmoil, 1636-1640," *WMQ*, XXXI (1974), 56n, 64, 66; Emery Battis, *Saints and Sectaries: Anne Hutchinson and the Antinomian Controversy in the Massachusetts Bay Colony* (Chapel Hill, 1962), vii; Richard B. Morris, *Fair Trial: Fourteen Who Stood Accused from Anne Hutchinson to Alger Hiss*, rev. ed. (New York, 1967), 3; Ann Fairfax Withington and Jack Schwartz, "The Political Trial of Anne Hutchinson," *NEQ*, LI (1978), 229; Selma R. Williams, *Divine Rebel: The Life of Anne Marbury Hutchinson* (New York, 1981), 84.

2. Philip F. Gura, *A Glimpse of Sion's Glory: Puritan Radicalism in New England, 1620-1660* (Middletown, Conn., 1984), 241; Battis, *Saints*, 5, 7-11.

3. Hosmer, ed., *Winthrop's Journal*, I, 299, 331n; William Hutchinson and others to JW, June 29, 1640, Forbes, ed., *Winthrop Papers*, IV, 260; Gura, *Glimpse*, 241; Battis, *Saints*, 11, 13; Wallace Notestein, "The English Woman, 1580 to 1650," in John Harold Plumb, ed., *Studies in Social History: A Tribute to G. M. Trevelyan* (London, 1955; rpt. Freeport, N.Y., 1969), 92.

4. Notestein, "English Woman," 94, 99-100, 103-105; Gura, *Glimpse*, 242; Battis, *Saints*, 43-44; Hall, ed., *Antinomian*, 380; Bremer, *John Winthrop*, 249.

5. Battis, *Saints*, 15, 38, 60, 62; Larzer Ziff, *The Career of John Cotton* (Princeton, 1962), 43.

6. JW, *Short Story*, 263; Hall, ed., *Antinomian*, 370-371; Battis, *Saints*, 4, 6.

7. Gura, *Glimpse*, 129, 243, 258; Battis, *Saints*, 90-92; J. H. Adamson and H. F. Folland, *Sir Harry Vane: His Life and Times (1613-1662)* (Boston, 1973), 118.

8. Hosmer, ed., *Winthrop's Journal*, I, 195, 206; JW, *Short Story*, 308; *Johnson's Wonder-working Providence*, 31, 50; Edwin S. Gaustad, *Liberty of Conscience: Roger Williams in America* (Grand Rapids, Mich., 1991), 52; Gura, *Glimpse*, 60; Edmund S. Morgan, "The Case against Anne Hutchinson," *NEQ*, X (1937), 638; James G. Moseley, *John Winthrop's World: History as a Story; The Story as History* (Madison, Wisc., 1992), 79; Battis, *Saints*, 39.

9. Hosmer, ed., *Winthrop's Journal*, I, 206; JW, *Short Story*, 205-206, 211; Battis, *Saints*, 101, 106; Michael P. Winship, *Making Heretics: Militant Protestantism and Free Grace in Massachusetts, 1636-1641* (Princeton, 2002), 41, 55, 140-141.

10. John Cotton, *The Way of Congregational Churches Cleared* (1648), in Hall, ed., *Antinomian*, 423; JW, *Short Story*, 210; Ziff, *Career*, 114; Battis, *Saints*, 105, 107-108, 137-138.

11. Gura, *Glimpse*, 243-244; *Johnson's Wonder-working Providence*, 127.

12. JW, *Short Story*, 209-210, 308; Gura, *Glimpse*, 69, 243-244; Morgan, "Case," 644; Jasper Rosenmeier, "New England's Perfection: The Image of Adam and the Image of Christ in the Antinomian Crisis, 1634-1638," *WMQ*, XXVII (1970), 458.

13. Thomas Shepard, *God's Plot: The Paradoxes of Puritan Piety Being the Autobiography and Journal of Thomas Shepard*, ed. Michael McGiffert (Amherst, Mass., 1972), 65; Gura, *Glimpse*, 244-245; Battis, *Saints*, 107; Adamson and Folland, *Vane*, 65.

14. Gura, *Glimpse*, 245; Battis, *Saints*, 56-57, 114.

15. John Cotton to Samuel Stone, Mar. 27, [1638], Sargent Bush, Jr., ed., *The Correspondence of John Cotton* (Chapel Hill, 2001), 274; Hall, ed., *Antinomian*, 372; Ziff, *Career*, 116-117, 127; Battis, *Saints*, 108-109.

16. Battis, *Saints*, 126-127.

17. John Wheelwright, *Mercurius Americanus* (1645), in Charles H. Bell, ed., *John Wheelwright, His Writings* (Boston, 1876), 214; Hosmer, ed., *Winthrop's Journal*, I, 211-212; JW, *Short Story*, 265; Adamson and Folland, *Vane*, 95.

18. Hall, ed., *Antinomian*, 161-165, 168-169; Gura, *Glimpse*, 250.

19. Hosmer, ed., *Winthrop's Journal*, I, 211-212, 216-218; Battis, *Saints*, 145-150; Mosely, *Winthrop*, 82.

20. Hosmer, ed., *Winthrop's Journal*, I, 215-216, 225; JW, *Short Story*, 254; Battis, *Saints*, 153-154; Mosely, *Winthrop*, 82; Adamson and Folland, *Vane*, 103, 107.

21. JW, *Short Story*, 248; Shepard, *God's Plot*, 65-66; Gura, *Glimpse*, 251-252; Battis, *Saints*, 165-168, 173.

22. JW, *Short Story*, 256-257; Wheelwright, *Mercurius*, 228; *Mass. Records*, I, 207; Hosmer, ed., *Winthrop's Journal*, I, 239-240; Battis, *Saints*, 184-185.

23. Hosmer, ed., *Winthrop's Journal*, I, 239-240; Hutchinson, *Collection*, I, 73; JW, *Short Story*, 262; Acknowledgment of Thomas Savage, c. Nov. 22, 1637, Forbes, ed., *Winthrop Papers*, III, 516; Acknowledgment of Samuel Wilbur, May 16, 1639, *ibid.*, IV, 121-122; Wheelwright, *Mercurius*, 195; *Mass. Records*, I, 207-208.

24. JW, *Short Story*, 262-263; "The Examination of Mrs. Ann Hutchinson at the court at Newtown," Nov. 1637, in Thomas Hutchinson, *The History of the Colony and Province of Massachusetts-Bay* (1764-1767), ed. Lawrence Shaw Mayo (Cambridge, Mass., 1936), II, 366-376; Ziff, *Career*, 136; Jean Cameron, *Anne Hutchinson, Guilty*

or Not? A Closer Look at Her Trials (New York, 1994), 85; Michael Winship, "'The Most Glorious Church in the World': The Unity of the Godly in Boston, Massachusetts in the 1630s," *Journal of British Studies*, XXXIX (2000), 96; Winship, *Making Heretics*, 7-8, 186.

25. "Examination," Hutchinson, *History*, II, 376-383; JW, *Short Story*, 270-271; Morris, *Fair Trial*, 23; Ziff, *Career*, 134-135,138-139; Morgan, "Case," 646; Battis, *Saints*, 198-202; Winship, *Making Heretics*, 176-177.

26. "Examination," Hutchinson, *History*, II, 382; William Haller, *The Elect Nation: The Meaning and Relevance of Foxe's Book of Martyrs* (New York, 1963), 122-123; Marilyn J. Westerkamp, "Anne Hutchinson, Sectarian Mysticism, and the Puritan Order," *Church History*, LIX (1990), 490. For Bilney see *DNB*, s. v. "Bilney, Thomas."

27. "Examination," Hutchinson, *History*, II, 383-384; JW, *Short Story*, 275; Dan 6: 16-24; Battis, *Saints*, 202-203.

28. "Examination," Hutchinson, *History*, II, 385-391; JW, *Short Story*, 274; Hosmer, ed., *Winthrop's Journal*, I, 240; Ziff, *Career*, 139, 141; Battis, *Saints*, 219.

29. Morris, *Fair Trial*, 11, 13; Withington and Schwartz, "Trial," 226.

30. "Examination," Hutchinson, *History*, II, 388; Jon Swan, "Apocalypse at Munster," *MHQ: The Quarterly Journal of Military History*, II (Spring 1990), 66-77; Thomas J. Curry, *The First Freedoms: Church and State in America to the Passage of the First Amendment* (New York, 1986), 11; Gaustad, *Liberty*, 3; Battis, *Saints*, 41-42.

31. *Mass. Records*, I, 211.

32. *Ibid.*, 212; Gura, *Glimpse*, 256-257; Battis, *Saints*, 212,232.

33. Hall, ed., *Antinomian*, 351; Hosmer, ed., *Winthrop's Journal*, I, 263-264; JW, *Short Story*, 301; Williams, *Rebel*, 188n; Battis, *Saints*, 243-244.

34. Hosmer, ed., *Winthrop's Journal*, I, 263-264; Hall, ed., *Antinomian*, 358, 362, 377; Battis, *Saints*, 239, 241.

35. Hall, ed., *Antinomian*, 372-374; Ziff, *Career*, 145-146; Battis, *Saints*, 245-247.

36. Hall, ed., *Antinomian*, 371-373, 385-386.

37. *Ibid.*, 384, 387-388.

38. Cotton to _____, June 4,[1638], Bush, ed., *Correspondence of Cotton*, 278; Hosmer, ed., *Winthrop's Journal*, I, 264; JW, *Short Story*, 281-282, 307; Carla Gardina Pestana, "The Quaker Executions as Myth and History," *Journal of American History*, LXXX (1993), 441.

39. Hosmer, ed., *Winthrop's Journal*, I, 264; *Johnson's Wonder-working Providence*, 185; Howard M. Chapin, ed., *Documentary History of Rhode Island* (Providence, 1916-1919), I, 59.

40. RW to JW, Apr. 16, 1638, Forbes, ed., *Winthrop Papers*, IV, 25-26; JW, *Short Story*, 214, 280-281; Hosmer, ed., *Winthrop's Journal*, I, 266-268, 277; Wheelwright, *Mercurius*, 196-198; Battis, *Saints*, 247-248; Gura, *Glimpse*, 263; Anne Jacobson Schutt, "'Such Monstrous Births:' A Neglected Aspect of the Antinomian Controversy," *Renaissance Quarterly*, XXXVIII (1985), 88-89; Valerie Pearl and Morris Pearl, eds., "Governor John Winthrop on the Birth of the Antinomians' 'Monster': The Earliest Reports to Reach England and the Making of a Myth," MHS, *Procs.*, CII (1990), 22.

41. Thomas Dudley to JW, Dec. 11, 1638, Forbes, ed., *Winthrop Papers*, IV, 86; Hosmer, ed., *Winthrop's Journal*, II, 7-8, 28; Cotton, *Way*, 437; Wheelwright, *Mercurius*, 198. For Hawkins, see Winship, "'Most Glorious,'" 76n12.

42. William Bradford to JW, Apr. 11, 1638, Forbes, ed., *Winthrop Papers*, IV, 23; RW to JW, Apr. 16, 1638, *ibid.*, 25-26; Hosmer, ed., *Winthrop's Journal*, I, 297, II, 39-40; JW, *Short Story*, 215.

43. Chapin, ed., *Documentary History of Rhode Island*, II, 19, 47, 55-57, 68, 84, 97; James Fulton Maclear, "New England and the Fifth Monarchy: The Quest for the Millennium in Early American Puritanism," *WMQ*, XXXII (1975), 240-242; Gura, *Glimpse*, 264.

44. Hosmer, ed., *Winthrop's Journal*, I, 284; JW, *Short Story*, 218; Gura, *Glimpse*, 265-266; Battis, *Saints*, 248.

45. Hosmer, ed., *Winthrop's Journal*, II, 137-138; *Johnson's Wonder-working Providence*, 186-187; Otto Hufeland, "Anne Hutchinson's Refuge in the Wilderness," in *Anne Hutchinson and Other Papers*, Publications of the Westchester County Historical Society, VII (White Plains, N.Y., 1929), 5, 8-10.

46. Hosmer, ed., *Winthrop's Journal*, II, 122, 166-167; *Mass. Records*, II, 67; Wheelwright, *Mercurius*, 197.

47. Shepard, *God's Plot*, 65, 74; Cotton, *Way*, 413-414; Ziff, *Career*, 147; William K. B. Stoever, *'A Faire and Easie Way to Heaven': Covenant Theology and Antinomianism in Early Massachusetts* (Middletown, Conn., 1978), 165-166; James Fulton Maclear, "'The Heart of New England Rent': The Mystical Element in Early Puritan History," *Mississippi Valley Historical Review*, XLII (1956), 636.

48. Edmund Browne to Sir Simonds D'Ewes, Sept. 7, 1638, Everett Emerson, ed., *Letters from New England: The Massachusetts Bay Colony, 1629-1638* (Amherst, Mass., 1976), 229-230; Cotton, *Way*, 425; Ziff, *Career*, 201-202; Gura, *Glimpse*, 219-220.

49. Hall, ed., *Antinomian*, 382-383; *Johnson's Wonder-working Providence*, 186. Michael P. Winship asserted that the feminist approach to Mrs. Hutchinson "is inadequate for an understanding of the overall controversy. . . ." Winship, *Making Heretics*, 294n65.

CHAPTER 4
MIANTONOMO

1. Bradford, *Plymouth*, 332n5. Modern spellings of Indian tribes have been inserted into quotations. The traditional spelling of Miantonomo's name is used and inserted into quotes where necessary. However, the sachem's name appears to have been pronounced "me-an-te-no-meah." See William Harris to Sir Joseph Williamson, Aug. 12, 1676, *Harris Papers*, Rhode Island Historical Society, *Coll.*, X (1902), 172.

2. Michael Leroy Oberg, "'We Are All the Sachems from East to West' : A New Look at Miantonomi's Campaign of Resistance," *NEQ*, LXXVII (2004), 479-480; Carolyn Merchant, *Ecological Revolutions: Nature, Gender, and Science in New England* (Chapel Hill, 1989), 89; Paul A. Robinson, "Lost Opportunities: Miantonomi and the English in Seventeenth-Century Narragansett Country," in Robert S. Grumet, ed., *Northeastern Indian Lives, 1636-1816* (Amherst, Mass., 1996), 28n; James D. Drake, *King Philip's War: Civil War in New England, 1675-1676* (Amherst, Mass., 1999), 110.

3. William Hubbard, *A Narrative of the Troubles with the Indians in New England* (1677), ed. Samuel G. Drake (New York, 1969), I, 42; Eric S. Johnson, "Uncas and the Politics of Contact," in Grumet, ed., *Northeastern*, 29; P. Richard Metcalf, "Who

Should Rule at Home? Native American Politics and Indian-White Relations," *Journal of American History*, LXI (1974), 652, 657.

4. William Hubbard, *A General History of New England from the Discovery to MDCLXXX* (1815) (New York, 1972), 33; Bradford, *Plymouth*, 87; Daniel Gookin, *Historical Collections of the Indians in New England* (1674), MHS, *Coll.*, 1st ser., 1(1792), 147; "Testimony of Roger Williams relative to the purchase of lands at Seekonk and Providence," Dec. 13, 1661, *The Complete Writings of Roger Williams* (New York, 1963), VI, 316; Neal Salisbury, *Manitou and Providence: Indians, Europeans, and the Making of New England, 1500-1643* (New York, 1982), 147-148.

5. John Winthrop, Jr., to JW, Apr. 7, 1636, Forbes, ed., *Winthrop Papers*, III, 246; Bradford, *Plymouth*, 203; Michael Leroy Oberg, *Dominion and Civility: English Imperialism and Native America, 1585-1685* (Ithaca, N. Y., 1999), 95-96; Neal Salisbury, "Native People and European Settlers in Eastern North America, 1600-1783," in Bruce G. Trigger and Wilcomb E. Washburn, eds., *The Cambridge History of the Native Peoples of The Americas*, Vol. 1 *North America*, Part 1 (Cambridge, 1996), 412.

6. Yasuhide Kawashima, *Igniting King Philip's War: The John Sassamon Murder Trial* (Lawrence, Kansas, 2001), 21; William S. Simmons, *The Narragansett* (New York, 1989), 31; "Testimony of Roger Williams relative to his first coming into the Narragansett country," June 18, 1682, *Williams Writings*, VI, 406-407.

7. RW, *A Key into the Language of America* (1643), in *Williams Writings*, I, 163.

8. Hosmer, ed., *Winthrop's Journal*, I, 89; *A Rhode Islander Reports on King Philip's War: The Second William Harris Letter of August, 1676*, ed. Douglas Edward Leach (Providence, 1963), 53; *Johnson's Wonder-working Providence*, 162.

9. Reginald Laubin and Gladys Laubin, *American Indian Archery* (Norman, Ok., 1980), 113, 121; Joseph B. Oxendine, *American Indian Sports Heritage* (Champaign, Ill., 1988), 91, 97-98; Chapin, ed., *Documentary History of Rhode Island*, I, 140.

10. Edward Winslow, *Good News from New England* (1624), in *The Story of the Pilgrim Fathers*, ed. Edward Arber (London, 1897), 517-519.

11. *Ibid.*, 519-520.

12. A suggestion that the bundle of arrows was actually an offer of alliance can be dismissed. See Joyce E. Chaplin, *Subject Matter: Technology, the Body, and Science on the Anglo-American Frontier, 1500-1676* (Cambridge, Mass., 2001), 107-108.

13. *Johnson's Wonder-working Providence*, 163-164; *PCR*, IX, 14.

14. RW, *Key*, 85; Hubbard, *Narrative*, I, 39-40; Alfred A. Cave, *The Pequot War* (Amherst, Mass., 1996), 66-67.

15. Hosmer, ed., *Winthrop's Journal*, I, 89; Hutchinson, *History*, I, 26-27; Robinson, "Lost," 21. For another mention of uninvited Indians entering houses, see *CR*, I, 52.

16. RW to [General Court of Commissioners of Providence Plantations?], Aug. 25, 1658, *The Correspondence of Roger Williams*, ed. Glenn W. LaFantasie (Hanover, N. H., 1988), II, 485 (cited hereafter as *RW Correspondence*); *ibid.*, 491; RW Testimony, Dec. 13, 1661, *Williams Writings*, VI, 316; Edwin S. Gaustad, *Liberty of Conscience: Roger Williams in America* (Grand Rapids, Mich., 1991), 48; Robinson, "Lost," 17-18.

17. Of the many accounts, the best is still Alden T. Vaughan, "Pequots and Puritans: The Causes of the War of 1637," in his *Roots of American Racism: Essays on the Colonial Experience* (New York, 1995), 177-199.

18. Hosmer, ed., *Winthrop's Journal*, I, 212; RW to Sir Henry Vane or JW, May 13, 1637, *RW Correspondence*, I, 79; *ibid.*, 82n8; John W. De Forest, *History of the Indians of Connecticut: From the Earliest Known Period to 1850* (Hartford, 1851; rpt. Hamden, Conn., 1964), 89; Salisbury, "Native People," 406.

19. Hosmer, ed., *Winthrop's Journal*, I, 184-185, 192-194; Cave, *Pequot War*, 107; Johnson, "Uncas," 32.

20. RW to Vane and JW, May 1, 1637, *RW Correspondence*, I, 72-73; Patrick M. Malone, *The Skulking Way of War: Technology and Tactics Among the New England Indians* (New York, 1991), 16, 22.

21. RW to Vane and JW, May 1, 1637, *RW Correspondence*, I, 72-73.

22. *Ibid.*, 72-74.

23. Hubbard, *Narrative*, II, 17; RW to Vane or JW, May 13, 1637, *RW Correspondence*, I, 78.

24. Peter Vincent, "A True Relation of The late Battell fought in New-England" (1638), in Charles Orr, ed., *History of the Pequot War: The Contemporary Accounts of Mason, Underhill, Vincent and Gardner* (Cleveland, 1897; rpt. New York, 1980), 102; De Forest, *Indians*, 125.

25. John Mason, "A Brief History of The Pequot War" (1735?), in Orr, *History*, 25; Vincent, "True Relation," 102; Hutchinson, *History*, I, 68; "John Hull's Diary of Public Occurences," in *A Library of American Puritan Writings: The Seventeenth Century*, ed. Sacvan Bercovitch, vol. 7 *Puritan Personal Writings: Diaries* (New York, 1982), 171-172; John A. Sainsbury, "Miantonomo's Death and New England Politics, 1630-1645," *Rhode Island History*, XXX (1971), 114; Kawashima, *Igniting*, 5.

26. Mason, "Brief History," 25.

27. Kevin A. McBride, "The Historical Archaeology of the Mashantucket Pequots, 1637-1900," in Lawrence M. Hauptman and James D. Wherry, eds., *The Pequots in Southern New England: The Fall and Rise of an American Indian Nation* (Norman, Ok., 1990), 101; John Underhill, "Newes from America" (1638), in Orr, *History*, 61.

28. Ian K. Steele, *Warpaths: Invasions of North America* (New York, 1994), 92-93; Armstrong Starkey, *European and Native American Warfare, 1675-1815* (Norman, Ok., 1998), 25-26.

29. James Drake, "Restraining Atrocity: The Conduct of King Philip's War," *NEQ*, LXX (1997), 134-136; Peter Charles Hoffer, *Law and People in Colonial America* (Baltimore, 1992), 21-22.

30. Underhill, "Newes," 83; Bradford, *Plymouth*, 296-297; Steven T. Katz, "The Pequot War Reconsidered," in Alden T. Vaughan, ed., *New England Encounters: Indians and Euroamericans, ca. 1600-1850* (Boston, 1999), 115.

31. Underhill, "Newes," 83.

32. *Ibid.*, 80-81.

33. *Ibid.*, 84; Francis Jennings, *The Invasion of America: Indians, Colonialism, and the Cant of Conquest* (New York, 1975), 223; *Oxford English Dictionary*, s. v. "admire," "naught."

34. *Ibid.* Jennings's thesis is supported in Michael Leroy Oberg, *Uncas: First of the Mohegans* (Ithaca, N. Y., 2003), 67, 235n11.

35. RW to JW, July 15, 1637, *RW Correspondence*, I, 101; Drake, *King Philip's War*, 28.

36. Vincent, "True Relation," 104-105; Bradford, *Plymouth*, 296.

37. RW to Vane or JW, May 13, 1637, *RW Correspondence*, I, 78. When RW used the phrase "cut off," he meant to behead. See RW to JW, after Sept. 21, 1638, *ibid.*, 183-184, 187n10 and Oberg, *Uncas*, 70.

38. RW to Vane or JW, May 13, 1637, *RW Correspondence*, I, 78.

39. *Ibid.*, 79; Hosmer, ed., *Winthrop's Journal*, I, 218; Hutchinson, *History*, I, 70. When the Pequots attacked Wethersfield, Conn., in April 1637, one woman and one child were killed. Scholars seem to have forgotten this. See Alden T. Vaughan, *New England Frontier: Puritans and Indians, 1620-1675*, 3d ed. (New York, 1995), 133.

40. RW to JW, July 10, 1637, *RW Correspondence*, I, 96-97; Mason to Commissioners of United Colonies, June 1649, *PCR*, X, 417-418.

41. RW to JW, Aug. 20, 1637, *RW Correspondence*, I, 112-114; Leach, ed., *Second Harris*, 53.

42. RW to JW, Aug. 20, 1637, *RW Correspondence*, I, 112-114; Edward Winslow, *Hypocrisie Unmasked: A True Relation of the Proceedings of the Governor and Company of the Massachusetts Against Samuel Gorton of Rhode Island* (1646), (Providence, 1916), 71; Oberg, *Dominion*, 116-117.

43. Israel Stoughton to JW, c. July 6, 1637, Forbes, ed., *Winthrop Papers*, III, 441-442; RW to JW, Aug. 20, 1637, *RW Correspondence*, I, 112-114.

44. Richard Davenport to JW, Aug. 23, 1637, Forbes, ed., *Winthrop Papers*, III, 491; RW to JW, c. Aug. 12, 1637, *RW Correspondence*, I, 110; RW to JW, c. Sept. 9, 1637, *ibid.*, 117; *ibid.*, 186n2; Johnson, "Uncas," 35.

45. RW to JW, May 27, 1638, *RW Correspondence*, I, 157-158; Lion Gardiner, "Leift. Lion Gardener his relation of the Pequot Warres" (1833), in Orr, *History*, 138-139.

46. RW to JW, c. Sept. 9, 1637, *RW Correspondence*, I, 118; RW to JW, c. June 14, 1638, *ibid.*, 163; Hosmer, ed., *Winthrop's Journal*, I, 238.

47. RW to JW, Jan. 10, 1637/8, *RW Correspondence*, I, 140; RW to JW, Feb. 28, 1637/8, *ibid.*, 145; RW to JW, May 27, 1638, *ibid.*, 157-158; John A. Strong, "Wyandanch: Sachem of the Montauks," in Grumet, ed., *Northeastern*, 19.

48. RW to JW, Feb. 28, 1637/8, *RW Correspondence*, I, 145; RW to JW, May 27, 1638, *ibid.*, 157-158; Gardiner, "Pequot Warres," 138-139.

49. RW to JW, Aug. 14, 1638, *RW Correspondence*, I, 176.

50. RW to JW, after Sept. 21, 1638, *ibid.*, 182-183; RW, *Key*, 101, 201.

51. RW to JW, after Sept. 21, 1638, *RW Correspondence*, I, 183-184; Treaty of Hartford, Sept. 21, 1638, in Vaughan, *New England Frontier*, 340-341; De Forest, *Indians*, 158.

52. McBridge, "Archaeology," 105; Johnson, "Uncas," 31; Kawashima, *Igniting*, 12.

53. Leach, ed., *Second Harris*, 53-55; Bradford, *Plymouth*, 330-331; Hubbard, *General History*, 446.

54. RW to JW, July 21, 1640, *RW Correspondence*, I, 202-203; Bradford to JW, June 29, 1640, Forbes, ed., *Winthrop Papers*, IV, 258-259; Bradford to JW, Aug. 16, 1640, *ibid.*, 275; Coddington to JW, Aug. 25, 1640, *ibid.*, 279; *CR*, I, 52.

55. RW to JW, Aug. 7, 1640, *RW Correspondence*, I, 206; Hosmer, ed., *Winthrop's Journal*, II, 6-7.

56. Hosmer, ed., *Winthrop's Journal*, II, 6-7, 14-15.

57. *CR*, I, 73; *PCR*, IX, 50-51; Winslow, *Hypocrisie*, 72-73; Hubbard, *General History*, 449; Strong, "Wyandanch," 53-54; Cave, *Pequot War*, 213. For what transpired in Maine, see Hosmer, ed., *Winthrop's Journal*, II, 77-78.

58. Roger Wunderlich, "Lion Gardiner, Long Island's Founding Father," in Tom Twomey, ed., *Awakening the Past: The East Hampton 350th Anniversary Lecture Series 1998* (New York, 1999), 44-45.

59. Gardiner, "Pequot Warres," 140-143.

60. "Relation of the Plott-Indian," MHS, *Coll.*, 3d ser., III (1833), 161-164; Hubbard, *General History*, 446-477.

61. Hubbard, *General History*, 446-447.

62. "Relation of the Plott," 161-164.

63. *Ibid.*

64. Winslow to JW, Jan. 7, 1643/4, Forbes, ed., *Winthrop Papers*, IV, 427-428; Benedict Arnold to JW, Jan. 19, 1643/4, *ibid.*, 432-433.

65. Bradford, *Plymouth*, 203; RW, *Key*, 176; Constance A. Crosby, "From Myth to History, or Why King Philip's Ghost Walks Abroad," in Mark P. Leone and Parker B. Potter, Jr., eds., *The Recovery of Meaning: Historical Archaeology in the Eastern United States* (Washington, D. C., 1988), 194-195; Salisbury, "Native People," 406-407; Karen Ordahl Kupperman, *Indians and English: Facing Off in Early America* (Ithaca, N. Y., 2000), 235.

66. RW to Vane or JW, May 13, 1637, *RW Correspondence*, I, 78; RW, *Key*, 159-161.

67. RW, *Key*, 85; Oberg, *Dominion*, 118.

68. Gardiner, "Pequot Warres," 139-140; "Relation of the Plott," 161-164; Winslow, *Hypocrisie*, 72-73.

69. *CR*, I, 73-74, 80; *Mass. Records*, II, 23-25, 28-29; Hosmer, ed., *Winthrop's Journal*, II, 75-80; Hubbard, *General History*, 447-448.

70. Winslow, *Hypocrisie*, 2; Hubbard, *General History*, 402, 404; Chapin, ed., *Documentary History of Rhode Island*, I, 168; *RW Correspondence*, I, 275n13.

71. Hubbard, *General History*, 404; Bradford, *Plymouth*, 96-97.

72. In 1656 RW reversed himself about the independence of the rebellious sachems. Apparently, RW's distaste for Gorton influenced his earlier statement. Arnold detested Gorton too and his testimony likely was affected by his feelings as well. RW to General Court of Massachusetts, May 12, 1656, *RW Correspondence*, II, 451, 453-454n6; Winslow, *Hypocrisie*, 2-3 and Epistle Dedicatory; Hubbard, *General History*, 401-402, 405, 451-452; Hosmer, ed., *Winthrop's Journal*, II, 122-126, 135-136; Sainsbury, "Miantonomo's Death," 122.

73. *PCR*, IX, 10-11; *Johnson's Wonder-working Providence*, 221; Sainsbury, "Miantonomo's Death," 117.

74. RW to John Winthrop, Jr., c. Apr. 7, 1649, *RW Correspondence*, I, 277-278; Timothy J. Sehr, "Ninigret's Tactics of Accommodation: Indian Diplomacy in New England, 1637-75," *Rhode Island History*, XXXVI (1977), 49.

75. *Johnson's Wonder-working Providence*, 220; RW, *Key*, 166.

76. *PCR*, IX, 11; Hosmer, ed., *Winthrop's Journal*, II, 130-131; De Forest, *Indians*, 189-191; Leach, ed., *Second Harris*, 55; Oberg, "'We Are All,'" 496.

77. Hubbard, *General History*, 450-451; Winslow, *Hypocrisie*, 71; Leach, ed., *Second Harris*, 55, 55n70; De Forest, *Indians*, 190-191; Simmons, *Narragansett*, 42.

78. John Haynes to JW, Feb. 17, 1643/4, Forbes, ed., *Winthrop Papers*, IV, 507; *PCR*, IX, 14-15; Oberg, *Dominion*, 120.

79. *PCR*, IX, 11-12; Leach, ed., *Second Harris*, 55-57.

80. *PCR*, IX, 11-12, 15; Hubbard, *General History*, 451-452; Winslow, *Hypocrisie*, 73-74; *CR*, I, 94-95.

81. Winslow, *Hypocrisie*, 80; RW, *Key*, 166; De Forest, *Indians*, 197-198; Kathleen J. Bragdon, *Native People of Southern New England, 1500-1650* (Norman, Ok., 1996), 226; Sainsbury, "Miantonomo's Death," 118.

82. Samuel Gorton, *Simplicities Defence against Seven-Headed Policy* (1646), in *Library of American Puritan Writings*, vol. 10, 89; Hosmer, ed., *Winthrop's Journal*, II, 134.

83. Winslow, *Hypocrisie*, 71 and Epistle Dedicatory.

84. Winslow to JW, Mar. 28, 1645, Forbes, ed., *Winthrop Papers*, IV, 18.

85. Leach, ed., *Second Harris*, 51, 59; Harris to Williamson, Aug. 12, 1676, *Harris Papers*, 171-172; Simmons, *Narragansett*, 44.

CHAPTER 5
SAMUEL MAVERICK

1. Oliver Ayer Roberts, *History of The Military Company of the Massachusetts, Now Called The Ancient and Honorable Artillery Company of Massachusetts, 1637-1888*, vol. 1 (Boston, 1895), 184, 187; Bremer, *John Winthrop*, 366; J. M. Sosin, *English America and the Restoration Monarchy of Charles II: Transatlantic Politics, Commerce, and Kinship* (Lincoln, Neb., 1980), 108, 113, 121; Richard S. Dunn, *Puritans and Yankees: The Winthrop Dynasty of New England, 1630-1717* (Princeton, 1962; New York, 1971), 157; Bailyn, *New England Merchants*, 126; Margaret E. Newell, "Robert Child and the Entrepreneurial Vision: Economy and Ideology in Early New England," *NEQ*, LXVIII (1995), 233n22.

2. Maverick, *Briefe Discription*, 247.

3. Endicott to Charles II, Dec. 19, 1660, *Mass. Records*, IV, part 1, 450-453.

4. Thomas Breedon to Council for Foreign Plantations, Mar. 11, 1660/1, *Clarendon Papers*, 16-19.

5. Maverick, *Briefe Discription*, 232-233, 236, 246; Banks, *Planters*, 56-57; Banks, *York*, I, 79, 135-136, 240; Mellen Chamberlain, *A Documentary History of Chelsea, 1624-1824* (Boston, 1908), I, 16-17.

6. Hosmer, ed., *Winthrop's Journal*, I, 50, 225, II, 247-248; *Johnson's Wonder-working Providence*, 63-64, 63n-64n; William Tompson to JW, May 25, 1638, Forbes, ed., *Winthrop Papers*, IV, 34 and II, 264n; John Josselyn, *Colonial Traveler: A Critical Edition of Two Voyages to New England*, ed. Paul J. Lindholt (Hanover, N. H., 1988), 12; Gardiner, *Vindication*, 37-38, 38n; Edmund S. Morgan, *The Puritan Dilemma: The Story of John Winthrop* (Boston, 1958), 190; Maverick's deposition on La Tour, Oct. 28, 1654, Photostat, MHS.

7. *Mass. Records*, I, 104; Hosmer, ed., *Winthrop's Journal*, I, 76, 96, 185-186; Josselyn, *Colonial Traveler*, 24; Charles Knowles Bolton, *The Real Founders of New England: Stories of Their Life Along the Coast, 1602-1628* (Boston, 1929), 157.

8. Hosmer, ed., *Winthrop's Journal*, I, 114-115, 136-137. Later, after Maverick began to oppose the Puritans, JW crossed out the word perpetual. Richard S. Dunn, "John Winthrop Writes His Journal," *WMQ*, XLI (1984), 196n.

9. *Johnson's Wonder-working Providence*, 64; Maverick to JW, Mar. 11, 1640/1, Forbes, ed., *Winthrop Papers*, IV, 324; *Mass. Records*, I, 140, 159; Darret B. Rutman, *Winthrop's Boston: Portrait of a Puritan Town, 1630-1649* (Chapel Hill, 1965), 70-71; *Suffolk Deeds* (Boston, 1880-1906), Liber I, 15; Chamberlain, *Chelsea*, I, 21, 28.

10. Hosmer, ed., *Winthrop's Journal*, I, 185-186; Maverick to JW, c. 1640, Forbes, ed., *Winthrop Papers*, IV, 167; Maverick to JW, Mar. 11, 1640/1, *ibid.*, 324; Dudley to Lincoln, Mar. 12, 1630/1, Young, ed., *Chronicles*, 322-323; Rutman, *Winthrop's Boston*, 185, 199; Bremer, *John Winthrop*, 345-346; William Prescott Greenlaw, "John Maverick and Some of His Descendants," *NEHGR*, XCVI (1942), 233.

11. Maverick to JW, Mar. 11, 1640/1, Forbes, ed., *Winthrop Papers*, IV, 324; Noble, ed., *Court Records*, II, 103.

12. Hosmer, ed., *Winthrop's Journal*, II, 47; Noble, ed., *Court Records*, II, 108-109.

13. Hosmer, ed., *Winthrop's Journal*, II, 47-48; Paul R. Lucas, "Colony or Commonwealth: Massachusetts Bay, 1661-1666," *WMQ*, XXIV (1967), 90.

14. "A Remonstrance and Petition of Robert Child, and others," Hutchinson, *Collection*, I, 214-223; Gura, *Glimpse*, 196-198; *DAB*, s. v. "Maverick, Samuel." Sometime in 1644 or 1645 Maverick had sent some unknown complaints about Massachusetts to England. Nothing seems to have resulted from it. Stephen Winthrop to John Winthrop, Jr., Mar. 1, 1644/5, *Winthrop Papers*, MHS, *Coll.*, 5th ser., VIII (1882), 200-201.

15. JW to J. Winthrop, Jr., Nov. 16, 1646, Forbes, ed., *Winthrop Papers*, V, 119-120; Hosmer, ed., *Winthrop's Journal*, II, 296-297, 307.

16. Hosmer, ed., *Winthrop's Journal*, II, 297.

17. *Ibid.*, 306-309, 316; *Mass. Records*, III, 166; Maverick to General Court, May 8, 1649, Photostat, MHS.

18. Maverick to General Court, May 1649, *Mass. Records*, III, 166-167; Maverick to General Court, Oct. 25, 1648, Photostat, MHS.

19. *Mass. Records*, III, 167, 200.

20. Vincent T. Harlow, *A History of Barbados, 1625-1685* (Oxford, 1926; rpt. New York, 1969), 268-269; S. Maverick to Nathaniel Maverick, Nov. 15, 1649, Photostat, MHS; Deed to George Briggs, Jan. 14, 1649/50, *ibid.*; Rutman, *Winthrop's Boston*, 70-71.

21. S. Maverick to N. Maverick, [1650], Photostat, MHS; S. Maverick to N. Maverick, Apr. 15, 1651, *ibid.*; S. Maverick to William Vassall and others, July 22, 1651, *ibid.*; Deed of Noddle's Island, July 31, 1656, *ibid.*; *Suffolk Deeds*, Liber I, 122-123; Harlow, *Barbados*, 54, 75-77.

22. Deed of Noddle's Island, July 31, 1656, Photostat, MHS; "John Sayre's Proposals," [1656?], *ibid.*; Deed of Noddle's Island, Feb. 9, 1656/7, *ibid.*; *Mass. Records*, III, 309-310, IV, part 1, 132.

23. *Suffolk Deeds*, Liber I, 262; S. Maverick to N. Maverick, Apr. 15, 1651, Photostat, MHS; S. Maverick to Governor and General Court of Massachusetts, Aug. 5, 1658, Washburn Papers, Vol. 1, MHS.

24. S. Maverick to Governor and General Court of Massachusetts, Aug. 5, 1658, Washburn Papers, Vol. 1, MHS; *Records of the Suffolk County Court, 1671-1680,* PCSM, XXX, *Coll.* (1933), 960; *Mass. Records,* IV, part 2, 381.

25. *Mass. Records,* III, 428, IV, part 1, 297; Maverick to General Court, May 1657, Photostat, MHS.

26. S. Maverick to Governor and General Court of Massachusetts, Aug. 5, 1658, Washburn Papers, Vol. 1, MHS; D. T. Witcombe, *Charles II and the Cavalier House of Commons, 1663-1674* (New York, 1966), 1.

27. Andrews, *Colonial Period,* II, 134; Morison, *Builders,* 257; Dunn, *Puritans and Yankees,* 124-125; Maverick, *Briefe Discription,* 244; Edward Godfrey to J. Winthrop, Jr., Oct. 5, 1661, *Winthrop Papers,* MHS, *Coll.,* VII (1865), 380. For the Maverick-John Winthrop, Jr., letters, see *ibid.,* 309-320.

28. Maverick to Clarendon, n. d., *Clarendon Papers,* 20-21; [Maverick] to Clarendon, n. d., *ibid.,* 22-25; Lucas, "Colony or Commonwealth," 98.

29. [Maverick] to Clarendon, n. d., *Clarendon Papers,* 26-28; Maverick to Clarendon, n. d., *ibid.,* 29-30. Maverick did not know that the Puritans had executed a man for masturbation and another for bestiality. Dunn, "Winthrop Writes," 209.

30. [Maverick] to Clarendon, n.d., *Clarendon Papers,* 26-27; Maverick to Clarendon, n.d.., *ibid.,* 31-32; Maverick to Clarendon, n.d., *ibid.,* 33.

31. Maverick, "A Representation of the state of affaires in New England . . . ," Feb. 1662/3, *ibid.,* 47; Maverick to Clarendon, n.d., *ibid.,* 30-31.

32. *Mass. Records,* IV, part 1, 451, 455-456.

33. *Ibid..,* IV, part 2, 37.

34. Maverick to Clarendon, n.d., *Clarendon Papers,* 38-41; Mayo, *Endecott,* 84-85; Israel Stoughton to John Stoughton, 1635, Emerson, ed., *Letters,* 144-145; Maverick, *Briefe Discription,* 242.

35. Maverick to Clarendon, Mar. 28, 1662/3, *Clarendon Papers,* 48-49; Sosin, *Charles II,* 106, 108; Noble, ed., *Court Records,,* II, 18; "Sir Joseph Williamson's Original Notes relating to New England, Written about 1663," MHS, *Procs.,* X (1867-1869), 381; John Corwin to _____, 1662, Photostat, MHS.

36. "Testimoniall from the Merchants," Mar. 20, 1662/3, *Clarendon Papers,* 49-50.

37. Sosin, *Charles II,* 106; "Instructions to . . . Colonel Richard Nicolls . . . ," Apr. 23, 1664, E. B. O'Callaghan, ed., *Documents Relative to the Colonial History of the State of New York* (Albany, 1853-1861), III, 51 (cited hereafter as *NYCD*); "Instructions . . . for the visitation of . . . Conecticott," Apr. 23, 1664, *ibid.,* 55; "Complaint of the intrusion of the Dutch into Manhattoes," July 6, 1663, *ibid.,* 46; Maverick, *Briefe Discription,* 245-246.

38. Sosin, *Charles II,* 108; David S. Lovejoy, *The Glorious Revolution in America* (New York, 1972), 127. For the conquest of New Netherland, see Robert C. Ritchie, *The Duke's Province: A Study of New York Politics and Society, 1664-1691* (Chapel Hill, 1977), 20-24.

39. Bailyn, *New England Merchants,* 126; Nicolls to secretary of state, Oct. 1664, *NYCD,* III, 68-69; Maverick to Nicolls, July 5, 1669, *ibid.,* 184; Maverick to J. Winthrop, Jr., Nov. 26, 1664, *Winthrop Papers,* MHS, *Coll.,* 4th ser., VII (1865), 311.

40. Maverick to Nicolls, Oct. 15, 1669, *NYCD,* III, 185; Maverick to Nicolls, July 5, 1669, *ibid.,* 182.

41. "Instructions to . . . Nicolls," Apr. 23, 1664, *ibid.,* 54.

42. "Instructions . . . to be considered and communicated only betweene themselves," Apr. 23, 1664, *ibid.*, 58.

43. *Ibid.*, 58, 60.

44. Witcombe, *Charles II*, 3.

45. Cartwright to Bennet, Jan. 16, 1664/5, *NYCD*, III, 83; Cartwright to Nicolls, Jan. 25, 1664/5, *ibid.*, 84; Cartwright to Nicolls, Feb. 4, 1664/5, *ibid.*, 87; "Report of the King's Commissioners concerning Massachusetts," n. d., *ibid.*, 111.

46. Cartwright to Nicolls, Feb. 4, 1664/5, *ibid.*, 87-88; Cartwright to Bennet, Feb. 7, 1664/5, *ibid.*, 89.

47. Carr, Cartwright, and Maverick to Bennet, May 27, 1665, *ibid.*, 96-97. For an account of the commission in these colonies, see Dunn, *Puritans and Yankees*, 157-168.

48. Cartwright to Nicolls, Apr. 19, 1665, *NYCD*, III, 94.

49. General Court to Charles II, Oct. 25, 1664, in Hutchinson, *History*, I, 445-449; Clarendon to Massachusetts, Mar. 15, 1664/5, *ibid.*, 450-451; Clarendon to Maverick, Mar. 5, 1664/5, *NYCD*, III, 92.

50. Bailyn, *New England Merchants*, 122; Deane to Clarendon, June 22, 1665, *Clarendon Papers*, 68-69; *Mass. Records*, IV, part 2, 218-219.

51. "Cartwright's Answer," Jan. 5, 1665/6, *Clarendon Papers*, 93-94.

52. *Ibid.*; "Instructions to . . . Nicolls," Apr. 23, 1664, *NYCD*, III, 53; Carr and Maverick to secretary of state, Nov. 20, 1665, *ibid.*, 107; *Mass. Records*, IV, part 2, 177.

53. *Mass. Records*, IV, part 2, 196. For the Puritan version, see Lucas, "Colony or Commonwealth," 104.

54. "Cartwright's Answer," Jan. 5, 1665/6, *Clarendon Papers*, 96.

55. "Declaration of the General Court of Massachusetts," May 23, 1665, *NYCD*, III, 95-96; Carr and Maverick to secretary of state, Nov. 20, 1665, *ibid.*, 107; Nicolls to Clarendon, Apr. 7, 1666, *Clarendon Papers*, 113-114.

56. Carr and Maverick to secretary of state, Nov. 20, 1665, *NYCD*, III, 107; Nicolls and others to General Court, May 24, 1664 [sic 1665], *ibid.*, 96.

57. Carr, Cartwright, and Maverick to Bennet, July 26, 1665, *ibid.*, 101-102; Maverick to Arlington, Aug. 25, 1668, *ibid.*, 173.

58. *Ibid.*; Carr and Maverick to secretary of state, Nov. 20, 1665, *ibid.*, 107-108; Massachusetts governor and council to Portsmouth constable, July 12, 1665, *ibid.*, 98; Carr, Cartwright, and Maverick to Bennet, July 26, 1665, *ibid.*, 101-102; *Mass. Records*, IV, part 2, 168; "Orders etc. of the Commissioners," June 23, 1665, James Phinney Baxter, ed., *Documentary History of the State of Maine, Vol. IV Containing the Baxter Manuscripts* (Portland, Me., 1889), 204. Cartwright appears not to have been present when the constable arrived. "Cartwright's Answer," Jan. 5, 1665/6, *Clarendon Papers*, 89.

59. Massachusetts governor and council to commissioners, [July 1665], *NYCD*, III, 98; Commissioners to Massachusetts governor and council, July 16, 1665, *ibid.*, 99.

60. Carr and Maverick to secretary of state, Nov. 20, 1665, *ibid.*, 107-108; Maverick to Nicolls, July 5, 1669, *ibid.*, 182, 184; Maverick to Arlington, Aug. 25, 1668, *ibid* 173-174; "Papers in the Case of Corbett," *Clarendon Papers*, 138-139.

61. Bellingham to Robert Boyle, May 31, 1665, *Clarendon Papers*, 66-67; Bellingham to Clarendon, May 30, 1665, *ibid.*, 60-62; "Cartwright's Answer," Jan. 5, 1665/6, *ibid.*, 99, 104, 105. The defense is in *Mass. Records*, IV, part 2, 157-265.

62. Maverick to Clarendon, Nov. 7, 1665, *Clarendon Papers*, 80; Nicolls to Arlington, Apr. 9, 1666, *NYCD*, III, 114.

63. "Cartwright's Answer," Jan. 5, 1665/6, *Clarendon Papers*, 100-101; Cartwright to Nicolls, Jan. 25, 1664/5, *NYCD*, III, 84.

64. "Cartwright's Answer," Jan. 5, 1665/6, *Clarendon Papers*, 89, 104; Maverick to Clarendon, July 24, 1665, *ibid.*, 73-74.

65. "Cartwright's Answer," Jan. 5, 1665/6, *ibid.*, 106; "Memoranda by Colonel Cartwright," n. d., *ibid.*, 107; Maverick to Clarendon, July 24, 1665, *ibid.*, 70; Maverick to Clarendon, Aug. 11, 1665, *ibid.*, 77-78.

66. Charles II to Massachusetts, Apr. 10, 1666, in Hutchinson, *History*, I, 453-454.

67. *Mass. Records*, IV, part 2, 315, 317; Maverick to Cartwright, n. d., *Clarendon Papers*, 126-128; Breedon and others to General Court, n. d., *ibid.*, 132-134; Nicolls, Carr, and Maverick to Massachusetts, Nov. 3, 1666, *ibid.*, 134-136; Maverick to secretary of state, Oct. 16, 1667, *NYCD*, III, 160; Nicolls to Morrice, Oct. 24, 1666, *ibid.*, 136; Maverick to Arlington, Aug. 25, 1668, *ibid.*, 173.

68. Carr and Maverick to Clarendon, Jan. 10, 1666/7, *Clarendon Papers*, 157-159; Nicolls to Morrice, Oct. 24, 1666, *NYCD*, III, 136-137.

69. Clarendon to Nicolls, Apr. 13, 1666, *ibid.*, 116; Maverick to Nicolls, July 5, 1669, *ibid.*, 184.

70. Dunn, *Puritans and Yankees*, 164; Robert Latham and William Matthews, eds., *The Diary of Samuel Pepys* (Berkeley and Los Angeles, 1970-1983), VII, 395, 397; Maverick to Nicolls, July 5, 1669, *NYCD*, III, 183-184.

71. Ritchie, *Duke's Province*, 80; Maverick to Sampson Bond, May 30, 1669, *Winthrop Papers*, MHS, *Coll.*, 4th ser., VII (1865), 317; Maverick to Nicolls, July 5, 1669, *NYCD*, III, 184; Maverick to Nicolls, Oct. 15, 1669, *ibid.*, 185; *DAB*, s. v. "Maverick, Samuel."

CHAPTER 6
KING PHILIP

1. Douglas Edward Leach, *Flintlock and Tomahawk: New England in King Philip's War* (New York, 1958), 243.

2. James Axtell and William C. Sturtevant, "The Unkindest Cut, or Who Invented Scalping?," *WMQ*, XXXVII (1980), 453. Revisionist works include Philip Ranlet, "Another Look at the Causes of King Philip's War," *NEQ*, LXI (1988), 79-100; James Warren Springer, "American Indians and the Law of Real Property in Colonial New England," *American Journal of Legal History*, XXX (1986), 25-58; Jill Lepore, *The Name of War: King Philip's War and the Origins of American Identity* (New York, 1998); Drake, *King Philip's War*.

3. William Apess, "Eulogy on King Philip, as Pronounced at the Odeon, in Federal Street, Boston" (1836), in Barry O'Connell, ed., *On Our Own Ground: The Complete Writings of William Apess, a Pequot* (Amherst, Mass., 1992), 283, 293, 298, 302. For Philip's paternity, see Appendix 2, "Who Was Philip's Father?"

4. *John Eliot's Indian Dialogues: A Study in Cultural Interactions* (1671), eds. Henry W. Bowden and James P. Ronda (Westport, Conn., 1980), 80, 164n19; Kristina

Bross, *Dry Bones and Indian Sermons: Praying Indians in Colonial America* (Ithaca, 2004), 50; Drake, *King Philip's War*, 10.

5. Daniel K. Richter, *Facing East from Indian Country: A Native History of Early America* (Cambridge, Mass., 2001), 251; Joshua David Bellin, "Apostle of Removal: John Eliot in the Nineteenth Century," *NEQ*, LXIX (1996), 4.

6. Oberg, "'We Are All the Sachems,'" 479-480, 496, 498-499. Oberg's remark about a united Indian resistance is contradicted by his book. See Oberg, *Uncas*, 189. The quotation summarizing Bellin is actually a translation by his editors. His jargon-filled essay is difficult to follow. Colin G. Calloway and Neal Salisbury, introduction to Calloway and Salisbury, eds., *Reinterpreting New England Indians and the Colonial Experience*, PCSM, LXXI, Coll. (2003), 18-19. For those interested in the mindless drivel, see Bellin, "'A Little I Shall Say': Translation and Interculturalism in the John Eliot Tracts," *ibid.*, 56-57.

7. John W. Tyler, foreword to Calloway and Salisbury, eds., *Reinterpreting*, 9; Jennings, *Invasion*, 55, 80, 164. Following Tyler's example, I should apologize for my first ancestor in America, Charles Runlett. During King Philip's War, an Indian war party that had killed several colonists captured him in New Hampshire. Runlett convinced one of the Indians to allow him to escape. How rude and impolite of my ancestor to escape rather than staying and enduring captivity or being killed. See Joseph Milton Odiorne, *A Rundlett-Randlett Genealogy, Mainly Descendants of Charles Runlett of Exeter, N. H., 1652?-1709* (Farmington, Maine, 1976), 1. On the use of the word "massacre," see Evan Haefeli and Kevin Sweeney, *Captors and Captives: The 1704 French and Indian Raid on Deerfield* (Amherst, Mass., 2003), 272. For related topics, see Appendix 3, "The PC Indian."

8. *Johnson's Wonder-working Providence*, 39-42; Bradford, *Plymouth*, 87; Sherburne F. Cook, "The Significance of Disease in the Extinction of the New England Indians," *Human Biology*, XLV (1973), 487-489.

9. Henry Warner Bowden, *American Indians and Christian Missions: Studies in Cultural Conflict* (Chicago, 1981), 98; William Wood, *New England's Prospect* (1634), ed. Alden T. Vaughan (Amherst, Mass., 1977), 102; William Bradford and Edward Winslow, *A Relation or Journall of the beginning and proceedings of the English Plantation setled at Plimoth in New England* (1622), (Ann Arbor, Mich., 1966), 37.

10. Winslow, *Good News*, 546-555; Frank Shuffleton, "Indian Devils and Pilgrim Fathers: Squanto, Hobomok, and the English Conception of Indian Religion," *NEQ*, XLIX (1976), 115.

11. Winslow, *Good News*, 548-549, 554-555.

12. *Ibid.*, 545, 555-556, 568-569; Bradford, *Plymouth*, 99, 116-118.

13. Hosmer, ed., *Winthrop's Journal*, I, 76, 269, II, 67; Louis B. Mason, *The Life and Times of Major John Mason of Connecticut: 1600-1672* (New York, 1935), 38; *New England's First Fruits* (1643) in Samuel Eliot Morison, *The Founding of Harvard College* (Cambridge, Mass., 1935), 428; Wood, *New England's Prospect*, 88-89.

14. Patrick M. Malone, "Changing Military Technology Among the Indians of Southern New England, 1600-1677," *American Quarterly*, XXV (1973), 50; RW, *Key*, 145, 180; Wood, *New England's Prospect*, 79.

15. John K. Mahon, "Anglo-American Methods of Indian Warfare, 1676-1794," *Mississippi Valley Historical Review*, XLV (1958-1959), 255; Josselyn, *Colonial Traveler*, 103-104; Malone, "Technology," 50-51; RW, *Key*, 200-201; Wood, *New England's Prospect*, 79; Ruth A. McIntyre, "John Pynchon and the New England Fur Trade,

1652-1676," in Carl Bridenbaugh and Juliette Tomlinson, eds., *The Pynchon Papers* (Boston, 1982-1985), II, 11.

16. Hubbard, *Narrative*, I, 46-47; *PCR*, III, 192; Betty Groff Schroeder, "The True Lineage of King Philip (Sachem Metacom)," *NEHGR*, CXLIV (1990), 211-214. Massasoit's date of death is uncertain.

17. *PCR*, III, 167, 192. On pigs, see Virginia DeJohn Anderson, "King Philip's Herds: Indians, Colonists, and the Problem of Livestock in Early New England," *WMQ*, LI (1994), 601-624, and also the exchange of letters between Anderson and myself that was published in *WMQ*, LII (1995), 575-580.

18. *PCR*, III, 192; Josselyn, *Colonial Traveler*, 92; Jane T. Merritt, *At the Cross-roads: Indians and Empires on a Mid-Atlantic Frontier, 1700-1763* (Chapel Hill, 2003), 57-58, 60. For more on the name game, see Appendix 1, "Philip's Name: A Cottage Industry."

19. John Cotton to I. Mather, c. Mar. 20, 1676/7, *The Mather Papers*, MHS, *Coll.*, 4th ser., VIII (1868), 233-234.

20. Hutchinson, *History*, I, 235n; J. Cotton to I. Mather, c. Mar. 20, 1676/7, *Mather Papers*, 232-234.

21. *PCR*, IV, 8, 25-26. Philip's letter printed in "Sachem Philip, His Answer to the Letter Brought to Him from the Governor of New-Plymouth," MHS, *Coll.*, 1st ser., VI (1799), 94, may have been written at this time.

22. *PCR*, III, 192, IV, 16-17, 24-25, 109-110; "A Letter from King Philip to Governour Prince," n. d., MHS, *Coll.*, 1st ser., II (1793), 40. Philip's letter was probably written in late 1662 or early 1663. Jennings, *Invasion*, 290n-291n.

23. Cotton Mather, *Magnalia Christi Americana; Or, The Ecclesiastical History of New-England* (1702), ed. Thomas Robbins (New York, 1967), I, 561-562; Bross, *Dry Bones*, 6.

24. Richard Baxter to Eliot, Jan. 20, 1656/7, *Some Unpublished Correspondence of the Reverend Richard Baxter and the Reverend John Eliot, the Apostle of the American Indians, 1656-1682*, ed. F. J. Powicke (Manchester, Eng., 1931), 21; Eliot to Baxter, Oct. 7, 1657, Jan. 22, 1667/8, *ibid.*, 22-23, 32; C. Mather, *Magnalia*, I, 567n6; Bross, *Dry Bones*, 34, 78.

25. Eliot to Humphrey Atherton, June 4, 1657, MHS, *Coll.*, 1st ser., II (1793), 9; Eliot, *A Late and Further Manifestation of the Progress of the Gospel in New-England* (1655), MHS, *Coll.*, 3rd ser., IV (1834), 271.

26. Eliot to Mr. Steele, Dec. 8, 1652, "Letters of the Rev. John Eliot, the Apostle to the Indians," *NEHGR*, XXXVI (1882), 294 (cited hereafter as "Letters of the Apostle"); James P. Ronda, "'We Are Well As We Are': An Indian Critique of Seventeenth-Century Christian Missions," *WMQ*, XXXIV (1977), 67; Matt 4: 18-22, 8: 21-22, 9: 9.

27. Eliot to Commissioners of the United Colonies in New England, Sept. 4, 1671, "Letters of John Eliot," MHS, *Procs.*, XVII (1879), 248-249; Bross, *Dry Bones*, 20, 63; James Axtell, *The Invasion Within: The Contest of Cultures in Colonial North America* (New York, 1985), 147-148; Rev 3:10, 16:14-16.

28. Eliot to Steele, Dec. 8, 1652, "Letters of the Apostle," 294.

29. C. Mather, *Magnalia* (ed. Robbins), I, 566; *Eliot's Indian Dialogues*, 121.

30. *Eliot's Indian Dialogues*, 61; Gookin, *Historical Collections*, 200. On Gookin's role, see Eliot, "An Account of Indian Churches in New-England, in a Letter Written A.D. 1673," MHS, *Coll.*, 1st ser., X (1809), 128-129.

31. Eliot to Commissioners of United Colonies, Aug. 25, 1664, *PCR*, X, 383.

32. Daniel Gookin, *An Historical Account of the Doings and Sufferings of the Christian Indians in New England, in the Years of 1675, 1676, 1677* (1677), AAS, *Transactions and Collections*, II (1836), 438-439; *Eliot's Indian Dialogues*, 121, 123.

33. C. Mather, *Magnalia* (ed. Robbins), II, 559; Eliot to Commissioners of United Colonies, Aug. 25, 1664, *PCR*, X, 384; "Letters of the Apostle," 298; William B. Trask, ed., "Rev. John Eliot's Records of the First Church in Roxbury, Mass.," *NEHGR*, XXXIII (1879), 297; I. Mather, *Diary, March 1675-December 1676, Together with Extracts from Another Diary by Him, 1674-1687* (Cambridge, Mass., 1900), 42; *The Present State of New-England with Respect to the Indian War* (1675), in Charles H. Lincoln, ed., *Narratives of the Indian Wars, 1675-1699* (New York, 1913), 24; Hubbard, *Narrative*, I, 60-61; *PCR*, IV, 25-26; David Bushnell, "The Treatment of the Indians in Plymouth Colony," *NEQ*, XXVI (1953), 208.

34. RW, *Christenings make not Christians, or a Briefe Discourse concerning that name Heathen, commonly given to the Indians* (1645), in *Williams Writings*, VII, 31.

35. Alden T. Vaughan and Daniel K. Richter, "Crossing the Cultural Divide: Indians and New Englanders, 1605-1763," AAS, *Procs.*, XC, part 1 (1980), 45.

36. "Cartwright's Answer," Jan. 5, 1665/6, *Clarendon Papers*, 90-91, 102; George D. Langdon, Jr., *Pilgrim Colony: A History of New Plymouth, 1620-1691* (New Haven, Conn., 1966), 157-158; Bushnell, "Treatment," 211; *PCR*, V, 6.

37. John Russell Bartlett, ed., *Records of the Colony of Rhode Island and Providence Plantations in New England* (Providence, 1856-1865), II, 193; *PCR*, IV, 151, 164-166.

38. *PCR*, IV, 151, 164-166.

39. *Rhode Island Records*, II, 266-278; Mason, *John Mason*, 310-314; *CR*, II, 548-551; "John Hull's Diary," 216.

40. RW to Mass. General Court, May 7, 1668, *RW Correspondence*, II, 577; RW to a Special Court of Commissioners, Oct. 18, 1677, *ibid.*, 740-741; I. Mather, *A Brief History of the Warr With the Indians in New-England* (1676), in Richard Slotkin and James K. Folsom, eds., *So Dreadfull a Judgement: Puritan Responses to King Philip's War* (Middletown, Conn., 1978), 107.

41. Eliot to Baxter, June 27, 1671, *Baxter Correspondence*, 62-63; *PCR*, V, 62.

42. Shuffelton, "Indian Devils," 116; John Pynchon to Winthrop or Allyn, Aug. 6, 1675, *Pynchon Papers*, I, 139; Hutchinson, *History*, I, 247n. On Philip's younger brother, see *PCR*, IV, 25. The identification of him as Takamunna is speculative, but it is based upon Takamunna having to sign a treaty resembling Philip's agreement of Sept. 1671. Takamunna, called "a sachem att Saconett," was clearly under Philip, who was then described by Plymouth as "chiefe sachem." *PCR*, V, 80.

43. Hutchinson, *History*, I, 237; Langdon, *Pilgrim Colony*, 159. The maneuver violated European military strategy because it alerted the colonists that war was possible. It was probably a ceremonial gesture, perhaps the last step before war. In 1675 the Narragansetts did the same thing to Warwick, Rhode Island. RW to J. Winthrop, Jr., June 27, 1675, *RW Correspondence*, II, 698.

44. *PCR*, V, 63; Taunton treaty, in I. Mather, *Brief History*, 151.

45. Pynchon to J. Winthrop, Jr., May 10, 1671, *Pynchon Papers*, I, 87; Leach, *Flintlock*, 27.

46. Leach, *Flintlock*, 27, *PCR*, V, 63-64, 73-75; "A Letter from Awasuncks to Governor Prince," Aug. 11, 1671, MHS, *Coll.*, 1st ser., V (1798), 195-196.

47. "Instructions from the Church at Natick to William and Anthony," Aug. 1, 1671, MHS, *Coll.*, 1st ser., VI (1799), 201-203. These instructions were written by "John Eliot, with the consent of the church."

48. *PCR*, V, 76; "James Walker's Letter to Governor Prince," Sept. 1, 1671, MHS, *Coll.*, 1st ser., VI (1799), 198.

49. *PCR*, V, 76-77.

50. "Walker's Letter," 198.

51. *Ibid.*; Prence to Awasuncks, Oct. 20, 1671, MHS, *Coll.*, 1st ser., V (1798), 197; "Articles of Agreement Between the Court of New-Plymouth and Awasuncks, the Squaw Sachem of Saconett," *ibid.*, 193-194; "Dartmouth Indians' Engagement," Sept. 4, 1671, *ibid.*, 194-195.

52. *PCR*, V, 76-77.

53. *Ibid.*, 77-79.

54. *Ibid.*, 79-80, X, 362; Langdon, *Pilgrim Colony*, 161.

55. Hubbard, *Narrative*, I, 58; Harris to Williamson, Aug. 12, 1676, *Harris Papers*, 163-164; Bushnell, "Treatment," 213-214; *PCR*, V, 97-98, 101, 106-107, 180; Langdon, *Pilgrim Colony*, 155. In 1671 Philip also sold some land in Massachusetts. See *Mass. Records*, IV, part 2, 498.

56. Eliot to Commissioners of the United Colonies, Sept. 4, 1671, "Letters of John Eliot," 248-249; Eliot to Mr. Ashurst, Dec. 10, 1671, *ibid.*, 250; I. Mather, *Brief History*, 87; Bross, *Dry Bones*, 53.

57. *PCR*, VIII, 190-191; Vaughan, *New England Frontier*, 328.

58. Hutchinson, *History*, I, 242; James P. and Jeanne Ronda, "The Death of John Sassamon: An Exploration in Writing New England History," *American Indian Quarterly*, I (1974), 92; *PCR*, X, 362; Hubbard, *Narrative*, I, 62; Gookin, *Doings and Sufferings*, 440-441.

59. Trask, ed., "First Church in Roxbury," 297; C. Mather, *Magnalia* (ed. Robbins), II, 559-560; Hubbard, *Narrative*, I, 63; *PCR*, V, 167; Rondas, "Death," 92; I. Mather, *Brief History*, 87.

60. JD to CT, Nov. 1, 1705, PRO, *Calendar of State Papers, Colonial Series, America and West Indies*, eds. W. Noel Sainsbury and others (London, 1860-1969), XXII, 659-660 (cited hereafter as PRO *Cal.*); "*de medietate linguae*," *Black's Law Dictionary With Pronunciations*, 5th ed. (St. Paul, Minn., 1979), 387; Kawashima, *Igniting*, 107.

61. Gookin to the Rulers and Constables of Natick, Sept. 2, 1682, Robert E. Moody, ed., *Saltonstall Papers*, MHS, *Coll.*, LXXX-LXXXI (1972-1974), I, 167; JD to CT, Nov. 1, 1705, PRO *Cal.*, XXII, 659-660; Kawashima, *Igniting*, 108.

62. *PCR*, V, 159, 167-168; Richter, *Facing East*, 103; Kawashima, *Igniting*, 109.

63. John Easton, "A Relacion of the Indyan Warre" (1675), in Lincoln, ed., *Indian Narratives*, 7-8; I. Mather, *Brief History*, 87; Jennings, *Invasion*, 295; Bushnell, "Treatment," 215.

64. *PCR*, X, 362-363.

65. Gookin, *Doings and Sufferings*, 440; Easton, "Relacion," 7; Francis Jennings, "Francis Parkman: A Brahmin among Untouchables," *WMQ*, XLII (1985), 309. On the importance of revenge among the natives, see Wilcomb E. Washburn, *The Indian in America* (New York, 1975), 17, 138.

66. *PCR*, X, 363; Josiah Winslow to Leverett, July 4, 1675, in Hutchinson, *History*, I, 242n-243n; RW to J. Winthrop, Jr., June 13, 1675, *RW Correspondence*, II, 691.

67. Winslow to J. Winthrop, Jr., July 29, 1675, *Winthrop Papers*, MHS, *Coll.*, 5th ser., I (1871), 428; Benjamin Church, *Entertaining Passages Relating to Philip's War* (1716), in Slotkin and Folsom, eds., *So Dreadfull a Judgement*, 400; George Madison Bodge, *Soldiers in King Philip's War* (Leominister, Mass., 1896), 104; Richard Smith, Jr., to Edward Rawson, Oct. 8, 1675, in Richard Smith, Jr., and others, *Further Letters on King Philip's War* (Providence, 1923), 12; Vaughan, *New England Frontier*, 312-313.

68. Church, *Entertaining*, 397-400.

69. George W. Ellis and John E. Morris, *King Philip's War* (New York, 1906), 60-61; *PCR*, X, 364; Harris to Williamson, Aug. 12, 1676, *Harris Papers*, 164-165.

70. Easton, "Relacion," 8-12.

71. *Ibid.*, 10, 14; Leach, *Flintlock*, 42-43.

72. Easton, "Relacion," 12; *PCR*, X, 364; *A Continuation of the State of New England* (1676), in Lincoln, ed., *Indian Narratives*, 62; Hubbard, *Narrative*, I, 64.

73. Bushnell, "Treatment," 210; Ellis and Morris, *War*, 46; Tobias Sanders to Fitz-John Winthrop, July 3, 1675, *Winthrop Papers*, MHS, *Coll.*, 5th ser., I (1871), 426-427; Hubbard, *Narrative*, I, 59; Vaughan, *New England Frontier*, 314, 398n9; Leach, *Flintlock*, 114.

74. Leach, ed., *Second Harris*, 29-31; Hubbard, *Narrative*, I, 86-88; C. Mather, *Magnalia* (ed. Robbins), II, 563; RW, *Key*, 74; Harry M. Ward, *The United Colonies of New England: 1643-90* (New York, 1961), 283; Leach, *Flintlock*, 40, 44, 54-56, 68-72.

75. Harris to Williamson, Aug. 12, 1676, *Harris Papers*, 169-170; Leach, ed., *Second Harris*, 31-33; Leach, *Flintlock*, 76-77.

76. Pynchon to J. Winthrop, Jr., Aug. 7, 19, 1675, *Pynchon Papers*, I, 140-141, 147.

77. Ward, *United Colonies*, 281; Ellis and Morris, *War*, 165-166.

78. Pynchon to Albany's English authorities, Sept. 8, 1675, *Pynchon Papers*, I, 150-151; Pynchon to Leverett, Sept. 8, 1675, Aug. 15, 1676, *ibid.*, 151-152, 168-169; Allen W. Trelease, *Indian Affairs in Colonial New York: The Seventeenth Century* (Ithaca, 1960), 231-236; Drake, *King Philip's War*, 122; John Easton, *A Narrative of the Causes which led to Philip's Indian War*, ed. Franklin B. Hough (Albany, 1858), 106, 114-116, 152.

79. I. Mather, *Brief History*, 100-101; *New-England's Present Sufferings under Their Cruel Neighboring Indians* (London, 1675), 6.

80. Jenny Hale Pulsipher, "'Our Sages are Sageles': A Letter on Massachusetts Indian Policy after King Philip's War," *WMQ*, LVIII (2001), 446-448; Leach, *Flintlock*, 165-166; Drake, *King Philip's War*, 4; Simon Schama, *A History of Britain: The Wars of the British, 1603-1776*, Vol. 2 (New York, 2001), 211.

81. Ellis and Morris, *War*, 167; *A New and Further Narrative of the State of New-England* (1676) in Lincoln, ed., *Indian Narratives*, 87-88; I. Mather, *Brief History*, 118, 121-122, 127-128; "James Quanapaug's Information," MHS, *Coll.*, 1st ser., VI (1799), 208.

82. RW to Leverett, Jan. 14, 1675/6, *RW Correspondence*, II, 712; Easton, *Narrative of Causes*, 124; Hutchinson, *History*, I, 258.

83. *New and Further Narrative*, 87-88, RW to JW, after Sept. 21, 1638, *RW Correspondence*, I, 182-183; RW, *Key*, 101; "Quanapaug's Information," 208; Leach, ed., *Second Harris*, 83-85.

84. Mary Rowlandson, *The Soveraignty and Goodness of God* (1682), in Alden T. Vaughan and Edward W. Clark, eds., *Puritans Among the Indians: Accounts of Captivity and Redemption, 1676-1724* (Cambridge, Mass., 1981), 46-47, 60, 67-68.

85. *A True Account of the Most Considerable Occurrences That have hapned in the Warrs Between The English and the Indians in New-England, From the Fifth of May, 1676, to the Fourth of August last* (London, 1676), 4.

86. Harris to Williamson, Aug. 12, 1676, *Harris Papers*, 178; Leach, ed., *Second Harris*, 61-63.

87. James Axtell, *The European and the Indian: Essays in the Ethnohistory of Colonial North America* (New York, 1981), 144-147; Pynchon to Leverett, Sept. 8, 1675, *Pynchon Papers*, I, 152.

88. Church, *Entertaining*, 421-428; *PCR*, V, 201-203.

89. Church, *Entertaining*, 441.

90. *Ibid.*, 441-447; Lepore, *Name of War*, 150.

91. Church, *Entertaining*, 447-452; Harris to Williamson, Aug. 12, 1676, *Harris Papers*, 177; *A True Account*, 1; Ellis and Morris, *War*, 273-274.

92. I. Mather, *Diary*, 24, 46-47; *PCR*, V, 173-174, 209-210, 243-244; *Mather Papers*, 689-690; Deut 24: 16.

93. Church, *Entertaining*, 411-412; Eliot to Massachusetts government, Aug. 13, 1675, *PCR*, X, 451-453; Hutchinson, *History*, I, 260; Eliot to Boyle, Nov. 27, 1683, "Letters from Rev. John Eliot of Roxbury to Hon. Robert Boyle," MHS, *Coll.*, 1st ser., III (1794), 183; Drake, *King Philip's War*, 160.

94. Trask, ed., "First Church in Roxbury," 297; Eliot to Boyle, Dec. 17, 1675, "Letters of John Eliot," 252.

95. Trask, ed., "First Church in Roxbury," 416; Eliot to Boyle, Dec. 17, 1675, "Letters of John Eliot," 252.

96. *Eliot's Indian Dialogues*, 53; Gookin, *Doings and Sufferings*, 485; I. Mather, *Diary*, 46; Mary Pray to James Oliver, Oct. 20, 1675, *Winthrop Papers*, MHS, *Coll.*, 5th ser., I (1871), 106; Pray to Oliver, Jan. 6, 1676, Smith and others, *Further Letters*, 22-23; Trask, ed., "First Church in Roxbury," 414-415.

97. Gookin, *Doings and Sufferings*, 452-453; William Kellaway, *The New England Company, 1649-1776, Missionary Society to the American Indians* (London, 1961), 118-119; Leach, ed., *Second Harris*, 67; *Present State of New-England*, 40-41; Trask, ed., "First Church in Roxbury," 298.

98. Trask, ed., "First Church in Roxbury," 297-298.

99. *Ibid.*, 415.

100. Eliot to Boyle, Dec. 17, 1675, John W. Ford, ed., *Some Correspondence Between the Governors . . . of the New England Company . . . and . . . the Missionaries of the Company and Others Between the Years 1657 and 1712* (London, 1896), 53; Eliot to Boyle, Mar. 15, 1682/3, "Eliot's Letters to Boyle," 181; Trask, ed., "First Church in Roxbury," 415.

101. Trask, ed., "First Church in Roxbury," 415; C. Mather, *Magnalia* (ed. Robbins), I, 566-567.

102. *PCR*, V, 240; *Rhode Island Records*, III, 64; Sydney V. James, *Colonial Rhode Island: A History* (New York, 1975), 98; Drake, *King Philip's War*, 191.

103. JD to Samuel Penhallow, Oct. 1, Dec. 13, 1711, Mar. 17, 1711/2, Belknap Papers, MHS; Haefeli and Sweeney, *Captors and Captives*, 195; Stephen Williams to

Benjamin Colman, June 24, 1735, in Nathaniel Appleton, *Gospel Ministers Must be fit for The Master's Use . . .* (Boston, 1735), iii.

104. Washington Irving, "Philip of Pokanoket: An Indian Memoir," in *The Sketch Book of Geoffrey Crayon, Gent.* (1819-1820), ed. Haskell Springer, *The Complete Works of Washington Irving*, Vol. 8 (Boston, 1978), 235, 246.

105. Easton, "Relacion," 16.

CHAPTER 7
SIR EDMUND ANDROS

1. Charles M. Andrews, ed., *Narratives of the Insurrections, 1675-1690* (New York, 1915), 223; Viola Florence Barnes, *The Dominion of New England: A Study in British Colonial Policy* (New Haven, 1923; rpt. New York, 1960); J. M. Sosin, *English America and the Revolution of 1688: Royal Administration and the Structure of Provincial Government* (Lincoln, Neb., 1982); Richard R. Johnson, *Adjustment to Empire: The New England Colonies, 1675-1715* (New Brunswick, N.J., 1981); Stephen Saunders Webb, *1676: The End of American Independence* (New York, 1984); Webb, "The Trials of Sir Edmund Andros," in James Kirby Martin, ed., *The Human Dimensions of Nation Making: Essays on Colonial and Revolutionary America* (Madison, Wisc., 1976), 23-53; Mary Lou Lustig, *The Imperial Executive in America: Sir Edmund Andros, 1637-1714* (Madison, N. J., 2002); Samuel Cooke, *A Sermon Preached at Cambridge, in the Audience of His Honor Thomas Hutchinson, Esq.* (1770), in A. W. Plumstead, ed., *The Wall and the Garden: Selected Massachusetts Election Sermons, 1670-1775* (Minneapolis, Minn., 1968), 340. For negative critiques of Webb, see Richard R. Johnson, "The Imperial Webb: The Thesis of Garrison Government in Early America Considered," *WMQ*, XLIII (1986), 408-430, and Ian Steele, "Governors or Generals?: A Note on Martial Law and the Revolution of 1689 in English America," *WMQ*, XLVI (1989), 304-314.

2. Webb, *1676*, 307, 311; Kenneth Murdock, *Increase Mather: The Foremost American Puritan* (Cambridge, Mass., 1921), 64, 158; Francis J. Bremer, "Increase Mather's Friends: The Trans-Atlantic Congregational Network of the Seventeenth Century," AAS, *Procs.*, XCIV (1984), 72.

3. Webb, *1676*, 312, 321, 324, 326, 328-329.

4. Dutch burgers to States General, 1674, *NYCD*, II, 738-739; Sir John Werden to Andros, Aug. 31, 1676, *ibid.*, III, 239; Pynchon to J. Winthrop, Jr., [Nov. 9, 1674], *Pynchon Papers*, I, 129-130; Sosin, *Charles II*, 247.

5. Webb, *1676*, 342-343.

6. *Ibid.*, 343-344.

7. Edward Randolph, "Report to the Council of Trade," [Oct. 12, 1676], *NYCD*, III, 241-242.

8. Thomas Dongan, "Report on the State of the Province," n. d., *ibid.*, 401; Sosin, *1688*, 74.

9. Duke of York to Andros, Apr. 6, 1675, Jan. 28, 1675/6, *NYCD*, III, 230-231, 235; Arthur Everett Peterson and George William Edwards, *New York As An Eighteenth Century Municipality* (New York, 1917), 11, 19; *Minutes of The Common Council of the City of New York, 1675-1776* (New York, 1905), I, 2.

10. Andros's commission, July 1, 1674, *NYCD*, III, 215; Andros, "A Short Account of the General Concerns of New-York," Mar. 1678, *ibid.*, 254; General Court of Conn. to Andros, July 10, 1675, *CR*, II, 580-581.

11. Governor and Council of Conn. to its towns, July 1, 1675, *CR*, II, 332; Andros to J. Winthrop, Jr., July 4, 1675, *ibid.*, 579; "Council Minutes concerning Indian Hostilities," July 4, 1675, Easton, *Narrative of Causes*, 44-45; Andros, "Short Account," *NYCD*, III, 254; Andros to governor of Mass., July 8, 1675, Peter R. Christoph and Florence A. Christoph, eds., *The Andros Papers . . . : Files of the Provincial Secretary of New York During the Administration of Governor Sir Edmund Andros, 1674-1680* (Syracuse, N.Y., 1989-), I, 184; Pynchon to J. Winthrop. Jr., [Dec. 17, 1674], *Pynchon Papers*, I, 131.

12. Andros to J. Winthrop, Jr., July 8, 1675, *CR*, II, 579; Governor and Council of Conn. to Chapman and Bull, July 8, 1675, *ibid.*, 334; Chapman and Bull to J. Winthrop, Jr., July 8, 1675, *ibid.*, 580; *ibid.*, 261-263; General Court to Andros, July 10, 1675, *ibid.*, 580-581.

13. Gershom Bulkeley to General Court, July 12, 1675, *ibid.*, 582.

14. Chapman and Bull to General Court, July 13, 1675, *ibid.*, 583-584. In 1687 Dongan reported that he had read "Memorandums" written by Andros that stated he wanted to make a surprise attack upon Saybrook. These memos were Andros's notes about Conn.'s charges against him. Dongan misread them. Dongan, "Report on New York," Feb. 22, 1687, E. B. O'Callaghan, ed., *The Documentary History of the State of New York*, vol. 1 (Albany, 1849), 187.

15. Duke of York to Andros, Jan. 28, 1675/6, *NYCD*, III, 235; Werden to Andros, Jan. 28, 1675/6, *ibid.*, 236, 238.

16. Andros, "Short Account," Mar. 1678, *ibid.*, 254; Werden to Andros, Aug. 31, 1676, *ibid.*, 238.

17. Andros to Lt. Gerrit Teunissz, Mar. 4, 1675/6, Christophs, eds., *Andros Papers*, I, 337; Andros, "Short Account," Mar. 1678, *ibid.*, 256; Randolph, "Report to Council," [Oct. 12, 1676], *ibid.*, 242; General Court to _____, Oct. 22, 1677, *Mass. Records*, V, 162; Trelease, *Indian Affairs*, 236.

18. Webb, *1676*, 365; Webb, "Trials," 30; Trelease, *Indian Affairs*, 232-233; Andros, "Short Account," Mar. 1678, *NYCD*, III, 254; Andros to LT, Apr. 16, 1678, *RP*, II, 303; Andros to governor and council of Mass., May 22, 1676, Christophs, eds., *Andros Papers*, I, 371.

19. "Orders in Council, 1660-1 to 1692," MHS, *Coll.*, 4th ser., II (1854), 287-288; William Stoughton and Peter Bulkley to Privy Council, Apr. 24, 1678, *NYCD*, III, 266; Order in Council, Apr. 24, 1678, *ibid.*, 267.

20. Trelease, *Indian Affairs*, 237; Commissioners of United Colonies to Andros, Sept. 6, 1678, *NYCD*, III, 273; Andros to Commissioners, Sept. 10, 1678, *ibid.*, 274; Commissioners to Andros, Sept. 14, 1678, *ibid.; DNB*, s.v. "Andros, Sir Edmund."

21. John E. Pomfret, *The Province of East New Jersey, 1609-1702: The Rebellious Proprietary* (Princeton, 1962; rpt. New York, 1981), 111, 121-122; Jasper Danckaerts, *Journal of Jasper Danckaerts, 1679-1680*, eds. Bartlett Burleigh James and J. Franklin Jameson (New York, 1913), 238-243.

22. Werden to Andros, May 24, 1680, *NYCD*, III, 283-284; Sosin, *Charles II*, 248-249; Michael Kammen, *Colonial New York: A History* (New York, 1975), 98; Ritchie, *Duke's Province*, 100-101.

23. Werden to Andros, May 24, 1680, *NYCD*, III, 283-284; Ritchie, *Duke's Province*, 122-123. For Lewin's legal problems in New York, see Christophs, eds., *Andros Papers*, III, xix, 192-193, 200-201, 226-227.

24. Peterson and Edwards, *Municipality*, 235; Patricia U. Bonomi, *A Factious People: Politics and Society in Colonial New York* (New York, 1971), 312; Andros, "Answer to Mr. Lewin's Report," Dec. 31, 1681, *NYCD*, III, 308; "Mr. Lewin's Report on the Government of New-York," 1681, *ibid.*, 302-306.

25. "Lewin's Report," 1681, *NYCD*, III, 302-306; *Common Council Minutes*, I, 13.

26. "Lewin's Report," 1681, *NYCD*, 302-306; West's commission, Nov. 8, 1680, *Common Council Minutes*, VIII, 146-147.

27. Werden to Andros, July 1, 1680, *NYCD*, III, 284; "Declaration of Deputy Mayor and Aldermen," Sept. 15, 1681, *Common Council Minutes*, I, 88-89.

28. Andros, "Answer to Lewin's Report," *NYCD*, III, 308-313; "Lewin's Report," *ibid.*, 302-306.

29. "Report to the Commissioners of the Duke of York's Revenue," n.d., *ibid.*, 314-316; Ritchie, *Duke's Province*, 124-125.

30. Andros, "Answer to Lewin's Report," *NYCD*, III, 308-313; Clarendon to Blathwayt, May 15, 1686, Samuel Weller Singer, ed., *The Correspondence of Henry Hyde, Earl of Clarendon, and of his Brother, Lawrence Hyde, Earl of Rochester* (London, 1929), I, 393.

31. William Penn to _____, July 30, 1683, *Pennsylvania Magazine of History and Biography*, XXXIX (1916), 233-234; Penn to Blathwayt and Gwyn, Nov. 21, 1682, Richard S. Dunn and Mary Maples Dunn, eds., *The Papers of William Penn* (Philadelphia, 1981-1986), II, 311.

32. Sosin, *Charles II*, 122-123; E. S. De Beer, ed., *The Diary of John Evelyn* (London, 1959), III, 584-585; "Orders in Council," MHS, *Coll.*, 4th ser., II (1854), 285; Michael Garibaldi Hall, *Edward Randolph and the American Colonies, 1676-1703* (New York, 1960), 20-21; Benjamin W. Labaree, *Colonial Massachusetts: A History* (Millwood, N.Y., 1979), 111; Johnson, *Adjustment*, 45.

33. C. Mather to John Richards, Nov. 13, 1682, Kenneth Silverman, ed., *Selected Letters of Cotton Mather* (Baton Rouge, 1971), 11-12; JD to Blathwayt, Aug. 1687, Blathwayt Papers, Colonial Williamsburg (cited hereafter as BPCW); JD to Blathwayt, Feb. 25, 1692/3, *ibid.*; Sosin, *Charles II*, 276-277, 295, 301; Hall, *Edward Randolph*, 28.

34. Randolph, "An answer to severall heads of enquiry concerning the present state of New-England," Sept. 20, Oct. 12, 1676, Hutchinson, *Collection*, II, 210-251; Randolph to Coventry, June 17, 1676, *RP*, II, 206; "The Business of New England," Apr. 8, 1678, *ibid.*, 296-297; Randolph to king, Feb. 6, 1678/9, *ibid.*, III, 34-35; Sosin, *Charles II*, 283-284; Johnson, *Adjustment*, 25.

35. Sosin, *Charles II*, 179-180, 285, 290-292, 297; Labaree, *Colonial Massachusetts*, 112; *Mass. Records*, V, 298; Randolph to king, June 13, 1683, *RP*, III, 236-237.

36. Sosin, *Charles II*, 297-298; Randolph to LT, May 29, 1689, *NYCD*, III, 579.

37. Sosin, *1688*, 68; J. M. Sosin, *English America and Imperial Inconstancy: The Rise of Provincial Autonomy, 1696-1715* (Lincoln, Neb., 1985), 165.

38. Randolph to Bishop of Asaph, Mar. 1685, *RP*, IV, 18; Randolph to Southwell, Aug. 1, 1685, *ibid.*, 29-30; Randolph to Archbishop of Canterbury, [July 7], 1686, Hutchinson, *Collection*, II, 291; Sosin, *Charles II*, 306-307; Webb, *1676*, 403-404;

Johnson, *Adjustment*, 51, 55; Stephen Saunders Webb, *Lord Churchill's Coup: The Anglo-American Empire and the Glorious Revolution Reconsidered* (New York, 1995), 98-99.

39. Andros's commission, June 3, 1686, in *Massachusetts Royal Commissions, 1681-1774*, PCSM, II, *Coll.* (1913), 44-56.

40. *Ibid.* and Andros's second commission, Apr. 7, 1688, *NYCD*, III, 537-542; Andros's instructions, Apr. 16, 1688, *ibid.*, 543-549.

41. Andros's instructions, Apr. 16, 1688, *NYCD*, III, 547.

42. Kenneth Silverman, *The Life and Times of Cotton Mather* (New York, 1984), 75; Johnson, *Adjustment*, 121.

43. Andros to Blathwayt, Dec. 23, 1686, BPCW; I. Mather, *Diary*, 54; T. B. Strandness, *Samuel Sewall: A Puritan Portrait* ([East Lansing], 1967), 146; Samuel Sewall, *The Diary of Samuel Sewall*, ed. M. Halsey Thomas (New York, 1973), I, 140; Randolph to Fitz-John Winthrop, Aug. 25, 1686, *Winthrop Papers*, MHS, *Coll.*, 6th ser., III (1889), 476.

44. Randolph to Blathwayt, Feb. 3, 1686/7, *RP*, VI, 211-212; Andros to Sunderland, Mar. 30, 1687, *Rhode Island Records*, III, 223; Andros to Fitz-John Winthrop, Apr. 9, 1689, *Winthrop Papers*, MHS, *Coll.*, 6th ser., III (1889), 486; Barnes, *Dominion*, 82, 85; Langdon, *Pilgrim Colony*, 216.

45. Randolph to Blathwayt, May 29, 1686, *RP*, VI, 171; Nathaniel Saltonstall to Andros, Sept. 24, 1687, Moody, ed., *Saltonstall Papers*, I, 181-182.

46. Randolph to LT, Sept. 2, 1685, *RP*, IV, 44-47; Randolph to LT, Aug. 23, 1686, *ibid.*, 117-118; Randolph to Blathwayt, Feb. 3, 1686/7, *ibid.*, VI, 212; Johnson, *Adjustment*, 56, 56n-57n; Sosin, *Charles II*, 252, 307; Sosin, *1688*, 20, 65, 70.

47. Johnson, *Adjustment*, 81; Langdon, *Pilgrim Colony*, 215; Sosin, *1688*, 72; Andros's instructions, Apr. 16, 1688, *NYCD*, III, 543-549; Andros to Blathwayt, July 11, 1687, BPCW.

48. Barnes, *Dominion*, 91-93; Langdon, *Pilgrim Colony*, 216; Andros to Blathwayt, Aug. 17, 1687, BPCW.

49. Andros to Blathwayt, Mar. 30, 1687, BPCW; Andros to Blathwayt, Aug. 31, 1687, *ibid.*; Andros to Blathwayt, Sept. 28, 1687, *ibid.*; Robert N. Toppan, ed., *The Andros Records*, AAS, *Procs.*, n.s., XIII (1899-1900), 259, 268; Sosin, *1688*, 73.

50. Andros to Blathwayt, Sept. 28, 1687, BPCW; "Proceedings agt. Wise and others," Oct. 1687, *RP*, IV, 171-182; Toppan, ed., *Andros Records*, 476-478, 480-482, 486.

51. Boston Declaration, Apr. 18, 1689, William H. Whitmore, ed., *The Andros Tracts* (Boston, 1868-1874; rpt. New York, 1967?), I, 14-15; Charges against West, *ibid.*, 164; Johnson, *Adjustment*, 391n; Andros to Blathwayt, Sept. 28, 1687, BPCW; Andros to Blathwayt, Nov. 28, 1687, *ibid.*; "Proceedings agt. Wise," Oct. 1687, *RP*, IV, 171-182; George Allan Cook, *John Wise: Early American Democrat* (New York, 1952), 57.

52. Meeting of Committee for Trade and Plantations, Oct. 23, 1686, *RP*, IV, 130; Thomas Hinckley to I. Mather, Oct. 16, 1691, *Hinckley Papers*, MHS, *Coll.*, 4th ser., V (1861), 288; Andros to Sunderland, Mar. 30, 1687, *Rhode Island Records*, III, 223.

53. Randolph to Blathwayt, Aug. 5, 1687, *RP*, VI, 225-226; Randolph to Blathwayt, Mar. 30, 1687, *ibid.*, 219; Andros to Blathwayt, Mar. 30, 1687, BPCW; Dongan, "Report to the Committee of Trade on the Province of New-York," Feb. 22, 1687, O'Callaghan, ed., *Documentary History*, I, 150-151.

54. Andros to Blathwayt, Sept. 28, 1687, BPCW; Langdon, *Pilgrim Colony*, 216-217; Toppan, ed., *Andros Records*, 248, 256, 259.

55. Randolph to Povey, May 21, 1687, Hutchinson, *Collection*, II, 297; Randolph to Povey, Jan. 24, 1687/8, *ibid.*, 300; William Stoughton and others, *A Narrative of the Proceedings of Sir Edmond Androsse* (1691), in Andrews, ed., *Insurrections*, 246.

56. Barnes, *Dominion*, 169-171; Randolph to Blathwayt, Apr. 2, 1688, *RP*, VI, 249-251; Randolph to Povey, May 21, 1687, Hutchinson, *Collection*, II, 298; Randolph to Povey, Jan. 24, 1687/8, *ibid.*, 300-301; Thomas Danforth to I. Mather, July 30, 1689, *ibid.*, 311-312; Toppan, ed., *Andros Records*, 252.

57. Johnson, *Adjustment*, 79-82; Langdon, *Pilgrim Colony*, 218-219; Barnes, *Dominion*, 184; William Pencak, *War, Politics, and Revolution in Provincial Massachusetts* (Boston, 1981), 15; Randolph to Blathwayt, May 21, 1687, *RP*, VI, 221-223; John Palmer, *An Impartial Account of the State of New-England: Or, The Late Government there, Vindicated* (1690), in Whitmore, ed., *Andros Tracts*, I, 48.

58. James and Jameson, eds., *Danckaerts Journal*, 248. For Randolph's petitions, see *RP*, IV, 171, 207. In 1676 Andros had been willing to treat unfenced land in New York City as legally "Vacant." "Order of the Governor in Councill," May 26, 1676, Christophs, eds., *Andros Papers*, I, 375.

59. Andros to Blathwayt, May 23, 1687, BPCW; *Mass. Records*, I, 5; Johnson, *Adjustment*, 79-82; Barnes, *Dominion*, 181; Samuel Sewall to I. Mather, July 24, 1688, *Mather Papers*, 517-518; Sewall, *Diary*, I, 172n, 173.

60. Stoughton and others, *Narrative*, 245; Sosin, *1688*, 74; Duke of York to Andros, Jan. 28, 1675/6, *NYCD*, III, 235.

61. Randolph to Povey, June 21, 1688, Hutchinson, *Collection*, II, 305-307; Randolph to governor of Barbados, May 16, 1689, *ibid.*, 316; Charges against Palmer and Graham, Whitmore, ed., *Andros Tracts*, I, 165, 167.

62. Randolph to Andros, July 28, 1686, *RP*, VI, 192-193; Randolph to Blathwayt, Mar. 14, 1686/7, *ibid.*, 214-215; Andros's commission, Apr. 7, 1688, *NYCD*, 542; Toppan, ed., *Andros Records*, 253, 257-259; Stoughton, *Narrative*, 241-242; Barnes, *Dominion*, 122-126.

63. Randolph to Blathwayt, Mar. 14, 1686/7, *RP*, VI, 214-215; Toppan, ed., *Andros Records*, 253, 257-259, 466, 468-469; Stoughton, *Narrative*, 241-242; Barnes, *Dominion*, 122-126.

64. Randolph to Archbishop of Canterbury, [July 7], Aug. 2, 1686, *RP*, II, 291-293, IV, 105-109 and *ibid.*, III, 326.

65. Sewall, *Diary*, I, 127-128, 135; Andros to Blathwayt, Mar. 30, 1687, BPCW; Andros to Sunderland, Mar. 30, 1687, *Rhode Island Records*, III, 223-224.

66. Sewall, *Diary*, I, 136, 139, 152, 165, 170-172; Randolph to Archbishop of Canterbury, Oct. 27, 1686, Hutchinson, *Collection*, II, 294-295; Ps 57: 1-3, 6.

67. Randolph to the committee, Mar. 25, 1687, *RP*, IV, 152; Randolph to Blathwayt, July 28, 1686, *ibid.*, VI, 194-195; Randolph to Blathwayt, Mar. 14, 1686/7, *ibid.*, 216; Randolph to Archbishop, Oct. 27, 1686, Hutchinson, *Collection*, II, 294-295; Andros, "Report of his Administration," May 27, 1690, *NYCD*, III, 722; Henry Wilder Foote, *Annals of King's Chapel: From the Puritan Age to the Present Day* (Boston, 1882-1896), I, 82.

68. Langdon, *Pilgrim Colony*, 214, 217.

69. "Act against Emigration," in Whitmore, ed., *Andros Tracts*, III, 92-93, 93n; Cotton Mather, *The Life of Sir William Phips* (1697), ed. Mark Van Doren (New York, 1929), 42-43; Stoughton, *Narrative*, 244.

70. Andros to Sunderland, Mar. 30, 1687, *Rhode Island Records*, III, 224; Randolph to Povey, Jan. 24, 1687/8, Hutchinson, *Collection*, II, 300; Randolph to Blathwayt, Mar. 31, 1687, *RP*, VI, 218.

71. "Humble Memorial of the New England Dissenters," c. 1688, *Mather Papers*, 700; Joshua Moody to I. Mather, Jan. 8, 1688/9, *ibid.*, 370; Sewall, *Diary*, I, 165-166; Palmer, *Impartial Account*, I, 46-47; Samuel Willard, *A Brief Discourse Concerning that Ceremony of Laying the Hand on the Bible in Swearing* (1689), in Whitmore, ed., *Andros Tracts*, I, 179-191.

72. Alice Lounsberry, *Sir William Phips* (New York, 1941), 178-179, 186; Viola F. Barnes, "The Rise of William Phips," *NEQ*, 1 (1928), 271, 273, 280-283, 285; Emerson W. Baker and John G. Reid, *The New England Knight: Sir William Phips, 1651-1695* (Toronto, 1998), 20-21.

73. Hall, *Edward Randolph*, 82; Sosin, *Charles II*, 296; Sosin, *1688*, 83; *Calendar of State Papers, Domestic Series, October 1, 1683-April 30, 1684*, eds. F. H. Blackburne Daniell and Francis Bickley (London, 1938), 344; Increase Mather, *Autobiography*, ed. Michael G. Hall, AAS, *Procs.*, LXXI (1961), 309.

74. George Ross to Randolph, June 6, [1684], *RP*, III, 305; Murdock, *Mather*, 184; Bradstreet to Randolph, Dec. 8, 1684, *RP*, III, 338; I. Mather, *Autobiography*, 309. The letter is in *RP*, III, 312-316.

75. Randolph to Shrimpton, July 18, 1684, *RP*, III, 310-311; Randolph to Povey, Oct. 19, 1688, *ibid.*, IV, 244-245; I. Mather to JD, Nov. 10, 1684, *ibid.*, III, 327-331; I. Mather, *Autobiography*, 309.

76. "Breefe in the case," n. d., *RP*, IV, 193; _____ to I. Mather, n. d., *ibid.*, 195; I. Mather to JD, Jan. 24, 1687/8, *ibid.*, 196-197; JD to Randolph, Dec. 15, 1687, *ibid.*, 192; "Pleas in the Case of Edward Randolph Against Increase Mather," Jan. 1687/8, *Mather Papers*, 703-704.

77. I. Mather, *Autobiography*, 322; Sewall, *Diary*, I, 155, 162; Randolph to Archbishop, Aug. 23, 1684, *RP*, III, 319; Randolph to Coventry, n. d., *ibid.*, VI, 81-82.

78. I. Mather, *Autobiography*, 321-323.

79. Thomas Gorges to Sir F. Gorges, July 7, 1641, Moody, ed., *Thomas Gorges Letters*, 31-32; *Oxford English Dictionary*, s. v. "arrest." See also John Wilds for Sarah Wilds, n. d., *SW*, III, 808.

80. Palmer, *Impartial Account*, I, 52; "Warrant for the Arrest of Increase Mather," Dec. 24, 1687, *RP*, IV, 193; Sewall, *Diary*, I, 155-156.

81. C. Mather, *Parentator* (1724), in Whitmore, ed., *Andros Tracts*, III, 128-129; I. Mather, *Autobiography*, 321; Boston Declaration, Apr. 18, 1689, in Andrews, ed., *Insurrections*, 180.

82. I. Mather, *Autobiography*, 322-323.

83. Beckles Willson, *The Great Company* (New York, 1900), 131-137, 140-141; David Ogg, *England in the Reigns of James II and William III* (Oxford, 1955), 190; Randolph to LT, May 29, 1689, *NYCD*, III, 580.

84. Randolph to LT, May 29, 1689, *NYCD*, III, 580; Randolph to Sir Nicholas Butler, Mar. 29, 1688, *RP*, VI, 242-243; Andrews, ed., *Insurrections*, 247n.

85. Johnson, *Adjustment*, 85; Andros to Blathwayt, June 4, 1688, BPCW; Randolph to Povey, June 21, 1688, Hutchinson, *Collection*, II, 304-305. The exact date of Andros's trek is uncertain. It was completed by June 4.

86. Randolph to Povey, June 21, 1688, Hutchinson, *Collection*, II, 304-305; Nicholson to [Povey?], Aug. 31, 1688, *NYCD*, III, 550-551; Denonville to Andros,

Oct. 23, 1688, *ibid.*, 571; Stoughton, *Narrative*, 247; Richard R. Johnson, *John Nelson: Merchant Adventurer* (New York, 1991), 46-47.

87. Nicholson to [Povey?], Aug. 31, 1688, *NYCD*, III, 550-551; Andros to Denonville, Sept. 19, 1688, *ibid.*, 557; Sewall, *Diary*, I, 174.

88. Andros, "Report of his Administration," May 27, 1690, *NYCD*, III, 723; Andros to Blathwayt, Oct. 19, 1688, BPCW; C. Mather, *Decennium Luctuosum* (1699), in Lincoln, ed., *Indian Narratives*, 187-188; Edward Tyng to Andros, Oct. 1, 1688, James Phinney Baxter, ed., *Documentary History of the State of Maine, 2nd ser.*, Vols. 4, 5, 6 *Containing The Baxter Manuscripts* (Portland, Me., 1889, 1897, 1900), VI, 435; Mary Beth Norton, *In the Devil's Snare: The Salem Witchcraft Crisis of 1692* (New York, 2002), 94-95, 353n32.

89. Thomas Treffry and others to Andros, Sept. 11, 1688, Baxter, ed., *Documentary History of Maine*, VI, 428; Treffry to Andros, Oct. 9, 1688, *ibid.*, 439; JD to Andros, Oct. 9, 1688, *ibid.*, 439-440; Tyng to Andros, Oct. 1, 1688, *ibid.*, 437; Johnson, *Adjustment*, 82.

90. C. Mather, *Decennium Luctuosum*, 187-188; Andros to Denonville, Oct. 1, 1688, *NYCD*, III, 566; Randolph to LT, Oct. 8, 1688, *ibid.*, 568-569; Andros to Blathwayt, Oct. 19, 1688, BPCW.

91. Andros to Blathwayt, Oct. 29, 1688, BPCW; Andros to Blathwayt, Nov. 10, 1688, *ibid.*; Andros to LT, Nov. 10, 1688, *ibid.*; Randolph to Blathwayt, Nov. 8, 1688, *RP*, VI, 281; Andros, "Report of his Administration," May 27, 1690, *NYCD*, III, 723; Fitz-John Winthrop to Andros, c. Dec. 1688, *Winthrop Papers*, MHS, *Coll.*, 6th ser., III (1889), 492.

92. Randolph to LT, May 29, 1689, *NYCD*, III, 581; Andros, "Report of his Administration," May 27, 1690, *ibid.*, 723; C. Mather, *Decennium Luctuosum*, 193.

93. Randolph to LT, May 29, 1689, *NYCD*, III, 581; *A Particular Account of the late Revolution at Boston* (1689), in Andrews, ed., *Insurrections*, 198, 209; Steele, "Governors," 311; Johnson, *John Nelson*, 50; Webb, *Lord Churchill's Coup*, 188.

94. C. Mather, *Magnalia Christi Americana*, Books I and II, ed. Kenneth B. Murdock (Cambridge, Mass., 1977), 292-293; Samuell Walker and others to king, Jan. 25, 1689/90, Whitmore, ed., *Andros Tracts*, I, 176-178.

95. C. Mather, *Magnalia* (ed. Murdock), 292-293; Baxter, ed., *Documentary History of Maine*, IV, 446-448, V, 28, VI, 472-473.

96. Langdon, *Pilgrim Colony*, 222; Johnson, *Adjustment*, 138-169.

97. Sosin, *1688*, 83-84.

98. *Ibid.*, 82-83, 88, 279n2; Johnson, *Adjustment*, 145; Langdon, *Pilgrim Colony*, 235.

99. Lounsberry, *Phips*, 201-202; Sosin, *1688*, 140; Johnson, *Adjustment*, 96.

100. C. Mather, *Phips*, 49-51; John West to Fitz-John Winthrop, Feb. 23, 1688/9, *Winthrop Papers*, MHS, *Coll.*, 6th ser., III (1889), 496-497.

101. Winslow's Declaration, Feb. 4, 1689, Whitmore, ed., *Andros Tracts*, I, 78-79; "C. D.," *New-England's Faction Discovered* (1690), Andrews, ed., *Insurrections*, 257; Steele, "Governors," 311; Ian K. Steele, "Origins of Boston's Revolutionary Declaration of 18 April 1689," *NEQ*, LXII (1989), 77, 79. For the English declarations, see Evans no. 465.

102. Langdon, *Pilgrim Colony*, 223; Sosin, *1688*, 92; "Samuel Mather's Account of the Preliminary to Revolt," in Michael G. Hall and others, eds., *The Glorious Revolution In America: Documents on the Colonial Crisis of 1689* (New York, 1964), 39-40;

Andros, "Report of his Administration," May 27, 1690, *NYCD*, III, 723-724; Ian K.
Steele, *The English Atlantic, 1675-1740: An Exploration of Communication and Community* (New York, 1986), 94, 96, 104; J. R. Jones, *The Revolution of 1688 in England*
(New York, 1972), 308; W. A. Speck, *Reluctant Revolutionaries: Englishmen and the
Revolution of 1688* (New York, 1988), 89.

    103. Randolph to LT, July 23, 1689, PRO *Cal.*, XIII, 101; Johnson, *Adjustment*,
93, 96; Silverman, *Cotton Mather*, 68, 70, 72, 436n; Lustig, *Imperial Executive*, 190-
191.

    104. John George to Pepys, June 12, 1689, in Andrews, ed., *Insurrections*, 216;
Nathaniel Byfield, *An Account of the Late Revolution in New-England* (1689), *ibid.*,
170; "A. B.," *An Account of the Late Revolutions in New-England* (1689), in Whitmore,
ed., *Andros Tracts*, II, 195-197; Thomas Danforth to I. Mather, July 30, 1689,
Hutchinson, *Collection*, II, 313; Steele, "Origins," 81.

    105. Andros, "Report of his Administration," May 27, 1690, *NYCD*, III, 723-724;
"A. B.," *Account*, II, 195-197; _____ to Hinckley, Apr. 22, 1689, Hutchinson, *History*, I, 318; "Summons to Sir Edmund Andros," Apr. 18, 1689, *Mather Papers*, 537-
538; Byfield, *Account*, 172; Sosin, *1688*, 92.

    106. C. Mather, *Phips*, 54; Byfield, *Account*, 174; John Riggs, "A Narrative of the
Proceedings at Boston," July 22, 1689, in John Gorham Palfrey, *History of New England* (Boston, 1885), III, 585n-586n; Boston Declaration, Apr. 18, 1689, in Andrews,
ed., *Insurrections*, 175-181.

    107. Randolph to LT, May 29, 1689, *NYCD*, III, 582; Palmer, *Impartial Account*,
I, 62; *A Particular Account*, 204.

    108. Andros, "Report of his Administration," May 27, 1690, *NYCD*, III, 724;
Andros, "Charges against the Government," Whitmore, ed., *Andros Tracts*, III, 31;
Sosin, *1688*, 94.

    109. "Reflections Upon the Affairs of New England," *Wyllys Papers*, Connecticut
Historical Society, *Coll.*, XXI (1924), 325-326; Pencak, *War*, 16-17; Johnson, *Adjustment*, 129; Benjamin Bullivant, *Journal of Dr. Benjamin Bullivant*, MHS, *Procs.*, XVI
(1878), 104.

    110. Randolph to Blathwayt, July 20, 1689, *RP*, VI, 291; Randolph to LT, Oct. 15,
1689, *ibid.*, IV, 298; "Reflections," *Wyllys Papers*, 332; Cuthbert Potter, *Journall and
Narrative of . . . Cuthbert Potter* (1690), in Newton D. Mereness, ed., *Travels in the
American Colonies* (New York, 1916), 8; Bullivant, *Journal*, 106.

    111. "An Information of What Entertainment Sir Edmund Androsse . . . Had . . .
upon Castle Island," Jan. 24, 1689/90, Whitmore, ed., *Andros Tracts*, I, 174-175; John
Coggeshall to Mass., Aug. 5, 1689, *ibid.*, III, 95; John Walley to _____, Aug. 5, 1689,
ibid., 99-100; Walley to _____, Aug. 8, 1689, *ibid.*, 100-101; Hutchinson, *History*, I,
332, 332n; Thomas P. Phelan, *Thomas Dongan: Colonial Governor of New York, 1683-
1688* (New York, 1933), 130-131.

    112. Randolph to Blathwayt, Oct. 8, 1689, *RP*, VI, 302; Randolph to Chaplain,
Oct. 28, 1689, *ibid.*, V, 20-21; Andros to Blathwayt, June 4, 1689, BPCW; Gertrude
Ann Jacobsen, *William Blathwayt: A Late Seventeenth Century English Administrator*
(New Haven, 1932), 134; "Order Discharging Sr Edmd Andros," Apr. 24, 1690,
Whitmore, ed., *Andros Tracts*, II, 173.

    113. Webb, "Trials," 44-45.

    114. Thomas Brinley to Francis Brinley, May 28, 1690, in Theodore B. Lewis, ed.,
"Sir Edmund Andros's Hearing before the Lords of Trade and Plantations, April 17,

1690," AAS, *Procs.*, LXXXIII (1973), 247, 249-250; "Reflections," *Wyllys Papers*, 327; "Report of the Council advising Andros's Acquital," Apr. 24, 1690, Whitmore, ed., *Andros Tracts*, III, 41-43.

115. Brinley to Brinley, May 28, 1690, Lewis, ed., "Andros's Hearing," 250; Nottingham to Blathwayt, Feb. 24-Mar. 6, 1690/1, Historical Manuscripts Commission, *Report on the Manuscripts of the Late Allan George Finch Esq. of Burley-On-The-Hill, Rutland*, Vol. 3 (London, 1957), 22; Webb, *1676*, 311; Sosin, *1688*, 170; *DNB*, s. v. "Andros, Sir Edmund."

116. Randolph to LT, May 29, 1689, *NYCD*, III, 581; Randolph to Nicholson, July 29, 1689, *RP*, IV, 288; Boston Declaration, Apr. 18, 1689, Andrews, ed., *Insurrections*, 181; Brinley to Brinley, May 28, 1690, Lewis, ed., "Andros's Hearing," 245.

117. Callieres to Seignelay, Jan. 1689, *NYCD*, IX, 403-408.

118. *Ibid.*; "Memoir to . . . Frontenac," June 7, 1689, *NYCD*, IX, 422-426; "Instructions for . . . Frontenac," *ibid.*, 427.

119. Willson, *Great Company*, 142-143, 146-168.

120. Sosin, *1688*, 64.

CHAPTER 8
SATAN

1. C. Mather, *Diary of Cotton Mather*, ed. Worthington Chauncey Ford (Boston, 1911-1912; rpt. New York, 1957), I, 147; Rev 12: 7-12.

2. Bengt Ankarloo, "Sweden: The Mass Burnings (1668-1676)," in Bengt Ankarloo and Gustav Henningsen, eds., *Early Modern European Witchcraft: Centres and Peripheries* (Oxford, 1990), 294-299.

3. John Putnam Demos, *Entertaining Satan: Witchcraft and the Culture of Early New England* (New York, 1982), 139, 182, 199; Norton, *Snare*, 32.

4. C. Mather, *Wonders of the Invisible World* (1693), in George Lincoln Burr, ed., *Narratives of the Witchcraft Cases, 1648-1706* (New York, 1914; rpt. 1975), 241-243 (except where noted, all references to Mather's *Wonders* are to Burr's edition); *SW*, II, 566-567; Norton, *Snare*, 8.

5. *SW*, II, 342-343, I, 211-212; Demos, *Entertaining*, 175-176.

6. *SW*, II, 474-477, III, 707-708, 823-826; Robert Calef, *More Wonders of the Invisible World* (1700), in Burr, ed., *Narratives*, 347; Paul Boyer and Stephen Nissenbaum, *Salem Possessed: The Social Origins of Witchcraft* (Cambridge, Mass., 1974), 12.

7. *SW*, III, 713-714, 971; Norton, *Snare*, 167.

8. John Hale, *A Modest Enquiry into the Nature of Witchcraft* (Boston, 1702), 21; *SW*, I, 159, II, 480, 681; Boyer and Nissenbaum, *Salem Possessed*, 13.

9. *SW*, I, 126-127; Boyer and Nissenbaum, *Salem Possessed*, 16; Norton, *Snare*, 213.

10. *SW*, I, 123-124, 308-309, III, 708.

11. C. Mather, "Enchantments Encountered," *Wonders of the Invisible World*, in Samuel G. Drake, ed., *The Witchcraft Delusion in New England* (Roxbury, Mass., 1866; rpt. New York, 1970), I, 21; Petition of Abigail Faulkner, Sr., to the General Court, c. June 13, 1703. *SW*, III, 967-968; Silverman, *Cotton Mather*, 438n-439n; 1 Sam 28; Baker and Reid, *New England Knight*, 144; Norton, *Snare*, 33.

12. *SW*, II, 484; Boyer and Nissenbaum, *Salem Possessed*, 11-12; Ankarloo, "Sweden," 290.

13. Sewall, *Diary*, I, 296; *SW*, III, 971; Norton, *Snare*, 278. Despite common belief, no one was burned at the stake in Salem. Bad Hollywood writers created that incorrect scenario.

14. C. Mather to Richards, May 31, 1692, Silverman, ed., *Mather Letters*, 39; Morgan, *Genuine Article*, 68.

15. John Proctor to Mr. Mather and others, July 23, 1692, *SW*, II, 689-690; C. Mather to Richards, May 31, 1692, Silverman, ed., *Mather Letters*, 38.

16. Calef, *More Wonders*, 375-376; Thomas Brattle, "Letter of Thomas Brattle, F. R. S.," Oct. 8, 1692, in Burr, ed., *Narratives*, 189.

17. Declaration of Mary Osgood and others, n. d., *SW*, III, 971; Margaret Jacobs to the court, n. d., *SW*, II, 491-492; *SW*, I, 132, 302, III, 777-778, 855; Daniel G. Payne, "Defending against the Indefensible: Spectral Evidence at the Salem Witchcraft Trials," *EIHC*, CXXIX (1993), 69.

18. *SW*, I, 73-74, II, 342-343, 504-505, 514, 615, III, 751; Boyer and Nissenbaum, *Salem Possessed*, 11-12.

19. Norton, *Snare*, 5, 12, 105; James E. Kences, "Some Unexplored Relationships of Essex County Witchcraft in the Indian Wars of 1675 and 1689," *EIHC*, CXX (1984), 179.

20. Thomas Putnam to John Hathorne and Jonathan Corwin, Apr. 21, 1692, *SW*, I, 165-166; Proctor to Mr. Mather and others, July 23, 1692, *SW*, II, 689-690; *ibid.*, 520-524; Brattle, "Letter," 184; Norton, *Snare*, 10; Bernard Rosenthal, *Salem Story: Reading the Witch Trials of 1692* (New York, 1993), 7.

21. David D. Hall, "The Mental World of Samuel Sewall," in David D. Hall and others, eds., *Saints and Revolutionaries: Essays on Early American History* (New York, 1984), 85; Rev 13: 18; Silverman, *Cotton Mather*, 107; Sewall, *Diary*, I, 60-61.

22. C. Mather, *A Midnight Cry: An Essay for our Awakening out of that Sinful Sleep, To which we are at This Time too much disposed* (Boston, 1692), 22, 23, 60.

23. *Ibid.*, 40, 48-49, 54, 59; Rev 20: 7-9.

24. C. Mather, *Wonders*, 211; C. Mather, "Enchantments Encountered," in *Wonders*, Drake, ed., *Witchcraft Delusions*, I, 17. For the confusion about Mather, see Silverman, *Cotton Mather*, 103, and Richard H. Werking, "'Reformation Is Our Only Preservation': Cotton Mather and Salem Witchcraft," *WMQ*, XXIX (1972), 282-283, 286.

25. *SW*, II, 439.

26. *Ibid.*, 454.

27. Mary K. Matossian, *Poisons of the Past: Molds, Epidemics, and History* (New Haven, 1989), 8-9, 13, 117-118; Nicholas P. Spanos and Jack Gottlieb, "Ergotism and the Salem Village Witch Trials," *Science*, CXCIV (24 Dec. 1976), 1390.

28. Matossian, *Poisons*, 117; Linnda R. Caporeal, "Ergotism: The Satan Loosed in Salem?," *Science*, CXCII (2 Apr. 1976), 23.

29. *SW*, II, 444-447; C. Mather, *Wonders*, 239-240; Laurie Winn Carlson, *A Fever in Salem* (Chicago, 1999), 35.

30. Matossian, *Poisons*, 14-17.

31. Samuel P. Fowler, ed., "Rev. Samuel Parris's Record of Deaths at Salem Village During His Ministry," *NEHGR*, XXXVI (1882), 188; Spanos and Gottlieb, "Ergotism," 1393; Rosenthal, *Salem Story*, 116-117.

32. *SW*, III, 847-848; Matossian, *Poisons*, 17.

33. *SW*, III, 849; Josselyn, *Colonial Traveler*, 128; Matossian, *Poisons*, 17; Peter Charles Hoffer, *The Devil's Disciples: Makers of the Salem Witchcraft Trials* (Baltimore, 1996), 70-71.

34. John Higginson, "An Epistle to the Reader," in Hale, *Modest*, 4-5; Marilynne K. Roach, "'That child, Betty Parris': Elizabeth (Parris) Barron and the People in Her Life," *EIHC*, CXXIV (1988), 5.

35. Hale, *Modest*, 132-133; Roach, "Betty," 6; Chadwick Hansen, "The Metamorphosis of Tituba, or Why American Intellectuals Can't Tell an Indian Witch from a Negro," *NEQ*, XLVII (1974), 4; Boyer and Nissenbaum, *Salem Possessed*, 1-2; Carol F. Karlsen, *The Devil in the Shape of a Woman: Witchcraft in Colonial New England* (New York, 1987), 271n31; Norton, *Snare*, 18.

36. *SW*, II, 507; Samuel P. Fowler, ed., "Biographical Sketch and Diary of Rev. Joseph Green, of Salem Village," in *Library of American Puritan Writings*, vol. 7, 221; "Salem Village Church Records," in Charles W. Upham, *Salem Witchcraft With an Account of Salem Village and History of Opinions on Witchcraft and Kindred Subjects* (Boston, 1867; rpt. New York, 1959), II, 513; Brattle, "Letter," 181-182; Norton, *Snare*, 23-24.

37. Hansen, "Tituba," 5; Bernard Rosenthal, "Tituba's Story," *NEQ*, LXXI (1998), 195-197; Roach, "Betty," 4; *SW*, III, 747-749, 753; Ruth Behar, "Sexual Witchcraft, Colonialism, and Women's Powers: Views from the Mexican Inquisition," in Asunción Lavrin, ed., *Sexuality and Marriage in Colonial Latin America* (Lincoln, Neb., 1989), 179-180, 183, 192; Calef, *More Wonders*, 343; Hale, *Modest*, 132-133.

38. *SW*, III, 747-749, 753; Caporeal, "Ergotism," 22; Behar, "Witchcraft," 182.

39. Deodat Lawson, *A Brief and True Narrative* (1692), in Burr, *Narratives*, 153; Roach, "Betty," 4; Norton, *Snare*, 333.

40. *SW*, III, 853.

41. Rosenthal, *Salem Story*, 15; Roach, "Betty," 11-13.

42. Hale, *Modest*, 23, 27; *SW*, III, 747-749, 753; Rosenthal, *Salem Story*, 14-15; Michael G. Hall, *The Last American Puritan: The Life of Increase Mather, 1639-1723* (Middletown, Conn., 1988), 256; Norton, *Snare*, 6, 26-28; Boyer and Nissenbaum, *Salem Possessed*, 3.

43. Norton, *Snare*, 7, 10, 21-22, 51, 53, 159, 305; John McWilliams, "Indian John and the Northern Tawnies," in Vaughan, ed., *New England Encounters*, 169-170; Rosenthal, *Salem Story*, 36, 41; Payne, "Defending," 71; *SW*, II, 374, 666-668, 670, 672. Such motives are similar to what happened on many college campuses in the 1990s. Some individuals would make mindless accusations, usually about racism, and gained substantial power. Some colleges even changed their curriculums to gain favor with these accusers.

44. Sewall, *Diary*, I, 289; Rebecca Eames to Sir William Phips, Dec. 5, 1692, *SW*, I, 284; ibid., 113, 185, II, 632; Brattle, "Letter," 187-188.

45. *SW*, I, 52, 327-328.

46. Ibid., 83-84, 288-289; Norton, *Snare*, 315-316.

47. *SW*, III, 806; Rosenthal, *Salem Story*, 39.

48. *SW*, I, 207-210, II, 658-661; Lawson, *Brief*, 156.

49. *SW*, I, 209, 250, II, 174 477, 550-552, 660-661, Norton, *Snare*, 315-316.

50. *SW*, I, 65-66, II, 520-524, 644, 647; Norton, *Snare*, 258.

51. *SW*, II, 390; Norton, *Snare*, 278.

52. *SW*, I, 49-50; Rosenthal, *Salem Story*, 98; Norton, *Snare*, 136-137.

53. *SW*, I, 251, II, 463, 466, 469, III, 705-706, 793, 802-803; Rosenthal, *Salem Story*, 45.

54. *SW*, I, 209-210.

55. *Ibid.*, 248-249, 251, 259-260, II, 603-605; Upham, *Salem Witchcraft*, I, 181; Norton, *Snare*, 44-47, 64-65.

56. George F. Dow, ed., *Records and Files of the Quarterly Courts of Essex County, Massachusetts* (Salem, 1911-1921), I, 137, 152, 172, IV, 275, VII, 77-78, 89, 89n-91n.

57. *SW*, II, 423; Norton, *Snare*, 114; Enders A. Robinson, *The Devil Discovered: Salem Witchcraft, 1692* (New York, 1991), 271.

58. *SW*, II, 600-601, 603; Norton, *Snare*, 22-23, 47; Boyer and Nissenbaum, *Salem Possessed*, 115, 149; Rosenthal, *Salem Story*, 192.

59. *SW*, II, 593.

60. *Ibid.*, 664, 677, 684-687; Norton, *Snare*, 71; Payne, "Defending," 77.

61. *SW*, I, 201-202, II, 357, 364, 368-369; Rosenthal, *Salem Story*, 88-89, 124.

62. *SW*, I, 93-97, 99-101; Calef, *More Wonders*, 356.

63. C. Mather, *Wonders*, 219-220; *SW*, I, 171, II, 405-408, 410-413, 415; Norton, *Snare*, 79-80, 120, 122, 131.

64. *SW*, I, 162-164, 166, 176; C. Mather, *Wonders*, 219-220; Boyer and Nissenbaum, *Salem Possessed*, 55-56; Norton, *Snare*, 58-59, 119-122, 125, 130, 149-150, 153-154; McWilliams, "Tawnies," 166.

65. *SW*, I, 153-154; C. Mather, *Wonders*, 217; Norton, *Snare*, 247, 307. Years later, Burroughs's children emphasized that he had been very thorough in teaching them their catechism, hardly a sign of devotion to Satan. *SW*, III, 982-983.

66. *SW*, I, 153-154, 160-162; Calef, *More Wonders*, 301; Rosenthal, *Salem Story*, 139-140.

67. George Burroughs to Andros, n. d., Baxter, ed., *Documentary History of Maine*, VI, 346.

68. Norton, *Snare*, 133, 137, 143-144.

69. *Ibid.*, 8.

70. Calef, *More Wonders*, 372; Norton, *Snare*, 233.

71. Calef, *More Wonders*, 348; Phips to Blathwayt, Oct. 12, 1692, *SW*, III, 861-862; C. Mather to William Stoughton, Sept. 2, 1692, Silverman, ed., *Mather Letters*, 43-44.

72. *SW*, II, 606-608; C. Mather to John Cotton, Aug. 5, 1692, C. Mather, *Diary*, I, 142.

73. Brattle, "Letter," 184-185; Samuel Sewall to Nathaniel Saltonstall, Mar. 3, 1692/3, Moody, ed., *Saltonstall Papers*, I, 211; Moody, "Nathaniel Saltonstall," *ibid.*, 52-53; Payne, "Defending," 71.

74. Calef, *More Wonders*, 357-358; C. Mather to Cotton, Aug. 5, 1692, C. Mather, *Diary*, I, 142.

75. Calef, *More Wonders*, 364-365.

76. *Ibid.*, 360-361; Brattle, "Letter," 177; Sewall, *Diary*, I, 294; Rosenthal, *Salem Story*, 144-145. See 2 Cor 11: 14.

77. Sewall, *Diary*, I, 294; *SW*, I, 178; Norton, *Snare*, 249.

78. David C. Brown, "The Case of Giles Corey," *EIHC*, CXXI (1985), 282-283, 287; David C. Brown, "The Forfeitures at Salem, 1692," *WMQ*, L (1993), 85; "Account of John Moulton," Sept. 13, 1710, *SW*, III, 985-986; Calef, *More Wonders*, 367.

79. Calef, *More Wonders*, 367; Sewall, *Diary*, I, 295.

80. Thomas Putnam to Samuel Sewall, n. d., *SW*, I, 246; Norton, *Snare*, 343.

81. Dow, ed., *Essex Quarterly Courts*, VI, 190n-191n.

82. *Ibid.*, 190, 191n; Putnam to Sewall, n. d., *SW*, I, 246; Sewall, *Diary*, I, 295.

83. Calef, *More Wonders*, 367-369.

84. *Ibid.*, 372. For the names and execution dates of the human victims, see Norton, *Snare*, 315-317.

85. *SW*, I, 53; Norton, *Snare*, 238-239, 275.

86. Thomas Newton to Isaac Addington, May 31 1692, *SW*, III, 867.

87. *SW*, I, 59, 122, II, 632-633.

88. *SW*, I, 168-169; C. Mather, *Wonders*, 217; Is 14: 12-14; Matt 4: 8-11; Norton, *Snare*, 371n80.

89. *SW*, I, 211-212, II, 665, 670; Robinson, *Devil Discovered*, 126.

90. Robert Pike to Corwin, Aug. 9, 1692, Upham, *Salem Witchcraft*, II, 538-544; Norton, *Snare*, 197, 266, 288-289. See John 8: 44 and 1 Sam 28: 13-14.

91. Calef, *More Wonders*, 372-373; Demos, *Entertaining Satan*, 38, 46, 404; Caporeal, "Ergotism," 21.

92. Calef, *More Wonders*, 369-370; Payne, "Defending," 81; Raymond Phineas Stearns, *Science in the British Colonies of America* (Urbana, Ill., 1970), 153, 402-403, 708; Baker and Reid, *New England Knight*, 154.

93. C. Mather, *Wonders*, 211; Payne, "Defending," 81.

94. Brattle, "Letter," 171, 182, 190.

95. *Ibid.*, 184-186; Silverman, *Cotton Mather*, 113-114; Rosenthal, *Salem Story*, 30; Baker and Reid, *New England Knight*, 154.

96. C. Mather to Cotton, Oct. 20, 1692, Silverman, ed., *Mather Letters*, 45-46; Silverman, *Cotton Mather*, 114, 117.

97. C. Mather to Stephen Sewall, Sept. 20, 1692, Silverman, ed., *Mather Letters*, 44-45; Brattle, "Letter," 177-178; Phips to Blathwayt, Oct. 12, 1692, *SW*, III, 861-862.

98. Baker and Reid, *New England Knight*, 147-150.

99. C. Mather, *Wonders*, in Drake, ed., *Witchcraft Delusions*, I, 216-217; Ankarloo, "Sweden," 299-300.

100. C. Mather, *Magnalia* (ed. Murdock), 329-330, 330n; Hale, *Modest*, 22-23.

101. John Miller, *New York Considered and Improved, 1695*, ed. V. H. Paltsits (Cleveland, 1903; rpt. New York, 1970), 123-125, 123n, 125n; "Note, Witchcraft in New York," NYHS, *Coll.*, II (1869), 274; C. Mather, *Phips*, 149-150; "Questions concerning Witchcraft, laid before the most reverend clergy from Belgium and France," MHS, *Procs.*, 2nd ser., I (1884), 354-358.

102. Phips to Earl of Nottingham, Feb. 21, 1692/3, *SW*, III, 864-865; *ibid.*, 919, 924, 926; Sewall, *Diary*, I, 299; Hale, *Modest*, 39; Norton, *Snare*, 290-292.

103. Pencak, *War*, 21, 28; Douglas Edward Leach, *Roots of Conflict: British Armed Forces and Colonial Americans, 1677-1763* (Chapel Hill, 1986), 34, 139-140; Barnes, "Rise of Phips," 278.

104. Chidley Brooke to Fletcher, Aug. 2, 1693, *NYCD*, IV, 58; Baker and Reid, *New England Knight*, 21-22.

105. Higginson to John How, Aug. 1, 1694, Moody, ed., *Saltonstall Papers*, I, 214-215; *ibid.*, 227n1.

106. Sewall, *Diary*, I, 354, 366-367.

107. C. Mather, *Diary*, I, 172, 216.

108. *SW*, III, 1015-1017; "Account of William Good," Sept. 13, 1710, *ibid.*, 994; Fowler, ed., "Green Diary," 98.

109. Calef, *More Wonders*, 305-306; *SW*, III, 1015-1017; "The Confession of Anne Putnam, when she was received to Communion, 1706," Upham, *Salem Witchcraft*, II, 510.

110. Hale, *Modest*, 132-133; Boyer and Nissenbaum, *Salem Possessed*, 78; Norton, *Snare*, 292, 408n59; Roach, "Betty," 20-25. Norton believed that Hale was referring to Susannah Sheldon. However, Hale, as related earlier, said that the divination was an opening wedge for the devil. Abigail, not Sheldon, was involved in the actual start of the troubles. See Norton, *Snare*, 311.

111. Morgan, *Genuine Article*, 57; Ranlet, *Richard B. Morris*, 58.

112. C. Mather, *A Town in its Truest Glory: A Brief Essay upon a Town Happy and Glorious* (Boston, 1712), 30-31; C. Mather, *Diary*, II, 112-113.

113. *SW*, II, 550-551.

CHAPTER 9
JOSEPH DUDLEY

1. Palfrey, *History*, IV, 246-248; Everett Kimball, *The Public Life of Joseph Dudley* (New York, 1911), v, 207, 219.

2. Johnson, *Adjustment*, 333-334; Silverman, *Cotton Mather*, 207-208.

3. *Boston News-Letter*, Apr. 4 - Apr. 11, 1720; Boyer and Nissenbaum, *Salem Possessed*, 133, 152. For Joseph, see Gen 37.

4. Benjamin Colman, *Ossa Josephi . . . A Sermon Preached After the Funeral of . . . Joseph Dudley, Esq.* (Boston, 1720), 34; I. Mather to JD, Jan. 20, 1707/8, "An Original Letter from Dr. Increase Mather, to Governour Dudley," MHS, *Coll.*, 1st ser., III (1794), 127-128.

5. *Mass. Records*, V, 151; Samuel Eliot Morison, *Harvard College in the Seventeenth Century* (Cambridge, Mass., 1936), II, 433n; Sewall, *Diary*, I, 576.

6. Coinage Committee Report, June 2, 1677, Photostat, MHS; Report on Salisbury Church, Sept. 13, 1677, *ibid.*; Report on Ministers' Salaries, Oct. 13, 1679, *ibid.*; JD's warrant, Dec. 6, 1679, Joseph Dudley Papers, MHS.

7. General Court Resolve, May 28, 1679, Photostat, MHS; Report on Navigation Acts, June 11, 1679, *ibid.*; Randolph, "Articles of high Misdemeanor," Feb. 15, 1681, Hutchinson, *Collection*, II, 266; Sosin, *Charles II*, 275.

8. *Mass. Records*, V, 346; "Instructions for JD and John Richards . . . ," Feb. 15, 1681/2, *ibid.*, 346-349.

9. *Ibid.*, 386-387; Instructions and General Court to JD and Richards, Mar. 30, 1683, *ibid.*, 390-392; Randolph to Clarendon, June 14, 1682, Hutchinson, *Collection*, II, 275; *RP*, III, 190-191, 203-204.

10. Richards to I. Mather, Dec. 12, 1682, *Mather Papers*, 499-500; JD to C. Mather, June 5, 1689, *Winthrop Papers*, MHS, *Coll.*, 6th ser., III (1889), 501-507; Sosin, *Charles II*, 292.

11. Randolph to Bishop of London, May 29, 1682, Hutchinson, *Collection*, II, 271.

12. Randolph to JD, Jan. 9, 1684, *ibid.*, 284; JD to Blathwayt, Dec. 1, 1683, BPCW.

13. *Ibid.*; Randolph to Shrimpton, July 26, 1684, *RP*, III, 317-318.

14. Randolph to Jenkins, Feb. 14, 1683/4, *ibid.*, 273-274; Randolph to LT, July 16, 1684, *ibid.*, 309-310; JD to Blathwayt, May 4, 1684, BPCW.

15. JD to Blathwayt, Nov. 4, 1684, BPCW; Sewall, *Diary*, I, 80-81, 85, 101-102.

16. JD to Randolph, Dec. 1, 1684, *Mather Papers*, 483; JD to Blathwayt, Sept. 20, 1685, BPCW; JD to Blathwayt, Sept. 28, 1685, BPCW; JD to Blathwayt, Nov. 2, 1685, BPCW; Sewall, *Diary*, I, 107.

17. Randolph to Blathwayt, May 17, 1686, *RP*, VI, 170; Randolph to Archbishop of Canterbury, [July 7], 1686, Hutchinson, *Collection*, II, 291; I. Mather, *A Narrative of the Miseries of New-England* (1688/9?), Whitmore, ed., *Andros Tracts*, II, 5; D. M. Brodie, "Edmund Dudley: Minister of Henry VII," Royal Historical Society, *Transactions*, 4th ser., XV (1932), 148-152.

18. JD's speech, May 17, 1686, "Dudley's Speeches," MHS, *Procs.*, VII (1864), 487-489; Randolph to Archbishop, [July 7], 1686, Hutchinson, *Collection*, II, 291.

19. JD's speech, May 25, 1686, Robert N. Toppan, ed., *Dudley Records*, MHS, *Procs.*, 2nd ser., XIII (1899-1900), 226-227; *Mass. Royal Commissions*, II, 37-43.

20. JD to Blathwayt, May 31, June 20, 1686, BPCW; Toppan, ed. *Dudley Records*, 240.

21. Toppan, ed., *Dudley Records*, 235-236, 246, 268, 277, 281, 285.

22. *Ibid.*, 232, 234; Sosin, *1688*, 69-70; JD to Samuel Sewall, June 30, 1686, Thomas Prince Papers, MHS.

23. JD to Blathwayt, July 31, 1686, *RP*, VI, 196; Randolph to LT, July 28, 1686, *ibid.*, IV, 101-102; Toppan, ed., *Dudley Records*, 241; Council to LT, c. June 1, 1686, *ibid.*, 240; Memorial to the king and others, c. June 1, 1686, *ibid.*, 244.

24. Toppan, ed., *Dudley Records*, 230, 238, 243-244, 256-258, 265; Jon Butler, *The Huguenots in America: A Refugee People in New World Society* (Cambridge, Mass., 1983), 13, 71-74, 80-81.

25. Toppan, ed., *Dudley Records*, 259, 262-265, 267, 270-271; Charges against JD, Whitmore, ed., *Andros Tracts*, I, 159-160.

26. Randolph to Blathwayt, Oct. 29, 1686, *RP*, VI, 200-201; Wharton's Deposition, Oct. 21, 1687, *ibid.*, 202-203; Randolph to Hayes, Nov. 20, 1687, *ibid.*, 205; Randolph to Sansom, June 30, 1686, *ibid.*, 183; JD to Blathwayt, Aug. 1687, BPCW; Theodore Dwight Bozeman, *To Live Ancient Lives: The Primitivist Dimension in Puritanism* (Chapel Hill, 1988), 283-284.

27. Theodore B. Lewis, "Land Speculation and the Dudley Council of 1686," *WMQ*, XXXI (1974), 258-259; John Frederick Martin, *Profits in the Wilderness: Entrepreneurship and the Founding of New England Towns in the Seventeenth Century* (Chapel Hill, 1991), 92.

28. Lewis, "Speculation," 261-262, 264-265, 270, Viola F. Barnes, "Richard Wharton, a Seventeenth Century Colonial," PCSM, *Transactions*, XXVI (1924-1926),

248-249, 262-263; JD to Blathwayt, Feb. 3, 1685, BPCW; Mass. Archives, vol. 126, pp. 30, 142-143.

29. JD to Blathwayt, May 31, 1686, BPCW; Randolph to Blathwayt, June 19, 1686, *RP*, VI, 176-177; Randolph to Blathwayt, July 12, 1686, *ibid.*, 187-189; Randolph to Southwell, July 10, 1686, *RP*, IV, 92-93; Hall, *Edward Randolph*, 102-103; Mass. Archives, vol. 126, p. 138.

30. Charges against JD, Whitmore, ed., *Andros Tracts*, I, 160. See the deeds in Mss. Large, MHS, and Oxford, Mass., Misc. Mss., NYHS.

31. Andros to Blathwayt, Mar. 30, July 11, 1687, BPCW; Barnes, "Wharton," 264-266; Sosin, *1688*, 61, 72; Lewis, "Speculation," 265-267, 269-270.

32. Cook, *Wise*, 49; C. Mather, *A Memorial of the Present Deplorable State of New-England* (1707), MHS, *Coll.*, 5th ser., VI (1879), 36; Johnson, *Adjustment*, 391; Charges against JD, Whitmore, ed., *Andros Tracts*, I, 157, 159.

33. Byfield, *Account*, in Andrews, ed., *Insurrections*, 174.

34. Charges against JD, Whitmore, ed., *Andros Tracts*, I, 159-160; JD to C. Mather, June 5, 1689, *Winthrop Papers*, MHS, *Coll.*, 6th ser., III (1889), 501-507.

35. Randolph to Blathwayt, July 20, 1689, *RP*, VI, 289-290; Robert Earle Moody and Richard Clive Simmons, eds., *The Glorious Revolution in Massachusetts: Selected Documents, 1689-1692*, PCSM, LXIV, *Coll.* (1988), 109, 113, 133; "The Petition of John Winslow," July 16, 1689, *ibid.*, 134; "Proposals to be considered by the General Convention," Aug. 14, 1689, *ibid.*, 136; Benjamin Davis to Edward Hull, July 31, 1689, *ibid.*, 398; Sir Henry Ashurst to [Lord Wharton?], Sept. 3, 1689, *ibid.*, 441.

36. JD to Bradstreet, Sept. 12, 1689, Prince Papers, MHS; Summons to JD, Oct. 16, 1689, *ibid.*; Randolph to Usher, Oct. 16, 1689, *RP*, VI, 307; Cook, *Wise*, 56, 60.

37. Moody and Simmons, eds., *Glorious Revolution*, 191-192, 192n, 204n; T. Brinley to F. Brinley, May 28, 1690, Lewis, ed., "Andros's Hearing," 249.

38. Stephen Saunders Webb, "William Blathwayt, Imperial Fixer: Muddling Through to Empire, 1689-1717," *WMQ*, XXVI (1969), 376; Sewall, *Diary*, I, 275.

39. Ritchie, *Duke's Province*, 212-213, 229-230; Sloughter to Nottingham, May 6, 1691, *NYCD*, III, 759-760; Jerome R. Reich, *Leisler's Rebellion: A Study of Democracy in New York, 1664-1720* (Chicago, 1953), 128; *Loyalty Vindicated; being an Answer to a Late False, Seditious and Scandalous Pamphlet* (1698), in *Documents Relating to the Administration of Leisler*, NYHS, *Coll.*, I (1868), 389; Thomas Newton to Francis Nicholson, Apr. 8, 1691, in Lawrence H. Leder, ed., "Captain Kidd and the Leisler Rebellion," *New-York Historical Society Quarterly*, XXXVIII (1954), 51; David William Voorhees, "The 'fervant Zeale' of Jacob Leisler," *WMQ*, LI (1994), 449, 467, 471.

40. JD to Blathwayt, Mar. 17, 1690/1, BPCW; Ritchie, *Duke's Province*, 230.

41. *Documents Relating to Leisler*, 351, 363-364; JD to Blathwayt, Apr. 6, 1691, BPCW; Reich, *Leisler's Rebellion*, 118-119; William Nicolls to Blathwayt, May 7, 1691, in Hall and others, eds., *Glorious Revolution*, 119.

42. Nicolls to Blathwayt, May 7, 1691, in Hall and others, eds., *Glorious Revolution*, 119; Lawrence H. Leder, *Robert Livingston, 1654-1728, and the Politics of Colonial New York* (Chapel Hill, 1961), 76n; Reich, *Leisler's Rebellion*, 121-122.

43. "Commission of Joseph Dudley as Deputy Governor of the Province of West New Jersey," Dec. 5, 1690, MHS, *Procs.*, XI (1869-1870), 204-205; Sloughter to Nottingham, May 6, 1691, *NYCD*, III, 761; Pomfret, *East New Jersey*, 276-277; JD to

Blathwayt, May 6, 1691, BPCW; *Diary of Lawrence Hammond*, MHS, *Procs.*, 2nd ser., VII (1891-1892), 160; Kimball, *Public Life*, 64.

44. Pencak, *War*, 21, 28.

45. JD to Blathwayt, Feb. 25, 1692/3, BPCW.

46. Johnson, *Adjustment*, 282-283, 338; Pencak, *War*, 27; Sosin, *Imperial Inconstancy*, 164; Kimball, *Public Life*, 64-65; Fletcher to Blathwayt, Aug. 18, 1693, Misc. Blathwayt Papers, NYHS; Baker and Reid, *New England Knight*, 153.

47. Robert C. Winthrop, Jr., ed., "Letters of Lord Cutts," MHS, *Procs.*, 2nd ser., II (1885-1886), 172, 176; Sewall, *Diary*, I, 587; William L. Sachse, *The Colonial American in Britain* (Madison, Wisc., 1956), 147; Kimball, *Public Life*, 69; Webb, *The Governors-General: The English Army and the Definition of the Empire, 1569-1681* (Chapel Hill, 1979), 492. While still in America, in July 1689 JD used the title Colonel, which then probably referred to militia rank. See Benjamin Davis to Edward Hull, July 31, 1689, Moody and Simmons, eds., *Glorious Revolution*, 398. On Cutts see *DNB*, s. v. "Cutts, John."

48. "Memorandum to Mr. Dudley," [c. 1693], Winthrop, ed., "Cutts Letters," 174; Cutts to JD, Apr. 1, 1698, *ibid.*, 189; Leonard Woods Labaree, *Royal Government in America: A Study of the British Colonial System Before 1783* (New Haven, 1930), 83; JD to Blathwayt, July 30, Nov. 10, 1705, BL 262, BL 263, Blathwayt Papers, Huntington Library.

49. Cutts to JD, May 31, 1695, Aug. 12, 1697, Winthrop, ed., "Cutts Letters," 182, 186.

50. John Higginson to JD, Aug. 2, 1694, Saltonstall Papers, MHS; Higginson to Howe, Aug. 1, 1694, *ibid.* On Nehemiah in Puritan thought, see T. H. Breen, *The Character of the Good Ruler: A Study of Puritan Political Ideas in New England, 1630-1730* (New York, 1970), 100.

51. JD to Blathwayt, Nov. 23, 1695, Feb. 9, 1696, BPCW; Sewall, *Diary*, I, 331-332; Jacobsen, *Blathwayt*, 344.

52. Johnson, *Adjustment*, 319; Sosin, *Imperial Inconstancy*, 200; Sir H. Ashurst to Wait Winthrop, July 10, 1701, *Winthrop Papers*, MHS, *Coll.*, 6th ser., V (1892), 89-90.

53. Reich, *Leisler's Rebellion*, 133-134; *Documents Relating to Leisler*, 348, 350-351; Stock, ed., *Procs. of Parliaments*, II, 118-119, 130-131.

54. Johnson, *Adjustment*, 261; Sosin, *Imperial Inconstancy*, 156, 166; Harry M. Ward, *"Unite Or Die": Intercolony Relations, 1690-1763* (Port Washington, N. Y., 1971), 32.

55. JD to his wife, May 6, 1696, Apr. 13, 1698, *Winthrop Papers*, MHS, *Coll.*, 6th ser., III (1889), 514, 517; JD to Paul Dudley, Dec. 23, 1700, *ibid.*, 520; Colman, *Ossa Josephi*, 36.

56. JD to Blathwayt, Aug. 22, 1701, Dudley-Blathwayt Papers, MHS; Sachse, *Colonial American*, 146.

57. Chamberlayne to JD, Sept. 22, 1702, *Winthrop Papers*, MHS, *Coll.*, 6th ser., III (1889), 531.

58. Pencak, *War*, 43; Webb, *Governors-General*, 10, 492; JD to Blathwayt, Aug. 19, 22, 1701, Dudley-Blathwayt Papers, MHS.

59. JD to C. Mather, May 10, 1701, Curwen Family Collection, AAS; C. Mather to JD, Aug. 25, 1701, Silverman, ed., *Mather Letters*, 65-66; Silverman, *Cotton Mather*, 204-205; Pencak, *War*, 44; G. B. Warden, *Boston, 1689-1776* (Boston, 1970), 60.

60. JD to Blathwayt, July 22, 26, 29, Aug. 5, 12, 15, 1701, Dudley-Blathwayt Papers, MHS; John Quick and Presbyterian ministers to I. Mather and Willard, July 28, 1701, BL 257, Blathwayt Papers, Huntington.
61. Byfield to JD, Aug. 7, 1701, BL 258, Blathwayt Papers, Huntington; "Extract of Severall Letters from New England," BL 256, *ibid.*
62. PRO *Cal.*, XIX, 610; Robert Worsley to JD, Nov. 19, 1701, C. E. French Collection, MHS; Albert Matthews, ed., *Notes on the Massachusetts Royal Commissions, 1681-1775*, PCSM, *Transactions*, XVII (1913-1914), 53-54.
63. Sewall, *Diary*, I, 470; JD's speech, June 16, 1702, Mass. Archives, vol. 108, 1-2.
64. Joshua Gee's deposition, Sept. 21, 1702, Chamberlain Collection, Boston Public Library; Dora Mae Clark, "The Impressment of Seamen in the American Colonies," in *Essays in Colonial History Presented to Charles McLean Andrews by His Students* (New Haven, 1931), 205; Silverman, *Cotton Mather*, 206; Johnson, *Adjustment*, 340.
65. I. Mather, *The Excellency of a Publick Spirit* (Boston, 1702), dedication; C. Mather, *Diary*, I, 464-465.
66. I. Mather to a lord, Dec. 8, 1703, "The Mathers and Sir Charles Hobby," PCSM, *Transactions*, XIX (1916-1917), 155; I. Mather to W. Ashurst, Dec. 5, 1709, *Documents From the Harvard University Archives, 1638-1750*, ed. Robert W. Lovett, PCSM, XLIX, *Coll.* (1975), 229; C. Mather, *Diary*, II, 15; Pencak, *War*, 46.
67. C. Mather to Lord Nottingham, Nov. 26, 1703, "Mathers and Hobby," 154; Hutchinson, *History*, II, 114; Johnson, *Adjustment*, 342-343; Silverman, *Cotton Mather*, 211.
68. JD to CT, Mar. 1, 1708/9, *DHM*, 253-254; JD to CT, Mar. 10, 1704/5, PRO *Cal.*, XXII, 447.
69. *The Acts and Resolves, Public and Private, of the Province of the Massachusetts Bay* (Boston, 1869-1922), VIII, 293; Johnson, *Adjustment*, 277-278, 397; Labaree, *Royal*, 353, 355; "Report of the British Board of Trade and Plantations, December, 1703," *New York Public Library Bulletin*, XI (1907), 490.
70. Labaree, *Royal*, 346, 353; *Massachusetts Acts*, VIII, 343, 358-359; CT to JD, May 26, 1704, *ibid.*, XXII, 137; JD to CT, Nov. 1, 1705, *ibid.*, 655-657.
71. Sewall, *Diary*, I, 596; JD to CT, Aug. 5, 1703, *DHM*, 148-149; JD to Nottingham, Dec. 10, 1702, PRO *Cal.*, XXI, 36; JD to CT, Nov. 1, 1705, *ibid.*, XXII, 655-657. On whales see JD to CT, Feb. 1, 1705/6, PRO *Cal.*, XXIII, 29-30; JD to _____, Mar. 25, 1705/6, Misc. Mss., MHS, and another letter of the same date in *ibid.* For private gifts see Paige to Popple, Sept. 20, 1706, PRO *Cal.*, XXIII, 226; Samuel Sewall to JD, July 14, 1715, *Letter-Book of Samuel Sewall (1686-1729)*, MHS, *Coll.*, 6th ser., II (1888), 47, 47n.
72. JD to Sunderland, Mar. 5-Mar. 9, 1708/9, HM 22303, Misc. Letters, Huntington; JD to assembly, Mar. 10, 1702/3, *DHM*, 125; JD's speech, Oct. 1702, *ibid.*, 133; Pemaquid committee report, Oct. 21, 1702, *ibid.*, 130-131.
73. "Representatives Answer," Nov. 16, 1703, *DHM*, 169-170; JD's speech, Sept. 5, 1705, *ibid.*, 225-226.
74. Hutchinson, *History*, II, 102; Pencak, *War*, 26; Sewall, *Diary*, I, 486; JD to CT, Mar. 1, 1708/9, *DHM*, 252; Warden, *Boston*, 80.
75. JD to CT, July 25, 1705, PRO *Cal.*, XXII, 588; CT to JD, Feb. 4, 1705/6, *ibid.*, XXIII, 43; Sewall, *Diary*, I, 523-524; Labaree, *Colonial Massachusetts*, 138; Pencak, *War*, 48; Francis Newton Thorpe, ed., *The Federal and State Constitutions*,

Colonial Charters, and Other Organic Laws of the States, Territories, and Colonies Now Or Heretofore Forming the United States of America (Washington, D. C., 1909), III, 1883.

76. JD to [CT], May 10, Dec. 19, 1703, PRO *Cal.*, XXI, 409, 881; JD to CT, Sept. 15, 1703, July 13, 1704, *DHM*, 154-155, 192, 197; Warden, *Boston*, 62; Haskins, *Law*, 165.

77. Pencak, *War*, 45.

78. David E. Van Deventer, *The Emergence of Provincial New Hampshire, 1623-1741* (Baltimore, 1976), 55; JD to Blathwayt, July 30, 1705, BL 262, Blathwayt Papers, Huntington; JD to Council of New Hampshire, Aug. 26, 1708, C. E. French Collection, MHS.

79. Lyman Horace Weeks and Edwin M. Bacon, eds., *An Historical Digest of the Provincial Press* (Boston, 1911), 176; Sewall, *Diary*, I, 532-537, 532n-535n; Strandness, *Sewall*, 79-80.

80. JD to CT, Dec. 1, 1713, PRO *Cal.*, XXVII, 253.

81. JD to CT, Sept. 17, 1702, *ibid.*, XX, 592; JD's speech, Oct. 21, 1702, *ibid.*, XXI, 39-40; JD to Nottingham, Dec. 10, 1702, *ibid.*, 34; JD to Fitz-John Winthrop, Jan. 18, 1702/3, *Winthrop Papers*, MHS, *Coll.*, 6th ser., III (1889), 118.

82. JD's speech, n. d., [c. June 1703], *DHM*, 134; Capt. Samuel Moodey to JD, July 20, 1710, *ibid.*, 302-303; JD to CT, Apr. 20, 1704, *ibid.*, 183; JD to [CT], May 10, 1703, PRO *Cal.*, XXI, 409; CT Journal, July 13, 1703, *ibid.*, 550; *Journal of the Commissioners For Trade and Plantations* (London, 1920), I, 102.

83. Cornbury to CT, June 30, 1703, *NYCD*, IV, 1061; JD to CT, Aug. 5, Sept. 15, 1703, *DHM*, 145, 151-152.

84. JD to CT, Sept. 15, 1703, *DHM*, 151-152; Kenneth M. Morrison, *The Embattled Northeast: The Elusive Ideal of Alliance in Abenaki-European Relations* (Berkeley, Calif., 1984), 158; J. C. Beckett, *The Making of Modern Ireland, 1603-1923* (New York, 1966), 150. For the atrocities, see "John Hornabrook's statement," n. d., *DHM*, 178-179.

85. JD to CT, Sept. 15, 1703, *DHM*, 153.

86. *Ibid.*

87. JD to CT, Sept. 15, 1703, Mar. 1, 1708/9, *DHM*, 156, 262-263; JD to CT, Apr. 8, 1712, PRO *Cal.*, XXVI, 257-258; Douglas Edward Leach, *Arms for Empire: A Military History of the British Colonies in North America, 1607-1763* (New York, 1973), 132.

88. JD to queen, Nov. 10, 1707, PRO *Cal.*, XXIII, 594; Cornbury to CT, June 30, 1703, *NYCD*, IV, 1061; Hunter to CT, July 24, 1710, *ibid.*, V, 168; JD to Sunderland, Mar. 5-Mar. 9, 1708/9, HM 22303, Misc. Letters, Huntington; Lawrence H. Leder, ed., *The Livingston Indian Records, 1666-1723* (Gettysburg, Pa., 1956; rpt. Stanfordville, N. Y., 1979), 202, 204-205, 212.

89. JD to Fitz-John Winthrop, May 27, 1703, *Winthrop Papers*, MHS, *Coll.*, 6th ser., III (1889), 129; JD to CT, Apr. 20, 1704, *DHM*, 180-181; John Williams, *The Redeemed Captive Returning to Zion*, 6th ed. (Boston, 1795; orig. pub. 1707; rpt. [New Canaan, Conn.?], 1966), 8; Haefeli and Sweeney, *Captors and Captives*, 95, 191.

90. JD's speech, Dec. 27, 1704, *DHM*, 209; JD's speech, n. d., *ibid.*, 248, Weeks and Bacon, eds., *Historical Digest*, 426; Leach, *Arms*, 135.

91. JD to CT, Sept. 15, 1703, Apr. 20, 1704, Mar. 1, 1708/9, *DHM*, 152-153, 181, 264; JD's speeches, Apr. 19, 1704, May 31, 1705, *ibid.*, 185, 217-218; JD to _____, Apr. 21, 1704, Parkman Transcripts, MHS; Privy Council to CT, July 15, 1706, Colonial Office 5 / 751 / no. 75, Library of Congress; Morrison, *Embattled Northeast*, 160.

92. Col. Thomas Noyes to JD, Jan. 6, 1709/10, *DHM*, 272; JD to CT, Jan. 31, 1709/10, *ibid.*, 278-280; JD to Fitz-John Winthrop, Mar. 6, 1703/4, *Winthrop Papers*, MHS, *Coll.*, 6th ser., III (1889), 179; JD to CT, Feb. 1, 1705/6, PRO *Cal.*, XXIII, 30-31.

93. JD's speech, Aug. 16, 1704, Weeks and Bacon, eds., *Historical Digest*, 120; JD to CT, July 13, 1704, *DHM*, 190; Kimball, *Public Life*, 111; Leach, *Arms*, 133; JD to CT, Mar. 10, 1704/5, PRO *Cal.*, XXII, 445.

94. JD to CT, Sept. 15, 1703, July 13, 1704, *DHM*, 153-154, 190-191; JD to CT, Mar. 10, 1704/5, PRO *Cal.*, XXII, 445.

95. JD to [Nottingham?], Dec. 19, 1703, PRO *Cal.*, XXI, 883; JD to CT, Apr. 20, 1704, *DHM*, 181-182; Isaac Addington to Blathwayt, Feb. 21, 1692/3, BPCW; JD to CT, Sept. 17, 1702, *Rhode Island Records*, III, 462-463; Rhode Island assembly to JD, *ibid.*, 463; Samuel Cranston to JD, Feb. 28, 1704/5, *ibid.*, 496-497.

96. JD to CT, Nov. 2, 1705, *Rhode Island Records*, III, 543-544; JD to CT, July 13, 1704, *DHM*, 190-191, 194-195; CT to JD, Apr. 18, 1705, Pepperrell Papers, MHS.

97. Sosin, *Imperial Inconstancy*, 189-190; *The Manuscripts of the House of Lords*, New Series, Vol. VII (London, 1921), 294; *Rhode Island Records*, IV, 16; Stock, ed., *Procs. of Parliaments*, III, 4, 76; CT to JD, Jan. 26, 1702/3, PRO *Cal.*, XXI, 156-157; Leach, *Arms*, 140; "quo warranto," *Black's Law Dictionary*, 1131.

98. Joseph Henry Smith, *Appeals to the Privy Council from the American Plantations* (New York, 1950), 424-425; Stock, ed., *Procs. of Parliaments*, III, 77. The Mohegans appear to have been using the name Uncas as a dynastic name in imitation of European forms.

99. JD to CT, Nov. 1, 1705, PRO *Cal.*, XXII, 659-660; Smith, *Appeals*, 425-426; CT to queen, Jan. 10, 1705/6, *Rhode Island Records*, IV, 15.

100. *Ibid.*

101. I. Mather, preface to C. Mather, *Winthropi Justa* (Boston, 1708; rpt. London, 1709), n. p.; Sir H. Ashurst to Lady Rachel Russel, c. 1709, *ibid.*; JD to Blathwayt, Feb. 1, 1705/6, Apr. 13, 1706, BL 265, BL 264, Blathwayt Papers, Huntington; Wait Winthrop to Fitz-John Winthrop, May 22, 1706, *Winthrop Papers*, MHS, *Coll.*, 6th ser., V (1892), 139.

102. Smith, *Appeals*, 427, 435, 442.

103. JD to Samuel Moody, Feb. 15, 1709/10, *DHM*, 293; Addington to Partridge, Feb. 28, 1709/10, *ibid.*, 294-295; JD to CT, Feb. 1, 1705/6, PRO *Cal.*, XXIII, 31; JD to Wait Winthrop, Mar. 25, 1708/9, Moody, ed., *Saltonstall Papers*, I, 286-288.

104. JD to queen, Nov. 10, 1707, PRO *Cal.*, XXIII, 594; JD to CT, Feb. 1, 1705/6, *ibid.*, 31; [Paul Dudley?], *A Modest Enquiry into the Grounds and Occasions of a Late Pamphlet, Intituled, A Memorial of the Present Deplorable State of New-England* (1707), MHS, *Coll.*, 5th ser., VI (1879), 73.

105. JD to CT, Feb. 1, 1705/6, PRO *Cal.*, XXIII, 31; JD to CT, Oct. 10, 1704, *ibid.*, XXII, 275; JD to CT, Oct. 2, 1706, HM 9916, Misc. Letters, Huntington; Weeks and Bacon, eds., *Historical Digest*, 332, 426, 435; Williams, *Redeemed Captive*, iii-vi;

Haefeli and Sweeney, *Captors and Captives*, 180-182, 325n33; Haefeli and Sweeney, "*The Redeemed Captive* as Recurrent Seller: Politics and Publication, 1707-1853," *NEQ*, LXXVII (2004), 347.

106. Weeks and Bacon, eds., *Historical Digest*, 346; JD to CT, Oct. 8, 1706, PRO *Cal.*, XXIII, 258-259.

107. JD to CT, Oct. 8, 1706, PRO *Cal.*, XXIII, 258-259; JD's speech, Aug. 7, 1706, Mass. Archives, vol. 108, 44-45.

108. Thorpe, ed., *Constitutions*, 1876, 1882; Hutchinson, *History*, II, 115-116; George M. Waller, *Samuel Vetch, Colonial Enterpriser* (Chapel Hill, 1960), 84; JD's speech, Aug. 7, 1706, Mass. Archives, vol. 108, 44-45.

109. Sewall, *Diary*, 549; JD to CT, Oct. 8, 1706, PRO *Cal.*, XXIII, 258-259; *Journal of Comm. for Trade*, I, 327-328.

110. Kimball, *Public Life*, 118, 184; Walker, *Vetch*, 87; Pencak, *War*, 49; N. Higginson and others to queen, [June 23, 1707], Hutchinson, *History*, II, 118; C. Mather, *Memorial of Present Deplorable State*; Paul Dudley to W. Wharton, Jan. 12, 1703/4, [C. Mather?], *The Deplorable State of New-England, By Reason of a Covetous and Treacherous Governour, and Pusillanimous Counsellors* (1708), MHS, *Coll.*, 5th ser., VI (1879), 109; H. Ashurst to Wait Winthrop, Sept. 16, 1704, *Winthrop Papers, ibid.*, 6th ser., V (1892), 133.

111. JD to queen, Nov. 10, 1707, PRO *Cal.*, XXIII, 594; CT to JD, July 23, 1708, *ibid.*, XXIV, 40; JD to Sunderland, Nov. 10, 1707, HM 22287, Misc. Letters, Huntington; Pontchartrain to Vaudreuil, June 9, 1706, *NYCD*, IX, 779; Hutchinson, *History*, II, 120; Sewall, *Diary*, I, 576; Kimball, *Public Life*, 119, 185-189; Pencak, *War*, 50-51; Waller, *Vetch*, 83.

112. Pencak, *War*, 51; Waller, *Vetch*, 99.

113. Colman, *Ossa Josephi*, 37; Morison, *Harvard Seventeenth*, II, 474, 548, 550-551, 555, 555n.

114. I. Mather to JD, Jan. 20, 1707/8, "Original Letter," 126-127; C. Mather to JD, Jan. 20, 1707/8, "An Original Letter from Dr. C. Mather, to Governour Dudley," MHS, *Coll.*, 1st ser., III (1794), 129; JD to Mathers, Feb. 3, 1707/8, "An Original Letter from Governour Dudley to Dr. Increase and Dr. Cotton Mather," *ibid.*, 135; 1 Thess 4:11; C. Mather to William Denison, n. d., in Morison, *Harvard Seventeenth*, II, 552-553; I. Mather to W. Ashurst, Jan. 19, 1709/10, *Harvard Documents*, XLIX, 230; H. Ashurst to G. Saltonstall, June 27, 1709, *Winthrop Papers*, MHS, *Coll.*, 6th ser., V (1892), 196.

115. Webb, "Blathwayt Imperial Fixer," 394; JD to _____, Nov. 26, 1704, Parkman Transcripts, MHS.

116. JD's speeches, Aug. 13, Oct. 29, 1707, Mass. Archives, vol. 108, 53-56; Winthrop Hilton to JD, July 16, 1707, Belknap Papers, MHS; JD to Sunderland, Mar. 5, 1707/8, HM 22287, Misc. Letters, Huntington; Ward, *Unite*, 107; Leach, *Arms*, 134.

117. JD's speech, July 13, 1709, *DHM*, 297; JD's speech, Oct. 26, 1709, Mass. Archives, vol. 108, 73-74; Leach, *Arms*, 143.

118. Gerald S. Graham, ed., *The Walker Expedition to Quebec, 1711* (Toronto, 1953), 105-107; JD and General Court to queen, Oct. 17, 1711, Gay Transcripts, X, 78-81, MHS; Leach, *Arms*, 151.

119. Samuel Moody to JD, July 20, 1710, *DHM*, 302-303; Vaudreuil to Pontchartrain, Oct. 31, 1710, *NYCD*, IX, 850-851; Pontchartrain to Vaudreuil, July 7, 1711, *ibid.*, 856.

120. JD to CT, Dec. 2, 1712, *DHM*, 335-337; JD to CT, Aug. 24, 1713, PRO *Cal.*, XXVII, 225; Indian treaty, July 13, 1713, *ibid.*, 229-230.

121. JD to W. Ashurst, Aug. 24, 1713, Misc. Mss., MHS; Francis Nicholson to JD, Dec. 25, 1714, PRO *Cal.*, XXVIII, 262-263; JD to CT, July 31-Aug. 4, 1715, *ibid.*, 252-253; *Journals of the House of Representatives of Massachusetts* (Boston, 1919-), I, 58; Charles E. Clark, *The Eastern Frontier: The Settlement of Northern New England, 1610-1763* (New York, 1970), 126.

122. Johnson, *Adjustment*, 272; Sewall, *Diary*, I, 494, 502, 544-545.

123. JD to CT, Mar. 1, 1708/9, *DHM*, 264-266.

124. *Ibid.*; JD to Blathwayt, July 30, 1705, BL 262, Blathwayt Papers, Huntington.

125. JD to CT, Mar. 1, 1708/9, *DHM*, 264-266.

126. CT to JD, Feb. 4, 1705/6, PRO *Cal.*, XXIII, 43; J. Campbell to Popple, Oct. 2, 1706, *ibid.*, 231; JD to CT, Oct. 2, 1706, *ibid.*, 234-236; H. Ashurst to Conn., Apr. 24, 1707, *Winthrop Papers*, MHS, *Coll.*, 6th ser., III (1889), 380; *CR*, IV, 546, 546n.

127. Colman, *Ossa Josephi*, 35; Samuel Myles to Beveridge, Jan. 4, 1703/4, Society for the Propagation of the Gospel Papers (cited hereafter as SPG Papers), Letter Series A, vol. 1, 162; Randolph to Lord Treasurer, Aug. 23, 1686, *RP*, IV, 113-115; Foote, *King's Chapel*, I, 151, 175, 177-178; Pennington, "Myles," 165.

128. Kimball, *Public Life*, 72; Pennington, "Myles," 160-161; Chamberlayne to JD, Apr. 10, 1703, *Winthrop Papers*, MHS, *Coll.*, 6th ser., III (1889), 536-537; John Boult to JD, Sept. 18, 1702, Misc. Bound Mss., MHS.

129. JD to Blathwayt, July 30, 1705, BL 262, Blathwayt Papers, Huntington; Vestry of King's Chapel to Compton, Jan. 29, 1711, Fulham Papers in Lambeth Palace, vol. 4, p. 37.

130. Foote, *King's Chapel*, I, 256; "An Answer of the Church of England in Brantrey . . . ," Sept. 1, 1710, Fulham Papers, vol. 4, p. 35.

131. "The Case of the Churchmen at Newbury," SPG Papers, Letter Series A, vol. 9, no. 14; "Petition of Inhabitants of West Precinct of Newbury to Bishop of London," n. d., *ibid.*, Letter Series B, vol. 1, no. 124; JD to SPG, Dec. 19, 1712, *ibid.*, no. 127.

132. *Ibid.*; Order of General Court, *ibid.*, Letter Series B, vol. 1, no. 124; Bridger to Dartmouth, Feb. 2, 1711, *ibid.*

133. Bridger to Church of England at Newbury, 1711, *ibid.*; "Petition of Inhabitants of West Precinct of Newbury to Bishop of London," *ibid.*; Bridger to Dartmouth, Feb. 2, 1711, *ibid.*; Joseph J. Malone, *Pine Trees and Politics: The Naval Stores and Forest Policy in Colonial New England, 1691-1775* (Seattle, 1964), 73; Sosin, *Imperial Inconstancy*, 41-42.

134. SPG to JD, Dec. 18, 1713, SPG Papers, Letter Series A, vol. 8, no. 3; JD to SPG, May 1, 1714, *ibid.*, vol. 9, no. 9; "The Case of the Churchmen at Newbury," *ibid.*, no. 14; JD to SPG, Dec. 19, 1712, May 1, 1714, *ibid.*, Letter Series B, vol. 1, nos. 127, 174; collector's statement, May 29, 1712, *ibid.*, no. 124; JD to Essex justices, Feb. 28, 1711/2, *ibid.*; Bridger to SPG, n. d., *ibid.*; "Proclamation of Gov. Joseph Dudley. . .," Feb. 28, 1711/2, Sewall, *Letter-Book*, I, 420-421; Sewall, *Diary*, II, 717; C. Mather, *The Diary of Cotton Mather D. D., F. R. S. for the Year 1712*, ed. William R. Manierre II (Charlottesville, Va., 1964), 25.

135. Samuel Lynde and others, *A Vindication of the Bank of Credit Projected in Boston from the Aspersions of Paul Dudley, Esqr.* (1714), in Andrew McFarland Davis, ed., *Tracts Relating to the Currency of the Massachusetts Bay, 1682-1720* (Boston,

1902), 150-155; Andrew McFarland Davis, *Currency and Banking in the Province of the Massachusetts Bay* (New York, 1901), II, 79-80; Pencak, *War*, 63-64; Warden, *Boston*, 71.

136.   JD to Popple, Oct. 3, 1714, PRO *Cal.*, XXVIII, 23; Byfield and others to CT, June 30, 1715, *ibid.*, 213; Byfield to John Leverett, June 19, 1714, Moody, ed., *Saltonstall Papers*, I, 314; Dummer to Colman, Jan. 15, 1714, "A Letter from Jeremiah Dummer, Esq. to Dr. Benjamin Colman," MHS, *Coll.*, 1st ser., V (1798), 198; Barbara A. Black, "Nathaniel Byfield, 1653-1733," in Coquillette, ed., *Law*, 101-102.

137.   Kimball, *Public Life*, 174, 193, 198; Johnson, *Adjustment*, 350-351; Hall, *Increase Mather*, 343; Hutchinson, *History*, II, 140; Pencak, *War*, 65-66; Dummer to JD, Feb. 19, 1710/1, June 5, 1711, Misc. Bound Mss., MHS.

138.   *Journal of House*, I, 3, 46-47; Sewall, *Diary*, II, 802, 804; Sewall, *Letter-Book*, II, 50; Hutchinson, *History*, II, 158-159; Kimball, *Public Life*, 199; Johnson, *Adjustment*, 347; Warden, *Boston*, 80.

139.   Sewall, *Diary*, II, 804-805; Johnson, *Adjustment*, 353; JD to _____, Nov. 16, 1716, "Letter of Governor Dudley," MHS, *Coll.*, 4th ser., II (1854), 308; Jeremiah Dummer, *Sir, I have Receiv'd of late* [London, 1729?], 1; Strandness, *Sewall*, 137-140.

140.   Sewall, *Diary*, II, 933-934, 943-945.

141.   *Boston News-Letter*, Apr. 4-Apr. 11, 1720; Sewall, *Diary*, II, 945.

142.   Heb 11:22; Sewall, *Diary*, II, 946; Colman, *Ossa Josephi*, i, 32-33; I. Mather, *Publick Spirit*, dedication; Hall, *Increase Mather*, 309.

CHAPTER 10
BENJAMIN COLMAN

1.   Everett Emerson, *Puritanism in America, 1620-1750* (Boston, 1977), 144; Charles H. Lippy, *Seasonable Revolutionary: The Mind of Charles Chauncy* (Chicago, 1981), 7; Niel Caplan, ed., "Some Unpublished Letters of Benjamin Colman, 1717-1725," MHS, *Procs.*, LXXVII (1965), 101.

2.   Ebenezer Turell, *The Life and Character of the Reverend Benjamin Colman, D. D.* (Boston, 1749), 47; Edwin Scott Gaustad, *The Great Awakening in New England* (New York, 1957), 148n39. There are two other short accounts of Colman. John Langdon Sibley and Clifford K. Shipton, *Biographical Sketches of Graduates of Harvard University* (Cambridge, Mass., and Boston, 1873-   ), IV, 120-137, contains a useful bibliography of his works. See also James W. Jones, *The Shattered Synthesis: New England Puritanism before the Great Awakening* (New Haven, 1973), 90-103.

3.   Turell, *Colman*, 1, 3-4.

4.   *Ibid.*, 5-9, 11-14, 31.

5.   Robert Middlekauff, *The Mathers: Three Generations of Puritan Intellectuals, 1596-1728* (New York, 1971), 219; Clayton Harding Chapman, "Benjamin Colman's Daughters," *NEQ*, XXVI (1953), 169; Jones, *Shattered Synthesis*, 91; David D. Hall, *The Faithful Shepherd: A History of the New England Ministry in the Seventeenth Century* (Chapel Hill, 1972), 221-222, 272-273.

6.   Robert G. Pope, *The Half-Way Covenant: Church Membership in Puritan New England* (Princeton, 1969), 182; David Levin, *Cotton Mather: The Young Life of the Lord's Remembrancer, 1663-1703* (Cambridge, Mass., 1978), 234, 290-291; Lippy, *Chauncy*, 8; Mason I. Lowance, Jr., *Increase Mather* (New York, 1974), 159.

7. Emerson, *Puritanism,* 142-143; Williston Walker, *Creeds and Platforms of Congregationalism* (New York, 1893; rpt. 1960), 475; Cook, *Wise,* 90-91; Colman to Wodrow, Jan. 23, 1719, Caplan, ed., "Colman Letters," 110-111.

8. John Nelson to Colman, May 20, 1699, Benjamin Colman Papers, MHS; William Brattle to Colman, May 16, 1699, *ibid.;* Leverett to Colman, May 25, 1699, *ibid.*

9. Pemberton to Colman, May 22, 1699, *ibid.;* Bradstreet to Colman, May 23, 1699, *ibid.;* Nelson to Colman, May 20, 1699, *ibid.* J. William T. Youngs, Jr., *God's Messengers: Religious Leadership in Colonial New England* (Baltimore, 1976), 82. On Noyes see Hutchinson, *History,* II, 188, 188n.

10. Nelson to Colman, May 20, 1699, Colman Papers; Noyes to Colman, May 14, 1699, *ibid.*

11. Turell, *Colman,* 44; Emerson, *Puritanism,* 143; Perry Miller, *Jonathan Edwards* (New York, 1949), 12; Nelson to Colman, May 20, 1699, Colman Papers.

12. Turell, *Colman,* 43; Walker, *Creeds,* 476; Cook, *Wise,* 93; Silverman, *Cotton Mather,* 147.

13. Colman and others, *A Manifesto or Declaration, Set forth by the Undertakers of the New Church Now Erected in Boston in New-England* (Boston, 1699), 1-2; Edmund S. Morgan, *Visible Saints: The History of a Puritan Idea* (Ithaca, 1963), 27-28; Turell, *Colman,* 179-180; Perry Miller, *The New England Mind: From Colony to Province* (Cambridge, Mass., 1953), 242.

14. Colman, *Manifesto,* 1-2.

15. *Ibid.* Another Boston church had allowed private relations since 1678. Walker, *Creeds,* 473.

16. Morgan, *Visible Saints,* 55, 88; Miller, *Mind to Province,* 242; Middlekauff, *Mathers,* 219; Colman, *Manifesto,* 3.

17. Colman, *Manifesto,* 3; Miller, *Mind to Province,* 242. Colman was not an early supporter of feminism. Women had no other form of influence in the Brattle Street Church. Men held all positions of authority, which greatly pleased Colman. See Colman to Wodrow, Dec. 9, 1717, Caplan, ed., "Colman Letters," 107.

18. Colman, *Manifesto,* 1-3.

19. Sewall, *Diary,* I, 418; Sewall, *Letter-Book,* I, 156.

20. Cook, *Wise,* 94; Sewall, *Diary,* I, 419; C. Mather, *Diary,* I, 325-327, 329-330; Salem ministers to authors of Manifesto, Dec. 30, 1699, Colman Papers; I. Mather and Allen to Colman, Dec. 28, 1699, *ibid.*

21. Middlekauff, *Mathers,* 220; Cook, *Wise,* 95; C. Mather, *Diary,* I, 332-333; Sewall, *Diary,* I, 421-422.

22. C. Mather, *Diary,* I, 325-327, 332-333; Cook, *Wise,* 96.

23. I. Mather, *The Order of the Gospel, Professed and Practised By the Churches of Christ in New-England* (Boston, 1700), 7-8, 12, 38, 61, 68, 71, 120. In Apr. 1700 the Cambridge ministerial association—undoubtedly at I. Mather's urging—condemned using the Lord's Prayer, as it "will not easily be cleared from the charge of superstition." Cambridge Association of Ministers, "Records of the Cambridge Association," MHS, *Procs.,* XVII (1879-1880), 276.

24. C. Mather, *Diary,* I, 325-327.

25. Colman and others, *Gospel Order Revived, Being an Answer to a Book Lately set forth by the Reverend Mr. Increase Mather* (New York, 1700), ii, v, vii, 15-16.

26. *Ibid.,* "Advertisement," n.p.; Bartholomew Green, *The Printers Advertisement* (Boston, 1701), 1, 4-5, 7-8, 10.

27. C. Mather, *Diary*, I, 375-376; C. Mather, *A Collection, of Some of the Many Offensive Matters, Contained in . . . The Order of the Gospel Revived* (Boston, 1701), preface, 5, 19-20. Silverman's suggestion that C. Mather indirectly inspired the creation of the Brattle Street Church is absurd. See Silverman, *Cotton Mather*, 148.

28. Cook, *Wise*, 100; Youngs, *Messengers*, 84; Sewall, *Diary*, I, 458.

29. Silverman, *Cotton Mather*, 155-156, 255; Sewall, *Diary*, I, 587-588; Colman to Stephen Sewall, June 18, 1717, Curwen Family Collection, AAS. The speech was C. Mather, A *Speech Made Unto his Excellency, Samuel Shute, Esq.* (Boston, 1717).

30. Emerson, *Puritanism*, 147; Miller, *Edwards*, 17, 20; Sibley and Shipton, *Harvard Graduates*, IV, 125; Theodore Hornberger, "Benjamin Colman and the Enlightenment," *NEQ*, XII (1939), 239-240; Teresa Toulouse, "'Syllabical Idolatry:' Benjamin Colman and the Rhetoric of Balance," *Early American Literature*, XVIII (1984), 265; Colman, *The Great God has magnified his Word* (Boston, 1742), 24, 30-31; Turell, *Colman*, 169-170.

31. C. Mather, "An Atestation" in Azariah Mather, *The Sabbath-Day's Rest, Asserted, Explained, Proved, and Applied* (Boston, 1725), 3; Jonathan Belcher to J. Belcher, Jr., Oct. 1, 1734, *The Belcher Papers*, MHS, *Coll.*, 6th ser., VII (1894), 125; Douglas C. Stenerson, ed., "An Anglican Critique of the Early Phase of the Great Awakening in New England: A Letter by Timothy Cutler," *WMQ*, XXX (1973), 483; George Selement, "Publication and the Puritan Minister," *WMQ*, XXXVII (1980), 223, 227.

32. Colman to Wodrow, Jan. 23, 1719, Caplan, ed., "Colman Letters," 110; "To ol' Master Janus," *New England Courant*, Sept. 2-Sept. 9, 1723; Colman, *Practical Discourses upon the Parable of the Ten Virgins* (London, 1707), 62-63.

33. Colman, *Practical Discourses*, 63-64.

34. Ola Elizabeth Winslow, *Meetinghouse Hill, 1630-1783* (New York, 1952), 151-152; Cook, *Wise*, 175-176; Patricia U. Bonomi, *Under the Cope of Heaven: Religion, Society and Politics* (New York, 1986), 68; Colman to Stephen Sewall, Aug. 26, 1712, Curwen Family Collection, AAS.

35. Winslow, *Meetinghouse*, 167; Colman, *The Government and Improvement of Mirth* (Boston, 1707), 5-6; Henry F. Jenks and others, eds., *Records of the Church in Brattle Square, Boston, 1699-1872* (Boston, 1902), 12-13.

36. Colman, *A Letter . . . to the Reverend Mr. Williams of Lebanon, Upon Reading the Confession and Retractions of the Reverend Mr. James Davenport* (Boston, 1744), 8; Silverman, *Cotton Mather*, 304; Turell, *Colman*, 176; Edwards to Colman, May 22, 1744, George S. Claghorn, ed., *The Works of Jonathan Edwards* (New Haven, 1998), XVI, 144-145; Charles W. Akers, *The Divine Politician: Samuel Cooper and the American Revolution in Boston* (Boston, 1982), 23.

37. Selement, *Keepers*, 44, 52, 71-72; Gaustad, *Great Awakening*, 123-124; Youngs, *Messengers*, 41; Colman to Stephen Sewall, Aug. 26, 1712, Curwen Family Collection, AAS.

38. Colman to Wodrow, Jan. 23, 1719, Caplan, ed., "Colman Letters," 108-109; C. C. Goen, *Revivalism and Separatism in New England, 1740-1800: Strict Congregationalists and Separate Baptists in the Great Awakening* (New Haven, 1962), 94.

39. Selement, "Publication," 219; Christopher R. Reaske, introduction to Turell, *Colman* (1972 rpt.), xii; David Harlan, *The Clergy and the Great Awakening in New England* (Ann Arbor, Mich., 1980), 60; Colman, *Jesus Weeping over His Dead Friend . . . A Sermon Preached . . . after the Funeral of the Reverend Mr. William Cooper*

(Boston, 1744), 28-29; Colman, *A Sermon Preach'd at the Ordination of Mr. William Cooper* (Boston, 1716), A2-A3; Jenks and others, eds., *Brattle Church Records,* 11.

40. Colman to Wodrow, Dec. 9, 1717, Caplan, ed., "Colman's Letters," 107; Colman to Wodrow, Mar. 1, 1720, *ibid.,* 118-119; Colman to Wodrow, June-July 1725, *ibid.,* 138.

41. Youngs, *Messengers,* 69-70; Stephen Foster, "English Puritanism and the Progress of New England Institutions, 1630-1660," in Hall and others, eds., *Saints and Revolutionaries,* 29; Carl Bridenbaugh, *Mitre and Sceptre: Transatlantic Faiths, Ideas, Personalities, and Politics, 1689-1775* (New York, 1962), 61.

42. Youngs, *Messengers,* 70-71; Walker, *Creeds,* 484-490.

43. Colman to Wodrow, Jan. 23, 1719, Caplan, ed., "Colman Letters," 114; C. Mather to Stirling, Sept. 16, 1715, Silverman, ed., *Mather Letters,* 185; Youngs, *Messengers,* 72-75; Walker, *Creeds,* 494.

44. Colman to Stephen Sewall, Apr. 9, 1718, Curwen Family Collection, AAS.

45. *Boston Gazette,* July 27-July 31, 1721; *Boston News-Letter,* Mar. 5-12, 1722; Hall, *Increase Mather,* 360; Silverman, *Cotton Mather,* 354; Colman to Wodrow, Feb. 13, 1721/2, Caplan, ed., "Colman Letters," 124; Colman to Stephen Sewall, June 4, 1722, Curwen Family Collection, AAS; Middlekauff, *Mathers,* 357; Colman, *Some Observations on the New Method Of Receiving the Small-Pox By Ingrafting or Inoculating* (Boston, 1721), 2-3, 16.

46. *Harvard College Records,* ed. Albert Matthews, PCSM, XVI, *Coll.* (1925), 436; Bridenbaugh, *Mitre,* 34-35; Turell, *Colman,* 45-46, 55; Harry S. Stout, *The New England Soul: Preaching and Religious Culture in Colonial New England* (New York, 1986), 131-132; Sibley and Shipton, *Harvard Graduates,* IV, 127.

47. *Harvard Records,* XVI, 516-517; Colman to Wodrow, Dec. 7, 1724, Caplan, ed., "Colman Letters," 135-136; C. Mather to Colman, Nov. 6, 1724, Silverman, ed., *Mather Letters,* 401; Silverman, *Cotton Mather,* 391-392.

48. Turell, *Colman,* 55-57, 136; *Mass. House Journals,* VI, 151, 196-198; Colman to Wodrow, Dec. 7, 1724, Caplan, ed., "Colman Letters," 135-136; Sibley and Shipton, *Harvard Graduates,* IV, 127.

49. Turell, *Colman,* 57-58; Colman to Wodrow, June-July 1725, Caplan, ed., "Colman Letters," 138; *Harvard Records,* XVI, 841; *Harvard Documents,* L, 545-546, 561.

50. Turell, *Colman,* 3n, 58-59, 224, 225n; Watts to Colman, Feb. 28, 1736/7, Henry F. Jenks, ed., "Letters of Dr. Watts," MHS, *Procs.,* IX (1894-1895), 352; Colman to Wodrow, June-July 1725, Caplan, ed., "Colman Letters," 138; Sewall, *Letter-Book,* II, 217, 219; Hollis to Colman, Aug. 12, 1725, *Harvard Documents,* L, 561.

51. *Harvard Records,* XVI, 559, 566-567, 569; Hollis to Colman, Aug. 21, 1725, *Harvard Documents,* L, 563.

52. Colman to Wodrow, Jan. 23, 1719, Caplan, ed., "Colman Letters," 111; Colman to Hoadley, May 6, 1719, in Turell, *Colman,* 143; James G. Leyburn, *The Scotch-Irish: A Social History* (Chapel Hill, 1962), 164-167.

53. A. L. Perry, "Scotch-Irish in New England," Scotch-Irish Society of America, *Proceedings and Addresses,* II (1890), 107-110; Colman to Wodrow, Nov. 23, 1722, Caplan, ed., "Colman Letters," 128; Leyburn, *Scotch-Irish,* 168.

54. Colman to Wodrow, Jan. 23, 1719, Caplan, ed., "Colman Letters," 111; Colman to Wodrow, Nov. 23, 1722, *ibid.,* 128-129.

55. Colman to Wodrow, Nov. 23, 1722, *ibid.*, 128-129; Colman to Wodrow, June-July 1725, *ibid.*, 138-139.

56. Perry, "Scotch-Irish," 110-115; Leyburn, *Scotch-Irish*, 237-238, 328, 331.

57. Frink to Colman, Jan. 21, 1735/6, Colman Papers; Perry, "Scotch-Irish," 115-118; Leyburn, *Scotch-Irish*, 239; Gaustad, *Awakening*, 59, 149n80; Charles Knowles Bolton, *Scotch Irish Pioneers in Ulster and America* (Boston, 1910), 166-169.

58. Colman to ____, Mar. 17, 1735/6, Colman Papers.

59. Perry, "Scotch-Irish," 119.

60. Carl Bridenbaugh, *Cities in the Wilderness: The First Century of Urban Life in America, 1625-1742* (New York, 1938), 391-392; Leyburn, *Scotch-Irish*, 240-241.

61. Colman to Kennett, Nov. 1712, Colman Papers; Youngs, *Messengers*, 79-80; Pennington, "Myles," 154, 159, 171, 177; Bridenbaugh, *Mitre*, 77; Lawrence H. Leder, *Liberty and Authority: Early American Political Ideology, 1689-1763* (Chicago, 1968), 69.

62. Henry Newman to Gibson, Feb. 26, 1725/6, Fulham Papers, vol. 4, p. 180-181; Youngs, *Messengers*, 84.

63. Colman to Gibson, Sept. 13, 1734, Fulham Papers, vol. 5, p. 137.

64. G. V. Bennett, *White Kennett, 1660-1728, Bishop of Peterborough: A Study in the Political and Ecclesiastical History of the Early Eighteenth Century* (London, 1957), 192; Colman to Kennett, Sept. 30, 1726, Feb. 19, 1728, Fulham Papers, vol. 4, pp. 192, 256; Colman to Newman, Jan. 22, 1725, *ibid.*, p. 153; Kennett to Colman, Sept. 15, 1713, July 28, 1716, "Bishop Kennett to Benjamin Colman," MHS, *Procs.*, LIII (1919-1920), 68, 70; Bridenbaugh, *Mitre*, 59; Arthur Lyon Cross, *The Anglican Episcopate and the American Colonies* (New York, 1902; rpt. Hamden, Conn., 1964), 98-99, 103-105.

65. Sewall to Saltonstall, Oct. 15, 1722, Sewall, *Letter-Book*, II, 144; Memorial of Cutler and Myles, June 10, 1725, *ibid.*, 184-186; Sewall, *Diary*, II, 997.

66. Matthias Plant to Gibson, Dec. 20, 1726, Fulham Papers, vol. 4, p. 206; Jeremiah Dummer to Gibson, June 20, 1727, *ibid.*, p. 218; Cutler to Gibson, Sept. 23, 1725, *ibid.*, p. 167; Myles to Gibson, Nov. 9, 1725, *ibid.*, p. 171; Price to Gibson, Nov. 20, 1739, *ibid.*, vol. 5, p. 257.

67. Colman to Shirley, Apr. 5, 1741, Benjamin Colman Misc. Mss., NYHS.

68. Turell, *Colman*, 168n; Sewall, *Diary*, II, 782.

69. Colman, *Some Reasons and Arguments Offered to the Good People of Boston and Adjacent Places for the Setting up Markets in Boston* (Boston, 1719), title page, 6; Colman, The *Religious Regards we owe to our Country, and the Blessing of Heaven assured thereunto* (Boston, 1718), 40; Colman, *Righteousness and Compassion: The Duty and Character of Pious Rulers* (Boston, 1736), 24, 26, 28-29, 31.

70. Wolfgang Michael, *England Under George I* (London, 1936-1939; rpt. New York, 1970), I, 48-49, II, 49; David Green, *Queen Anne* (London, 1970), 311, 334n; Colman to George Curwin, Aug. 30, 1714, Curwen Family Collection, AAS,

71. Michael, *George I*, I, 1, 9-10, 204, II, 49; Bridenbaugh, *Mitre*, 66-67.

72. Colman to Stephen Sewall, June 18, 1717, Curwen Family Collection, AAS; Michael, *George I*, I, 7; Ebenezer Pemberton, *A Brief Account of the State of the Province of the Massachusetts-Bay in New England, Civil and Ecclesiastical* (Boston, 1717).

73. Pemberton, *Brief Account*, 2-4, 8; Colman to Wodrow, May 27, 1719, Caplan, ed., "Colman Letters," 115.

74. Bridenbaugh, *Mitre,* 37-38; Francis G. Walett, ed., *The Diary of Ebenezer Parkman, 1703-1782* (Worcester, Mass., 1974), 26; "To His Most Excellent Majesty King George," May 31, 1727, Colman Papers.

75. Leonard W. Cowie, *Henry Newman: An American in London, 1708-43* (London, 1956), 215-216, 221.

76. Pencak, *War,* 70-73; Colman to Wodrow, Dec. 7, 1720, Caplan, ed., "Colman Letters," 122; Cowie, *Newman,* 216-217.

77. Colman to Stephen Sewall, June 18, 1717, Curwen Family Collection, AAS; Colman to Wodrow, Dec. 7, 1720, Caplan, ed., "Colman Letters," 122; Jack N. Rakove, *The Beginnings of National Politics: An Interpretive History of the Continental Congress* (New York, 1979), 36; Watts to Colman, Mar. 4-5, 1729/30, "Watts Letters," 331-332.

78. Cowie, *Newman,* 216-217; Foote, *King's Chapel,* I, 528-529; Hutchinson, *History,* II, 302-303; J. Belcher to J. Belcher, Jr., May 8, 1740, Jan. 27, 1740/1, *Belcher Papers,* 291, 367; Colman to J. Belcher, Aug. 22, 1743, "Original Letter from Reverend Benjamin Colman, D. D. to the Honourable Jonathan Belcher, Esquire," MHS, *Coll.,* 2nd ser., II (1814), 186-187. For Belcher's administration, see Michael C. Batinski, *Jonathan Belcher, Colonial Governor* (Lexington, Ky., 1996).

79. Colman to Shirley, Apr. 5, 1741, Colman Misc. Mss., NYHS.

80. Colman to Belcher, Aug. 22, 1743, MHS, *Coll.,* 2nd ser., II (1814), 186-187; John A. Schutz, *William Shirley: King's Governor of Massachusetts* (Chapel Hill, 1961), 85, 109; Byron Fairchild, *Messrs. William Pepperrell: Merchants at Piscataqua* (Ithaca, 1954), 187.

81. Colman, *A Sermon Preached Before the Governour and Council July 22d, 1708: Being the Day of the Proclamation of the Happy Union of the Two Kingdoms of England and Scotland* (Boston, 1708), 30; Colman, "Some Memoirs for the Continuation of the History of the Troubles of the New-English Colonies from the Barbarous and Perfidious Indians, Instigated by the more Savage and Inhuman French of Canada and Nova Scotia," MHS, *Coll.,* 1st ser., VI (1799), 109-110.

82. Thomas Hubbard to Pepperrell, July 4, 1745, *Pepperrell Papers,* MHS, *Coll.,* 6th ser., X (1899), 308; Colman to Pepperrell, July 3, 1745, *ibid.,* 306-307.

83. Colman to Pepperrell, Nov. 9, 1745, *ibid.,* 395; Colman to a minister, Jan. 16, 1745/6, Colman Misc. Mss., NYHS; Leach, *Roots of Conflict,* 73.

84. Conrad Wright, *The Beginnings of Unitarianism in America* (Boston, 1955), 9; Carl Bangs, *Arminius: A Study in the Dutch Reformation* (New York, 1971), 13, 15, 17, 220-221; Youngs, *Messengers,* 85-86.

85. Jones, *Shattered Synthesis,* 91; Hornberger, "Enlightenment," 229; Miller, *Mind to Province,* 242; Wright, *Unitarianism,* 65.

86. Sibley and Shipton, *Harvard Graduates,* VIII, 663; Charles Edwin Jones, "The Impolitic Mr. Edwards: The Personal Dimension of the Robert Breck Affair," in William J. Scheick, comp., *Critical Essays on Jonathan Edwards* (Boston, 1980), 21, 24-27; Youngs, *Messengers,* 87; William Cooper, *The Work of Ministers represented under the Figure of Sowers* (Boston, 1736), 19; W. Cooper to Colman, Nov. 25, 1735, Colman Papers; Colman to Williams and Hopkins, Dec. 29, 1735, *ibid.; Boston Gazette,* Nov. 3-Nov. 10, Nov. 24-Dec. 1, 1735.

87. Colman, *The Holy Walk and Glorious Translation of Blessed Enoch* (Boston, 1728), 29-30.

88. J. Williams to Colman, July 2, 1728, Colman Papers; Silverman, *Cotton Mather*, 193.

89. Colman to Watts, quoted in Watts to Gibson, Oct. 11, 1738, Fulham Papers, vol. 5, p. 226; Gaustad, *Awakening*, 50, 52; Edwards to Colman, May 19, 1737, Colman Papers; Miller, *Edwards*, 136-137.

90. William Howland Kenney, 3d, "George Whitefield, Dissenter Priest of the Great Awakening, 1739-1741," *WMQ*, XXVI (1969), 76-78; Gaustad, *Awakening*, 50; "Harvard College Testimony," in Alan Heimert and Perry Miller, eds., *The Great Awakening: Documents Illustrating the Crisis and Its Consequences* (New York, 1967), 341; Colman and others, *Three Letters to the Reverend George Whitefield* (Philadelphia, 1739), 6; Woolverton, *Colonial Anglicanism*, 190; Frank Lambert, "'Pedlar in Divinity': George Whitefield and the Great Awakening, 1737-1745," *Journal of American History*, LXXVII (1990), 824.

91. Watts to Colman, May 23, 1740, "Watts Letters," 374-375.

92. Kenney, "Whitefield," 89.

93. George Whitefield, *A Continuation of the Reverend Mr. Whitefield's Journal* (Boston, 1741), 76-77.

94. *Ibid.*, 50-52; Colman to William Harris and others, Oct. 3, 1740, Colman Papers; Bonomi, *Under the Cope*, 149; Lambert, "Pedlar," 814, 824.

95. Whitefield, *Journal*, 53-54; John Pollock, *George Whitefield and the Great Awakening* (Garden City, N.Y., 1972), 158-159; Colman to Harris and others, Oct. 3, 1740, Colman Papers; Edwards to Colman, Mar. 19, 1736/7, Claghorn, ed., *Works of Edwards*, XVI, 65-66.

96. Whitefield, *Journal*, 55-56, 59-60.

97. *Ibid.*, 71, 74-75.

98. Colman to Whitefield, c. 1741, in Jules Herbert Tuttle, ed., "The Glasgow-Weekly-History, 1743," MHS, *Procs.*, LIII (1919-1920), 197-198; W. Williams to Colman, July 1, 1740, Colman Papers; Colman, *Souls Flying to Jesus Christ* (Boston, 1740), 5-6, 14-15, 21-22.

99. Gaustad, *Awakening*, 55.

100. Cutler to Gibson, Dec. 5, 1740, Fulham Papers, vol. 5, p. 269; Colman, *Souls Flying*, 26, line 28; "Harvard Testimony," Heimert and Miller, eds., *Documents*, 346.

101. Lippy, *Chauncy*, 34-35; Gaustad, *Awakening*, 55; Colman to Whitefield, June 3, 1742, in Tuttle, ed., "Glasgow-Weekly," 214; Colman, *Word of God*, 31-32. For Croswell, see Leigh Eric Schmidt, "'A Second and Glorious Reformation': The New Light Extremism of Andrew Croswell," *WMQ*, XLIII (1986), 214-244.

102. Jones, "Impolitic," in Scheick, comp., *Edwards Essays*, 27; Jonathan Ashley, *The Great Duty of Charity* (Boston, 1742), preface; W. Cooper to the publishers, Jan. 5, 1742/3, *Boston Gazette*, Jan. 11, 1743.

103. *Boston Gazette*, Feb. 1, 1743; Jonathan Ashley, *A Letter from the Reverend Mr. Jonathan Ashley To the Reverend Mr. William Cooper* (Boston, 1743), 3-4.

104. Colman and others, *The Declaration of A Number of the Associated Pastors of Boston and Charles-Town*, July 1, 1742, in Richard L. Bushman, ed., *The Great Awakening: Documents on the Revival of Religion, 1740-1745* (New York, 1970), 50-51; news account, *ibid.*, 51-53; James Davenport, *The Reverend Mr. James Davenport's Confession and Retractions* (1744), *ibid.*, 53-55; Harry S. Stout and Peter Onuf, "James Davenport and the Great Awakening in New London," *Journal of American History*,

LXX (1983), 556-557, 575; Goen, *Revivalism,* 25, 25n; Benjamin Lord to publisher, Apr. 4, 1743, *Boston Gazette,* Apr. 12, 1743.

105. *Boston Gazette,* Dec. 13, 20, 1743; Colman, *Dead Friend,* ii, 32-33; Colman, *Letter to Williams,* 4-5.

106. Colman, *Dead Friend,* ii; Akers, *Politician,* 15-16.

107. Colman, *Letter to Williams,* 2-8.

108. *Ibid.,* 6; *Whitefield's Journals,* in Bushman, ed., *Great Awakening,* 65; Goen, *Revivalism,* 30; Walett, ed., *Parkman Diary,* 111.

109. Caleb Cushing and others, *A Letter From Two Neighbouring Associations of Ministers in the Country, To the Associated Ministers of Boston and Charlestown, relating to the Admission of Mr. Whitefield into Their Pulpits* (Boston, 1745), 2-4, 6-7; Walett, ed., *Parkman Diary,* 111.

110. "Rustico Clerus" to Fleet, Dec. 14, 1744, *Boston Evening Post,* Dec. 17, 1744; Habersham to Timothy, Oct. 1, 1744, *ibid.,* Dec. 24, 1744; *ibid.,* Dec. 3, 1744; *Boston Gazette,* Dec. 4, 1744.

111. "The Layman's sincere and humble Address," *Boston Evening Post,,* Dec. 10, 1744; "A Letter from the Country," *ibid.,* Nov. 19, 1744; "To the Reverend Ministers of the Town of Boston, that admire Mr. George Whitefield," *ibid.,* Dec. 17, 1744; "To the Reverend Mr. Whitefield," *ibid.,* Dec. 24, 1744; *ibid.,* Dec. 3, 1744.

112. "J.S." to the publisher, Dec. 6, 1744, *ibid.,* Dec. 10, 1744; "A.X." to Fleet, *ibid.,* Dec. 24, 1744; *Boston Gazette,* Dec. 4, 1744.

113. Colman to Whitefield, Jan. 14, 1744/5, Colman Papers; *Boston Gazette,* Jan. 15, 22, Feb. 5, Apr. 9, 1745.

114. *Boston Evening Post,* Mar. 30, 1747; *Boston Gazette,* Mar. 31, June 30, 1747.

115. "A.C." to Fleet, July 29, 1747, *Boston Evening Post,* Aug. 3, 1747; *Boston Gazette,* Aug. 4, 1747; Colman to ____, July 25, 1747, Colman Papers.

116. Turell, *Colman,* 227; *Boston Evening Post,* Aug. 31, 1747; Akers, *Politician,* 18-19; Walett, ed., *Parkman Diary,* 160.

117. *Boston News-Letter,* Sept. 3, 1747; *Boston Gazette,* Sept. 22, 1747.

EPILOGUE

1. Ezra Stiles, *A Discourse on the Christian Union* (Boston, 1761), 50-51.

2. Malcolm Freiberg, "Thomas Hutchinson: The First Fifty Years (1711-1761)," *WMQ,* XV (1958), 46; Page Smith, *John Adams* (Garden City, N.Y., 1962), I, 3.

3. Peter Shaw, *The Character of John Adams* (Chapel Hill, 1976), 59; Rakove, *Beginnings of National Politics,* 93; Smith, *Adams,* I, 263.

4. John Adams to Nathan Webb, Sept. 1, 1755, *Papers of John Adams,* ed. Robert J. Taylor (Cambridge, Mass., 1977-), I, 1.

5. Thomas Hutchinson to Robert Hale, Dec. 20, 1755, Moody, ed., *Saltonstall Papers,* I, 411-412, 411n1.

6. Linda Rodriquez, "Salem Eyes Witch-trial Pardon," *Boston Herald,* Oct. 31, 2004, p. 22; Rosenthal, *Salem Story,* 204.

7. Cameron, *Anne Hutchinson,* 222.

8. Morgan, *Genuine Article,* 15; Hansen, "Tituba," 11. See Webb, *1676, passim.*

9. William G. McLoughlin, "Anne Hutchinson Reconsidered," *Rhode Island History,* XLIX (1991), 14.

10. Satan, of course, is not meant to be included in the sentiments expressed in this paragraph.

APPENDIX 1
PHILIP'S NAME: A COTTAGE INDUSTRY

1. Jennings, *Invasion*, is a good example.
2. Lepore, *Name of War*, xx.
3. *Ibid.*; Jeremy Dupertuis Bangs, ed., *Indian Deeds: Land Transactions in Plymouth Colony, 1620-1691* (Boston, 2002), 326; Eleise Pokonoahkit to chief officer, May 7, 1666, PRO *Cal.*, V, 380; *Eliot's Indian Dialogues*, 120; *PCR*, VIII, 190-191; George R. Horner, "Massasoit and His Two Sons: Wamsutta and Metacom," *Bulletin of The Massachusetts Archaeological Society*, LVI (1995), 21; Jennings, *Invasion*, 290n.
4. Drake, *King Philip's War*, 248n2.
5. RW, *Key*, 129; Peter Berresford Ellis, *The Celts: A History* (New York, 1998), 28.
6. Ives Goddard, "Eastern Algonquian Languages," in *Handbook of North American Indians*, Vol. 15: *Northeast*, ed. Bruce G. Trigger (Washington, D.C., 1978), 70-71; Bert Salwen, "Indians of Southern New England and Long Island: Early Period," *ibid.*, 160; Simmons, *Narragansett*, 61; Edward G. Gray, *New World Babel: Languages and Nations in Early America* (Princeton, 1999), 113.
7. Jacob Muttamakoog to Eliot and others, July 6, 1676, in *A True Account*, 6-7. Lepore quoted this letter but did not realize its significance. Lepore, *Name of War*, 252-253n38.
8. Josselyn, *Colonial Traveler*, 101; RW, *Key*, 163; Hutchinson, *History*, I, 235; Winslow, *Good News*, 586-587; Francis Higginson, *New-Englands Plantation* (1630), (Salem, Mass., 1908), 104; Slotkin, *Regeneration*, 79.

APPENDIX 2
WHO WAS PHILIP'S FATHER?

1. Schroeder, "True Lineage," 211-214.
2. Lepore, *Name of War*, 252n37; "N.S.," *Present State of New-England*, 26; "N. S.," *Continuation of the State*, 69-70. For the full titles of the works of "N. S.," see Lepore, *Name of War*, 243. Missing in the following accounts is one basic fact. Schroeder believed that "N. S." could actually be "Nathaniel Southworth, brother-in-law to Captain Benjamin Church." Church had considerable expertise and knowledge about Philip. This appendix will assume that "N. S." was Saltonstall. Schroeder, "True Lineage," 213.
3. Horner, "Massasoit," 20-22; Lepore, *Name of War*, 252n37.
4. Terence G. Byrne and Kathryn Fairbanks, "Sunconewhew: 'Phillip's Brother'?," *Bulletin of The Massachusetts Archaeological Society*, LVII (1996), 50-57.
5. Dennis P. Walsh, "King Philip (Metacom) Redux: Massasoit's Son or Grandson?," *NEHGR*, CLVII (2003), 116-123.
6. Nathaniel Morton, *New England's Memorial* (Cambridge, Mass., 1669), dedication, 144.

7. Josselyn, *Colonial Traveler*, xxvi, 103, 175n114; Greenlaw, "John Maverick," 236; Walsh, "King Philip," 119.

8. Josselyn, *Colonial Traveler*, 71, 113.

9. *Ibid.*, 105.

10. *Ibid.*, 185, 148-197; Morton, *Memorial*, 133, 199.

11. "N. S.," *Continuation of the State*, 69-70; Morton, *Memorial*, 24, 112-113, 160-161. Note, especially, that the anonymous author employed Morton's spelling of Massasoit's name.

12. Saltonstall to Andros, Sept. 23, 24, 1687, Moody, ed., *Saltonstall Papers*, I, 181-182; Saltonstall to Rowland and Elizabeth Cotton, Aug. 23, 1694, *ibid.*, 94; militia journal, 1684, *ibid.*, 168-174, 171; Samuel Sewall to Elizabeth Saltonstall, Apr. 29, 1710, *ibid.*, 296; Morton, *Memorial*, 196; Byrne and Fairbanks, "Sunconewhew," 54; Walsh, "King Philip," 118n6, 119. Although Walsh is correct that Robert E. Moody had "no credence" that Saltonstall was "N. S.," Moody added that "I may be mistaken." Moody, "Nathaniel Saltonstall (1639?-1707)," in Moody, ed., *Saltonstall Papers*, I, 49, 56, 56n26.

13. Pynchon to John Winthrop, Jr., or John Allyn, Aug. 6, 1675, *Pynchon Papers*, I, 139; Lepore, *Name of War*, 303n1; Byrne and Fairbanks, "Sunconewhew," 55-56; Eric B. Schultz and Michael J. Tougias, *King Philip's War: The History and Legacy of America's Forgotten Conflict* (Woodstock, Vt., 1999), 366n36. For more on oral tradition, see Appendix 3.

14. Bangs, ed., *Indian Deeds*, 326, 387.

15. RW, *Key*, 216; Lepore, *Name of War*, xx; Axtell, *The European and the Indian*, 126-127.

16. See note 14.

17. "N. S.," *New and Further Narrative*, 90, 90n4; *Harris Papers*, 171n; *RW Correspondence*, II, 692n4; Morton, *Memorial*, 113n; Horner, "Two Sons," 22; Byrne and Fairbanks, "Sunconewhew," 54.

18. *Eliot's Indian Dialogues*, 126.

19. *Oxford English Dictionary*, s. v. "father." The word also had complicated meanings in the Indian languages of New England. RW, *Key*, 56n49.

APPENDIX 3
THE PC INDIAN

1. RW, *Key*, 22-23. Joyce E. Chaplin has questioned the usefulness of "Native American." See Chaplin, *Subject Matter*, 329n2.

2. Lepore, *Name of War*; Drake, *King Philip's War*.

3. Lepore, *Name of War*, 328; Drake, *King Philip's War*, 4, 13.

4. Ann Marie Plane, review of *King Philip's War*, *NEQ*, LXXIII (2000), 673. For Leach's career, see Samuel T. McSeveney, "Douglas Edward Leach," *Perspectives*, XLII (May 2004), 47, and Paul Conkin, "A Life of Scholarship and Service: Douglas Edward Leach," in *Uncommon Sense*, No. 118 (Spring 2004), 23-24. Although Leach has been thoroughly castigated, no one, apparently, has noticed Samuel Eliot Morison's rather antediluvian introduction to Leach's book. See Leach, *Flintlock*, ix-x.

5. Calloway and Salisbury, "Introduction: Decolonizing New England History," in Calloway and Salisbury, eds., *Reinterpreting*, 13-15; John W. Tyler, foreword to *ibid.*, 10.

6. Ellis, *Celts*, 180.

7. Haefeli and Sweeney, *Captors and Captives*, 274-275.

8. Devon A. Mihesuah, introduction to Mihesuah, ed., *Natives and Academics: Researching and Writing about American Indians* (Lincoln, Neb., 1998), 3.

9. Simmons, *Narragansett*, 53.

10. Deborah Gussman, "'O Savage, Where Art Thou?': Rhetorics of Reform in William Apess's *Eulogy on King Philip*," *NEQ*, LXXVII (2004), 458, 458n16; reader report in author's possession.

11. Mihesuah, introduction to Mihesuah, ed., *Natives and Academics*, 7.

12. Ron His Horse Is Thunder, comments in "A Long Time Coming," *Smithsonian*, XXXV (Sept. 2004), 60.

13. RW, *Key*, 43.

A Note on the Sources

The first edition of this book had an extensive bibliography. This note will concentrate on recent publications along with the scholarship on Miantonomo and the Salem witchcraft trials, subjects new to this edition of *Enemies of the Bay Colony*.

Anyone interested in the history of early New England should examine the assorted collections, proceedings, and journals put out by venerable institutions such as the Massachusetts Historical Society, the New England Historic Genealogical Society, the American Antiquarian Society, and the Colonial Society of Massachusetts. Searching through the extensive runs of these organizations' publications, especially those issued before 1900, is guaranteed to produce a rich harvest.

Two valuable collections of primary sources, *The Correspondence of John Cotton* (2001), ed. Sargent Bush, Jr., and Jonathan Edwards's *Letters and Personal Writings* (1998), ed. George S. Claghorn (vol. 16 of *The Works of Jonathan Edwards)*, are both highly recommended.

Secondary sources are more erratic. Michael P. Winship's *Making Heretics: Militant Protestantism and Free Grace in Massachusetts, 1636-1641* (2002) is a major contribution, but Francis J. Bremer's *John Winthrop: America's Forgotten Founding Father* (2003) is not. Bremer seemingly could not decide whether to write a biography or a study of Puritanism in both Old and New England. Puritanism won out. The tome does have much on religion. Edmund S. Morgan's *The Genuine Article: A Historian Looks at Early America* (2004) is a compendium of his book reviews, some of which have relevance to Puritanism. Evan Haefeli and Kevin Sweeney co-authored *Captors and Captives: The 1704 French and Indian Raid on Deerfield* (2003), which is the definitive account of that famed event. An astute reader will have noticed that Richard W. Cogley's *John Eliot's Mission to the Indians before King Philip's War* (1999) is cited nowhere in *Enemies of the Bay Colony*. The explanation is straightforward. *John Eliot's Mission* is a disappointment; Eliot deserves better. Kristina Bross, *Dry Bones and Indian Sermons: Praying Indians in Colonial America* (2004), must be used with caution.

King Philip remains a popular subject. Yasuhide Kawashima, *Igniting King Philip's War: The John Sassamon Murder Trial* (2001), is a summary of the scholarship on Philip. Two other books, however, are very significant. Jill Lepore, *The Name of War: King Philip's War and the Origins of American Identity* (1998), is primarily a cultural history while James D. Drake, *King Philip's War: Civil War in New England, 1675-1676* (1999), is more interested in the war itself. Lepore strongly praised Edward G. Gray's work, published as *New World Babel: Languages and Nations in Early America* (1999). However, a reader should be warned that his book is mostly about printed Bibles and so has limited value. As for Gray's ideas about Indian languages, I thought that the relevant articles in vol. 15 of the *Handbook of North American Indians* (1978), ed. Bruce G. Trigger, were superior.

Sir Edmund Andros has not been forgotten. Stephen Saunders Webb, *Lord Churchill's Coup* (1995) did not irritate me as much as his earlier works, largely because it is really about English history. Mary Lou Lustig produced *The Imperial Executive in America: Sir Edmund Andros, 1637-1714* (2002), which is adequate but very conventional and follows Webb's lead. Lustig has somehow made Andros seem boring. She also neglected to mention the biography of Andros in *Enemies of the Bay Colony,* which is critical of Webb, her mentor—a coincidence no doubt.

Miantonomo, Uncas, and the Pequots remain controversial. A collection of Indian biographies edited by Robert S. Grumet, *Northeastern Indian Lives, 1636-1816* (1996), has a good essay on Uncas by Eric S. Johnson. A valuable contribution about Pequot archaeology by Kevin A. McBride is in Lawrence M. Hauptman and James D. Wherry, eds., *The Pequots in Southern New England: The Fall and Rise of an American Indian Nation* (1990). The most extensive history of the Pequot conflict, Alfred A. Cave's *The Pequot War* (1996), has some important insights.

The same can not be said for Michael Leroy Oberg, *Uncas: First of the Mohegans* (2003). Although Oberg's *Dominion and Civility: English Imperialism and Native America, 1585-1685* (1999) is a good effort, his biography of Uncas is not. The chapters on Miantonomo, with some exceptions, could have easily been written several decades ago. *Uncas: First of the Mohegans* has little to offer.

It would be impossible to summarize the scholarship relating to the Salem witchcraft trials or New England witchcraft in general. Four of the most important books are: Paul Boyer and Stephen Nissenbaum, *Salem Possessed: The Social Origins of Witchcraft* (1974); John Putnam Demos, *Entertaining Satan: Witchcraft and the Culture of Early New England* (1982); Bernard Rosenthal, *Salem Story: Reading the Witch Trials of 1692* (1993); and Mary Beth Norton, *In the Devil's Snare: The Salem Witchcraft Crisis of 1692* (2002). I have disputes with each one, but they are all significant.

Primary sources about Salem are contained in three volumes edited by Boyer and Nissenbaun, *The Salem Witchcraft Papers: Verbatim Transcripts of the Legal Documents of the Salem Witchcraft Outbreak of 1692* (1977). These transcripts were actually produced by the WPA of Franklin D. Roosevelt's New Deal. Bernard Rosenthal is working on a revised edition.

Finally, readers might like to consult my essays on Joseph Dudley, Paul Dudley, Sir Christopher Gardiner, and Philip in the reference source, *American National Biography*.

Index

witchcraft, 32;
  confessions and, 147-49, 154-55,
    157, 162-63;
  in Andover, 162-63, 165-66;
  in Salem Village, 3, 145-71, 184,
    246, 294n13;
  in Sweden, 145, 147, 162, 168;
  spectral evidence and, 147, 156-
    60, 164, 166-69;

  touch test and, 146, 156, 159, 167
Wollaston, Richard, 9-10
Worcester, Mass., 226-27, 245
Wyandanch, 50, 52
Yale, 2, 228
Zouch Phoenix, 9
Zuckerman, Michael, 11

About the Author

P hilip Ranlet is an adjunct assistant professor of history at Hunter
College of the City University of New York. His scholarly works
include *The New York Loyalists* and *Richard B. Morris and American
History in the Twentieth Century*, both published by the University Press
of America.